Risk Management in Law Firms

Strategies for Safeguarding the Future

Consulting Editor: **Hermann J Knott**

Consulting editor
Hermann J Knott

Editorial board
Anthony E Davis
Markus Hartung
Richard Harrison

Managing director
Sian O'Neill

Editorial services director
Carolyn Boyle

Production manager
Neal Honney

Group publishing director
Tony Harriss

Risk Management in Law Firms: Strategies for Safeguarding the Future
is published by
Globe Law and Business
Globe Business Publishing Ltd
New Hibernia House
Winchester Walk
London SE1 9AG
United Kingdom
Tel +44 20 7234 0606
Fax +44 20 7234 0808
www.globelawandbusiness.com

Printed and bound by Gomer Press, Llandysul, SA44 4JL

ISBN 9781909416444

Risk Management in Law Firms: Strategies for Safeguarding the Future
© 2014 Globe Business Publishing Ltd

All rights reserved. No part of this publication may be reproduced in any material form (including photocopying, storing in any medium by electronic means or transmitting) without the written permission of the copyright owner, except in accordance with the provisions of the Copyright, Designs and Patents Act 1988 or under terms of a licence issued by the Copyright Licensing Agency Ltd, 6-10 Kirby Street, London EC1N 8TS, United Kingdom (www.cla.co.uk, email: licence@cla.co.uk). Applications for the copyright owner's written permission to reproduce any part of this publication should be addressed to the publisher.

DISCLAIMER
This publication is intended as a general guide only. The information and opinions which it contains are not intended to be a comprehensive study, nor to provide legal advice, and should not be treated as a substitute for legal advice concerning particular situations. Legal advice should always be sought before taking any action based on the information provided. The publishers bear no responsibility for any errors or omissions contained herein.

Table of contents

Part I. Structure and management of law firms

Optimal legal forms _____ 7
    Richard Turnor
    Maurice Turnor Gardner LLP

Governance structures _____ 19
    Anthony E Davis
    Hinshaw & Culbertson LLP
    Jaime Fernández Madero
    Fernández Madero Consulting
    Markus Hartung
    Bucerius Center on
    the Legal Profession
    Richard Turnor
    Maurice Turnor Gardner LLP

Professional indemnity _____ 33
insurance: practical considerations in an increasingly international market
    Janet M Henderson
    Brit Syndicate 2987
    Ernst Millaard
    Aon Global Risk Consultants

Part II. Client work

Conflicts of interest _____ 51
    Anthony E Davis
    Hinshaw & Culbertson LLP
    Frank Maher
    Legal Risk LLP
    Andrew Scott
    Clyde & Co LLP

Confidentiality and disclosure _____ 71
    Frank Maher
    Legal Risk LLP
    Andrew Scott
    Clyde & Co LLP

Engagement letters _____ 85
    Heather Hibberd
    Legal Practitioners' Liability Committee
    Andrew Scott
    Clyde & Co LLP

Client risk _____ 97
    Simon Chester
    Heenan Blaikie LLP
    Anthony E Davis
    Hinshaw & Culbertson LLP
    Frank Maher
    Legal Risk LLP

Precedent databases and _____ 117
knowledge management
    Martin Schulz
    German Graduate School of
    Management and Law
    Luis Felipe Mohando
    SORAINEN

Review processes and ———— 129
client satisfaction: handling
high-risk cases
    Tracey Calvert
    Oakalls Consultancy Limited
    Anthony E Davis
    Hinshaw & Culbertson LLP
    Richard Harrison
    Clyde & Co LLP

Managing the client ———— 143
engagement
    Tracey Calvert
    Oakalls Consultancy Limited
    Abhijit Joshi
    AZB & Partners
    Frank Maher
    Legal Risk LLP
    Angeline Poon
    Rajah & Tann LLP

Part III. Data protection

Data protection and ———— 157
privacy in the United States
    Steven M Puiszis
    Hinshaw & Culbertson LLP

Data protection and ———— 167
privacy in Europe
    Silvia C Bauer
    Silke Gottschalk
    Luther

Part IV. Money laundering

Money laundering ———— 175
    Sue Mawdsley
    Legal Risk LLP
    Suzie Ogilvie
    Freshfields Bruckhaus Deringer LLP

Part V. HR issues

Hiring – identifying ———— 189
the key risks
    Ruth Bonino
    Chris Holme
    Clyde & Co LLP

Lateral hiring of partners ———— 197
– the hiring process
    Ruth Bonino
    Chris Holme
    Clyde & Co LLP

Integration of lateral hires ———— 205
    Anthony E Davis
    Hinshaw & Culbertson LLP

Personal development ———— 209
policies
    Jaime Fernández Madero
    Fernández Madero Consulting

Part VI. Financial risk

Financial risk management ———— 213
in law firms
    Anthony E Davis
    Hinshaw & Culbertson LLP
    Frank Maher
    Legal Risk LLP
    Wolfgang Weiss
    University of Applied Arts, Coburg

Non-lawyer ownership of ———— 227
law firms and outsourcing
of legal services
    Anthony E Davis
    Hinshaw & Culbertson LLP
    Heather Hibberd
    Legal Practitioners' Liability
    Committee
    Frank Maher
    Legal Risk LLP

Part VII. Cyber risk

Mitigating law firms' ———— 239
cyber risk
    Steven M Puiszis
    Hinshaw & Culbertson LLP

Part VIII. Globalisation

The globalisation of ———— 255
legal services
    Friedrich R Blase
    Holland & Knight
    Julia Graham
    DLA Piper
    James W Jones
    Georgetown University Law Center

Part IX. Brand and reputation

The effects of risk ———— 271
management on brand and
reputation management
    Georg-Christof Bertsch
    Bertsch.Brand Consultants
    Simon Chester
    Heenan Blaikie LLP
    Jane Hunter
    Aon Risk Solutions

About the authors ———— 295

Optimal legal forms

Richard Turnor
Maurice Turnor Gardner LLP

1. **Introduction**

    Within the professional lifetime of many lawyers who are still in practice today, law firms were almost invariably structured as general partnerships. They were based in, and advised on the law of, only one jurisdiction. The legal landscape is almost unrecognisable now, and it is changing faster than ever.

    This chapter describes the changes law firms have experienced and outlines the key issues to consider when structuring a legal practice. It also attempts to anticipate how law firm structure may evolve over the next 10 years. It follows the almost universal market practice of calling the proprietors of a law firm partners when they work as lawyers in the business, whether the firm is structured as a general partnership, a limited liability partnership, a company or a complex international organisation comprising a variety of entities.

2. **General partnership**

    Traditionally, lawyers could only practise as sole practitioners, as partners in general partnerships, as employees of such firms or in house. English barristers generally practise as sole practitioners to this day, even though they collaborate in Chambers. Slaughter and May is an example of a well-known London law firm that is still structured as a general partnership.

    A law firm general partnership arises when one or more lawyers are practising jointly together, using a shared name and sharing profits on an agreed basis. There is generally no requirement to file accounts publicly. The partnership simply needs an agreement to regulate its internal affairs, and while this agreement need not be in writing, in practice a well-governed law firm partnership invariably has a written agreement.

    General partnerships are very flexible and capable of being adapted to almost any business model. The business can be funded with capital, retained profits or debt. Profits can be shared equally, or according to a simple lock step, or a firm can adopt a sophisticated system designed to reward and incentivise good performance. Arrangements can be made for outgoing partners to be paid a share of unrealised gains in the value of the firm's assets, including goodwill, or their capital and undistributed profits can simply be repaid to them. A small firm can be managed through regular partners' meetings. A large firm can adopt the most sophisticated governance and risk management structures and processes. Arrangements can generally be made for the business to be passed through successive generations in any way that suits the firm. There is generally no obligation to file annual returns or accounts on a public registry. Were it not for professional liability issues, and for regulations preventing profit sharing with foreign lawyers from some jurisdictions, perhaps most law firms, like Slaughter and May, would still practice in this form.

The main reason why so many firms have moved away from the general partnership structure is exposure to claims. In most jurisdictions, all general partners are exposed to all the liabilities of the firm. If one partner or member of staff provides negligent advice, and this causes loss to a client, the client can generally recover the whole loss from any partner, whether involved or not, leaving that partner to recover contributions from the others. In England and Wales, by virtue of the 'holding out' rule in Section 14 of the Partnership Act 1890, third parties may be entitled to assume that all those described to the world as partners in the firm are actually general partners, even if they are in fact only employees, and they are liable accordingly. As the world became increasingly litigious and claims became ever larger, and as firms became larger and the task of mutual assurance and supervision became more difficult, so the pressure to allow lawyers to practise with limited liability grew.

Many jurisdictions have the concept of a 'limited partnership', comprising one or more general partners and a number of 'limited partners'. The limited partners are investors who are entitled to share in the profits but protected from losses provided that they avoid participation in management. In return, they provide funding for the firm's activities. Limited partnership has not caught on as a vehicle for law firms, perhaps mainly because of regulations in most jurisdictions that still preclude outside investors.

3. **Company**

The risk associated with practising in partnership prompted calls to allow lawyers to practise through limited liability companies. Even though, during the 1970s and 1980s, this became permitted in many jurisdictions, relatively few firms chose to go down this route, even though the company is attractive from a liability and governance standpoint and many of the flexible arrangements for funding, profit sharing and succession in a partnership can be replicated with careful structuring.

One factor that inhibited the use of companies was the requirement to publish accounts, thus revealing the firm's profitability (or the lack of it) and other valuable commercial information. Another was the fact that companies are generally opaque for tax purposes and that the effective rates of tax on profits, salaries and dividends combined has often been less favourable. Another practical problem with a company is that the means has to be found of passing the shares from generation to generation of partners in a way that is attractive to incoming and outgoing partners and that does not involve complex valuation issues and expensive tax consequences. This can be a challenge in tax jurisdictions such as the United Kingdom.

Subsidiary companies, owned by the main firm, have often been established to conduct related businesses or overseas operations. The subsidiaries usually employ lawyers who are remunerated by way of salary (and some of whom may also be partners in the main firm). The shares in the subsidiary devolve as an asset of the main firm. In such cases it is important to bear in mind that the company's shares are exposed to the insolvency of the entity that owns them. In cases where it is intended to avoid this, ideally they should be held in a non-practising entity held directly by the partners (see below in relation to the *verein* approach).

The company may yet have its day. In the United Kingdom, for example, some law firms have taken this form for a number of years. Many think that others will follow suit in order to benefit from lower rates of tax on undistributed company profits, the ability to finance the business from retained profits and tax reliefs available when selling shares at a gain on retirement. There has been renewed interest in practising through limited companies following the implementation of the new regime for taxing members of LLPs (assuming that the Finance Bill 2014 becomes law). A company may also be a convenient way to structure a law firm which is to seek outside investors.

4. **Limited liability partnership**

The tax and other difficulties associated with companies, combined with increasing concerns about the unlimited liability of partners, led to calls for a new kind of hybrid entity. 'Limited liability partnerships' (LLPs) emerged in the United States, in response to these calls.

Typically, like limited partnerships, US LLPs are partnerships in the sense of businesses conducted jointly by the partners, but the partners in a US LLP are generally entitled to protection from personal liability to professional indemnity claims arising other than by reason of their own personal fault. The responsible partners, and the assets of the business itself, remain exposed. A US-style LLP is just as flexible as a general partnership and is taxed accordingly in most jurisdictions. It has been widely taken up in the United States.

Other jurisdictions followed with equivalent structures. One such jurisdiction was the United Kingdom, which introduced the Limited Liability Partnerships Act 2000. LLPs are available both in Scotland and in England and Wales. The draftsmen of this legislation felt that the courts of other jurisdictions would be more likely to respect the limited liability of a body corporate than a partnership, for reasons of comity between nations. The legislation therefore provides for the UK-style LLP to be a body corporate and not (despite the name) a partnership. Large sections of UK company and insolvency law apply to UK LLPs even though they have no share capital and, in the United Kingdom at least, they are generally treated as tax transparent like a partnership. The fact that UK LLPs are bodies corporate led to a concern that some tax jurisdictions might treat them as opaque for tax purposes, but generally those fears have proved to be unfounded. Most of the major international firms of London origin have adopted this route, even though the UK LLP (unlike its US counterpart) has to publish its accounts.

In the United Kingdom, firms that have adopted the form of LLPs generally continue to refer to the proprietors as partners. This means that they have to take great care to ensure that clients and others are informed that in fact they are not partners but members of an LLP, because otherwise, under the holding out rule in Section 14 of the Partnership Act 1890, they would remain exposed as if they were actually general partners.

5. **Growing complexity**

As clients have expanded their operations overseas, their legal advisers have sought to protect their relationships and to compete for their business by their own international expansion. They have had to find pragmatic solutions to the many regulatory and tax issues arising as a result.

Some firms have mostly expanded in an organic way. Typically, the process begins with one or two partners and a small team being posted to a particular jurisdiction in response to client demand. Since they only practise the law of the firm's home jurisdiction, there is usually little or no local regulation. In the first few financial periods, the branch is often loss making. It therefore frequently makes sense for the office to operate as a branch of the home firm and for those partners posted overseas to receive a profit share from the main firm, so that all the partners benefit from the losses for tax purposes. In other cases it may be more tax efficient for those posted overseas to become local employees, so that their salaries are deductible as an expense in the home jurisdiction for tax purposes, but the salary is not subject to the high rates of tax applicable to a share of the profits of the main firm.

As the branch becomes more established, there may be a need to advise on local law and to recruit local lawyers. This creates pressure to set up a separate entity, because otherwise all the partners in the main firm may become subject to regulation both in the branch and at home. It is for that reason that most of the US firms with a London office have established a separate UK LLP to conduct the practice in London.

As the operations of the branch become profitable in their own right, local tax and double taxation issues arise. There may be a requirement for all partners to file tax returns in both jurisdictions. There may also be a desire to insulate the main partnership from liabilities arising in the branch, and vice versa. These factors add to the pressure to establish the branch as a separate entity in its own right.

Firms have often sought to achieve international scale more rapidly, by means of merger or alliance with, or acquisition of, firms in other jurisdictions. In the early years, alliances have often been little more than loose affiliations, but as they have built up a shared brand and a common culture, so the need for a structured approach to worldwide governance and profit sharing has grown. Acquisitions and mergers have often resulted in the addition of yet another separate entity to the organisation.

Thus, as firms have expanded internationally, they have tended to evolve into complex, multi-entity legal practices. As a result, it has become more and more challenging to structure profit sharing so that it is fair, consistent with a global model, responsive to local market conditions and not unduly complex for tax purposes. At the same time, it is necessary to take into account professional liability issues and to make sure that all the elements of the organisation adhere to the firm's core values and work together to deliver a worldwide strategy. Thus there is a need for robust international governance. Firms have developed a range of solutions.

6. **Global corporate group**

One might have thought that the obvious solution would be to establish an international group, with a separate holding entity established in a suitably tax-efficient jurisdiction. A separate subsidiary would then be established to carry on operations in each jurisdiction. The holding company would provide the overarching governance and the means of sharing worldwide profits. Some firms have indeed established wholly owned subsidiary companies in jurisdictions where this does not present a tax or regulatory problem, but generally firms have not so far adopted the global corporate group model.

One reason for this is regulation. In some jurisdictions it has not been permissible to practise law through anything other than a traditional general partnership. In others, although companies and limited liability partnerships have been permitted, ownership and control has been restricted to a limited number of recognised professions. In England and Wales, for example, only members of recognised professions which are considered to be subject to similar professional standards and oversight can generally be direct or indirect owners or managers of recognised bodies, authorised to practise as solicitors. While it is now possible to apply to become a licensed body with non-lawyer owners and managers, an international corporate approach remains relatively rare.

Another reason is international taxation. The tax issues associated with a corporate structure are referred to in section 3 above, and these difficulties can multiply exponentially when several jurisdictions are involved.

7. Multiple partnerships and LLPs

Many firms, and especially those that have expanded mainly in an organic way, deal with these tax and regulatory issues by means of multiple partnerships and LLPs.

Typically, a separate LLP is established to practise law in each jurisdiction where the LLP is tax transparent and permitted to practise in that form. Sometimes the same LLP practises in more than one jurisdiction. In jurisdictions where LLPs are not yet permitted, or taxed on an unfavourable basis, it may be necessary to use a general partnership (or a subsidiary company– see section 6 above). Each LLP has its own direct relationship with its clients. Where a transaction involves more than one network entity, care is taken to make sure that it is clear in engagement letters which entity is responsible for which aspect of the assignment, thus seeking to restrict exposure to only one entity. While it may in practice be impossible for the remainder of the network to allow one of its entities to fail (after all, the Enron debacle led to the collapse of Arthur Andersen worldwide), the isolation of each part of the global organisation from claims against other parts may at least put the organisation in a stronger negotiating position when seeking to settle a catastrophic claim. Some international practices may prefer to be able to say to their clients and counterparties that all assets of the worldwide organisation (but not personal assets of the partners) are available to meet claims, and require inter-entity agreements to achieve that result.

All the partners practising in a jurisdiction generally become partners in the LLP or partnership established to conduct the practice there. They receive a share of profits from that LLP and it is only taxed locally. Where insufficient profits are generated locally to provide them with their intended share of the global profits of the international legal practice, they generally receive a top-up profit share from one or more other entities in the organisation, and have to be members of those entities as well. The top-up element is taxable in the jurisdiction of source as well as in the jurisdiction of tax residence, with appropriate double taxation reliefs applying.

The top-up profits usually come from the original entity where the whole international legal practice originated, in which all, or nearly all, partners worldwide are members and which is expected every year to generate more profits than it needs to provide the global profit shares of its own local partners. This entity is referred to below as the 'headquarters entity'.

That leaves the issue of how to deal with any profits generated locally that exceed those needed to provide the partners who practise locally with their intended shares of global legal practice profits. It can be difficult to eliminate these surplus profits by means of licence fees, royalty payments and payments for services provided by the headquarters entity because of international transfer pricing rules. Sometimes this is resolved by arranging for the headquarters entity itself to hold a direct interest in the local entity, which entitles it to the surplus profits. The interest is either held directly, or it is held via a trust declared by the partners in the local entity.

Sometimes, this approach is inappropriate because some of the members of the headquarters entity are not members of professions recognised in the local entity jurisdiction. Professional indemnity considerations also often make it undesirable for one practising entity to hold an interest in another. Tax issues may also arise if the headquarters entity is not treated as tax transparent in the jurisdiction of the local entity or if that jurisdiction regards the trust through which the interest is held as opaque for tax purposes. One approach that is often used to deal with these issues may be for the headquarters entity to nominate a number of 'valve partners' to become members of the local entity. Any surplus local profits can then be allocated to the valve partners, whose profit shares in the headquarters entity are adjusted downwards to take into account their shares of these local profits. Those partners who cannot, perhaps for tax and regulatory reasons, be members of the headquarters entity have to be remunerated wholly through a local entity.

However complicated the structure has to be, it is more crucial than ever for complex international practices that the entire organisation should have a clear governance structure with established reporting lines, responsibilities and accountabilities. A variety of techniques has been developed. One approach is for all, or nearly all, members of each local entity to be members of the headquarters entity as well, so that the headquarters entity can provide overarching governance for the entire organisation. Its constitutional documents can include a range of controls, including duties to behave consistently with global values and with the directions of the management of the headquarters entity (so far as consistent with local regulation). The valve partners can be selected by the management of the headquarters entity and provided with controlling votes locally where permitted by local regulation. The constitutional documents of the headquarters entity and all local entities can include restrictive covenants seeking to reduce the risk of former partners poaching clients and staff, to the extent enforceable. The headquarters entity can also enter into licences and service level agreements whereby the local entity is permitted to use the name and other intellectual property of the network, and the headquarters entity agrees to provide back-office and other services, and these agreements can be used also to cement the organisation and to make it very difficult for a local entity that breaks away to operate successfully thereafter.

In practice there may be a risk that the form of a carefully designed structure like this is ignored, and that in reality the organisation operates exactly as if it were a single worldwide entity. Only global consolidated accounts are produced and the only meetings and decisions that take place do so at a global level. This creates the risk that it might be argued by rebel partners, by tax authorities and by creditors that the structure is really a single worldwide general partnership, and that the complex structure is a sham. It is therefore important to ensure that the substance of the way the organisation works reflects its form.

8. **The Swiss *verein* approach**

More and more international law firms are now moving towards a model first developed by the major international accounting firms. These firms tended to expand more by alliance than organically, and very often they share profits on a local rather than a global basis. Their alliances and mergers have often been structured by setting up a non-practising entity in a suitable low or no tax jurisdiction. Sometimes, a Swiss corporate entity, known as a *verein*, has been used, and this term has come to be used, inaccurately, as a generic term for this kind of structure. This chapter refers to such a non-practising entity as an "overarching vehicle".

Under these arrangements, sometimes all the partners remain partners in their local practising entities but also become members of the overarching vehicle, and sometimes the practising entities themselves become the members of the overarching vehicle. The constitutional documents of the overarching vehicle set out the global governance arrangements. Its management team is responsible for global management and is accountable to its board. Local entities are managed by their own management teams, members of which are also members of the overarching vehicle, or of a firm which is a member of the over-arching vehicle, and the overarching vehicle very often owns the name and other intellectual property of the global organisation and licenses it to the local practising entities. Restrictive covenants and the like are to be found both in the local constitutional documents and in those of the overarching vehicle itself.

Law firms that have expanded by merger have often adopted this kind of approach, and it is becoming more popular as a means of resolving intractable regulatory, tax and governance issues in increasingly complex global structures. Having established an overarching vehicle, the headquarters entity referred to in section 7 above can become just another local entity. All of its non-legal businesses, and any associated trust, fiduciary and other businesses, can be transferred to the overarching vehicle, and if the latter takes a similar legal form to the headquarters entity, it may be possible to do this without serious commercial and tax consequences as between the members. The global governance issues can be addressed in the constitutional documents of the overarching vehicle.

The benefit of this kind of approach is that the degree of control exercised by the overarching vehicle can be designed to comply with local regulatory requirements, and the name and intellectual property, and perhaps any associated trust and fiduciary businesses, can be held in a non-practising entity where there is less risk of exposure to claims. Profit sharing and limitation of liability issues can continue to be dealt with as described in section 7 above and the profits distributed by subsidiaries of the overarching vehicle can be used to even up profit shares of partners in the local operating entities in order to achieve the desired global shares. It may be possible for non-lawyers to participate in governance at the level of the overarching vehicle, and in profits of the non-legal businesses, without falling foul of local regulations.

Thus the verein approach may help law firms to achieve the best of all worlds.

9. **Remaining liability problems: 'lifeboat arrangements'**
In many international structures, it remains necessary, for regulatory reasons, to practise through a general partnership in some jurisdictions. Thus partners practising in those jurisdictions remain exposed to claims against the firm or themselves in the manner described in section 2 above. The same is true of any valve partners who become partners in order to extract surplus profits or to exercise central control. Such partners will generally only have the right to seek contributions from the other partners in the general partnership, and not from partners in LLPs and other limited liability entities practising in other jurisdictions.

A range of products, often called 'lifeboat arrangements', has been developed to reassure those partners that they will not be left hung out to dry, but without reducing the limited liability protection available to other partners. One approach is for the partners in limited liability entities to promise to pay a capped amount to the family of any partner who is bankrupted as a result of a liability claim. Because the promise is made by non-bankrupt partners to the family of the bankrupt partner, the benefit of the promise should be protected from the insolvency of the bankrupt partner. The non-bankrupt partners can then insure the potential risk of a claim by the families of the bankrupted partners. The insolvency law issues arising tend to make the documentation of these arrangements very complex.

10. **Structural reorganisation**
A law firm wishing to reorganise its structure faces a range of challenges. First, it needs to decide what kind of structure will best support its culture and strategy. The key issues will of course include the proposed arrangements for governance, profit sharing and control of risk, especially limitation of liability. It is important, however, to take into account the tax and regulatory environments in which the firm operates. For a firm operating from a single office, the decision may be relatively straightforward, but the addition of each overseas office multiplies the issues and the likely complexity of the structure.

For international legal practices, the best approach to a restructuring project may be to create a small central team with responsibility for the overall project, supported by the internal and external advisers needed to ensure that all the relevant issues are taken into account and the project is designed and delivered efficiently. The starting point is to decide how the overall organisation is to be funded and governed and how its profits are to be shared. Having clarified the desired structure from a commercial point of view, the central team needs to check with local technical teams whether any tax or regulatory issues arise in their jurisdictions as a result, and (if so) to identify potential solutions. The central team will also need to circulate a plan of the steps required to achieve the reorganisation. This may involve transfers of staff, assets and liabilities from the existing to new entities. Again this will need to be tested with the local technical teams in order to identify and deal with any tax and other issues arising. It is desirable to make the constitutional documents of all the practising entities and the documents creating the relationships between entities as standard and consistent as possible. The central team will need to create templates so that the local teams can review and comment on them and develop local versions that take into account local considerations.

Of course it will also be necessary to win the support of partners worldwide for the proposed restructuring. It is important to clarify at an early stage what decisions will be required to authorise the reorganisation, and the majorities and notice periods required. In order to achieve a successful vote, it may also be desirable to put out the proposed structure for wider consultation, to invite comments and questions both in writing and at road shows, and to provide reasoned explanations of why particular suggestions have, or have not, been adopted. It will be important to ensure that every partner understands the particular impact that the proposals will have on him or her.

11. Non-lawyer investors

Ownership by non-lawyers of entities authorised to practise law, as is now permitted in Australia and England and Wales, opens up a range of new possibilities. While the legal practice may still be conducted by a company, a partnership or an LLP, and the senior lawyers may still participate as partners, members, shareholders or directors and employees, the involvement of outsiders will change the dynamics.

Investors participating directly, or through a publicly listed company or private equity fund, will expect the highest standards of governance. They will expect the appointment of a management team they are confident will deliver value for them, as well as for those working in the business. They will also expect an approach to rewards and incentives that takes account of the market conditions and the contribution of those working in the business and that aligns their interests with those of the business and its investors. Even though there is no fundamental reason why they should not participate with those working in the business through a partnership or LLP, investors may prefer to see the practice conducted through a company structure simply because that is the kind of structure with which they will be familiar.

A new form of authorisation may be required by the firm's regulator. In England and Wales, for example, under the Legal Services Act 2007 and the SRA Authorisation Rules, a licensable body of this kind has to undergo a different authorisation process from a traditional law firm, even though, once authorised, the regulatory regime is very similar. It may be very difficult for firms with outside investors to become fully integrated into an international legal practice so long as local regulations in some jurisdictions prevent sharing profits with, or ownership and control by, non-lawyers. Structuring around these difficulties may present a considerable challenge.

12. **Structure of the future law firm**

In the future, law firms will have to adapt to changing market conditions and an evolving regulatory and tax environment. They will have to keep their structures under review and to take steps to ensure that they remain optimal.

The larger legal advisers to international business will continue to extend their international reach as their clients take advantage of the globalisation process. In circumstances where the international harmonisation of law firm regulation and taxation seems as remote as ever, it seems likely that their structures will increase in complexity and that they will need to ensure that complexity does not get in the way of culture, client service and strategy. It is unlikely that many of such international legal practices will take the opportunity to seek outside investors, for the time being, because of the associated regulatory problems.

Increased competition in mature markets seems likely to lead to further consolidation, both within particular jurisdictions and internationally. As the size and complexity of law firms increase, so it will become increasingly difficult to keep the entire practice together. Particular practice and geographic areas may cease to be aligned with the global model, and groups of partners may spin off and form separate boutique firms with far simpler structures.

Client demand for innovative ways of delivering legal services and fee pressure will also drive structural change, as firms explore the means of providing better value to their clients. Examples of such innovations already being pioneered include offshoring, legal process outsourcing, zero hours contract lawyers who are available on demand, and online legal services. There is no reason why a traditional practice should not establish these services as an adjunct to their own, thus raising new structuring issues. Can such a linked business be held through an entity that is not exposed to claims? Should it perhaps be held by an overarching vehicle that does not practise? How should any goodwill value generated over time be shared between different generations of partner, and between working partners and outside investors? How should the structure be designed for tax efficiency and for regulatory compliance purposes?

More and better regulation will drive change forward, as regulators insist on an improved approach to governance and structures have to be adjusted accordingly. Only one thing is certain: the structure of the legal industry is bound to look very different 10 years from now.

13. **Some key structuring considerations for an international practice**

The following international issues of principle should first be considered:
- How will global operations of the international practice be funded and how will that funding be made available to the practices in each jurisdiction?
- Should any of the funding be provided by outside equity investors?
- How will global capital and revenue profits be shared and how will surplus profits in one jurisdiction be shared with partners practising in other jurisdictions?

- How will the international practice be governed? Should governance take place through a practising headquarters entity or through a non-practising overarching vehicle?
- How should the practising entities themselves in each jurisdiction be governed?
- Should the name and other intellectual property of the international practice (and any subsidiary companies) be held by a practising headquarters entity or through a non-practising overarching vehicle, bearing in mind the risk of claims?
- How should the name and other intellectual property rights be made available to other entities in the international practice, and on what terms?
- What kind of support services should be provided globally to local entities, and on what terms?
- What restrictions should affect outgoing partners and outgoing entities that cease to be part of the international practice?
- Should partners practise with limited liability wherever possible, and should attempts be made to prevent assets of one entity in the international practice being affected by the liabilities of another?
- What protection should be provided for any partners who have to become partners in a general partnership owing to local regulations in a particular jurisdiction?

The following technical issues should then be considered in every jurisdiction where an international legal practice operates:
- What kinds of vehicle are permitted by local regulators and do they have limited liability?
- Will the courts of the relevant jurisdiction respect the limited liability of partners practising through entities established in other jurisdictions that are involved in the same client matters?
- How do the costs of incorporation, administration and regulatory compliance of the different available structures compare?
- How do the different structures compare in relation to filing and disclosure requirements?
- Are there any restrictions on who can have an ownership interest in a law firm, have influence over it and share its profits, and what are they?
- How will the regulator in the relevant jurisdiction regulate overseas branches of the entity?
- Do any applicable regulatory requirements affect the way the entity in the relevant jurisdiction can be governed? For example, is there anything to prevent the entity or its members agreeing to comply with directions from an overarching vehicle or headquarters entity?
- What kind of structure is most tax efficient in relation to profits allocated among the partners practising locally?
- If the local entity does not generate sufficient profits to meet the intended profit shares of those practising through it, what is the most tax-efficient way of topping up their shares from other entities?

- If the local entity generates profits that are surplus to local requirements, what is the most tax-efficient method of sharing them with the partners of the international practice who practise elsewhere?
- What is the local tax treatment of royalties and service charges paid to the headquarters entity or overarching vehicle, and what transfer pricing issues arise?
- Will transferring the name and other intellectual property of the international practice to the entity that is to hold it, and any licence to the entity in the relevant jurisdiction, have any local tax consequences?
- What kind of entity is most tax efficient when partners retire or their profit shares go down?

Governance structures

Anthony E Davis
Hinshaw & Culbertson LLP
Jaime Fernández Madero
Fernández Madero Consulting
Markus Hartung
Bucerius Center on the Legal Profession
Richard Turnor
Maurice Turnor Gardner LLP

1. **Purpose of governance**

    A law firm must be well governed if it is to succeed in a complex, competitive and fast-changing world.

    At the most basic level, somebody needs to be responsible for ensuring that there is an infrastructure enabling the firm to operate effectively. The infrastructure must accommodate all aspects of day-to-day operational management, including finance, human resources (HR), information technology, risk, compliance, knowledge management and business development.

    Infrastructure alone is not enough. A strategy gives direction to the efforts of everyone involved in the business and enables the firm to allocate resources effectively. Somebody must have responsibility for developing and maintaining the firm's strategy, and somebody must set measurable aims as part of the strategy, so that everyone in the business knows exactly what is required of them and so that their performance can be evaluated and managed. The strategy needs to be capable of responding to changing circumstances and should leave entrepreneurial partners with the freedom to pursue their own opportunities in a way that is aligned with the broader strategy. Someone also needs to take responsibility for ensuring that the firm understands the ever-changing risks which threaten it and its strategy, and for ensuring that controls are in place to mitigate those risks.

    The firm will be able to develop a more effective strategy, and will have a better view of the associated risks, if it understands how the world is changing, and what that means for its clients and therefore for the firm. Developing and maintaining this vision will require vigilance, active enquiry and deep thought from the firm's leaders.

    Finally, at the highest level, shared values help everyone in the business to react constructively to contentious issues. Articulating agreed values and securing universal adherence to them requires both leadership and engagement from everyone working in the business. Even if a merged firm combines businesses with very different histories and cultures, it should still be able to develop core values with which everyone can identify. These values are likely to include:

    - integrity;
    - a focus on the interests of clients;
    - dedication to quality and hard work;
    - a disciplined approach to financial sustainability;

- consensus about how profits are shared;
- acceptance that decisions made after due process must be respected;
- intolerance of bad practice;
- respect for everyone and for local culture; and
- concern for the present and future success of those working in the business.

2. Principles of governance

Even though the values listed above probably apply to almost all law firms and indeed to professional service firms generally, there needs to be a structured approach to governance. This structured approach is normally referred to as corporate governance, or good corporate governance. Literature and research on corporate governance in law firms hardly exists, but law firms have been able to borrow from research and best practice developed for other types of corporation. Bearing in mind that traditional law firms (not structured as corporations but as partnerships or limited liability partnerships (LLPs)) are different because of their non-hierarchical ownership structure, let us briefly remind ourselves what corporate governance is all about:

According to a commonly held view (as is summarised in Wikipedia, for example):

Corporate Governance refers to the system by which corporations are directed and controlled. The governance structure specifies the distribution of rights and responsibilities among different participants in the corporation (such as the board of directors, managers, shareholders, creditors, auditors, regulators, and other stakeholders) and specifies the rules and procedures for making decisions in corporate affairs. Governance provides the structure through which corporations set and pursue their objectives, while reflecting the context of the social, regulatory and market environment. Governance is a mechanism for monitoring the actions, policies and decisions of corporations. Governance involves the alignment of interests among the stakeholders.

This rather general definition of corporate governance is not sufficient. Therefore, certain principles of corporate governance have been developed further, which can be taken into account when setting up a structure. These principles can be summarised as follows (more thoroughly discussed at www.oecd.org/daf/ca/corporategovernanceprinciples/31557724.pdf):

- rights and equitable treatment of shareholders;
- interests of other non-shareholder stakeholders, including employees, investors, creditors, suppliers, local communities, customers and policy makers;
- role and responsibilities of the board;
- integrity and ethical behaviour; and
- disclosure and transparency.

To this we would add the need for the role of everyone in the business, from the most junior to the board itself, to be clear, understood and to receive constructive support, challenge and oversight from another member of the firm.

All these principles are applicable to professional service firms, and to law firms in particular, irrespective of their size. Corporate governance is by no means only applicable to large law firms. Small and medium-sized firms have to measure themselves against these principles as well.

There is a major difference between governance structures in law firms and other corporations, however. As a general rule, governance structures go hand in hand with hierarchies and clear reporting lines. In many law firms, non-hierarchical structures and equity amongst partners are essential for the culture of the firm and for the commitment of the partners. There is no empirical evidence, but we would make the point that every law firm with a strong culture, including strong glue amongst partners, seems to be more successful than law firms lacking such partnership ethos: though again empirically unproven, it is the ownership and entrepreneurial spirit of the partners that drive a firm forward. That has to be borne in mind when it comes to setting up a governance structure in a law firm. Law firms fail if they organise this process like a standard corporation: unlike corporations, law firms have to make sure that partners as owners buy into the governance structure. This applies to the first and third of the above-mentioned principles in particular: respect for the rights and equitable treatment of shareholders, otherwise known as equity amongst partners, is essential. This is one of the major obstacles when it comes to (hierarchical) structures in law firms: striking the right balance between the independence of lawyers (as partners and owners) and the structural requirements of modern law firms. It seems to be a conundrum: law firms fail if their governance structures are not accepted by partners, and yet they also fail without such structures.

So, do not even think about just copying and pasting the structural elements described below. Rather, try to find the ideal set-up for your own firm. It may well differ from the ideal for other law firms, even for your closest competitors. Bear in mind that governance structures have a lot to do with culture, and therefore your governance structure should be aligned with your culture and your strategic goals, not with the governance structure of your competitors.

3. Governance structure and process

3.1 Management team

Everyone in the firm has their part to play in the delivery of its strategic plan. In a larger practice, leadership of the service departments is provided by the finance director, the general counsel responsible for all legal issues affecting the firm, the risk manager, the IT director, the HR director, the business development or marketing director and so on. In client-facing roles, leadership is provided by the leaders of the firm's key offices and practice lines.

However, not all of these leaders need to be members of the core management team. This team is likely to be more effective if it is small and nimble. The core team might include a managing partner or CEO, a finance director and the general counsel. The other operational leads can then report to this team and look to it for the resources and support they need.

Sometimes the managing partner is directly elected by the partners and sometimes he or she is appointed by the board or management committee. Generally, the managing partner has considerable latitude to appoint the other members of his or her core team, and often to appoint the managers of different offices and practice lines as well. Thus the managing partner can build teams with members who work well together and all of whom are made answerable to him or her.

Whereas there is now general acceptance that functions such as finance, human resources and information technology need to be led by a specialist, many firms still believe that only a long-serving partner can have a deep enough understanding of the firm to enable him or her to fulfil a senior leadership role and to command the respect of partners. This view is now showing signs of changing. Apart from the general counsel and practice leaders, none of these posts necessarily needs to be filled by a lawyer. Outside investors are certainly unlikely to share the view that only an insider, who may lack any comparable outside management experience, can fill the managing partner role. They may insist on filling the post with the best possible person by means of a well-conducted search, as happens in most other industries. There is a growing belief in some quarters that any firm could benefit from this sort of approach, whether or not it has outside investors, and even if an appointee has no history in the firm or experience as a lawyer.

Perhaps an internal appointee as managing partner, supported by a team of externally appointed managers, provides the best of all worlds.

3.2 Board

Consistently with the principles of governance, the management team should itself be subject to challenge and oversight. The partners as a group may be able to fulfil this need in a small firm, but time spent on these issues inevitably distracts them from looking after the interests of clients and developing the firm's business. In any firm with more than (say) fifteen partners, and especially in an international firm, effective oversight is therefore best delegated to a board, which can also provide the management team with support and advice. This board might be a unitary board which includes the core management team. In order to secure effective challenge, the unitary board should include a majority of members who have the standing and experience to provide effective oversight. Alternatively, a firm might choose to establish a separate supervisory board.

3.3 Chair

Chairing the board is a crucial function, whichever route is chosen. This role is generally fulfilled by a senior partner who exercises his or her independent judgement in setting the agenda, ensuring that all strategic issues are properly discussed and that sufficient time is set aside to consider more routine, but equally vital, risk management issues. This task is performed in consultation with the management team and with the non-management members of the board. The chair also has an important task of ensuring that views are gathered from the wider partnership and considered appropriately. Very often, the senior partner also takes on the role of a mediator, resolving internal partner relationship issues, and of an ambassador, representing the firm externally. Sometimes these different roles are separated and different office holders chair meetings of the board, act as mediator and act as ambassador.

3.4 Accountability to the partners

The managing partner, senior partner/board chair and members of the supervisory board, or the non-management members of the unitary board, can be made directly accountable to the partnership as a whole by means of an electoral process. Individual partners are invited to stand for the managing and senior partner posts, perhaps with a requirement of a minimum number of nominations. Some firms arrange for other board places to be filled by treating different offices or practice groups as constituencies that can elect their own representatives to the board. Others, and especially very large firms where the constituency route is impracticable, arrange for everyone to vote for the candidates for every role, perhaps using the standard transferable vote or a similar system, and require that those standing must have the support of a minimum number of partners through a nominations process. The firm's constitutional documents specify the way in which votes are cast and counted, and any external arrangements for supervision of elections (in England and Wales, for example, the Electoral Reform Society is often asked to supervise). In order to avoid over-politicisation of the electoral process, limits can be placed on the resources (whether temporal or monetary) that can be devoted to electioneering. Ideally the timing of elections would be staggered so as to ensure continuity of the firm's corporate memory.

3.5 Committees, external support and non-executive directors

In a complex business, it may not be practicable to expect the full board to oversee all aspects of governance, and so aspects are delegated to committees.

For example, an audit and finance committee might assume responsibility for risk and financial stability issues, reporting to the board and supported by the finance team and perhaps by a separate internal risk team. The finance director is likely to be a member of this committee, but a majority of independent members is likely to be included, in order to ensure effective oversight. Its agenda is likely to cover both audit and finance and the audit part of any meeting is likely to be attended by the firm's external auditors, who will be accountable to the firm through the meeting. Some internal audit functions may also be outsourced, perhaps to a different firm from the external auditors. These two sets of auditors can provide the firm with an external perspective on best practice.

Responsibility for strategy may also be delegated, ensuring that there is a body which devotes the whole of its agenda to the consideration of the firm's vision and strategy. The strategy committee would work closely with the management team and would report to the board.

Some issues may be more appropriate for a committee that is entirely independent of management. For example, a remuneration committee comprising directly elected members, or independent members of the board, can be made responsible for or for supervising any decisions regarding the allocation of profits between members. A nominations committee could be made responsible for appointing external non-executive directors.

Law firms have been slow to use external non-executive directors even though their corporate clients regard the oversight, external experience and advice of appropriate non-executives as an essential part of their own corporate governance. Perhaps this reluctance stems from a belief that the internally elected board members, who are charged with oversight of the management team, can already fulfil this function adequately. The danger of only appointing insiders to the board, however, is that the firm can become insular and may miss opportunities and risks that could have been be picked up by someone with relevant external experience.

3.6 Compliance officers

In England and Wales there is now a regulatory requirement for the appointment of two compliance officers, one of whom (the compliance officer for legal practice (COLP)) must be a lawyer. Both the COLP and the compliance officer for finance and administration (COFA) must either be employees of, or principals in, the business. They must have the experience, standing and authority needed to enable them to ensure that there is a systematic approach to compliance and risk management and that breaches of compliance are recorded and (if material) reported to the Solicitors Regulatory Authority (SRA). The COLP and COFA now form a *de facto* part of the governance structure of firms in England and Wales, and the SRA expects them to ensure that risks associated with the firm's involvement in an international organisation are also managed. There is no prohibition against the managing partner being the COLP or COFA, or against the same person fulfilling both roles, but combining compliance officer and management roles means that the opportunity of a layer of oversight and challenge will have been lost and conflicts of interest may arise.

3.7 Governance structures of international and global firms

The objectives and principles of governance are exactly the same for an international as for a domestic practice, but the more widespread and complex a practice is, the greater the governance challenges become. Quite apart from such differences as culture, market conditions and profitability, the very fact that a firm is international inevitably means that its internal structure must be more complex. The challenge is how to establish a workable system for governing a complex structure established for tax, regulatory and other reasons.

Overall worldwide governance is normally vested in an overarching entity, however the organisation is structured. The structure is likely to provide for a global managing partner or CEO, a global management team, a global chair or senior partner, a global board, global committees and so on.

This overarching entity may itself practice as a law firm, or it may act as holding company for some of the organisation's businesses (such as trustee and fiduciary businesses). It may simply provide information technology, HR, business development and other support to the organisation as a whole. It may also set the values, standards and strategy applicable to the whole organisation, and everyone within the organisation may be contractually committed to compliance with the directions of its board (so far as permitted by regulation in each jurisdiction).

Even so, governance arrangements must respect the form of the global structure if it is not to be treated as a sham. Day-to-day management of local practising entities should be left to their individual management bodies. In larger practices, local practising entities may have sophisticated governance structures of their own. Depending on local tax and regulatory requirements, it may be possible to provide for the overarching entity to appoint the management of local practising entities, or at least to exercise control through those with majority votes.

A further challenge is how to make the partners worldwide feel like part of a global firm even if the firm has its origins in a particular jurisdiction. It will be helpful to locate some of the firm's central management functions in one place, not necessarily in the location where the firm's history began. For example, it may be possible to move many back-office functions to a neutral low-cost jurisdiction. It is important to encourage candidates from different locations to stand for senior roles and helpful to vary the location of meetings. Avoiding language which suggests that the seat of power is in a particular jurisdiction (such as referring to anywhere else as an 'overseas office') is helpful when trying to establish a genuinely global culture.

3.8 Outside investors

Jurisdictions such as England and Wales and Australia now permit outside investment in law firms. A private equity fund or public company holding an interest in a law firm is likely to demand a more structured approach to governance that is compliant with best practice in the corporate world.

4. Tools of governance

4.1 Reporting

Complete transparency of information is fundamental to effective governance of a law firm (whatever business structure has been adopted). Both management and the firm's owners (whether shareholders, LLP members or partners and all referred to in this chapter as 'partners') must ensure that all relevant information about the firm and its business and professional performance are regularly circulated and discussed. The recent demise of some well-known law firms is ample evidence of what can happen when management does not provide the partners (as well as the firm's lenders) with complete information.

Transparency is accomplished by regular (monthly, or at least quarterly) reporting of the basic metrics of the firm's operations. The reports should include basic financial information regarding cash, income and expenses, as well as the level of work in the firm generally and in its separate offices and practice areas if the firm is so structured. Many firms circulate even more detail, breaking down each or many of these categories by individual partner.

Additionally, the firm's leadership groups should keep and circulate minutes of their meetings. In this way, the owners are in a position to ask questions on a timely basis, and matters requiring wider discussion can be aired in a timely manner. Standard topics are likely to include:
- profitability and budgeting;

- the level of work in each practice area;
- headcount and hiring, and human resource management of professional and support staff;
- major developments in the addition or loss of significant clients, marketing and client development activities;
- major initiatives that will involve extraordinary expenses, such as special IT expenses;
- real estate (leases, office issues); and
- information technology, including data security.

Sometimes it may be necessary to exclude especially sensitive commercial discussions from the minutes prepared for wide circulation, perhaps in order to reduce the risk of a leak during sensitive negotiations, to protect the privacy of individual partners who are subject to scrutiny or to protect legal privilege. In those cases, the board members will need to record the reasons for withholding that information. It may also be appropriate to ask a core group of non-management opinion makers to work with and provide support and challenge to the management team on behalf of all partners. It is also important to consider whether withholding that information from other partners may have an adverse impact on them, and if so, what are the means of mitigating that impact.

4.2 Meetings on and off site

The frequency of meetings varies widely between firms. Very small firms often arrange weekly or fortnightly meetings of the partners, who effectively operate like a board. As firms get bigger, they tend towards weekly meetings of the management team, perhaps monthly board meetings and less frequent meetings of the whole partner body. Partner meetings are also an opportunity to hold elections, or to announce appointments relating to management changes in accordance with the firm's business and constitutional documents. For practical reasons, some of the very large international firms can hold only infrequent (perhaps annual or biannual) meetings of the partners as a whole. Decision making and elections are then often conducted via the firm's intranet and email between partner meetings, and partner meetings are held informally off site. This approach is perfectly acceptable provided that there is a steady flow of complete and accurate information as discussed above, and effective oversight and accountability in the periods between meetings.

There is significant value to holding partner meetings off site, and away even from a firm's headquarter offices, whether the meetings are for decision making or not. This can help to ensure that one office does not dominate and other offices feel like equal partners in a global firm. It is also important for the partners to recognise the need to take time away from practice and the ordinary routine in order to gather together and discuss collective professional and business issues. Although these events can involve significant expense, the value in terms of maintaining and building the firm's culture and expressing common purpose and objectives is critical to every firm's long-term stability and well-being. Even in hard economic times, it is not a prudent cost saving to postpone or defer these meetings. On the contrary, those are the moments when the group's need to coalesce around a common strategy is more important than ever.

4.3 **Agenda setting and board papers**

As noted above, the senior partner (in consultation with the management team, the board and partners generally) often has responsibility for ensuring that all the relevant issues are properly considered at the appropriate level and in a timely way.

Board agendas and agendas for board-level committees will inevitably include a number of standing items, such as reviewing management accounts and key risks, and it is important that time should be set aside for these as well as for consideration of more strategic matters and urgent one-off items. Reports would normally be distributed in advance of periodic full partner body meetings and the firm's leaders should lead discussions, covering the same general headings as the regular periodic reports.

Board papers should be clear, so that discussion can be as well informed as possible. They should be as brief as is consistent with clarity and transparency, and expressed in plain language. It is rarely appropriate to clutter board papers with the detailed working papers of the management team, though it may be necessary to include correspondence with the firm's external advisers and other relevant materials that need to be taken into account.

Papers for full partner meetings, likewise, should be as brief and as clear as possible and should give partners all the information they need to take into account in the discussions proposed at the relevant meeting.

4.4 **Use of technology**

Technology can be very helpful as a means of communicating and organising board papers. iPads and similar devices, combined with an appropriate App such as Boardpad, can be very useful means of avoiding a proliferation of paper and of facilitating meetings and voting.

Indeed, it is debatable whether a truly international or global practice could exist at all were it not for technology. An intranet site can be used to give worldwide partners access to information about the firm's governance structure, reporting lines, values, practice standards, policies and procedures. It can also be used as a secure and accessible place to record relevant financial information, board papers, minutes and so on. Email and webcasts provide an excellent means of communication with a partner body located in many different places and time zones, and thereby of disseminating information about values, the firm's vision, strategy and the capabilities of different practice groups to help one another's clients.

The topic of information technology generally is covered extensively in other chapters of this work. For present purposes it is sufficient to note that in order to practice law effectively, law firms of all sizes must be technologically proficient. This involves an understanding of the necessary components of hardware and software in order to be able to provide services to clients, and an understanding of the precautions required in order to preserve clients' confidential information. What is appropriate for any given firm will depend on its location, on the type of practice in which it engages and the type of clients it serves. What is reasonable for a small firm with a single office working solely on decedents' estates is likely to differ fundamentally from the needs of a global firm serving highly regulated financial institutions. But all law firms have one thing in common in the modern world – the need to manage their IT operations effectively in order to meet these twin requirements of serving clients efficiently using appropriate technology, while also taking all reasonable steps to protect and preserve client confidentiality. In very small firms, this may be delegated to an outside consultant, but in firms of any significant size this will necessarily require staff led by qualified individuals with the necessary skills to assure the firm that both of these responsibilities will be met at all times.

4.5 **Risk management**
Law firms need to have a clearly defined risk management structure in place that is fully supported by the firm's leaders. This will normally have the following components.

A General Counsel is normally appointed and designated to oversee all of the risk management and compliance functions. These will include ultimate responsibility for client intake with special reference to conflicts of interest, insurance, claims, contracts, compliance with regulatory standards of all kinds (both professional ethics rules and those imposed by government agencies such as money-laundering regimes, data security and so on) and the development and promulgation of firm-wide policies and procedures to assure continuing compliance with those policies throughout the firm. The General Counsel also act as the firm's lawyer whenever issues arise involving the firm's professional duties or the activities of individual lawyers. Depending on the size of the firm, the role may be accomplished by one individual on a part-time basis, or an individual overseeing an Office of the General Counsel with deputies and subordinates in each separate area of responsibility.

In some jurisdictions, such as in England and Wales, the function is either inclusive of or parallel to the role of compliance officer (the COLP and COFA). That role, whether subsumed in or separate from the general counsel function, will have the obligation to maintain a register of incidents where breaches of policies and procedures have occurred.

A risk register can be very helpful. It is normally built up from the risks perceived at the grass roots of the firm, and it is a convenient and clear way of recording, organising and grading them so that the firm's leaders can monitor them appropriately. The register categorises groups of risks that threaten the firm or its strategy (eg, financial, competitive and compliance-related risks). It also records the controls in place to mitigate each risk, evaluates the risk's likelihood and potential impact, and names the person or persons charged with monitoring and reporting on each risk. It can also specify the frequency with which reports on particular risks should be made to the board or appropriate committee. High-risk and new items can be flagged in red or amber, and routinely discussed as a standing item at every relevant board or committee meeting. It is important that the register should be a dynamic document, which is regularly reviewed and updated. A number of off-the-peg software packages are available to support the risk register.

This bottom-up approach can be supplemented by a top-down counterpart in the form of a 'board assurance framework'. This document would record what senior management regards as the firm's strategic priorities, the person in charge of delivering each priority, the relevant risks and the measures in place to ensure delivery of the strategy. This dual approach may help to ensure full coverage of all risks threatening the firm and its strategy. Both documents will be very helpful when it comes to agenda setting.

Many firms have recognised the benefit of regular file reviews. Reviews might be limited simply to checking compliance with the firm's policies and procedures on such matters as client acceptance, file closing and document retention. Reviews might also extend to the regular assessment of the quality of work of individual partners, although this will require much more experienced reviewers. The review might be conducted internally (in which case some firms retain retired partners and staff to help) or by peer firms or external consultants. Whatever the approach, care must be taken to ensure that client confidentiality is protected. In some jurisdictions, such as several of the Australian states, regulators have established explicit requirements for firms to articulate in writing clear standards for their operations and require the regular review of compliance with those standards in order to reduce significantly grievances and claims.

If the firm's accounts are audited by external auditors, they will normally wish to test the robustness of risk management controls, as part of testing the reporting of liabilities. They may also be able to comment on market developments and best practice in the light of their wider experience.

In the case of larger and more complex firms, an internal audit function may be helpful to support the General Counsel and his or her team. This might be established as an internal function, or (like many corporates) the firm might retain an external 'internal' auditor such as an accounting firm (not necessarily the same firm as the external auditors because of the risk of conflicting duties). A budget for internal auditing work would normally be agreed at the beginning of each year, together with the internal audit priorities for that year. The internal auditors can then look into the area specified in depth and report to the appropriate board or committee. In this way the internal auditors can help the firm to identify areas where its operations could be less costly or more efficient and (over time) help it to become more effective.

5. A Latin-American perspective

The Latin-American legal market has only partially developed from a management perspective, with few exceptions. Latin-American firms have been traditionally managed in an informal and family-like manner. Partners normally take decisions based on intuition and on a case-by-case basis. As owners, they are reluctant to accept controls and rules unless strictly necessary. Consequently, you could find different partners applying different criteria to similar situations. This informal approach tends to influence all aspects of a firm's management, including risk management.

To be successful, risk management policies require certain general conditions such as a clear vision and set of values, discipline, consistency, long-term objectives, an adequate rewards and compensation system, intense training and coaching and, most importantly, a strong culture that supports such policies. All these aspects are difficult to achieve in immature markets, especially if you consider all these conditions together. Some firms make progress in some aspects but lag behind in others that, in many cases, result in failures because of inconsistencies and contradictions.

Given all the above, some best practices and suggested solutions that work in more sophisticated legal markets might be difficult to apply or even understand in less-developed markets. Law firms are organisations with a high level of political or cultural content. That means that their functioning is not primarily defined by technical or efficiency criteria from a management perspective but by (1) the type of agreements and understandings that their members are able to produce, and (2) the general cultural environment – legal, economic and sociological – in which they operate. As a result, norms and processes are not necessarily adopted because of their expected operational efficiency, but because of the value or cultural content that the participants see in them. The horizontal structure of law firms and the autonomy with which lawyers work make it only harder to apply rules in which they do not believe.

Consequently, leaders of Latin-American law firms, and of international practices establishing operations in the region, should be cautious about simply rolling out solutions that are considered appropriate in other jurisdictions. There is a risk of these solutions being rejected, or simply ignored, if members cannot recognise their value to their specific situation. Does that mean that these law firms, and those establishing operations in the region, should not look into what other more sophisticated markets have done? On the contrary, the experience of more developed markets is an excellent source of potential solutions since problems, at the end of the day, are quite similar across jurisdictions. But the key to that exercise is that leaders of Latin-American firms become able to process any foreign ideas through the lens of their own practices and cultures. Otherwise, adopting sophisticated solutions will require autocratic decisions with little support from the remaining partners, and we know how far that can go.

Having said all the above, as legal markets become more global and sophisticated, law firms also need to aspire to more professional standards in dealing with risk management, and that implies a shortening of the gap between local and international standards.

An effective governance system – in relation to both processes and principles – is one of the pillars that would allow successful results in a risk management strategy. Governance issues should be covered from two perspectives:

5.1 Decision-making level

Any successful risk management programme will require a high level of support from partners. They need to understand why this is important for the firm and themselves, and commit to apply what has been decided, both at a personal and group level. Since tensions will be created and negative reactions are likely to occur, it is key that partners are part of the decision-making process and, after approval, they commit to a successful implementation. This is not a matter only relevant to the managing partner or a management committee, but to all the firm.

In order to achieve this, firms need to:
- become knowledgeable about standards used in other jurisdictions and how these can be useful for the firm's own practice;
- determine how much conflict those standards have with their present practices and cultural values, in the firm and in the market;
- discuss with partners which standards would be useful to adopt, their pros and cons and difficulties for implementation and be creative in finding the right balance between what would be desirable and what is realistic;
- make a joint strategic decision over the direction they want to take and how they are going to make change happen.

5.2 Implementation level

Once a clear decision has been taken and the partners' buy-in is guaranteed, an adequate implementation strategy should be established. Some basic recommendations at this stage could be:
- A risk management programme should be simple to understand and apply. Anything considered too bureaucratic and complex is bound to fail. It is better have fewer rules and systems that actually work.
- Invest time, energy and resources to make this strategy understandable for all the organisation, and get their commitment to apply it.
- Partners in charge of practice groups should be part of the governance structure, to ensure effective implementation and follow-up.
- Effective communication between partners is very important to avoid inconsistencies and solve problems effectively.
- A small group should be empowered to resolve conflicts in a fast and efficient manner, to avoid endless discussions and implementation deadlocks. This group should also invest time in problem-case analysis so that the firm can learn from prior experience.
- Sufficient time and energy should be applied to provide adequate education to the lawyers, both from a technical and cultural perspective. Only through direct communication – and not just emails – will partners and associates understand the importance and objectives of a risk management system.
- Be consistent in its application, and be ready to bear the costs when results are not positive.
- Be ready to accept faults and mistakes, and do not become disappointed. This is not a project to be completed overnight, but rather a continuous exercise. You have to be persistent. An enduring commitment from all the organisation is key to the success of any significant change.

Professional indemnity insurance: practical considerations in an increasingly international market

Janet M Henderson
Brit Syndicate 2987
Ernst Millaard
Aon Global Risk Consultants

1. **Introduction**

   This book seeks to help law firms minimise risk and professional liability exposure but there comes a point when some issues simply cannot be avoided and despite the firm's best efforts, bad things happen to good people. Such risks pose a real financial danger and professional indemnity (PI) insurance can protect the firm's balance sheet from such exposure. There are law firms around today that simply would not exist if they hadn't purchased adequate professional liability insurance in the past. A robust PI policy with a reputable carrier is therefore a practical necessity, and viewed with the proper perspective, can provide substantial peace of mind in a troublesome climate.

   In some parts of the world it is still rare for lawyers to face lawsuits brought by clients alleging legal malpractice. However, in the United States, the United Kingdom and an increasing number of other territories the number of lawsuits brought against lawyers has increased significantly, the severity (size) of verdicts and settlements has been greatly enlarged, and perhaps even more alarmingly, it is not at all uncommon any more for lawyers to be sued by non-clients for perceived wrongdoing. Sometimes lawyers just get caught in the crossfire of litigants in the adversarial system or are simply obvious targets for clients living in an increasingly litigious society and looking for someone to blame for bad outcomes.

   Professional indemnity (PI) insurance, as we will refer to it in this chapter, can also be referred to as errors and omissions (E&O) insurance, which is non-specific and refers to liability insurance for professionals in general, or lawyers professional liability (LPL) insurance, which is a term most commonly used in the USA.

2. **How does the policy work?**

   The detailed answer to this question can depend upon where in the world the lawyer is practising, but in an attempt to give a globally acceptable answer: a (PI) policy protects lawyers and their firms in the event that a third party seeks financial recompense for a perceived professional mistake in rendering legal services to a client. In understanding what is covered, it is just as important to understand what your policy does not cover. This chapter is not large enough to give detail for each territory or product but below is a broad global standard.

PI policies generally only address professional services. 'Professional services' is a term which is nearly always defined specifically in the policy, either in the definitions section or in the language of the insuring agreement. PI policies generally exclude the following:

- Bodily injury, property damage, emotional distress – professional liability policies are intended to cover economic losses occasioned by professional malpractice; they are not intended to cover personal injuries or damage to tangible property. Most US policies also exclude emotional distress damages but if your policy is based on a wide civil liability form, such as UK and most European policies, this cover is not expressly excluded.
- Fee disputes, disgorgement of legal fees – even when disgorgement of legal fees is not addressed in a policy exclusion, cover is usually prohibited in most policy language. The operative definition of damages excludes from their scope legal fees paid to the insured.
- Known claims, pre-existing claims – sometimes a carrier addresses through exclusionary language its intent that cover is not available for claims that the insured knew or should have known about prior to the policy period, or for claims reported to prior carriers.

2.1 Structure of a PI policy

Although they are not always neatly identified, all policies contain essentially four parts: declarations, the insuring agreement, conditions, and exclusions. Only when all these elements of the policy are read together is it possible to determine what is and is not covered, and to what extent.

(a) Declarations page

The declaration page declares what the coverage is and to whom it belongs.

(b) Insuring agreement

The insuring agreement creates the coverage that is provided.

The language describes in broad terms what risks fall within the protection of the policy, who (besides the named insured) is considered insured under the policy, and what events or occurrences trigger coverage. In short, the insuring agreement states in broad terms what protection is being purchased under the policy.

(c) Conditions

The conditions describe the obligations of the insured in the event of a claim, and specify certain conditions that must exist for coverage to apply.

For example, this is where the policy states:
- what an insured is required to report in the event of a claim;

- when reporting is required;
- geographic limitations on where the policy will apply; and
- extended reporting endorsement options.

Essentially, the conditions portion of the policy contains the terms and conditions of coverage of claims.

(d) *Exclusions*

All policies contain clauses that delineate or limit coverage for certain acts or under certain circumstances. These clauses address acts or events that are not covered under the policy. Examples include:
- liabilities not arising out of professional services (such as personal injury or property damage);
- 'moral' risks (such as fraud or intentional acts);
- statutory fines and penalties;
- sanctions;
- punitive damages;
- bodily injury.

Exclusions may also address and exclude known risks or risks that were not disclosed to the carrier in the application.

2.2 Other important policy features

(a) *Definitions*

Today, virtually every policy contains a definitions section, where key terms in the policy are defined for the purposes of interpretation and understanding. Frequently defined terms are in bold quotation marks where they appear throughout the policy for ease of reference. The definitions section is generally a part of the insuring agreement; it specifies the meaning of terms used in the policy, such as 'professional services', 'claim', and even 'damages'.

(b) *Reporting requirements*

Language within the policy, frequently in the conditions section, specifies the insured's obligations to report certain events to the carrier in order to trigger or preserve coverage. It is essential to understand these requirements because compliance with reporting requirements is typically a condition precedent to coverage.

(c) *Cooperation clause*

Also usually under conditions, this language creates a contractual obligation by the insured to cooperate with the carrier in investigating, defending and settling claims or determining coverage. A typical cooperation clause prohibits the assumption of another's risk.

(d) *Other insurance*
These clauses dictate the application of this policy when other policies of insurance provide coverage for the same risk. It is frequently designed to limit coverage to situations only where no other insurance applies. Alternatively, it may limit coverage to an excess basis if other insurance applies.

(e) *Endorsements*
Endorsements are specialised additions to a policy, which modify coverage contained within the policy by further defining the insuring agreement or conditions. Endorsements are often attached to the policy as a separate page and may expand or limit coverage.

(f) *Coverage territory*
Usually a condition to the policy, this clause specifies either or both: where the insuring event must have occurred and where the claim must be made for coverage to apply. Normal practice in almost all countries of the world is to provide worldwide coverage excluding the United States, but sometimes work conducted in the United States is included with special clauses and restricted limits.

(g) *Limits*
The per-claim or 'any one claim' limit refers to the most the carrier will pay for a single claim or all claims from any number of claimants arising out of the same act or omission made under the policy during that policy period.

The aggregate limit refers to the most the carrier will pay for multiple claims made during a single policy period. Larger firms outside the United States should try to avoid an aggregate limit where possible in order to ensure that all clients can rely on the coverage of the firm's policy. In reality, however, US firms must accept an aggregate limit.

(h) *Claims expenses*
A critical term of every policy is how it treats claims expenses in relation to the per-claim limit. This information should be located on the declarations page, but may also exist within the policy. Claims expenses are usually defined in policies as the costs of investigating, adjusting and defending claims. Most often claims expenses include defence costs, expert fees, mediation and arbitration fees, and court costs. The term never includes internal costs of the insurance carrier itself, such as the salaries of its in-house adjusters or investigators, or the costs of investigating coverage or adjusting the claim.

This term is critical because every policy limit either includes (costs inclusive) or excludes (costs in addition) claims expenses. In the United States and some other territories the per-claim policy limit includes claims expenses. This means the policy has only that limit available, not just for payment of a judgment or settlement, but also for defence costs.

In some parts of the world carriers offer defence expenses outside limits coverage, or a defence allowance, either automatically as part of the insuring agreement or as an option for purchase. With this type of policy, the per-claim limit does not include defence costs. The defence allowance is sometimes stated in the declarations and the amount the carrier will pay for claims expenses can carry its own separate limit. However, in the United Kingdom, Europe and in much of Australia the costs available in addition to the indemnity limit are not capped.

(i)   *Deductibles*

Most policies include a provision that requires the insured to pay the first amount of a claim, up to a certain quantum, which is that insured's deductible. The deductible amount is always stated in the declarations page, and carriers offer differing amounts as deductibles, depending upon the size of the firm, the type of practice and the premium paid.

While the deductible always applies to the first monies paid out for a claim, it may or may not apply to defence costs. Some policies provide defence costs without a deductible as an additional coverage for purchase. Otherwise, the insured's obligation to pay the deductible is triggered by the first amounts paid out, whether they are for defence or indemnity. Because many more claims require defence costs than ultimately require indemnity payments, the application or non-application of a deductible to defence costs is an important provision in any policy.

For larger firms, carriers will require a self-insured retention instead of a deductible. A self-insured retention differs from a deductible in that the insured actually retains the risk of loss up to a certain amount, and the carrier has no obligation to defend or pay the claim until the self-insured retention is exhausted.

It should be apparent from the above that there are no redundant terms in PI policies. Policies therefore need to be read carefully, and from beginning to end, if their scope and limitations are to be fully understood.

3. Geographical differences

Most countries have a system that sets rules that every lawyer has to take out an individual policy or a policy per firm with minimum terms in order to be permitted to practise law. This is the case in the United Kingdom, Ireland, Canada, Australia, Italy, Switzerland, Norway, the Netherlands, Germany and many more.

The bar association, law society or controlling legal body sets the compliance rules for the policies.

3.1 United Kingdom

In the United Kingdom the rules surrounding PI insurance have undergone some changes in recent years. There is also, of course, the clear distinction in the United Kingdom between solicitors and barristers. For the purpose of this chapter we are only addressing coverage for solicitors. There are minimum terms and conditions of cover, which form Appendix 1 of the Solicitors' Indemnity Insurance Rules. At the time of writing the minimum limits required are £2 million for any one claim for sole practitioners or partnerships and £3 million for limited liability partnerships (LLPs) or limited companies.[1] These are minimum limits and firms may obtain higher levels of insurance if they wish. It is not unusual for a large firm to have cover of £300 million for any one claim.

As the PI policy is also the instrument for the profession to show that it is well aware of its privileged condition, it is important that those individual policies give appropriate protection when a mistake is made. That is why there is a minimum limit of indemnity every lawyer or solicitor has to carry, there are a restricted number of insurance approved companies that can insure the primary PI limits (admitted carriers) and there is an agreed wording with a very broad "civil liability"-based cover.

On October 1 2013 the Assigned Risks Pool was abolished. This used to provide coverage backed by the group of admitted insurance companies for the lawyers who were refused cover by insurers in the open market. Today, in the absence of the Assigned Risks Pool, any law firm that is absolutely unable to obtain admitted coverage must cease practice within 60 days.

3.2 Continental Europe

In most European countries there is a mandated minimum PI insurance limit that every lawyer has to take out regardless of his or her practice. Lawyers often have very specialised knowledge and in most countries only a lawyer is allowed to represent clients in court (one exception is Sweden). Because of this monopoly and high degree of specialised knowledge lawyers are often not permitted to limit their liability.

The minimum requirements can differ for partnerships or LLPs (where allowed) compared to individual lawyers. In Austria, for example, a sole practitioner has to buy a limit of €400,000 per act committed and if the law firm is organised as a limited company (GmbH) it has to purchase insurance with a limit of at least €2.4 million per act committed.

The minimum amount insured differs from country to country. There are only a few countries where no insurance is required.

Maximum amounts are not specified in any country but for the large European practices limits of €300 million per claim and even higher amounts are available.

In several countries it is necessary to show a certificate of insurance to the bar association before the lawyer is admitted to the bar. Usually a minimum amount insured is sufficient. This can only be the case where the coverage has to be taken out by the individual lawyer (eg, in Germany).

Multinational practices in Europe can be complicated to control. If a German lawyer wants to practice in Italy he still needs to be compliant with German rules and regulations. The same is true for a UK solicitor who wants to work from the Paris office. This is despite the fact that restrictions on the freedom of services in the EU are prohibited.[2] As there are substantial differences in PI insurance requirements for lawyers in different EU countries, it always makes sense to check these rules when lawyers work cross border or are licensed to work in more than one country.

---

1   In May 2014, the Solicitors Regulation Authority launched a consultation paper, inviting responses to proposals that, among other things, the level of mandatory PI cover should be reduced to £500,000; an aggregate limit on claims (possibly of £1.5 million) should be introduced; and compulsory cover should be limited to claims made by individuals, small and medium-sized enterprises, trusts and charities. At the time of writing, the outcome of this consultation is unknown.
2   Article 56 of the Treaty on the functioning of the EU (formerly Article 49 TEC).

3.3 United States

Each state has its own Bar Association, which can sometimes help with insurance needs for smaller firms or firms that only practice in that state. However, if the firm is larger or has a national or international footprint then insurance is generally purchased with a commercial carrier or in the subscription market, that is to say that the insurance placement is split and placed with various commercial carriers to spread the risk. Commercial carriers are either admitted or non-admitted (non-admitted is also known as 'surplus lines'). PI limits are usually on an aggregate basis.

An admitted carrier is licensed by the particular state to which it is admitted, and is fully regulated by that state. Each state has rigorous requirements that must be met in order to qualify as an admitted carrier, and these requirements differ from state to state. Those insured by admitted carriers are likely to benefit from a guarantee fund, which protects policyholders if that carrier fails.

In the 1970s and early 1980s, malpractice insurance was not easily obtained, to the extent that the situation was described as a crisis. That crisis led to efforts by many state bar associations to form their own malpractice insurance companies to provide professional liability insurance to their members, most of which still exist today.

3.4 Canada

In Canada, each province governs the minimum standards of PI coverage purchased. For most provinces C$1 million is required but in Quebec C$10 million is the minimum limit per firm. This large Quebec limit used to be supplied for a negligible contribution (a single dollar per lawyer at one point) but now commands a higher, though still incredibly reasonable, cost from the Barreau du Québec.

3.5 Australia

Each state within Australia has its own law society and lawyers are required to obtain a minimum limit of A$2 million per firm of approved coverage, regardless of the firm's size.

3.6 Global law firms

Global firms have much to consider in ensuring that local insurance regulations are complied with in all jurisdictions in which they wish to practice. It could be that the most cost-effective way of purchasing insurance is in two tranches, one that will include US exposures and a separate tower for all other worldwide offices excluding the United States. However, global coverage is much more accessible than it used to be. A reputable PI broker will be able to source appropriate global coverage for a well-managed firm that can provide civil liability coverage where required as well as aggregated limits for US-exposed work. One global policy limits the chances of a claim falling through the cracks when coverage is inconsistent relating to cross-firm work performed by lawyers from offices in the United States and elsewhere working as a single legal team.

4. Cover considerations

The two primary goals of obtaining PI coverage are as follows:

- to provide clients with adequate protection in the event of an error; and
- to protect the firm and lawyers' assets from exposure to malpractice liability.

With that in mind, we have suggested below some aspects about the purchase of insurance that are worthy of consideration.

4.1 Bar association versus commercial market coverage

Rules and regulations differ from country to country. In many countries the bar association takes out a policy protecting all lawyers admitted to the bar. Each lawyer has the same coverage and in most cases pays the same price/premium per year. Sometimes the premium is related to fee income and sometimes deductibles and premiums can differ. Examples of such collective schemes are regional bars in France, Spain, a few bar associations in Germany, Belgium, Austria, the Czech Republic, Hong Kong and many more.

In most European countries there is usually more freedom to purchase PI insurance commercially. Bar associations sometimes require lawyers and law firms to send proof of their cover to the bar association so that it can check that every lawyer is insured. Some countries require proof of insurance before a lawyer is admitted to the bar.

(a) *Bar association policy advantages*
- Every lawyer is covered.
- Every lawyer has the same extensive policy conditions.
- The bar association usually pays the premium so there are no disputes over non-payment of the premium.
- In most cases the bar association will have a say in claims that are disputed.
- Lawyers who stop practising remain covered as long as the policy stays in place (this depends on the policy conditions but is true in most cases).
- Claims can be monitored and it is possible to help lawyers prevent claims or take action when claims are coming from the same cause.

(b) *Bar association policy disadvantages*
- Every lawyer gets the same cover and some lawyers do not buy any additional cover even though their clients and their practice justify a higher limit. And the reverse, of course, is that sole practitioners with hardly any risk get the same insurance and pay the same premium as larger, riskier practices.
- It is difficult to move cover from one insurer to another as the knowledge, both in claims handling and in professional terms, is concentrated with the insurers that handle the policy of the bar association.
- The local practices of international law firms are usually required to take out the local bar coverage for their local lawyers. Coverage can differ from their corporate policy and there could be differences in claims handling between the local policy and the corporate policy. Problems can arise if multinational clients and projects require that lawyers from different countries work together in one team and make a mistake. Who has made the mistake and

which policy should respond, the bar policy or the policy of the international firm? This can also be an issue for smaller firms that cooperate with law firms in other countries.

(c) **Advantages of a commercial carrier**
- Premium can differentiate depending on risks and claim activity.
- International firms can rely also on their corporate coverage in cases where an admitted policy needs to be taken out (eg, Brazil, Switzerland).
- Insurance can assist in marketing. Some clients will demand specific arrangements in the PI policies of their law firms.
- Deductibles can differ.

(d) **Disadvantages of a commercial carrier**
- It is difficult to check that every lawyer has bought insurance.
- Is the bar association liable when a lawyer is uninsured?
- An insurance company can fail to pay claims.
- Policy conditions can differ.

4.2 Claims made policies v acts committed/losses occurring policies

In most countries in the world liability policies are triggered when a claim or circumstance is reported to the insurance company. This is called a 'claims made' policy.

In a few countries it is still possible to purchase an 'acts committed' or 'losses occurring' policy. This means that the policy pays the claim that is or was in place when the act was committed that caused the damage.

An example can help to understand the difference between the two:

A lawyer makes a mistake in drafting a contract for a client in 2010. The mistake is discovered in 2014 and the lawyer reports the claim to his insurance company.

In the claims made system the policy that is in place in 2014 will respond and in the acts committed/losses occurring system the policy that was in place in 2010 will respond.

With an acts committed/losses occurring policy, once you purchase coverage for a given period, you are covered indefinitely for any claims that arise out of your conduct during that insured time.

(a) **Advantages of claims made policies**
- The limit of the policy is in line with the current claim environment. Claims have the tendency to increase over time and therefore the insured amount usually increases over time. In this example it could be that the limit of indemnity of the policy was £1 million in 2010 and increased to £5 million in 2014. In a claims made system £5 million would be the maximum available for this claim.
- The claims made system is better for the insurance company because when the policy is cancelled new claims can no longer be made.

(b)   Disadvantages of claims made policies
- Special arrangements need to be made for coverage to continue after the lawyer stops practising. Normally the policy will stop when the lawyer stops practising. However, this does not mean that a claimant who has suffered a loss will not pursue a claim, who may also be able to pursue the heirs of the lawyer. Therefore it is important to arrange coverage after retirement and automatic cover in case of death or other circumstances that make it necessary for the lawyer to stop practising.

(c)   Advantages of acts committed policies
- The best feature of the acts committed coverage is the fact that when the lawyer has this type of coverage during his whole professional career he/she only pays an annual premium and when he/she stops practising he/she and his/her heirs will remain covered for as long as is legally required.

(d)   Disadvantages of acts committed policies
- The biggest difficulty of the act committed system is the amount insured. The lawyer has to buy an amount that is sufficient to protect him/her against future claims. The time between the claim and the mistake can be 10 years or longer, making it difficult to predict what the right amount will be.
- The insurance company still needs to exist to be able to pay the claim.

4.3   Each and every claim v aggregate limits

In most policies there is a maximum liability limit per year for the insurance carrier. For example, in Europe, coverage is often €1 million per claim with a maximum of €2 million per year for all claims together. This last amount is called an aggregate limit for all claims together. The aggregate limit can be the same as the maximum amount per claim. This effectively means that one claim can wipe out the whole coverage. As it is often difficult to predict what amount will be paid when a claim comes in, this straight aggregate limit should be avoided where possible, though this is difficult to do in the United States. Twice the limit per claim should be considered the bare minimum and in some countries no aggregate limit is possible (eg, the United Kingdom for minimum standard limits), which means that the limit of the policy can be paid an unlimited number of times. Certainly for larger firms this can be a very important issue because it guarantees that each case has coverage. Usually insurance companies will limit their exposure on US claims, even if they agree to each and every claim cover for the rest of the world.

4.4   Adequate limits

There is no precise mathematical formula available to help a lawyer or law firm decide how much coverage is enough. Frequently, less thought is given to this aspect of purchasing coverage than the decision of which broker to use. Even more frequently, a policyholder continues with the same limits renewal after renewal, with no consideration of anything but the premium.

Importantly, when choosing limits lawyers must consider the fact that they are personally exposed to liability and defence costs at the lowest and highest layers of exposure. That is, they have to pay for all sums falling within the deductible, and all sums awarded above the upper limit of the policy.

The following factors should be considered:
- The danger of personal exposure – what is the firm's comfort level (or that of its partners) with the potential of uncovered exposure?
- The firm's practice profile and degree of risk involved in its particular practice area – does the firm practise in a high exposure area, such as intellectual property or class action lawsuits?
- The size of transactions and potential damages created by errors – what is the size of the firm's typical transaction, case or claim?
- The frequency and severity of the firm's claims history – has the firm experienced losses (or near losses) in the past, and what was the highest level of exposure?
- The financial ability of the firm to absorb the costs of defence or payment of claims – to what extent (in both the low and high layers) can the firm afford to self-insure its exposures?
- The financial ability of individual partners or shareholders to absorb the costs of defence or payment of claims – to what extent are the firm's members willing and able to contribute to uninsured exposure? Is there disparity in this answer among the various members?
- The degree to which the individual partners have insulated themselves from (or accepted) joint and several liability by choosing among available alternative business models – is the firm a general partnership, limited liability partnership or limited liability corporation?
- The effect of the economy on the number and size of claims – claim frequency and severity is thought to fluctuate with the economy, with professionals more likely to be sued in a tough economic climate.

4.5   Use of a broker

Insurance brokers act as intermediaries between insurance companies and consumers. A broker will help the law firm to consider its own specialised needs when deciding how to purchase coverage, as each method has its own advantages and disadvantages. They can usually provide access to a greater number of carriers and can save firm resources by showing a single application to competing companies. Brokers can also convey the firm's best attributes to insurers to help obtain the best possible coverage and premium for that individual firm.

5.   **How can you get the best from your insurer?**

No matter what the market conditions, you will get the best from your carrier by establishing an open and honest relationship with them. Working in partnership with your carrier over a prolonged period of several years will ensure the best understanding between you. Carriers are much more likely to give favourable terms to a long-standing, faithful client because liability is a long-term exposure with a claims development 'tail' of approximately five to seven years. Insurers will look at a firm's past record of insurance relationships and if the firm has moved carriers frequently they are more likely to receive a loaded rate as the chance of long-term loyalty is considered less.

Each year before completing the application for renewal or for coverage with a new carrier, the law firm should survey all its lawyers for known circumstances that might give rise to claims. This effort should be sincere and thorough. Reporting potential claims provides the benefit of locking in coverage no matter when the actual claim is made. Lawyers should be encouraged to report potential claims; not reporting them can lead to coverage being lost.

The firm should always require written acknowledgement from the existing carrier that it received notice of the potential claims. If a claim is made, this provides a written record that it was reported to the carrier during the policy period.

The importance of giving written notice to a claims-made carrier whenever facts or circumstances occur that could give rise to a claim cannot be overstated. Reporting such situations in writing is the only certain way of triggering coverage for them, should a claim ultimately be made. Lawyers should not be afraid that early reporting will bring retaliation or an increase in premium. Those reactions are highly unlikely. Insurance companies are in the business of handling claims and they expect to receive reports. They would rather know about a potential claim earlier rather than later. Insurers are usually more comfortable with long-term insured relationships where the insured tends to over report, and in fact reports out of an abundance of caution, leaving little guesswork as to what else might be out there.

When listing a claim to your carrier on renewal or on an application for a new carrier, address head on the causes of the claim. Demonstrate that the firm has addressed the cause for the claim and has taken appropriate measures to prevent a recurrence.

The purpose of an insurance carrier in requiring lawyers to complete an application for coverage is to obtain as much information as possible in order to assess and evaluate the risk that the lawyers present to the potential insurer. Underwriters do their best to predict, with the information given, what the risk is of the applicant drawing a claim and the likely severity of any such claim. Underwriters use general guidelines and risk factors based on prior experience that have substantial value in reaching their ultimate goal, which is to charge an appropriate premium, commensurate with the risk presented.

It is essential that the insurance application be completed with all due deliberation and effort. An application should always be typed, neat, legible and complete. No question should be left unanswered; if a question is not applicable, state that as the answer. In addition, the better an underwriter knows a firm, the better job they can do of tailoring coverage to that firm.

Risk management is the most influential aspect of rating outside the firm's location and practice area. Demonstration of a proactive risk management approach with a good understanding and embedded protocols will achieve a significant discount to standard rates. However, if a firm is not taking risk management seriously, it will often not even be entertained for quotation by the more discerning carriers.

6. What can you expect when a claim occurs?

At any time that a lawyer becomes aware of an error or circumstances that might lead to a claim being made the situation should be reported promptly to the carrier. Full information should be provided, sufficient for the carrier to link a claim that may eventually be made to the circumstances reported in the first place. This practice can prevent the unfortunate problem that occurs when a claim is made and reported and a dispute erupts over whether the claim was known to the insured and therefore not covered by the policy.

Every policy defines the term 'claim'. A typical policy defines it as a demand for money or services made against the insured.

Although policy language differs from carrier to carrier on how, when and to whom to report claims, the following guidelines comply with most, if not all, carriers' requirements (if in doubt, follow the strict language of the applicable policy).

- Report claims and circumstances immediately they occur. Report any incidents or errors that may give rise to a claim as soon as practicable after they occur.
- Provide details of any potential claim, the name of the potential claimant(s), the lawyer(s) involved, the date and specific nature of the error, omission or dispute, the amount of potential exposure (if known).
- Respond promptly to your carrier's requests for additional information.
- Report promptly any change in circumstance regarding the potential claim to the carrier.

Once a claim is made against you and you have reported it to the appropriate carrier, you have a duty to cooperate with your carrier in the investigation of that claim.

- Be prepared to provide a copy of your entire file to the insurance carrier and counsel retained to defend you.
- Ask your defence counsel to send you copies of his or her invoices for legal services and costs. This will help you to stay apprised of what is happening, but it is especially important if you have a declining limits policy, because as defence expenses are incurred they reduce the indemnity sum available to settle/pay the claim.
- Do not keep correspondence, notes, or memoranda regarding the claim in the underlying client file. Invariably the claimant will request a copy of his or her entire file; your thoughts on your liability, your defence, or the potential damages should not be mixed in with your file on the client's representation.
- During the investigation, defence and settlement of your claim, make yourself available to your claims representative and your defence lawyer. Help them help you through this difficult process.
- When the claim is resolved and the claim file closed, communicate with the carrier in order to find out how much was spent on defence and indemnification. Those figures have an impact on your aggregate limit

availability for the remainder of that policy period; they may also affect the premium charged by your carrier for the next policy.
- Once the claim has concluded, take the time to extract, and thereby benefit from, the costly lessons that can be learned. What was the error that led to the claim? What was the underlying cause of the error? Was it a system failure, such as a docketing error, or is it possibly symptomatic of a larger problem? Frequently, lawyer errors arise out of substance abuse, dependency, overworking, burnout or depression. Law firms should take care to question whether any such issues contributed to the claim. What procedures, safeguards, or other mechanisms can be implemented to prevent a recurrence of the problem(s) leading to the claim?

7. Difficult or unusual coverage issues

7.1 New lawyers joining the firm

Usually coverage automatically attaches to lawyers employed by the named insured in the middle of a policy year, though there is often a threshold limiting the number of lawyers that can be added mid-term without additional charge. A standard policy will only cover the new lawyers' actions from the date they join the firm though prior acts coverage can sometimes be purchased for an additional premium. The firm should consider very carefully indeed before purchasing prior acts coverage relating to the newly employed lawyers. To expose the firm's limit and record to acts committed while the lawyer was practising at a completely different firm, when your firm had no control over intake procedures, ethics or practice protocols is extremely dangerous.

7.2 Cyber/privacy exposure

A fast-evolving type of insurance policy has originated with the technology and information age and the potentially unforeseen exposure it brings. This type of policy is designed to cover breaches in technology security and the risks of technology failure. Most other policies have exclusions for these specialised types of risk. Some carriers imply that cover for such exposure is included within their PI product but unless it gives a separate and distinct limit for privacy breach and the first-party costs associated with notifying clients and individuals of the breach and its potential effects, then the cover is not fully provided and a separate specialist insurance is the only way to ensure protection.

7.3 Limitation of liability

Is the lawyer allowed to limit his liability towards his or her client and to the general public?

In most countries a contractual limitation of liability with a specific client is possible. Some countries will not allow such limitation below a certain amount.

A more important issue with respect to the limitation of liability is the question of whether lawyers are allowed to work in an organisation that limits their liability by law. Limited liability partnerships or even limited liability companies are allowed in many countries. For the larger law firms where there are differences in practice, differences in fee income and differences in exposure, it may well be necessary to organise limited liability to take care that all practices are still represented. Does a family lawyer want to run the risk that he or she will be involved in a large claim just because a colleague in the mergers and acquisitions section has made a costly mistake? The limited liability company can help to resolve this disparity to a more acceptable level.

Does this have a bearing on the PI insurance? Yes, it does in some countries. For limited liability companies the minimum amount that needs to be insured is often higher than for partnerships or individual lawyers (eg, in the United Kingdom, Germany and Austria).

7.4 What happens when I retire?

Many lawyers worry about their liability once they have retired from practice. As mentioned earlier, if they have been able to purchase 'acts committed' policies for all their years of practice and their carrier is still in existence then they have no need to worry. Also, for lawyers practising as part of an LLP, the firm's ongoing insurance will cover their work for many years to come as it is the firm's policy that assumes the liability.

However, for sole practitioners or traditional partners in various parts of the world the coverage varies. For example, in most European countries the lawyer who stops practising will remain responsible for claims made against them for periods ranging from 10 to 30 years. When they have passed away the liability could rest on their heirs.

For sole practitioners who cannot rely on a collective policy purchased by the bar association it is of great importance that, upon retirement, their individual insurance policy stays in force for as long as is legally required.

When there are bar policies in place the problem is usually non-existent as the bar policy will also provide coverage for retired members.

In the United Kingdom the primary policy will provide six years of run-off cover as set down in the rules of the Law Society of England and Wales. If there are excess policies in place then those policies do not usually provide any run-off cover.

There is a tendency in Europe for claims made policies to provide full run-off cover for all insured lawyers who stop practising.

Wherever you practise check your policy wording on this important issue.

7.5 Law firms working in an international network

Many law firms have international partner firms to whom they refer clients in need of legal assistance abroad and of course they get clients referred from those same partner firms. In the unfortunate case that a mistake is made the client often seeks compensation from the firm which referred the case to its foreign partner. The insurance company can pay the claim and seek recourse from the foreign firm that actually made the mistake. However, things could get difficult if the insurance company refuses to pay the claim because the referring law firm has not done anything wrong.

To avoid such circumstances it is advisable for all network partners to purchase their PI policy with the same carriers and perhaps combine excess policies to create purchasing power. The large multinational brokers are well capable of structuring a network policy with primary policies in every country according to local rules and regulations. As this is a highly specialised area there are not many brokers and carriers who are offering these multinational network policies, but it is well worth the effort to seek them out for networks that want to protect their clients.

8. Checklist

Below is a brief checklist of tasks and timings to ensure the best outcome for your PI policy renewal.

8.1 Three months before renewal

- Discuss with your broker the requirements for renewal:
  - obtain a copy of the application form and review the questions;
  - ask about changes in available coverage since last year;
  - highlight any new geographical locations with differing insurance needs;
  - discuss hot topics of exposure that may need to be addressed; and
  - discuss adequacy of your current limits.
- Ask all lawyers to report on any claims or potential claims.
- Collate financial data regarding fees, practice split etc needed for the application.

8.2 Two months before renewal

- Send your completed, signed application form for the broker to seek renewal terms.
- Discuss with your partners the firm's appetite for risk retention (ie, deductibles and limits).
- Consider other insurances such as cyber insurance.
- Discuss the suitability of the renewal quotes and alternative structures offered when quotes are received.

8.3 Thirty days before renewal

- Conduct the final survey of lawyers relating to potential claims in order to complete the No material changes declaration required by insurers if the application form was signed more than 30 days prior to inception.
- Finalise details of the chosen programme and proceed to give a clear firm order to insurers in good time prior to the inception date.

9. Conclusion

Remember that a law firm's ability to bargain for better PI coverage depends upon the attractiveness of that law firm to the underwriters. A faithful firm with a clean claims history, which demonstrates a proactive risk management protocol, will always have more bargaining power than one that has regularly switched carriers and/or evidenced substantial claims problems in the past.

It is essential that lawyers within law firms take individual responsibility for understanding how PI insurance works, what coverage is afforded them by their present employers, and what options are available for protection should a change in circumstance occur. This is especially so in the legal profession today, where lawyers are increasingly mobile among firms, and even move in and out of the practice with regularity. Get involved and ensure adequate PI protection is purchased, demand quality coverage. This is not just a cost of doing business, it is real protection that has far-reaching, personal value for each lawyer.

Conflicts of interest

Anthony E Davis
Hinshaw & Culbertson LLP
Frank Maher
Legal Risk LLP
Andrew Scott
Clyde & Co LLP

1. **Introduction**

    The duty of a lawyer not to act where there is a conflict of interest is one of the most fundamental duties a lawyer owes to a client. This is so whether the conflict is between the interests of two clients, or between the lawyer's own interests and those of the client. In this chapter, we refer to these as 'client conflicts' and 'own interest conflicts' respectively.

    The consequences for a law firm and the lawyers concerned of acting where there is a conflict of interests may be significant. Reputational damage may be severe, there may be disciplinary consequences, clients may be lost and fees may have to be written off. The firm may also be liable to compensate the client.

    The rules that apply vary from jurisdiction to jurisdiction and it is not intended that this chapter should provide a detailed analysis of all the rules that may be found around the world, but we shall consider some examples by way of illustration.

    Lawyers are under a professional duty to avoid conflicts, not merely to undertake conflict searches. Conflict searches alone do not prevent conflicts – it is the decisions made by lawyers, based on those searches and other information known to them, that are critical. Where a conflict or potential conflict is identified, the firm may have to:

    - turn down an engagement; or
    - exclude an office or particular lawyers from a multi-jurisdictional team if this would put them in breach of their own professional body's rules; or
    - limit the retainer.

    It is important to keep in mind that conflicts do not just arise at the beginning of a proposed instruction – they may arise at any time, and those arising during the course of a retainer may be harder to spot and more difficult to handle.

    First, let us look at the two types of conflict in general terms, though we do so appreciating that there will be many variations between how the rules are expressed in different jurisdictions.

    1.1 **Client conflicts**

    Lawyers are generally prohibited from acting for a client in circumstances where there is a conflict, or a significant risk of conflict, between the interests of that client and another client in relation to the same or a substantially related matter.

    In some jurisdictions, this may only apply to current clients, the interests of former clients being protected instead by the continuing duty to keep the former client's affairs confidential after termination of the retainer. In other jurisdictions, particularly in the United States, the lawyer may be subject to an express duty not to act against the interests of a former client.

This will encompass all situations where doing the best for one client in a matter will result in prejudice to another client in that matter or a related matter.

Prohibited conflicts between the interests of clients may be obvious, such as acting for buyer and seller of the same asset, where negotiations are required on price or other key terms, or acting for opposing parties in litigation; they may, however, be more subtle, because the achievement of a client's objective on one matter, for example succeeding on a disputed point of law in litigation over the disputed meaning of a rent review clause on property X, may adversely affect the interest of another client in a dispute over a similarly worded rent review clause on property Y.

Identifying conflicts in less obvious cases may present challenges to the establishment of effective systems and, once identified, may require the exercise of professional judgment. Key to the decision-making process will be whether the lawyer can act in the best interests of the client. Sometimes, the fact that one is even asking the question whether there is a conflict is sufficient to identify that there is one.

1.2 **Conflict between the duty of confidentiality and the duty to disclose**
A lawyer generally owes clients a duty to continue to keep their affairs confidential after the retainer has concluded. The lawyer also owes clients a duty, during the currency of the retainer, to inform them of any information the lawyer has in his or her possession that may be material to the current client's instruction. The effect of these two duties may be to create a conflict between the duty of confidentiality owed to the former client and the duty of disclosure owed to a current client. It may be possible in some circumstances to overcome this difficulty with the consent of each client, but otherwise the lawyer may be unable to act.

1.3 **Own interest conflicts**
Conflicts between the interests of the client and the lawyer's own interests are particularly serious. While there may be exceptions in the case of client conflicts, for example permitting the lawyer to act in certain circumstances with client consent, there will be no exceptions where there is an own interest conflict.

1.4 **Liability for breach**
A lawyer who acts for a client when there is a conflict of interest, whether with the interests of another client or with the lawyer's own interest, may be liable to compensate the client. That may mean an award of damages, or in some jurisdictions, an account of profits.

By way of illustration, an example in the English courts was the case of *Hilton v Barker Booth & Eastwood*.[1] The defendant solicitors acted for both a seller (Mr Hilton) and a buyer (Mr Bromage) on a commercial property transaction, contrary to the

---

1   [2005] UKHL 8.

conduct rules then in force. The solicitors failed to disclose to the seller that they knew that the buyer had a criminal record for bankruptcy offences which had resulted in imprisonment. They also failed to disclose that they were lending money to the buyer to complete on part of the transaction. After the contract was completed, the buyer defaulted and Mr Hilton was left with substantial losses, which led to his bankruptcy. Attempts at recovery from the buyer failed.

The solicitors defended the claim on two bases. First, the conviction was a matter of public record. Secondly, had the claimant instructed other solicitors, those other solicitors would not have known of the conviction and, they said, their breach therefore caused no loss. The defence succeeded initially but the claimant won on appeal. Put simply, the solicitors were in breach of duty to Mr Hilton, and could not complain if they had put themselves in that position by their own actions.

Note the comments of one of the judges on appeal, Lord Scott of Foscote:

The reason why it would have been a breach of the solicitors' duty to Mr Bromage to inform the appellant of Mr Bromage's bankruptcy and criminal conviction was not because the information was "confidential" but because it was their duty as Mr Bromage's solicitors to do their best to further Mr Bromage's interests in the transaction in respect of which Mr Bromage had instructed them.[2]

The firm was found liable to compensate the claimant.

1.5 Reputational risk – and sanctions

For a lawyer, reputation is all. The loss of client confidence, and the risk of disciplinary action and publicity, may be the most significant driver for ensuring that the firm has effective systems. In a recent case in New York, a prominent litigation firm was sanctioned by the court, in a decision that castigated the firm for failing to identify, and then for failing to withdraw when the conflict was pointed out, in a case where it had sought to act adversely to a party for whom it had negotiated the same agreement that was now in dispute.[3]

1.6 Lawyers may be bound by more than one set of rules

Firms with lawyers who qualified in other jurisdictions need to be aware that those lawyers may be subject to more than one set of professional rules. This can be an issue particularly for non-US firms who employ US lawyers, as the US rules may be more restrictive, and it may in some instances be necessary to consider excluding a US lawyer from a particular engagement if the involvement of that lawyer would put him or her in breach of their own bar rules. Significant problems can arise when a firm is operating in multiple jurisdictions where the rules governing conflicts differ.

2. Differing rules in outline

In this section we set out a brief outline of the applicable conflicts rules in a selection of jurisdictions in order to illustrate how they may vary and to raise awareness of

---

2 At paragraph 7.
3 *Madison 92nd St Assoc, LLC v Marriott Int'l, Inc*, No 13 Civ 0291, (CM), 2013 WL 5913382 (SDNY Oct 31, 2013).

how different lawyers who are asked to advise on the same matter may be subject to different restrictions. It is of course essential to refer to the rules themselves when considering their application to any given situation.

Identifying the differences in rules is important to gaining an understanding of the issues that, depending on the nature of the firm's practice, may need to be addressed in establishing systems for checking and managing conflicts.

2.1 United States

The American Bar Association (ABA) Model Rules of Professional Conduct serve as models for the ethics rules of most states in the United States, although the actual rules adopted in the individual states may vary significantly from the Model Rules and from each other. Model Rule 1.7 of the Model Rules[4] provides: "a lawyer shall not represent a client if the representation involves a concurrent conflict of interest". The rule explains that a concurrent conflict of interest exists if either "the representation of one client will be directly adverse to another client", or "there is a significant risk that the representation of one or more clients will be materially limited by the lawyer's responsibilities to another client, a former client or a third person or by a personal interest of the lawyer".

The ABA's comment on Model Rule 1.7[5] explains that "a lawyer may not act as an advocate in one matter against a person the lawyer represents in some other matter, even when the matters are wholly unrelated". This is stricter than, for example, in England and Wales. However, notwithstanding the general prohibition referred to above, Model Rule 1.7 does permit the lawyer to act in defined circumstances provided each client gives informed consent in writing.

Model Rule 1.8 addresses own interest conflicts in a variety of scenarios, including prohibiting lawyers from entering into business transactions with clients unless the terms are fair and reasonable to the client and disclosed in writing, and the client has been informed of the desirability of seeking independent legal advice. The client must provide informed consent in writing.

The rule also prohibits lawyers from using information related to representation for the benefit of the lawyer or a third party, such as another client, and from soliciting gifts from clients.

Model Rule 1.9 prohibits a lawyer from acting against a former client on "the same or a substantially related matter in which that person's interests are materially adverse to the interests of the former client"; there is an exception where there is informed written consent from the former client. The rule is particularly concerned with confidentiality. We shall look later at what may be meant by "the same or substantially related matter".

Model Rule 1.10 provides: "While lawyers are associated in a firm, none of them shall knowingly represent a client when any one of them practicing alone would be prohibited from doing so by Rules 1.7 or 1.9". However where the restriction under

---

4   www.americanbar.org/groups/professional_responsibility/publications/model_rules_of_professional_conduct/rule_1_7_conflict_of_interest_current_clients.html.
5   www.americanbar.org/groups/professional_responsibility/publications/model_rules_of_professional_conduct/rule_1_7_conflict_of_interest_current_clients/comment_on_rule_1_7.html.

rule 1.9 arises from the disqualified lawyer's prior firm, an ethical screen or information barrier may be used, subject to compliance with specified requirements.

2.2 England and Wales

The Solicitors Regulation Authority (SRA) regulates solicitors in England and Wales. Solicitors form by far the largest branch of the legal profession in the UK, and it is the rules applying to them that we shall look at in this section. Other lawyers, such as barristers, have separate regulators with their own rules.

Conflicts of interest are governed by Chapter 3 of the SRA Code of Conduct 2011. As mentioned earlier, the position in relation to former clients is governed by the confidentiality principles addressed in Chapter 4 of the Code of Conduct.

Chapter 3 prohibits solicitors from acting where there is conflict, or a significant risk of conflict, between two or more current clients, or between the lawyer and the client. There are two exceptions in relation to client conflicts, but none in relation to own interest conflicts. In each case there are requirements that must be satisfied, including a requirement for informed consent in writing and that it is reasonable to act for both parties.

The first exception is where the clients have a 'substantially common interest' and have provided informed consent in writing. It must be in the clients' best interests. A 'substantially common interest' is defined in the SRA Glossary as "a situation where there is a clear common purpose in relation to any matter or a particular aspect of it between the clients and a strong consensus on how it is to be achieved and the client conflict is peripheral to this common purpose".

It is debatable, therefore, whether this is in fact an exception at all, as the implied underlying premise is that there is no conflict.

The second exception is where the clients are 'competing for the same objective', sometimes referred to as the 'auction exception'. This is defined as "any situation in which two or more clients are competing for an 'objective' which, if attained by one client will make that 'objective' unattainable to the other client or clients and 'objective' means ... an asset, contract or business opportunity which one or more clients are seeking to acquire or recover through a liquidation (or some other form of insolvency process) or by means of an auction or tender process or a bid or offer which is not public". There must be no other conflict in relation to the matter, and "unless the clients specifically agree, no individual acts for, or is responsible for the supervision of work done for, more than one of the clients in that matter".

Importantly, these are the only exceptions. There is a general note that consent may cure a conflict. If, under the SRA rules, there is a conflict and neither of the two exceptions applies, the firm cannot act. An information barrier will not cure a conflict – it can only have an application where there is an issue in relation to confidential information, and then only subject to strict conditions.

Firms are also required to "have effective systems and controls in place to enable [them] to identify and assess potential conflicts of interests". They must have systems and controls for identifying both client and own interest conflicts appropriate to the size and complexity of the firm and these must also extend to the identification of commercial conflicts.

In contrast to the United States, the knowledge of one person is not imputed to others in the firm.

2.3 Europe

Europe encompasses many different jurisdictions, each with their own different rules. Rules may, for example, only prohibit acting in the same matter, rather than related matters. Whether clients can waive a conflict may vary from state to state. There may also be differences in whether lawyers who encounter a conflict between the interests of two clients may continue to act for one, or must cease acting for both. Rules on confidentiality, often referred to as professional secrecy, may in many countries be enforced by the criminal law.

The Council of Bars and Law Societies in the European Union (CCBE) has a Code of Conduct applicable to cross-border work, the conflict position of which is broadly equivalent to English rules, save that there is no reference to 'related matters' and the 'common interest' and 'auction' exceptions do not feature.[6]

2.4 Common law

Common law jurisdictions are not only subject to regulatory rules but may also be subject to the common law itself. If the rules are the same, then this may not matter greatly, but it can in certain circumstances expose lawyers to 'double jeopardy' – the risk of complying with one set of obligations to the letter, but finding oneself in breach of other obligations. Breach of bar or law society rules may expose a lawyer to disciplinary sanction, but breach of the common law may expose the lawyer to a claim for damages, an account of profits and an order restraining the lawyer from acting further.

The provisions of the SRA Code of Conduct in England and Wales are broadly in line with the common law, save that clients may waive a conflict at common law but under the SRA Code of Conduct this does not permit the lawyer to act unless one of the two exceptions (common interest or the 'auction exception') applies.

2.5 Duties continuing after the retainer

We have already looked at ABA Model Rule 1.9 in section 2.1 above. It will be recalled that this prohibits a lawyer who has formerly acted for one client subsequently acting for another party in the same or a substantially related matter if the other party's interests are materially adverse to the former client's interests, unless that former client consents in writing.

In England and Wales, the fiduciary duty owed to a client generally ceases when the retainer comes to an end, but, as in other jurisdictions, the duty of confidentiality continues, so it is important to ensure that one can identify when the retainer has come to an end. Lawyers are often bad at tidying up the loose ends when a matter is all but concluded and this can mean that the retainer has not ended, and a current client conflict arises that could have been avoided. Failing to identify that one instruction was not in fact concluded was an issue, albeit only one of many, in the recent English case of *Georgian American Alloys v White & Case*.[7]

---

6 See www.ccbe.eu/fileadmin/user_upload/NTCdocument/EN_CCBE_CoCpdf1_1382973057.pdf.

2.6 Acting against current clients

An important area of difference between jurisdictions is whether a lawyer is prohibited from acting in any matter against a current client, or only where the two instructions are in the same or related matters. The ABA Model Rules adopt the restrictive approach, preventing the lawyer from acting against a current client unless the client consents and the matter is unrelated. In England and Wales, and many other jurisdictions, the restriction applies only to the same or related matters, but there may of course still be a commercial conflict which would in practice preclude the lawyer from acting.

3. Who is the client?

3.1 Subsidiaries and affiliates

The complexities of commercial life mean that many clients are part of larger groups of companies or affiliated in other ways. This can introduce additional layers of complexity to checking and managing conflicts. Rules may even specify that different legal entities in the same group are to be treated as one, as the Swedish Bar rules provide.[8] But even where that is not the case, there may either be a commercial conflict, or client-imposed terms may preclude the lawyer from acting.

3.2 Corporate clients and directors or employees

Care needs to be taken when acting for corporate clients because, intentionally or otherwise, the lawyer may assume duties to individual directors, managers or employees. It is important to ensure that, if a duty is not intended to arise, the individuals are made clear about the position.

The interests of the person conveying the instructions may be identical to those of the company, or they may diverge. An example in England and Wales and doubtless many other jurisdictions would be the defence of a claim by an employee for harassment and discrimination in the workplace. The employee may allege that a particular supervisor has been instrumental in the behaviour of which he or she complains. The supervisor may confess privately to the lawyer that some of the allegations may be true. The lawyer needs to be absolutely clear about where his or her duties of loyalty lie.

The solution to this scenario will be fact sensitive and may be subject to differences in the applicable conflicts rules. It is not therefore possible to provide a definitive answer to resolve this issue. By way of general guidance, however, in England and Wales, the lawyer should first identify whether the supervisor is a client, which certainly will be the case if the supervisor is a party to the proceedings and the lawyer is on the court or tribunal record as acting for him or her, and may be so in other circumstances too.

In that event, the lawyer has received confidential information from one client (the supervisor) while acting for another (the employer). It may be to the supervisor's

---

7 [2014] EWHC 94 (Comm).
8 Rule 3.2.3 of the Code of Professional Conduct for Members of the Swedish Bar Association www.advokatsamfundet.se/Documents/Advokatsamfundet_eng/Code_of_Professional_Conduct_with_Commentary.pdf.

detriment to communicate the information to the employer, as the employer may withdraw funding of the supervisor's costs and may bring disciplinary proceedings. The lawyer would have to have the supervisor's consent to pass the information to the employer, but would be exposed to a conflict breach in seeking it. It may therefore be necessary to cease acting for the employer. That may create a commercial conflict in itself and it may be simpler to cease acting for both parties.

Even if the supervisor is not, on the facts, a client, the lawyer may still owe duties of care and possibly confidentiality. It is therefore important to identify clearly if the lawyer is acting solely for the employer and to confirm this in writing to the supervisor. Either way, it is important to appreciate the risk at the outset and consider the extent to which it can be addressed in the terms of engagement and correspondence and other communications with those concerned.

Kirschner v K&L Gates[9] was a case where the law firm was instructed by a special committee of the board, which had been set up to investigate certain allegations of impropriety by senior executives of a company. However, despite the firm's attempt in the engagement letter to identify the special committee, as opposed to the company, as its client, the special committee was found to have had no separate legal existence, and the lawyers therefore owed their duties to the company as a whole.

4. Acting for two or more clients

Whenever a lawyer agrees to act for two or more clients, the potential for conflict must be considered – not just at the point of instruction, but how a conflict may arise in future. It is not inevitable that their interests will diverge. For example, a lawyer acting for a married couple on the purchase of property may have no reason to anticipate that their interests will differ at all. But in other cases the position may be more complex. Practice may vary in different jurisdictions, but a firm may be instructed by an insurer to act for a defendant in the defence of a liability claim and have no reason to suspect that there will be any reason why the defendant may not be entitled to insurance cover, but may discover facts later that would entitle the insurer to decline cover.

Identifying at the outset where things may go wrong may save a lot of problems later. Depending on the circumstances, it may be that the clients should be told to seek separate representation at the outset, or it may be possible to manage the situation in advance, for example by limiting the retainer to aspects on which there is no significant risk of conflict and, where conduct rules allow, by agreeing for which client the lawyer may continue to act in the event that a conflict does arise. Although that may not ultimately be determinative, it can make it easier to have the conversation with the client.

In the United States, regardless of the jurisdiction, it will be critical to make disclosure of the nature and risks associated with the conflicts, including the clients' rights as to the future use of confidential information and what will happen if actual conflicts arise, and to obtain informed consent, before undertaking any joint representation of multiple clients in the same matter.

---

9   2012 Pa Super LEXIS 541 (Super Ct Pa May 14 2012).

It will be easier in practice to limit the retainer when dealing with a sophisticated client.

4.1 Common interest

The 'substantially common interest' exception has already been mentioned in the context of the rules that apply in England and Wales, along with the observation that in reality it may be that there is no conflict. Examples may be members of a family setting up a company together. If there are any areas of conflict, they must be substantially less important than the common purpose and should be excluded from the retainer. It may be that the parties can obtain separate advice on areas where their interests do not correlate, whether from another lawyer or another professional, such as their accountant.

Another example, given in earlier SRA guidance notes,[10] is acting for different tiers of lenders (for example senior lenders and mezzanine lenders) and/or different parties (for example arrangers/underwriters and bond/security trustees) entering into a financing transaction where there is already an agreed or commonly understood structure with regard to the ranking of their respective claims, the content of their respective obligations and associated commercial issues.

4.2 Co-purchasers

Co-purchasers of a property or a business may pose no conflict threat. However, it cannot be assumed that that is so without examining the circumstances, as they may have different interests that need protecting. How their interests are to be dealt with in the event of the death of a natural person who co-owns property is just one example.

4.3 Lender and buyer

In England and Wales it is generally accepted practice for a lawyer to act for both an institutional lender and a private client purchasing a home for his or her own occupation. Provided there is no conflict, the rules permit this subject to certain conditions. The lender client's instruction must be on certain prescribed terms. The practice is permitted because both lender and buyer have a common interest in obtaining good title to the property. This example of acting for more than one client is, however, a good example of how things can go wrong, as there have over the years been countless claims by institutional lenders alleging that the lawyers failed to disclose material information to them obtained in the course of acting for the buyers. The result has been to render many firms who provide private client services uninsurable, and insurance is a prerequisite for authorisation to practise.

In the United States many states treat dual representation of lender and buyer as improper and the inherent conflicts as unwaivable, while some follow rules similar to those described above in England and Wales.

---

10   To the now-repealed Solicitors' Code of Conduct 2007, but which still holds good in the writers' opinion.

4.4 Joint ventures

There may be circumstances where it is appropriate for a law firm to act for two or more joint venture partners, but it is essential that they should have agreed between themselves the key terms governing their relationship.

4.5 Insurer and insured

It is common in many jurisdictions for law firms to act for an insurer and the insured. In England and Wales this will generally be when the law firm is on an insurer's panel. We identified previously the risk of an insurance coverage issue creating a conflict. The lawyer must also, however, be alert to the interests of the insured in the conduct of the defence.

In the United States it is common to inform the insured of the lawyer's obligations towards the insurer, and in Florida the regulators have established specific language for such notification.[11]

In the English case of *Groom v Crocker*,[12] the solicitors, on instructions from the defendant's motor insurers, admitted liability without the insured's consent; it was part of a deal with other insurers on another claim. The insured succeeded in a claim against the solicitors. The significance of the decision is that a solicitor on the court record for the insured owes duties to the insured as he does to any other client.

4.6 Clients competing for the same objective

This exception, outlined above in relation to the rules in England and Wales, will only apply to sophisticated clients. It might apply where a firm acts for competing bidders, but may also be relevant when acting for more than one creditor on an insolvency matter. Many (but not all) firms in the United States view these engagements as inherently risky, because of the danger that an unsuccessful client will sue the firm for working harder on behalf of the successful bidder. In addition to being an ethical conflict (being adverse to the interests of another current client), it is also viewed as a business conflict that should be identified and considered before accepting instructions.

5. Outside Counsel Guidelines and client-imposed rules

5.1 Imposition of terms

Increasingly, large institutional clients are seeking to impose their own ethical rules on law firms, sometimes even by sending their terms after the initial instruction has been agreed, and stating that their terms apply in preference to the law firm's terms. The clients' terms may be contained in Outside Counsel Guidelines or some other contractual document.

5.2 Difficulties in identifying the impact

Client-imposed terms may have a wide impact. They may seek to bar the firm from acting against not only the client itself but also its subsidiaries, associated entities

---

11 Florida Rules of Professional Conduct 4-1.8.
12 [1939] 1 KB 194.

and affiliates. It may be difficult in practice to work out who those are, and even the client may not be able to supply a list. The problem can be exacerbated by changes in company ownership during the course of a retainer. The challenges this may present to conflict checking cannot be overstated.

5.3 Central firm control to agreement of terms

The imposition of a client's terms in this way is a risk management issue for the law firm, because unless there is a central system for logging the acceptance of such terms, they may be breached unwittingly by another member of the firm agreeing a retainer. It also makes it essential that there is some central control mechanism before such terms are agreed to ensure that the firm's own interests are protected: it is not unknown for a client to appoint a law firm to a panel, impose terms which prevent the firm from acting against it, and then give the firm no instructions at all. The agreement of such onerous terms should not therefore take place without the involvement of senior management.

6. Own interest conflicts

6.1 Personal appointments

Examples of own interest conflicts may arise where a lawyer is appointed as a director or trustee, or under power of attorney, or as a holder of part-time judicial or government office. It is essential that the firm's conflict checking procedures are capable of identifying these conflicts, and it follows that the firm should generally insist on its members obtaining prior authorisation before accepting such appointments.

6.2 Financial interests

Examples of financial interests giving rise to own interest conflicts may include buying property from a client, borrowing money from a client, or receiving a testamentary gift, unless the client is receiving independent legal advice.

Referral arrangements may also give rise to financial interests. In one bitterly contested claim in which one of the authors acted for a leading English law firm, the claimants alleged that the firm had failed to act in their best interests, out of deference to the corporate finance house from whom they derived a large amount of their work.

Another example was where a firm of accountants provided tax advice to clients and wanted to instruct a law firm to draft wills and trust documents. The accountants were anxious to maintain their relationship with the client and wished to avoid the lawyers having contact with the clients as far as possible. Lawyers must be jealous in guarding their independence in circumstances such as this, anxious though they may be not to offend the introducer of work.

Referrals may also operate in the other direction, particularly with the recommendation of other advisers and independent experts, which must always be in the best interests of clients, regardless of the lawyers' own interests which may be in maintaining cross-referral of work.

Where lawyers can lawfully act for two (or more) parties, they should be alert to the risk that a disaffected client may assert that they have done so in order to secure two sets of fees. The prejudicial value of such an assertion may outweigh its probative value, and it is rare for such allegations to influence the outcome, but it is important to be aware of the risk nonetheless.

6.3 Potential claims

An important example of an own interest conflict is where the lawyer may have advised on a contract that subsequently ends up in litigation. There may be an issue about whether the lawyer's previous advice was correct and the lawyer may be bound to advise the client to seek independent advice from another firm, particularly if the client may have grounds for a professional liability claim against the lawyer.

Similarly, in other cases where the lawyer is aware that the client may have reason to make such a claim, the lawyer will generally be unable to continue acting unless the client has had independent legal advice.

7. Related matters

In many jurisdictions the conflict rules prohibit acting where there is a conflict on the same or related matters. This raises the question of what is a 'related matter'. An example would be acting for a client that is negotiating with publishers for the publication of a novel, and receiving an instruction from another client alleging that the novel is plagiarised and breaches copyright.[13]

An American decision in New Jersey provides another illustration. In *City of Atlantic City v Trupos*[14] a law firm represented the city of Atlantic City in certain real estate tax appeals in 2006 and 2007. The firm ceased acting and later represented some taxpayers in an appeal of 2009 real estate tax assessments. The city applied to the court to restrain the law firm from acting, asserting that the firm's former representation of the city and current representation of the taxpayers were substantially related. The New Jersey Supreme Court held that the matters were not substantially related.

The Court held that matters are substantially related if: (1) the lawyer received confidential information from the former client that can be used against that client in the subsequent representation of parties adverse to the former client; or (2) facts relevant to the prior representation are both relevant and material to the subsequent representation. The city's application failed because it did not identify any potentially harmful confidential information that it shared with the law firm, and because the firm's prior work for the city involved different properties, valuers and relevant facts.

One of the most high-profile conflict cases in recent times was the English case of *Marks & Spencer v Freshfields Bruckhaus Deringer*[15] (albeit decided under earlier conflicts rules). The facts were that Philip Green instructed Freshfields on a bid to

---

13　This example is taken from the guidance notes to the now-repealed Solicitors' Code of Conduct 2007 in England and Wales.
14　201 NJ 447, 992 A2d 762 (2010).
15　[2004] EWCA Civ 741.

take over Marks & Spencer. However, Freshfields had acted for Marks & Spencer on litigation matters, and on contracts with George Davies over the Per Una product line – an engagement that was not concluded. This was one of the most successful and profitable Marks & Spencer lines and was fundamental to the value of the business. Marks & Spencer applied for an injunction to restrain Freshfields from acting. They alleged that Freshfields had acquired a substantial amount of confidential information in the course of acting for them, including information about the supply chain and contracts, pricing policies, supply volumes and their attitude to termination and renewal of the same.

Freshfields argued, among a variety of points, that the conflict rule only prevented them acting if they acted on the same transaction. Both the Judge and the Court of Appeal rejected this argument. The conflict rules were not limited to same transaction cases. There simply had to be a reasonable or sufficient degree of relationship between the two matters.

8. Commercial or business conflicts

In general, subject to the rather more onerous rules in the United States, which, as we have seen, prohibit acting against current clients without consent, in many jurisdictions there may be no legal or bar association rule against acting for competitors of an existing client, or for enterprises whose interests may be opposed to an existing client's general business interests. The firm may act against existing clients unless it is in the same or a related matter, or there is a risk to confidential information.

In practice, however, commercial conflicts (referred to as 'political conflicts' in Germany) may be a more significant issue than legal ones. So, for example, the lawyer who derives substantial fees from real estate work for a client may not even wish to consider seeking the client's consent to acting against it on behalf of another client in litigation.

Some clients may try to control the situation, as we have seen in section 5.1 above, through Outside Counsel Guidelines or other contractual provisions.

It is sensible for the lawyer to think ahead and ask "What comes next"? It is too easy to take on each client as he or she walks through the door, without considering whether this may preclude a more significant and lucrative instruction further down the line.

9. Changes during the life of a matter

Compliance is not confined to conflict checking at the start of a retainer. Lawyers must remain constantly alert to changes in circumstances which may necessitate a review of the conflict position.

The most difficult conflict issues are those that emerge during a matter. For a particularly stark example of this, see *TSB v Robert Irving & Burns*,[16] where English solicitors acting for real estate valuers on instructions of their professional indemnity insurers arranged a conference with counsel partly for the purpose of extracting

---

16 [2000] 2 All ER 826.

information from the valuer that might enable insurers to decline indemnity. The insurers were prohibited by the court from relying on any material obtained through this process.

9.1 Changes in, or additional, parties

Examples include a change in the identity of a proposed buyer of a business when acting for the seller, or the addition of another defendant to litigation.

9.2 Changes in ownership of the client and takeovers

A lawyer may be acting for a corporate client, for example in litigation, unaware that the client is being acquired by another company. If the litigation lawyer's firm is not instructed in relation to corporate matters, it may be wholly unaware that this is even happening. The risk is that the lawyer's earlier conflict check may have given rise to a false sense of security, and the introduction of a new owner may give rise to unforeseen conflicts with other clients. On becoming aware of the change, it will be necessary to re-do conflict checks and, depending on the circumstances, it may be necessary to cease acting.

10. Information barriers/ethical screens

Information barriers are also referred to as ethical screens or Chinese walls, though the last term has largely fallen from favour in many jurisdictions. These may serve to protect confidential information. They do not, however, neutralise a conflict, and unless the rules of a particular jurisdiction allow a lawyer to act with client consent where there is a conflict, they will not be of assistance for any purpose other than protection of confidential information.

11. Client consent/waivers

In the United States, when conflicts are considered to be waivable (see Model Rule 1.7 and 1.8[17]) the general requirements are: (sometimes 'full') disclosure of the nature of the conflicts; an explanation of the advantages and disadvantages to the client of waiving the conflict and the alternatives available to the client; and the client's consent, which is sometimes required to be memorialised in writing, and sometimes needs to be signed by the client. These requirements together are often referred to as 'informed consent', a definition of which may be found in Model Rule 1.0 (e)[5].[18]

11.1 Sophisticated versus unsophisticated clients

Traditionally, courts in the United States did not distinguish between sophisticated and unsophisticated clients, holding lawyers to every element of the requirements of disclosure and consent, even where the client was a large company with a substantial number of in-house counsel staff. Recently, however, this has begun to change. In the decision in *Galderma Laboratories, LP v Actavis Mid Atlantic LLC*,[19] the United

---

17   See note 3 above.
18   See www.americanbar.org/groups/professional_responsibility/publications/model_rules_of_professional _conduct/rule_1_0_terminology.html.

States District Court explicitly held the company to a waiver signed by its long-time in-house counsel, noting that the company was huge, regularly employed multiple outside law firms, and that the company's General Counsel had come from a law firm background and should be taken to understand what he had signed and be bound by that agreement. On the other hand, many courts, especially state rather than federal courts, continue to ignore the distinction, and to require full compliance with the ethical rules.

11.2 Do you want to act with consent even where permitted?

Law firms always need to consider the potential wider implications of asking a client for waivers. This goes back to the underlying issue of loyalty discussed at the beginning of this chapter. On the other hand, where a large company seeks a narrow type of legal assistance, firms may be unwilling (or commercially unable) to accept such engagements without waivers.

11.3 Advance waivers

This raises the topic of seeking waivers in advance of accepting engagements. Again, while courts traditionally frowned on these, on the grounds that neither a law firm nor a client could adequately predict the nature of future conflicts, the balance of power between firms and their clients is increasingly recognised as being more even – if not leaning in favour of clients rather than the law firms. Given that clients are seeking to impose guidelines (see section 5 above) on their outside counsel, the request for advance waivers is the law firm's counter. Again, however, the less sophisticated the client, the more it will be necessary to identify with great specificity the scope of the waivers before these are likely to be enforced. At a minimum, clients should be advised of their right to obtain separate counsel before agreeing to grant such waivers, and some firms actually insist on clients obtaining such advice before they will proceed based on such waivers.

12. Associated firms

12.1 Networks

Many firms seek to enlarge their international footprint by joining associations. The purpose will be to build up a referral network. Some networks may be closer than others. There have been examples of firms united under a common brand and, while they are separate firms, it will be difficult to avoid a perception that they are one firm and conflict rules should therefore be applied as though they were.

The corporate whistleblower Michael Woodford, in his book *Exposure: Inside the Olympus Scandal*,[20] describes his removal from his post as president of Olympus in Japan, and his return to England where he decided to expose the major fraud that had taken place in the company. He explains how he instructed a leading London

---

19   Case No 3:12-cv-2038 (ND Tex February 21 2013).
20   Michael Woodford, *Exposure: Inside the Olympus Scandal: How I went from CEO to Whistleblower* (Penguin Group US, 2012).

law firm. He was initially impressed but eight days later they informed him they could no longer act, as a German firm in the same worldwide alliance had already been instructed. He observed that their apology was not enough, having accepted him as a client and sent him an invoice. He commented that experiences such as this give lawyers a bad name.

Consideration should be given to whether it is necessary to obtain (the specific) consent of the proposed client to share information with other members of the network in order to undertake checks.

12.2 Vereins

Many international professional service firms use the Swiss verein as the corporate vehicle for their network structure. It allows firms to work together without being in a single corporate group. They operate together commercially, if not legally. The conflict issues therefore are really the same as for networks, but the perception that it is one firm will be reinforced to the outside world and make it practically impossible to act when there is a conflict.

13. Managing and avoiding conflicts

13.1 Limiting the scope of the retainer

Lawyers are often lax in the way they define their retainer in an engagement letter, but it can be an important means of managing conflicts.

Key to the definition of 'client conflict' is whether the lawyer owes separate duties to act in the best interests of two or more clients in relation to the same or related matters, so if the lawyer excludes an aspect of the matter on which there is a conflict, it may still be possible to act. However, this is subject to important limitations. It must be reasonable to limit the retainer, and the client must be capable of understanding the limitation, so it may work very well in the case of a sophisticated commercial client, but not work in the case of an elderly and vulnerable private client.

13.2 Common interest

We covered the issue of substantial common interest in section 4.1. This may offer a route by which it is proper to act for more than one client. However, the decision to act for more than one client, even where it is proper to do so, means in reality that the risk of it going wrong is carried by the lawyer. It may become necessary to cease acting for either or both parties, and it may be difficult in practice to charge for the work already done.

13.3 The risks of general files

Commercial clients may wish to have a retainer with a law firm under which they can contact the lawyer on an *ad hoc* basis for incidental advice, with terms agreed and already in place. This may be highly convenient, but it is also carries risk. It means that the limits of the retainer may not be defined, and, significantly for present purposes, conflict checks may not be carried out. It may be a fact of commercial life that such arrangements exist, but measures need to be taken to guard against conflicts.

First, if the firm does decide to allow general matters, they should never be used for transactional work or litigation. It may be that there are no counterparties to the matters on which advice is sought, for example where the client seeks advice on its internal policies and procedures, which may mitigate the risk.

Secondly, it may be prudent to impose a maximum amount of time, say, one hour, that can be allocated to a specific query on a general file without opening a separate file.

Thirdly, some firms require a new file to be opened each year. Although the protection this adds may be rather limited, it may serve as a reminder of the need for caution.

Firms that simply ban general files altogether should not ignore the ingenuity of lawyers in finding ways around procedures. In some cases, they do so by tacking a general query onto another matter which is open. A partner in one firm that had banned general files told one of the writers that, instead, he "now uses compliance files".

Education is an important part of the process of managing risk, and file audit too has a crucial role to play.

In an ideal world, general files would not exist, but real life may sometimes dictate that they do.

13.4   Avoiding the small instruction that precludes a large one

Lawyers need to be alert to the risk that by taking on a small instruction they may prevent the firm acting on a much larger matter. Sometimes the risk is foreseeable, in other cases it will not be.

13.5   Confidential information from prospective clients or tenders

There is always a risk when a firm is invited to tender for work it receives confidential information that then precludes it from acting for another party. Prospective clients should therefore form part of the conflict-checking process.

13.6   Written policies

Firms should have written policies on conflicts. These must be communicated to all staff, not just fee earners. Training is important, first to help avoid the risk of mistakes happening, and secondly, because in the event of a disciplinary investigation, it may assist the firm to show itself in a better light if it can demonstrate that it has trained its staff.

Like all policies, the conflict policy should be subject to annual review to ensure that it takes account of changes in the firm's systems, its client base, its practice areas, and, most importantly, that lessons are learned when things have gone wrong and appropriate changes made.

13.7   Conflict checking

As stated earlier, lawyers are under a professional duty to avoid conflicts, not merely to undertake conflict searches. Ideally, conflict checking will be combined with the whole client inception process, including risk assessment of the client and the matter, and anti-money laundering checks. In the larger firms, this will be a centrally run process with a dedicated team, though it must be appreciated that the decision on whether to act rests with the lawyers.

In section 9 we saw how changing circumstances during the lifecycle of a matter may necessitate a further conflict check.

Search terms are an important consideration. These should take account of data integrity – spelling errors and differences, particularly with foreign names, and especially if they use different alphabets. Project names, used to preserve confidentiality, may mean that a subsequent search fails to identify a matter. Failing to include an asset description may also prevent a later search picking up prior involvement in a related matter with unconnected parties.

Corporate structures, groups, affiliates and the involvement of individuals as shareholders, directors or officers may present additional challenges.

It is important, too, to ensure that the conflict checking procedure is not focused solely on client conflicts – it must address own interest conflicts too.

Finally, ensure that conflicts checks are carried out before any work is commenced; some firms help to encourage compliance by preventing time recording until checks have been done. There should be a record of all checks undertaken.

14. Checklist

- For each new jurisdiction where the firm will practise, ascertain the applicable conflict rules and how these compare with the rules applicable to the firm's operations in other jurisdictions.
- Ascertain whether the firm's conflict checking arrangements need to be adapted to address differences identified.
- Put in place process initiatives to minimise conflicts risk, for example:
  - request an advance conflicts waiver, where appropriate;
  - close client matters as soon as completed.
- Decide what guidance and training may be required as to:
  - applicable conflicts rules;
  - firm procedures and processes;
  - the need to stay alert to fresh conflict issues arising as matters develop;
  - the circumstances in which it may be permissible to act for more than one client in respect of the same matter, and necessary safeguards.
- Establish a process for review and logging of client-imposed terms.
- Establish an escalation process aimed at objective decision making, in the interests of the firm, on whether to accept instructions where:
  - there is a potential commercial conflict;
  - the client insists on acceptance of onerous conflict provisions (ie, over and above locally applicable requirements);
  - the client will not accept advance conflicts waivers, where these are sought.
- Establish a process for disclosure, approval and logging of partner and staff

outside appointments (directorships, trusteeships, powers of attorney, etc).
- Establish rules to restrict the use of general files and other workarounds that may expose the firm to conflicts risks.
- Where a conflict is identified, consider whether it can be cured by:
  - waiver, or do applicable rules preclude this?
  - limiting the retainer, assuming the client understands and agrees?
- Ensure that conflicts processes also cover the need to identify situations where acceptance of a new instruction may put a former client's confidential information at risk, and establish procedures to deal with this.

Confidentiality and disclosure

Frank Maher
Legal Risk LLP
Andrew Scott
Clyde & Co LLP

1. Introduction

1.1 The client's perspective

Confidentiality – or 'professional secrecy', as it is termed in European jurisdictions – is at the heart of the lawyer–client relationship. For convenience, we shall use the term 'confidentiality' in this chapter in relation to professional secrecy.

While the right of a client to consult a lawyer in confidence is respected in most jurisdictions, there is considerable variation, depending on jurisdiction, in the detail of the rights and duties of lawyers and their clients in relation to confidentiality. Some of the differences are outlined here in order to raise awareness that when dealing with lawyers from other jurisdictions or acting in cross-border matters, a lawyer may need to enquire about the position.

Firstly, there are differences in relation to the jurisprudential principles giving rise to those rights and duties – whether by statute, conduct rules or (as in common-law jurisdictions), judge-made law, and whether they are subject to criminal liability for breach.

Secondly, the rules may vary according to their extent – whether, for example, confidentiality applies to correspondence between lawyers and if so in what circumstances. In some jurisdictions, certain correspondence between lawyers may be confidential, such that it cannot be disclosed to the client. There are also variations in whether confidentiality applies to documents or information obtained by the lawyer from parties other than the client during the course of the retainer.

Thirdly, confidentiality is increasingly subject to exceptions imposed by law – particularly in the field of legislation on anti-money laundering and counter-terrorist financing, but also tax law and investigations by competition authorities.

The underlying purpose of the protection afforded by confidentiality rules is to ensure the proper administration of justice, and to ensure that clients can freely consult with lawyers without perceiving a need to hold back part of their case.

Putting to one side the important variations in the applicable rules, clients expect their lawyers to keep their affairs confidential. The focus of this chapter will be on what steps lawyers need to take, and what risks they need to guard against, to satisfy the duties they owe.

1.2 The interaction with conflicts of interest

As we shall see, lawyers also have duties to disclose material information in their possession to their clients. When acting for two clients, A and B, in the same or substantially related matters, if appropriate measures have not been taken, the lawyer may be subject to conflicting duties – to keep client A's information confidential, yet at the same time to disclose client A's information to client B.

This may also be the case where A is a former client: the duty of confidentiality will continue after the lawyer–client retainer has ended. Whereas in some jurisdictions that would not strictly be regarded as a conflict of interest, the steps that have to be addressed are similar and will form part of the firm's system for checking conflicts of interest and ensuring compliance with the firm's professional obligations.

1.3   **Types of information – paper, electronic, knowledge**
The information that must be kept confidential may come in many forms – whether on paper, electronic, or knowledge within the firm. Rules differ between jurisdictions on whether the knowledge of one person in the firm is attributed to all others, but even where it is not attributed to others in this way, the scenario outlined in the previous paragraph, of acting for two clients either simultaneously or in sequence, may still require steps to be implemented to protect the confidential information of client A.

1.4   **Potential clients and tenders**
Confidentiality issues are not confined to current and former clients: they also arise in connection with prospective clients. So lawyers need to be wary of the risk, when pitching for work, that they may receive confidential information that would preclude them from acting against the potential client, even though they may ultimately be unsuccessful in their attempt to obtain the work.

An example of this was the Canadian case of *Ainsworth Electric Co v Alcatel Canada Wire Inc*.[1] Alcatel invited a number of law firms to submit proposals to act for it in a dispute with Ainsworth. One of the firms that submitted a proposal was Goodman Phillips & Vineberg (Goodman). A representative of Alcatel had a one-and-a-half hour meeting with two representatives of Goodman. The anticipated litigation was discussed, along with Goodman's proposals for staffing and their proposed charging. A second meeting of similar length took place. No documents were provided to Goodman. Goodman was not instructed.

Initially, a partner in another law firm acted for Ainsworth. The partner then joined Goodman and brought the case with him. The fact that Goodman had pitched for the work was not picked up in the lateral hiring process.

Alcatel applied to the court to have Goodman disqualified from acting. There was an evidential dispute as to whether Alcatel had provided confidential information to Goodman. The judge held:

> In my view, there was a "solicitor-client" relationship between Alcatel and the Goodman firm as that phrase is understood in law, even though Alcatel was just "shopping" and had not actually or formally retained the Goodman firm in this case. Goodman clearly owed Alcatel a duty of confidentiality.[2]

---

1   1998 14845 (ON SC).

However, he held that Goodman had rebutted any inference that such confidential information as had been conveyed by Alcatel to them would be used to Alcatel's detriment and there was no real risk of prejudice to Alcatel. The judge therefore declined to disqualify Goodman from acting.

The case highlights the risk of pitching for work which, if unsuccessful, may in some cases preclude the firm from acting on other matters, and also highlights the risks of lateral hiring. It is highly desirable that firms record potential clients on their conflict systems so matters such as this can be identified.

1.5 Continuing duty after termination of retainer

The duty of confidentiality will continue after the retainer terminates. Even though information obtained confidentially may, with the passage of time, become public knowledge, in many jurisdictions the lawyer may still be precluded from using the knowledge to the advantage of another client.

1.6 Interaction with legal professional privilege (in common-law jurisdictions)

In common-law jurisdictions, legal professional privilege is the right of the client to withhold documents and advice from production. Privilege is the right of the client, but confidentiality is the duty of the lawyer. However, confidentiality is a precondition to the existence of the privilege.

2. The duty of confidentiality

2.1 Absolute

Lawyers and their staff are under a duty to keep the affairs of clients confidential. Subject only to a few limited exceptions, of which examples are given below, this duty is an absolute one. So it was held in the English case of *Bolkiah v KPMG*[3] that:

> the duty to preserve confidentiality is unqualified. It is a duty to keep the information confidential, not merely to take all reasonable steps to do so. Moreover, it is not merely a duty not to communicate the information to a third party. It is a duty not to misuse it, that is to say, without the consent of the former client to make any use of it or to cause any use to be made of it by others otherwise than for his benefit.

2.2 Crime fraud exception

In many, and probably most, jurisdictions confidentiality will be subject to a crime-fraud exception, meaning that there is no confidentiality protection where the client is using the lawyer to enable him or her to commit a criminal act. In English law, this exception also applies to cases where a party other than the client intends a lawyer–client communication to be made for that purpose, for example where an innocent client is being used by a third party.[4]

---

2   At paragraph 39.
3   [1998] UKHL 52, [1999] 2 AC 222 at page 235 G-H.
4   *R v Central Criminal Court ex p Francis & Francis* [1989] 1 AC 346.

2.3 Other exceptions

There may also be other exceptions to the principle that confidentiality is absolute. For example, more often than not, it may be necessary for the lawyer to communicate with a third party in order to advance the client's case, whether it be litigation or a transaction, and it will be necessary to communicate with the other party or its lawyers and perhaps others. Client consent to communicate in this way may be implied, but the lawyer should nonetheless consider whether it is necessary or desirable to obtain express consent.

Money-laundering and counter-terrorism legislation will often provide an exception to the duty of confidentiality, to enable the lawyer to report suspicion to the authorities.

2.4 Information in the public domain

In the English case of *Hilton v Barker Booth & Eastwood*,[5] the law firm was acting for two clients with conflicting interests. It knew that one had a criminal conviction, which was in the public domain, but unknown to the other client. As it was a matter of public record, it could not be confidential. However, the lawyers would have been in breach of their duty to advance the convicted client's case had they disclosed the conviction.

3. The duty of disclosure

Lawyers will generally be under a duty to disclose material information in their possession to the client. If they hold information on behalf of one client, or former client, which is subject to the duty of confidentiality, but is relevant to a second client's instruction, this may put them in breach of duty to one or other client: they cannot discharge their duty to one client without breaching their duty to the other.

3.1 Disclosure prohibited by law

There may be circumstances where disclosure is prohibited by law, particularly under 'tipping off' provisions in anti-money laundering legislation.

3.2 Modifying the duty

It may be possible to modify the duty of disclosure by agreement. An example of where this may happen in practice is where the law firm acts for two competing bidders in a corporate transaction. The firm may be asked to act for the two clients and will generally use different teams if it does so (always assuming it is not prohibited by its bar rules from acting for competing bidders). Nonetheless, it is necessary to keep each client's bid information confidential.

But the situation may also arise where the firm acts for successive clients in connection with the same or related matter, for example a potential buyer of property who decides not to proceed. A subsequent client may wish to instruct the firm on buying the same property. However, it is necessary to examine the facts carefully. It may be one thing if the first client dropped out due to inability to secure

---

5   [2005] UKHL 8.

funds, but quite another if it was due to an adverse survey report which suggested the property was defective and overpriced – material information that the second client would be bound to want to know.

In practice, the difficulty may be that it is not possible to ask a client to agree to a modification of the duty of disclosure without at the same time breaching confidentiality to the other client by disclosing that the lawyer has acted for that client.

Caution is needed here, however, as it is important that clients understand what they are being asked to agree to and that it is in their best interests to do so. In practice, this may be restricted to sophisticated clients. For these purposes, a sophisticated client may be one who has independent legal advice either from another law firm or its own in-house counsel; beyond that, it is difficult to be specific without examining the full facts in context.

The danger is always that the consenting client, on subsequently discovering the information which was kept back from it, will say that it would never have consented had it known the full picture. The risk of that rests with the lawyer, and the client might be forgiven for saying that the lawyer chose to proceed in order to facilitate the collection of two sets of fees.

3.3 Joint instructions

The lawyer may act for two or more clients who have a common interest. Examples of this might be co-purchasers, lender and buyer in relation to property, co-litigants and the defence of an insured party to litigation on instructions from an insurer.

In general, the instruction will be on the basis that there are no secrets as between the respective clients who are each equally entitled to the information in the lawyer's possession. If either seeks to provide information on the basis that it will not be communicated to the other client, the lawyer needs to consider carefully whether it is proper to continue acting for both.

4. Material information

4.1 What is material information?

What is material information will be fact sensitive. The danger for the lawyer, particularly when obtaining consent to act for two clients, either simultaneously or sequentially, is that the issue may be judged with hindsight and from the client's perspective.

4.2 'Soft' information

Knowledge of clients' affairs can come in more than one form – it may be very specific, or it may be something more subtle – knowledge, from experience of acting for clients, of how they work, their approach to particular issues, strategy and tactics – which North Americans refer to as 'playbook' knowledge. A judicial definition of this appeared in the US case of *In re: North American Deed Company, Inc*:[6]

> [T]he heart of this concept is possession of extensive and relevant information about a

---

[6] 334 BR 443, 454 (Bankr D Nev 2005) at page 15, 7-13.

client obtained directly or as a byproduct of confidential communications, or at least through communications that would not have been made if the client had known that the law firm would be able to use the information against the client in later litigation. Subsequent use of that information could thus give the law firm an unfair advantage over the former client based in no small part on exploitation of these fruits of confidential communications.

This type of conflict can be particularly difficult to determine. In many cases it may come down to an issue of commercial relationships with clients – where there may be no legal objection to the firm acting, but where it would not want to act against an important client from which it received a regular stream of work.

4.3 Accidentally received information

Sometimes documents or information may be disclosed to the lawyer by the opposing party by mistake. Whether the lawyer is then under an obligation to notify the opponent of the mistake and whether the lawyer should or should not disclose this to the lawyer's own client will very much depend on the detail of the circumstances and the jurisdiction.

5. Information barriers

5.1 When they can be used

Information barriers are also referred to as 'ethical screens' and have in the past been described in many reported cases (and are still described in some jurisdictions) as 'Chinese Walls', though the latter term may now be regarded as inappropriate. Cases where information barriers may be used include situations where:

- the firm acts for two clients on a related matter;
- the firm has recruited staff from another firm who may have acquired confidential information while acting for another party to a matter on which the firm is instructed;
- the firm acts in a particularly sensitive matter, which might, for example, involve price sensitive market information or a high-profile client;
- the firm is acting for competing bidders, where permitted by law or rules of conduct to do so.

Information barriers are not a quick fix: it has been said that they "serve as barriers for reassuring clients, not for neutralizing conflicts".[7]

Where relying on an information barrier, it must be reasonable in all the circumstances and permitted under relevant local law and regulatory requirements.

Information barriers can require considerable care to implement, and they cannot exist in one person's mind. To survive a hostile challenge, the authorities in England have held that they must be part of the established structure of the firm,[8]

---

7   Shapiro, *Tangled Loyalties*, University of Michigan Press (2002), page 403.
8   This was said to be a requirement in *Bolkiah v KPMG*, though in *Young v Robson Rhodes* [1999] 3 All ER 524, Laddie J said "The crucial question is: 'will the barriers work?' If they do, it does not matter whether they were created before the problem arose or are erected afterwards."

that staff must be trained in them regularly, and that further training must be provided to relevant staff when they are implemented. It is also worth noting that in the event of such a challenge, the outcome may be unpredictable, even before an experienced commercial judge.[9] In the leading case of *Bolkiah v KPMG*,[10] it was said that the firm should be restrained from acting unless satisfied on the basis of clear and convincing evidence that effective measures have been taken to ensure that no disclosure will occur.

5.2 **Information that may need to be protected (including time records, billing, library searches)**

An effective information barrier where required by the rules involves far more than password protecting documents in a document management system: firms hold data in a variety of forms, and the people issues are just as important. In practical terms, it may involve detailed consideration of issues such as use of shared facilities, use of meeting rooms (even clearing waste-paper bins after meetings), library research services, shared support staff, digital dictation, financial and accounting information and departmental meetings.

5.3 **Requirements for an information barrier**

The requirements may vary by jurisdiction. However, there was a useful summary of most of the English common-law requirements in guidance notes to the (repealed) Solicitors' Code of Conduct 2007,[11] which substantially summarised the common law and therefore provides valuable assistance. It read as follows –

(a) *that the client who or which might be interested in the confidential information acknowledges in writing that the information held by the firm will not be given to them;*

(b) *that all members of the firm who hold the relevant confidential information ("the restricted group") are identified and have no involvement with or for the other client;*

(c) *that no member of the restricted group is managed or supervised in relation to that matter by someone from outside the restricted group;*

(d) *that all members of the restricted group confirm at the start of the engagement that they understand that they possess or might come to possess information which is confidential, and that they must not discuss it with any other member of the firm unless that person is, or becomes a member of the restricted group, and that this obligation shall be regarded by everyone as an on-going one;*

(e) *that each member of the restricted group confirms when the barrier is established that they have not done anything which would amount to a breach of the information barrier; and*

(f) *that only members of the restricted group have access to documents containing the confidential information.*

The note continued by adding that the following arrangements may also be

---

9 See for example, *Koch Shipping v Richards Butler* [2002] EWCA Civ 1280.
10 [1998] UKHL52.
11 See guidance note 44 to Rule 4.04.

appropriate, and might in particular be necessary where acting in a common interest situation or for competing bidders:

(g) that the restricted group is physically separated from those acting for the other client, for example, by being in a separate building, on a separate floor or in a segregated part of the offices, and that some form of "access restriction" be put in place to ensure physical segregation;

(h) that confidential information on computer systems is protected by use of separate computer networks or through use of password protection or similar means;

(i) that the firm issues a statement that it will treat any breach, even an inadvertent one, of the information barrier as a serious disciplinary offence;

(j) that each member of the restricted group gives a written statement at the start of the engagement that they understand the terms of the information barrier and will comply with them;

(k) that the firm undertakes that it will do nothing which would or might prevent or hinder any member of the restricted group from complying with the information barrier;

(l) that the firm identifies a specific partner or other appropriate person within the restricted group with overall responsibility for the information barrier;

(m) that the firm provides formal and regular training for members of the firm on duties of confidentiality and responsibility under information barriers or will ensure that such training is provided prior to the work being undertaken; and

(n) that the firm implements a system for the opening of post, receipt of faxes and distribution of email which will ensure that confidential information is not disclosed to anyone outside the restricted group.

5.4 Implementation and monitoring

The courts may impose additional requirements for an information barrier to those set out above. In particular, the guidance arguably falls short of that required by law, in that it does not specify a requirement for monitoring the effectiveness of the information barrier and compliance with undertakings.[12]

6. People risks

6.1 Working outside the office

Working outside the office poses risks to confidentiality. First, there are risks associated with information technology, such as the use of mobile devices and home computers.

Secondly, there is the risk of working in surroundings where confidentiality cannot be assured, such as working on public transport.

6.2 Social media

The immediacy of social media, such as Facebook, LinkedIn, Twitter and the like carries significant risk. It is too easy to divulge information. Lawyers and their staff

---

12 See the terms of the order applied in *GUS Consulting GmbH v Leboeuf Lamb Greene & Macrae* [2006] EWCA Civ 683.

need to be alert to the risks even when withholding the name of the client, because others may be able to fill in the missing pieces and identify the matter.

6.3 JK Rowling's lawyer

It is important, too, that lawyers and their staff do not discuss client matters in a social setting. This was amply illustrated by the case of the lawyer who acted for JK Rowling, the well-known author of the Harry Potter books. JK Rowling had written another novel under an assumed name in order to conceal her identity. Her lawyer disclosed this to his wife, who told her friend, and the matter rapidly reached the press. The lawyer was fined and his firm paid substantial damages.

7. Information security

7.1 Cyber risk

Law firms have been referred to as "the soft underbelly of corporate America" by the US government. Meanwhile, the UK government created the National Cyber Security Programme, and a taskforce of a dozen major UK professional organisations, associations and professional services firms has been set up to help companies to deal with the growing cyber security threat from organised crime networks, nation states and others. It has published a practical guide, Cyber-Security in Corporate Finance.[13]

Two examples of cyber risk are worth noting here. The first was the case of ACS Law. The firm was acting against approximately 5,000 individuals accused of illegal file-sharing. Their clients claimed that their copyright in music, software, computer games and films had been infringed. The firm's website was subject to a malicious hacking attack, resulting in the loss of personal data relating to the 5,000 individuals. The lawyer and firm were fined.

The second example is of seven Canadian law firms whose systems were reported to have been hacked in connection with an unsuccessful $40 billion bid to acquire Potash Corporation of Saskatchewan by BHP Billiton. Confidential client data on high-value corporate transactions can be of considerable worth to competing parties.

7.2 Bring your own device

The increasing use of devices such as smartphones owned by staff has put pressure on firms to ensure that appropriate levels of security are maintained. Firms will need to ensure they have control over client data and the right to insist on wiping data from the device when staff leave.

7.3 Business continuity issues

Damage to firms' IT systems or premises could put client confidentiality at risk and should therefore be considered when preparing and reviewing the firm's business continuity plan.

---

13 Available at www.icaew.com/~/media/Files/Technical/Corporate-finance/Corporate-finance-faculty/tecpln12526-cyber-web.pdf.

7.4 Premises

It is important to consider confidentiality and information security issues in connection with the firm's premises. For larger firms, is there electronic access control? Would staff challenge someone they did not know wandering around areas where client work was taking place?

There have been instances of firms being subject to regulatory investigation because confidential documents were visible through office windows.

7.5 Working from home

Home working may suit those who need flexible working arrangements, but what steps are taken to ensure that client information is kept confidential? Do staff take paper files home? This may be particularly important in cases where the firm holds sensitive personal data. Are staff emailing material to their home email address so they can work on their home computer?

7.6 Client requirements

Increasingly, corporate, institutional and public sector clients may impose specific information security requirements and may audit firms to ensure their requirements are met.

7.7 ISO27001 certification

This is an international standard for information security management. More and more corporate law firms are applying for certification under the standard as a means of demonstrating to clients that certain minimum standards are being met.

7.8 Departing partners and staff

Lawyers traditionally regard client precedents as their own and may seek to take them with them when they leave the firm, which will generally risk breaching the duty of confidentiality in the absence of client consent. Firms should be alert to the risk of departing partners and staff taking paper copies, emailing documents home or taking copies on recordable media such as USB drives or DVDs. Larger firms will have technological means of detecting and/or preventing this.

8. Data protection and freedom of information

As well as the duty to preserve the client's confidential information, there may be statutory requirements under data protection legislation. Those who act for public sector clients may also need to take account of freedom of information legislation where applicable.

9. Outsourcing

Outsourcing also poses a risk to confidentiality. It is important to obtain agreement from contractors to preserve client confidentiality. The firm should also obtain client consent to the use of outsourced services.

10. Financial risks to confidentiality

10.1 Charging the firm's assets
Those who seek to borrow money on the security of the firm's debt or other assets, such as IT equipment, should be alert to the risk to client confidentiality and should consider carefully how this may be protected contractually and in practice.

10.2 Factoring bills
Factoring bills, under which the benefit of the debt due from the client is assigned to a finance company that pays the law firm a proportion up front, have not been allowed in the United Kingdom due to the risk to client confidentiality.

11. Lateral hires

11.1 The need for conflict checks
Earlier, we looked at the case of *Ainsworth Electric Co v Alcatel Canada Wire Inc*.[14] The risks in relation to lateral hiring may be further illustrated by reference to the English case of *GUS Consulting GmbH v Leboeuf Lamb Greene & Macrae*.[15] GUS was party to an arbitration with DCL-KF involving allegations of fraud over shares in the Russian company Gazprom. The team acting for DCL at Debevoise & Plimpton left to join Leboeuf Lamb Greene & Macrae, and took the case with them. Leboeuf had acted for GUS in earlier transactions relating to the means by which shares were held, and which had been put in issue in the arbitration.

Leboeuf had not identified the conflict when the lateral hires joined them as it related to a former client, but had then put in place a 'conscientious and sophisticated ethical wall system' barring the DCL team from access to the GUS files. The firm's former client's honesty and integrity was under attack.

GUS applied for an injunction to restrain Leboeuf from acting for DCL in the arbitration.

The information barrier included controls on access to computerised documents and archived files, and files were physically stamped as restricted. However, the order of the judge at first instance also contained the following undertakings by Leboeuf to the court:

1) *By 5pm on Friday 4 November 2005 the Defendant will cause changes to be made to its working arrangements at its London offices so that the Arbitration Team ... will not occupy office space on the same floor as those who have previously carried out work for [GUS] and are still with the Defendant, and who are listed in the table attached to this order ("the relevant partners and staff");*

2) *The Defendant will, as soon as is reasonably practicable, issue an instruction in writing by e-mail to the relevant partners and staff that they are not to discuss that work with any member of the Arbitration Team or amongst themselves;*

3) *None of the Arbitration Team will seek any information about [GUS] from any of*

---

14 1998 14845 (ON SC).
15 [2006] EWCA Civ 683.

the relevant partners and staff, nor seek access to any paper or electronic files concerning [GUS];

4) None of the relevant partners and staff will discuss [GUS] work amongst themselves or with any member of the Arbitration Team;

5) The Defendant will until otherwise agreed by the Claimant or approved by the Court;

   (a) at all times maintain the ethical wall presently in place,

   (b) take reasonable steps to monitor the effectiveness of the ethical wall,

   (c) take reasonable steps to monitor compliance with undertakings (2)-(4) set out above.

6) The Defendant will, during the months of April and October of every year during the currency of LCIA Arbitration 2371;

   (a) issue a fresh instruction repeating the instruction in paragraph (2) above,

   (b) verify that there has been no breach of the ethical wall presently in place, and that the integrity of the ethical wall is maintained,

   (c) notify the Claimant in writing that it has taken the steps referred to in 6) (a) and (b) above.

The Court of Appeal held that Leboeuf had shown that the risk of disclosure was more theoretical than real. It was important that the information related to transactional matters conducted some years before. The Court also said that one had to stand back from the adversarial process and assess how likely the risk of disclosure really was.

11.2 Practical difficulties

A practical problem with lateral hires may be that conduct rules may prevent full conflict searches being carried out, due to the need to preserve client confidentiality. In the United States, Rule 1.6(b)(7) of the American Bar Association (ABA) Model Rules of Professional Conduct provides that a lawyer may disclose client confidential information "to the extent the lawyer reasonably believes necessary ... to detect and resolve conflicts of interest arising from the lawyer's change of employment or from changes in the composition or ownership of a firm, but only if the revealed information would not compromise the attorney–client privilege or otherwise prejudice the client".

Eminently sensible though this is, there is no similar provision in England and the writer is not aware of any such provision elsewhere.

12. Secondments (in and out)

Increasingly, commercial clients require secondments to and from the law firms they instruct. This can be helpful in fostering relations and increasing understanding, but it does pose risks to confidentiality. The inbound secondees may potentially gain access to the client's competitors, which would almost certainly be unwelcome to the other clients, and the outbound secondee may gain access to confidential information relating to other, competing firms, such as charging rates. Consideration should be given to the terms of the secondment agreement, and to treating the secondees in the way one would treat new staff and departing staff.

13. **International firm structures – sharing information**

    International firms usually comprise more than one legal entity. Terms of business should, where appropriate, address the need to share data with other legal entities. Consideration will need to be given to local conduct rules. It may be necessary to obtain the consent of potential clients to share details with other legal entities in the firm structure in order to carry out conflicts checks.

14. **Training**

    It has been said that confidentiality is in lawyers' DNA, but the complexity of the rules, which vary from jurisdiction to jurisdiction and the hazards one may encounter, including those described in this chapter, mean that nothing can be taken for granted. In addition, it should not be assumed that support staff and unqualified fee earners have the same level of understanding. Firms should therefore consider training staff, particularly in relation to information barriers.

15. **Document retention**

    Firms should have document retention policies and should address the ownership and retention of documents in the terms of business for clients. Particular care should be taken when disposing of documents, whether electronic or paper, to ensure that client confidentiality is preserved.

16. **Written policies**

    The firm should have written policies covering the key issues set out in this chapter. It is particularly important to do so in relation to information barriers, if the firm anticipates implementing them, as in some jurisdictions (particularly England), *ad hoc* arrangements are unlikely to suffice.

17. **Checklist**
    - For each new jurisdiction where the firm will practise, ascertain the applicable confidentiality rules and how these compare with the rules applicable to the firm's operations in other jurisdictions.
    - Ascertain the exceptions to confidentiality, the circumstances in which they apply, and what it may be sensible to say about them in the firm's engagement letters and terms of business.
    - Consider procedures to restrict, or otherwise manage, the receipt of confidential information when pitching for work (to reduce the risk, if the pitch is unsuccessful, of such information preventing the firm from taking on matters for other clients).
    - Ensure that interactions with potential clients (including pitch activity) are recorded in the firm's conflict checking systems.
    - Have a clear policy and procedures for implementing information barriers where these are appropriate, including template letters for seeking client consent.
    - Have appropriate policies and procedures in place in relation to information security and specifically:

- working outside the firm;
- home working;
- use of own devices;
- use of social media;
- outsourcing;
- premises security;
- leavers.
- Understand applicable data protection requirements and have in place appropriate policies and procedures in respect of them.
- Establish a practical policy for managing conflict and confidentiality risks in respect of proposed lateral hires.
- Have in place appropriate templates (including as to confidentiality) for secondments.
- Consider arrangements that may be needed in order to share information and data between different entities within a group structure.
- Provide training on the above as appropriate.

Engagement letters

Heather Hibberd
Legal Practitioners' Liability Committee
Andrew Scott
Clyde & Co LLP

---

1. **Introduction**

    Having in place appropriate engagement terms is one of the most important tools on the lawyer's risk management workbench. Well-drafted engagement terms will set out clearly who the lawyer is acting for, the work to be done, any limitations on liability, the basis of charging and other important information and caveats with a view to managing risk. In some jurisdictions the provision of some information to clients (in the form of client-care letters or fee agreements) is mandatory in certain circumstances; but engagement terms have a wider purpose and benefit that should not be underestimated.

    Engagement terms may appear in a number of guises. In some jurisdictions, particularly England and Wales, usual practice is to issue an engagement letter accompanied by a detailed set of terms of business. In other jurisdictions a simpler form of letter is more usual. There are also jurisdictions where the issue of any form of engagement terms is relatively unusual – but a sophisticated firm practising in such a jurisdiction is unlikely to be content with issuing nothing. Firms that practise internationally may, if the jurisdictions in which they operate have similar regulatory and business cultures, be able to adopt a single template engagement letter and terms of business for use in all of them, with the terms of business perhaps containing some alternative clauses which are applicable only in certain jurisdictions. It is more likely, however, that international firms will have a suite of engagement letter templates and terms of business for use in the different jurisdictions in which they do business. It may also be that different templates will exist for different practice areas, although having a plethora of different templates can be unhelpful because of the difficulty of keeping them all updated and the risk that the wrong one will be selected for a particular matter.

    Complications can arise where a client puts forward its own standard terms, whether in the form of a service level agreement, counsel guidelines or a more formal contractual document. Care is needed to ensure that such documents are reviewed centrally before agreement, and processes for this and other purposes related to the formalisation of engagement terms are considered at the end of this chapter.

2. **The client**

    2.1 **Who are you acting for?**

    The first and obvious issue to be clear about in the engagement letter is who the firm is acting for. Often this may appear straightforward – the client will be the individual who approaches the firm or the company he or she represents. But appearances can be deceptive, and lawyers need to think carefully about who they will be acting for and who they will not be acting for, and record this in the engagement letter.

Examples of situations which may not be straightforward include the following:
- The firm is asked by an in-house lawyer at the parent company of a group to act on behalf of one of its subsidiaries. Is the client the subsidiary or the parent or both? At any rate the firm will not want to accept duties to other group subsidiaries and it is sensible to include standard wording in the engagement letter template to make clear that only the particular group company or companies for which work is done will be clients, and other members of the group will not be. This will also help with conflicts management.
- In all situations where the firm is instructed by a company, care is needed to determine whether any duty will be accepted to the company's directors and officers with whom the firm will be dealing. There are dangers inherent in leaving this question dangling, highlighted elsewhere in this book. The safe default is not to accept any such duties and to incorporate standard language in the engagement letter template to make clear that individual directors and officers will not be clients.
- A firm may receive instructions from an individual or group of individuals who are setting up a company. Are these individuals the client, or is it the company? It may well be that the identity of the client will switch once the company is set up, when the law firm will start acting on the company's behalf, and if this is the case it would be wise at that point for the firm to bring its retainer from the individuals to an end and issue new engagement documentation to the company.
- Firms may receive instructions from someone acting on behalf of another individual or entity. Examples would include requests from another law firm to help out on a matter they are dealing with; or instructions from someone holding a power of attorney; or instructions from a spouse in respect of property which both spouses own jointly. All of these situations require care. The firm needs be sure who the client is, that there is no risk that the client's interests might be prejudiced by the instructions of the intermediary and that the intermediary does have authority to give instructions.

Firms will also want to be sure that individuals giving instructions on behalf of companies have the necessary authority to do so. Typically firms will specify in the engagement letter who in practice they will be dealing with at the client company and include a standard warranty of authority, though from time to time more assurance on this aspect may be needed.

2.2 More than one client

It is a given that firms can only act for more than one client in respect of the same matter if there is no conflict between them. However, while that may be so at the outset, there will often be the potential for interests to diverge later, and firms can sometimes help themselves by including in the engagement letter language designed to mitigate the effects of this.

An example arises where firms (in those jurisdictions where they are permitted to do so) represent both a defendant and its insurer in litigation. Commonly the source of such instructions will be the insurer, who will appoint the firm to consider policy coverage as well as acting in the defence of the claim. If at the outset there is an obvious and material coverage issue the firm cannot act for both and each would require its own lawyers; but otherwise the situation may be managed by language in the engagement letter with the insurer pointing out the insurer's rights as regards policy coverage and the firm's duties to it in respect of this issue. Typically this would include making clear to the insured that the firm's advice to the insurer regarding policy coverage would not be shared with the insured.

It may also be desirable where a firm is acting for two or more parties to a matter to seek to agree who (if anyone) the firm will continue to represent if differences emerge between the clients at a later date.

3. Scope and responsibilities

It is essential to clarify from the start, in the engagement letter, what the firm is retained to do. The scope of the engagement should be carefully delineated and described. Save where the instruction is of a routine nature for an experienced client, simplistic descriptions such as 'acting in relation to the purchase' are best avoided.

Many claims against lawyers arise from a failure on the lawyer's part to fully understand and articulate in writing the scope of the retainer, particularly where it has been limited in some way. This failure leaves the firm open to allegations later that the scope was much wider than envisaged and consequently that the firm has been negligent in not dealing with, or advising on, a particular issue. An English example is *Hurlingham Estates Ltd v Wilde & Partners*.[1] In this case the client complained that a company acquisition and related property transaction had given rise to an unexpected tax charge. The partner handling the matter, who had little tax knowledge, claimed that he had pointed this out to the client, but there was no record in an engagement letter or other document that this had happened or that the firm's retainer had been limited in any way. The firm was therefore liable to compensate the client in respect of the tax charge, which could have been avoided by a simple change to the structure of the transaction. Given the particular pitfalls of tax law, firms will often now provide in their terms of business that they will not advise on tax unless specifically agreed in the engagement letter. However, relying on a blanket carve-out in respect of this or other matters may not in itself suffice. If there is an aspect, such as tax, which the firm will not be dealing with but which will need to be factored in to a particular matter, the firm may need to make sure that the client is aware of this and takes appropriate advice elsewhere.

Claims also occur where the lawyer discusses the scope and initially documents it but then the scope changes when the client asks for further things to be done,

---

1 [1997] 1 Lloyd's Rep 525.

usually as a result of a further issue emerging, and that change is not documented. This 'retainer creep' can leave the firm exposed because the scope of the retainer is no longer set out fully in writing, making it easier to argue that it was wider than the firm itself understood. It is therefore important to remind fee-earners of the need to update engagement letters where appropriate, or issue fresh ones.

The scope section should also include any essential aspects that the client has agreed to deal with, including the time frame if important. So, for example, an engagement letter might set out that the client has agreed to collate and provide particular documents by a certain time, or deal with various bodies to obtain necessary licences for a business purchase. Template terms of business may include more general expectations of clients, that they will provide complete and accurate information to the firm and give clear and prompt instructions, for example.

4. Limiting liability

The extent to which a law firm and its individual lawyers are able to restrict their legal liability to clients in the event that something goes wrong will depend on local legislation and regulation. Some jurisdictions permit lawyers to cap their liability to clients, subject to certain restrictions, but many do not. There are also other means by which the lawyer's obligations to clients can potentially be limited. In this section we will look at the different options that may be available.

4.1 Liability capping

Some jurisdictions permit lawyers to agree a monetary cap with clients in the event that something goes wrong. In England and Wales the Solicitors Regulation Authority (SRA) permits solicitors to agree such caps provided they are set at an amount not less than the minimum level of professional indemnity insurance that is compulsory for the practice (currently either £2 million or £3 million depending on the nature of the practice vehicle). The SRA, understandably, require that such caps are properly brought to the client's attention and freely agreed to. Similar arrangements occur in various states in Australia provided the firm is a member of a limited liability scheme, permitted by professional standards legislation in participating jurisdictions, which places insurance and risk management standards on firms.

Liability capping, where permissible, may also be subject to local legal requirements. Within the United Kingdom capping is subject to the terms of the Unfair Contract Terms Act 1977. This makes void any attempt to limit liability for death or personal injury (hopefully a relatively rare contingency in the context of a legal practice) and makes other liability restrictions applied in the course of business subject to a reasonableness test, which is applied retrospectively by the court should the efficacy of the restriction ever be called into question. Among various factors, the higher the amount of the cap, the more likely it is to be upheld as reasonable. For larger firms the overriding concern is likely to be to set caps at a level that is likely to be upheld should they ever be needed in the context of a major claim. Care will be needed in drafting standard engagement letters and terms of business and in guiding the firm's lawyers to ensure that liability capping is appropriately structured and drawn to the client's attention and that it is also made clear to the client that the cap is negotiable if necessary.

Many jurisdictions, including those of the United States and Canada, do not permit liability capping and it may be a breach of professional ethics rules even to attempt this. The situation in Europe depends very much on the law of the relevant member state.

4.2 Other ways of limiting liability

The importance of defining the client and the scope of the engagement have already been mentioned. Where permissible, a law firm may also seek to restrict its liability in a number of other ways. These include:
- Agreeing that only the firm (assuming it is an incorporated vehicle) will be liable if something goes wrong and that individual partners and employees will not have liability. This is a standard approach in the United Kingdom where the practice is a limited liability partnership or company, but will not be permissible in jurisdictions that do not permit lawyers to limit their liability.
- Agreeing that the law firm will only be liable for its fair share of any loss or damage the client may suffer if something goes wrong. Such a clause, if carefully worded, can provide greater certainty that the firm will not be responsible for losses that the client brought upon itself or that were caused by other advisers. Wording might, for example, make clear that the client cannot seek to recover more from the firm because another adviser is now insolvent or set a liability cap at a low level. In Australia proportionate liability laws achieve this outcome where all parties caused the same loss.
- Where the firm practises through multiple entities, structuring arrangements so that the client is only able to sue one entity if something goes wrong. This may be done by treating the entity first approached by the client as the lead entity, with which the client contracts. If the matter has an international element and services are required from another firm entity, the lead entity will arrange those services for the client and assume responsibility for them.

The efficacy of these and other arrangements will vary from jurisdiction to jurisdiction. Firms need to review carefully how best to take advantage of the protections that are legitimately available to them.

Additionally, firms will wish to consider:
- placing a restriction on the client's ability to share the firm's advice and work product with others, or to use these for a purpose outside the immediate engagement; and
- making clear that they are not responsible for the work of others to whom tasks may have to be sub-contracted, such as local counsel or experts. This of course will not be a complete absolution of responsibility: the firm will still owe obligations in respect of its selection of other advisers (if it selects them) and in respect of the briefing it gives them, and it is unlikely to avoid responsibility entirely if there is something very obviously wrong with the other adviser's work product.

5. **Charges**

An engagement letter is the obvious place to provide information to the client about the basis on which the firm will charge for its work and an estimate of likely cost. Some jurisdictions impose legal or regulatory obligations on law firms in these respects. So, for example, the SRA Code of Conduct requires a high level of transparency about charges, extending to an obligation on solicitors to consider whether the anticipated outcome for the client justifies the likely outlay. In the United States there is generally at least a requirement to document the proposed basis of charging in matters that will involve court proceedings. In Australia most of the state jurisdictions have their own similar legislative requirements, under which firms must provide the basis on which legal costs will be calculated and estimates of costs for the whole of the matter for many clients, with exceptions for defined sophisticated clients. In Europe it will vary from jurisdiction to jurisdiction.

The engagement letter and terms of business can be used to deal with additional points such as:
- how expenses and disbursements will be dealt with;
- whether a payment on account or a retainer is required;
- the firm's policy on the payment of interest where it holds client funds;
- the time by which payment of bills is required and the consequences of late payment.

6. **Managing conflicts and confidentiality**

The engagement letter and terms of business may be an appropriate place for information that needs to be provided to the client about the management of conflicts of interest and confidentiality. So if in a US context, for example, disclosure of existing representations and consent to the firm acting are required, an engagement letter may be the appropriate place to record these; so too if the firm seeks any other form of conflict waiver.

Increasingly engagement letters and terms of business may include:
- a generic form of advance conflict waiver, in those jurisdictions such as the United States that adopt a loyalty-based approach to client conflicts;
- where loyalty-based conflict provisions do not apply, but the firm also has a presence in a jurisdiction where they do, a provision confirming that conflict questions arising out of the engagement will be determined in accordance with local rules.

Terms of business may also typically deal with aspects of the firm's duties of confidentiality to its clients, including circumstances where the duty may be overridden (for example by duties to the court or statutory duties in respect of money laundering and similar issues). In certain jurisdictions, firms may also seek through their standard terms of business advance consent to the use of information barriers should a situation subsequently arise where the firm's duty of confidentiality to the client conflicts with a potential duty of disclosure to another client. However, the efficacy of general provisions of this nature is untested.

7. **Files and documents**

The engagement letter or terms of business should set out how the law firm will manage the documents and files that are created or come into its control during the retainer and when the retainer ends.

Each jurisdiction will have rules on which documents belong to the client and which are the property of the law firm. Sometimes these will define when documents must be returned to the client and how long they must be kept by the law firm after the retainer is finished and when any documents can be destroyed. There may also be legislation that governs the destruction of documents generally.

The contents of firms' document retention and destruction policies are beyond the scope of this chapter and will be heavily dependent on local jurisdictional requirements. Policies will typically need to balance such factors as the obligation to return (or keep safely) valuable original documents; any regulatory requirements to maintain records for a particular period; the potential desirability (though views may vary) of having files available if a claim materialises during applicable limitation periods; the strict legal ownership of papers; and any data protection requirements to delete certain types of data once they are no longer needed. The aim in the engagement letter and terms of business will be to convey the essentials of the firm's policy and obtain any consents needed, for example to the destruction of papers after a certain period.

Firms may also have rights to retain files and papers if the client terminates their engagement and does not settle outstanding bills. Firms may wish to clarify in their terms of business when such rights (a lien) may arise.

8. **Communications**

Agreeing at the start how the client and lawyer will communicate during the matter, and how often, will help avoid misunderstandings and improve communication.

Email communication will often be the preferred medium, but emails are often written very casually and quickly and are not proofread which can lead to mistakes and misunderstandings. There can be expectations that email will be read as soon as it is sent which can cause problems if the matter is urgent but not read by the recipient in time. Many lawyers will receive vast amounts of email each day and it can be very easy for an email to be lost.

Firms may therefore set out ground rules for email in the engagement letter. These might include:
- a requirement that the subject heading should always include either the name of the matter or the file number and short description of the content or purpose of the email;
- a statement that emails will not always be read as soon as they are received but will generally be read within a specified time;
- a direction that if the matter is urgent a phone call should be made instead of an email or to highlight that an email has been sent and to check it has been received and read.

Firms will also often include in terms of business a warning about the security risks inherent in the use of email, with an indication that clients who are concerned about these risks contact them to explore alternatives.

9. **Termination provisions**

It is wise to set out in engagement letters and terms of business the circumstances in which the firm can terminate its retainer. What is permissible will vary from jurisdiction to jurisdiction but typically firms will reserve to themselves the right to terminate if a request for money on account (retainer) is not met, bills are left unpaid, the client does not meet other important obligations or if continuing to act would breach legal or ethical requirements. Terms of business can be used to set out the consequences of termination in such circumstances.

It can also be helpful to identify when an engagement that runs its course will be regarded as concluded, so that it is clear when the client relationship ends. It is helpful to do this because lawyers are not known for their attention to housekeeping and long-finished files can often sit open in the firm's system. For this reason, particularly in jurisdictions that apply the loyalty approach to client conflicts, firms will often specify that their engagement and (unless instructed on another matter) the client relationship will terminate once their work on the matter is completed and a file bill is rendered.

10. **Other information**

In some, though by no means all, jurisdictions, there will be legal or regulatory obligations to convey certain information to clients over and above the items outlined above. Examples include:
- providing information about, and securing agreement to, the use of client data for certain purposes, where such matters are subject to local law and regulation (such as the Data Protection Act in the United Kingdom and equivalents elsewhere);
- providing information about the firm's complaints policies, and specifically who to contact if a problem arises;
- explaining the client's rights if it is unhappy with the level of charges made;
- providing information about the firm's insurance arrangements, where this is mandated by applicable regulation.

An engagement letter template may also be a good place to record certain other information that it is helpful for the firm to know has been communicated to the client. Examples, in a litigation context, might include information about the client's duties to provide disclosure (discovery) of documents, and its obligations to preserve documents safely in the meantime, or about the client's potential exposure to adverse costs or other sanctions in the event of failure to comply with court orders or timetables. Obviously the extent to which it is useful or necessary to convey such information will depend on the jurisdiction.

11. **Law and jurisdiction**

It will be helpful, particularly if the client is not resident in the relevant jurisdiction or the matter has an international dimension, to specify which law will apply in the event that a dispute arises between the client and the firm. Typically this will be the law of the jurisdiction in which the firm, or particular office, is trading, although if the office is simply a representative office and does not practise local law it may be appropriate to specify the law of the jurisdiction where the firm's principal office is located.

It is also desirable to specify where and how disputes are to be resolved. Usually such a provision will require that disputes be dealt with in the courts of the jurisdiction where the firm, or particular office, is trading. However, if the firm deals with many overseas clients, it is worth reserving the option to initiate proceedings (for example to recover unpaid fees) in the jurisdiction where the client or its principal assets are based.

It is also worth considering the option of arbitration, both because of the more private nature of such proceedings and also because it may be easier to enforce an arbitration award in certain overseas jurisdictions than it is to enforce a court order.

12. Firm policies and processes

There is little point in pulling together standard engagement letter templates and terms of business if they are not used. Moreover, if part of the purpose of having engagement letters is to comply with local regulatory requirements the firm will find itself in breach of those requirements if engagement letters are not sent out on a systematic basis. Firms therefore need appropriate policies and procedures to ensure that this happens.

The measures firms put in place to achieve this will depend significantly on their internal culture and the type of work carried out. If a firm deals with a high volume of routine matters for a disparate client base, it may be possible to treat the issue of an engagement letter as a mandatory step in the matter inception process, but such an approach will not work in other contexts. Other options may include requiring issued engagement letters to be logged within a stated period, with a follow-up for defaulters. Internal compliance auditing is also an option, though less immediate in its impact.

Whatever the route taken, firms need to ensure that their standard templates, including terms of business, are readily available and signposted and that lawyers have the necessary guidance, backed up by appropriate training, to use them effectively. A central compliance function to which questions and difficulties can be referred is also helpful.

A common question raised by lawyers, and sometimes clients, is whether it is necessary for the firm to issue a full engagement letter and terms of business every time a good client sends through another instruction. One way of dealing with this is to have available an alternative template, for use in such situations, which covers generically the type of work that the client will be referring to the firm. On receipt of subsequent instructions the client team then just needs to confirm that the new matter will be dealt with under that existing arrangement and convey whatever information may be required about the specific matter (such as which lawyers will be working on it and the likely cost). It is good practice to update such arrangements at least annually.

Review of the firm's charging rates is a good opportunity to send out new letters and ensure that the client has the latest version of the firm's terms of business.

One other process issue to consider is that more sophisticated clients are increasingly putting forward their own standard terms when retaining lawyers. These may be in the form of a service level agreement, counsel guidelines or a more formal contractual document. The problem inherent in such documents is that they will not include all the liability protections and other information that law firms will wish, or may be required, to communicate to clients, and they may also seek to commit the firm to onerous conflicts restrictions (such as seeking to apply US loyalty-based requirements in jurisdictions where these do not apply) or to very broad indemnities or other onerous provisions. For this reason it is wise to set up a process for the central review of all such documents, with the aim of trying to negotiate the sting out of the more awkward provisions. This will not always be achievable, in which case there should be an appropriate escalation procedure to take the issue of whether the terms should be accepted out of the hands of the prospective matter partners and have it considered in the overall interests of the firm by one or more independent partners. This role is often undertaken by the risk management partner or department in larger firms.

Firms should not lose sight of the fact that even if clients' own terms are unobjectionable, there is no logical reason why the firm's own standard terms of business should not also be included in the mix. This might be done by agreeing with the client that both sets of terms will apply, with the client's taking precedence in the event of any conflict.

Finally, firms will also want to ensure that wherever they agree to act on the basis of a client's own terms these are, once finalised, centrally logged and accessible to others in the firm who may have future dealings with that client.

13. Checklist

- What format should be adopted: engagement letter with standard terms of business, or engagement letter only?
- Will it work to have a single template (with some alternative provisions) for all jurisdictions and practice areas, or are variants required?
- What prompts should be included (along with guidance and training) to get lawyers to focus on the importance of being clear who the client is? Can standard wording be added to help with this?
- Does the firm commonly act for two or more clients in respect of the same matter, and if so should standard wording be provided for this?
- What prompts and other guidance should be included as regards the scoping in and scoping out of particular issues?
- Are the firm and its individual lawyers permitted to limit liability to clients? If so, should liability capping be adopted, and at what level should caps be set? What prompts and guidance should be included to maximise the prospects of a cap being effective if needed?
- What other means can appropriately be used to manage the extent of the firm's liability to clients and others?

- What legal and regulatory requirements are there to provide information about the firm's likely charges? What would it be sensible to provide in any event?
- Are there conflicts-related issues that can appropriately be managed through generic engagement letter provisions, and if so how should this be done?
- What should be said about the firm's obligations of confidentiality and disclosure?
- What needs to be communicated about the firm's document retention and destruction policies?
- Should something be said about means of communication, including email risk?
- How will the firm bring its engagement to an end, either because there is a particular need to do so or because the matter is concluded?
- Is there other information that the firm is obliged to provide in each of the jurisdictions in which it practises and that needs to be or could usefully be conveyed in the engagement letter and terms of business?
- Is there anything else it would be useful to use the engagement letter and terms of business to convey?
- How does the firm want to deal with choice of law and dispute resolution?
- How will the firm's client teams be made aware of and trained on the firm's requirements in respect of engagement letters and terms of business?
- What systems will be put in place to ensure letters are sent?
- What systems will be put in place to ensure that clients' own terms are centrally reviewed (with an appropriate escalation procedure) and logged?

Client risk

Simon Chester
Heenan Blaikie LLP
Anthony E Davis
Hinshaw & Culbertson LLP
Frank Maher
Legal Risk LLP

---

1. **Why this topic matters**

    Clients instruct lawyers for a number of reasons; partly for the obvious reasons that they wish to know their legal rights or want help with a problem or process, but also because they want to transfer risk to their lawyer – and sometimes because they wish to gain the cloak of respectability associated with the lawyer's profession. Risks presented by clients are among the most difficult that law firms face.

    Risk can be transferred in a variety of ways, depending on the nature of the instruction. For example, a client buying property wants to know that the title is good, without unforeseen claims by third parties or boundary and access disputes. The law firm's liability, and its insurance, gives the client that assurance.

    Increasingly, clients are asking how well firms manage risk: they need to know that the firm is insured, but in addition they want the risk that the advice and process is correct to rest with the firm. They want assurance that the firm will do things right every time.

    Public sector and corporate clients are increasingly examining firms' information security measures and business continuity plans in great detail and subjecting them to rigorous audits.

    When things go wrong, and courts have to decide whether a given loss should be borne by the law firm or the client, the courts will look at the retainer to determine which risks were transferred and which were not. That will be clearer in some cases than others.

    Against this background, lawyers should be cautious about their choice of client and not simply accept every client who walks through the door. That is not to say that law firms should only act for upright citizens and their corporate equivalents: otherwise no firm would ever do criminal work. Instead, it is about aligning the client's risk profile with that of the law firm.

    If firms can manage the client engagement risk, a significant proportion of risk issues fall into place. By this we mean: acting for the right clients on work that firms are competent to do and with the right resources for the work, and having a clear agreement at the outset as to what is included and excluded in the engagement, as well as the price to be paid.

    Claims can come from many sources (obviously from lenders, investors, beneficiaries and the like) but clients are the main source. The need for risk management does not end at the point of client engagement; the need to stay alert to the good client who turns bad is key, and in some cases anti-money laundering legislation may require ongoing monitoring.

New clients are a particular risk, and law firm insurers identify them as such. You should ask: why have they instructed you? Are they merely seeking the benefit of being associated with your firm and its reputation? If they have stopped using other lawyers, why did they do so? The answer may provide an indicator of potential problems – unwillingness to pay, or unrealistic expectations, for example.

Lawyers who have been sued often say that they "knew they were trouble from the start", yet they took the matter on and lived to regret it.

2. Warning tales

2.1 Phillip Griffiths's story

It is not only the risk of a claim for damages which should concern lawyers: there is the risk of criminal liability too.

Phillip Griffiths was an English solicitor who inadvertently became entangled in the affairs of drug-dealers and ended up going to jail.

Griffiths acted for an estate agent, Pattison, in buying a house for £43,000. In fact, it was worth £150,000, but it had a mortgage on it for £43,000. Pattison was buying the house from drug dealers, who, having been convicted, were awaiting sentence. The purpose of the transaction was to hide their assets from government confiscation. Before the transaction took place, the police had served a 'production order' on Mr Griffiths, under anti-money laundering legislation, requiring him to produce documents relating to other property transactions involving the drug dealers.

The court accepted that Griffiths knew enough about local property prices to appreciate that the transaction was at a substantial undervalue. Griffiths said that Pattison had told him that he had some friends in financial trouble and that Pattison was buying out the mortgage to help them.

Pattison was convicted of entering into a money laundering arrangement, by agreeing to buy a house from a drug dealer at an undervalue in the hope of avoiding confiscation proceedings. Mr Griffiths was found guilty of failing to report reasonable suspicions of money laundering, despite clear signs that the transaction was unusual. He was sentenced to 15 months' imprisonment, reduced on appeal to six months.[1]

2.2 Enron's lawyers share the blame

When Enron collapsed, it was one of the largest corporate failures in history. The court-appointed Examiner concluded in his Second Interim Report that through the pervasive use of structured finance and accounting techniques involving Special Purpose Entities (SPEs), Enron had so engineered its numbers that its financial statements bore little resemblance to reality. In 2000 alone, Enron's use of six accounting techniques produced 96% of its reported net income and 105% of its reported funds flow from operating activities, and enabled it to halve its reported debt.[2]

---

1   *R v Phillip Griffiths and Leslie Pattison* [2006] EWCA Crim 2155.
2   From $22.1 billion to $10.2 billion.

The involvement of Enron's accountants, Andersen, and their subsequent demise was the subject of extensive press coverage. But the infamous transactions could not have happened without the involvement of lawyers – and the Examiner focused on them too. Enron employed over 250 in-house attorneys and retained hundreds of law firms, some of whom assisted in the SPE transactions. Some also produced legal opinions that Andersen needed to let Enron get its desired accounting treatment.

The Examiner concluded that the evidence showed that the lawyers knew that their opinions did not address the accounting issues as they should, were involved in transactions without economic substance or rational business purpose and delivered tax opinions that enabled Enron to 'generate' accounting income from projecting future tax savings. The reputational harm was huge.

2.3 Tax opinions bite back

The global financial crisis has increased governments' focus on maximising tax revenue and reducing both the artificial avoidance and the (criminal) evasion of tax. In the United States, professional services firms targeted by the Internal Revenue Service for creating aggressive tax shelters included law firm Jenkens & Gilchrist, which paid a $76 million fine and closed its doors. One partner had earned $93 million in fees from tax-shelter work. Another firm had recently merged with the tax-shelter specialists, blinded by the supposed profitability. The firm's failure demonstrated the perils of not doing appropriate due diligence on your future partners.

Professor Milton C Regan, in a detailed analysis of the firm's demise,[3] observed that law firms may be less willing to examine the impact of client activities on third parties out of concern to avoid jeopardising relationships with clients who do not want their lawyers to get in the way of their commercial objectives.

2.4 Real estate fraud

Lawyers can become unwittingly involved in mortgage fraud in many ways, which have cost law firms' insurers vast sums of money.

They included cases where:
- the borrower's identity was false;
- the lawyer thought he was acting for both husband and wife on a sale, but the husband forged the wife's signature on sale documents;
- buyers pretended that they were buying property as their main home but in fact intended to rent it (which may affect their willingness to repay the lender); and
- perhaps most commonly where the price they are paying is materially less than the declared price, meaning that often the property is worth less than the mortgage advance.

---

[3] Milton C Regan, Jr., Taxes and Death: The Rise and Demise of an American Law Firm (April 23 2010). *Studies in Law, Politics and Society: Law Firms, Legal Culture, and Legal Practice*, Vol. 52, 107–144, Austin Sarat, ed., JAI Press, 2010; Georgetown Law and Economics Research Paper No 11-08. Available at SSRN: http://ssrn.com/abstract=1802697.

The Law Society of England and Wales has highlighted useful indications of warning signs in its Mortgage Fraud Practice Note.[4] Be alert to cases where:
- the client or the property is located a long distance from the law firm – one might ask why they are choosing that firm to act for them;
- the property has been owned for less than six months; and
- back-to-back transactions or sub-sales, which may be devices to engineer uplift in the apparent value of the property to trick the lender into making a larger loan than otherwise justified.

Sometimes lawyers can try too hard to assist a client in achieving completion of a transaction. An illustration of this occurred in the English case of *Santander v RA Legal*,[5] a claim which arose from a conveyancing fraud in which the solicitors who purported to act for the seller, Sovereign, did not in fact do so.

The key point is that the buyers' solicitors were also criticised for signing a title report to the lender, certifying that there was good clear title to the property, when in fact there was an outstanding conveyancing point to be checked. Their intention was to expedite release of the advance on the basis that it would not be used if the title issue turned out to be a problem. There was no finding of dishonesty in this case, but the court fired a warning shot at solicitors who adopt this practice in the future. Prudence suggests to leave the risk of delay with the client. The moral of the story is: do not let clients' problems become your problem.

3. Potential risks to the firm

Risks to the law firm can include:
- Not getting paid – Credit risk is an issue you should always think about. Sometimes the firm's exposure is mitigated by the clients' insurers paying (but that may be subject to coverage disputes, or even insurer insolvency). Be aware of the risk of clients who later argue that the bill should be sent to a third party – while sometimes this is quite proper, it may also show something more suspicious, such as misuse of company funds or, by fabricating a business expense without a business purpose, tax fraud.
- Getting sued for malpractice – Problematic clients may give rise to liability for damages, whether to the client or, less often, third parties, such as investors or opposing parties (most likely in the case of fraud). Even though these may be insured, you will soon find that in the future insurance is more expensive, more difficult or even impossible to obtain, so the comfort of being insured may be illusory.
- Professional discipline – The lawyer who acts for a client who is involved in rogue activities may risk professional disciplinary action as well as liability for damages. Most professional codes will require the lawyer to put the duty to the public above pursuit of the client's demands at all costs. Examples of this

---

4 www.lawsociety.org.uk/advice/practice-notes/mortgage-fraud/#mf4. Also see *Cheshire Mortgage Corporation Ltd v Longmuir & Co's Judicial Factor, Blemain Finance Ltd v Balfour & Manson LLP* [2012] CSIH 66 and *Excel Securities v Masood* [2010] Lloyds Rep PN 165.
5 [2014] EWCA Civ 183 a.

are in the American Bar Association (ABA) Model Rule 1.2 (d) and, in England, the Solicitors Regulation Authority (SRA) Principles, the guidance notes for which state:

Where two or more Principles come into conflict, the Principle which takes precedence is the one which best serves the public interest in the particular circumstances, especially the public interest in the proper administration of justice.[6]

- Accessory liability – Acting for rogue clients may also expose firms to liability for damages for assisting them. Some English examples have involved complex facts and serious allegations of dishonesty against the lawyers. In a number of cases lawyers were found liable, although a significant proportion has been appealed successfully by the lawyers.[7] However, this illustrates an important risk management point: no lawyer wishes to spend years of his or her professional life facing litigation, allegations of dishonesty and disputes with insurers over coverage, even if they do ultimately obtain some degree of vindication on appeal. Do not go anywhere near a court in the first place.
- Criminal liabilities – As we have seen, acting for rogue clients may expose lawyers to criminal liability. This might be for fraud or under anti-money laundering legislation, as in the case of Griffiths, mentioned at paragraph 2.1
- Reputational risk – Lawyers often fear the big claim that may sink a firm, but such events are almost unknown. The demise of Enron's accountants, Andersen, did not occur because of liability claims: it arose from the destruction of its reputation from involvement in corporate failures including Enron; and illustrates amply the point that reputation is the most valuable asset any professional practice has.

3.1 Secondments

Increasingly, commercial clients ask their lawyers to second staff to them, and, less often, they wish to second staff to the law firm. This can provide valuable benefits in understanding the client's needs and can provide opportunities for new instructions, though one will always fear that the client will want to keep the firm's better associates for itself. There are risks associated with secondments.

- Supervision – Secondments to the client may take many forms. The client may have a large in-house legal team, making it little different from a law firm, and the client's general counsel or other lawyer may take responsibility for supervision, though doubtless part of the expected deal will be that the junior lawyer will have recourse to the seconding firm. In other cases, however, the secondment may be to a subsidiary which has no legal team, or to a client with no lawyers at all. In those cases supervision responsibility will remain with the firm.
- Conflicts – Care needs to be taken, particularly with inbound secondments,

---

6   SRA Principles, note 2.2.
7   See, for example, *Twinsectra v Yardley* [2002] UKHL 12 and *Attorney General of Zambia v Meer Care & Desai* [2008] EWCA Civ 1007. For Australian examples of accessory liability in helping clients strip assets, see *ASIC v Somerville* [2009] NSWSC 934, *ASIC v Somerville* (No 2) [2009] NSWSC 998.

because the secondee may have knowledge of matters which, depending on the facts and the local laws, may give rise to conflict issues.
- Confidentiality – Care needs to be taken, because:
  - the secondee to the client will gain knowledge of relationships that the client has with other law firms, including charging rates and terms. If the client is an insurance company, there may also be issues in relation to those whom it insures;
  - the inbound secondee gives rise to significant issues for the law firm – would the client's competitors be happy in the knowledge that the secondee may have access to their matters? Probably not, and yet the exposure to a wider variety of work is probably a driver for the client making the request in the first place. Some large firms decline inbound secondments.
- Liability – Liability issues should be agreed and documented at the outset. If the secondee to the client is working under the supervision of the client's general counsel rather than the firm, one would expect the client to accept responsibility for acts and omissions, but it is a point for discussion.
- Insurance – Insurance will probably not cover the secondee unless specific agreement is reached with the firm's insurers, so settle this with insurers, notwithstanding the client's deal. In England and Wales, the compulsory SRA Minimum Terms and Conditions of Insurance provide that secondees in each direction are insured, but this only extends to the compulsory primary layer of cover and not any top-up cover.

3.2 Financial risks

Law firms may seem like perpetual motion machines in which payment for work may come much later – after a closing or a victory in court. One of the authors has just experienced a major law firm dissolution. Only when the music stopped was it possible to see just how often a successful lawyer representing valued clients would be found to have clients whose value did not extend to paying their accounts. Assurances of profitability made at the time when the firm's profits were divided were illusory. In retrospect, accounts receivable and unbilled time should have been closely tracked, not to monitor or punish the partner, but simply so the firm could be aware of what was real and what might not be.

Cash is not king – beware of it. However attractive receiving cash may be, in an era where money-laundering regulations require detailed reporting, a better policy is simply to discourage its use. Similarly, accepting equity in an illiquid private company or property such as paintings is likely to prove problematic, especially if their value has been overstated.

Finally, institute a firm rule against letting clients use the lawyers' trust accounts where there is no underlying transaction (ie, as a banking facility). Your insurance may not cover you if you are acting as a bank. And if there's a dispute, you may lose the file or end up as a witness.

3.3 Money laundering

We have already seen (at 2.1) the example of Mr Griffiths who was imprisoned for failing to report a suspicious transaction involving his client as required by UK money-laundering legislation.

3.4 Whistle-blower obligations

Section 307 of the Sarbanes-Oxley Act, implemented in the United States after Enron collapsed, empowered the Securities and Exchange Commission (SEC) to issue rules setting "minimum standards of professional conduct for attorneys appearing and practicing before the Commission in any way in the representation of issuers".

The relevant provisions are in the SEC Rules of Professional Conduct, Part 205. They require an attorney to report evidence of a material violation of securities law or breach of fiduciary duty or similar violation by the company or any agent of it to the chief legal counsel or chief executive officer of the company, and if an appropriate response is not received, the attorney must report the evidence to the company's audit committee or to the board. In Canada, the Rules of Professional Conduct require in-house counsel to whistle-blow up the corporate ladder. In the most serious cases, an in-house counsel whose warnings are ignored may be required to resign.

4. Precautions

Having identified some of the risks that clients can pose and obligations that can arise, we now need to turn to what we can do to identify potentially problematic clients and what we can do to mitigate the risks.

4.1 Identifying problematic clients

The objective of every client intake management system must be to maximise the firm's acceptance of 'good' clients and to ensure – as far as humanly possible – the rejection of 'bad' clients. And the difference, in a broad sense, is easy to understand. Good clients are those whose matters are within the competence of the firm, and the individual lawyers assigned to them, and who have the ability and willingness to pay an appropriate fee. Bad clients are those for whom the firm is unlikely to reach acceptable outcomes, who are likely to refuse to pay fees, and, if dissatisfied, bring claims of malpractice, demand disgorgement of fees already paid, file complaints with regulators, bring the firm into public disrepute and generally waste everyone's time and energy in unproductive activities. In this section we discuss some of the more common categories of these undesirable clients to assist firms in improving their screening methodologies to avoid accepting their proffered engagements.

(a) *Politically exposed persons*

Unless the firm is set up with the specific objective of taking on high-profile individuals, politically exposed individuals, whom the public are likely to view with disfavour (and, by association, their lawyers) are likely to be 'bad' clients. Few firms would want to represent individuals in President Vladimir Putin's inner circle in today's environment; those willing to do so have specialised practices that specifically cater to such clients. What is important is to identify this kind of client by doing appropriate background checks – often using basic research tools such as Google – before embarking on such engagements.

(b) **Secretive clients**
This class of client – which may overlap with the last group – are dangerous because by being unwilling to tell their lawyers all of the pertinent information relating to their matters they make it impossible to obtain desired outcomes. Further, secretiveness often signals that there is an unethical or outright unlawful purpose behind their need for counsel. Good intake interviews (rather than accepting clients after five minutes on the telephone, or based on a single email with no interview) are critical to identifying this class of client up front.

(c) **Unorthodox sources of funds**
Clients who cannot pay reasonable fees are the single worst kind of client from a law firm's point of view. There are only three reasons why clients do not pay fees: they do not have the funds; they are unhappy with the outcome obtained and/or with the total fee sought; or they never intended to pay in the first place. If clients propose to pay in cash, or to use a complicated mechanism involving transfers from third parties abroad, it is likely that more than one of these factors is in play. Establishing a firm policy of requiring a significant retainer (advance payment), and establishing that the funds come from a legitimate bank account in the client's own name, is a critical first step.

(d) **Clients who lie**
Few (if any) clients tell their lawyers the entire story behind their proposed engagements without prompting. But that is quite different from clients whose evident *modus operandi* is telling lies. Again, a critical element of good intake procedures is an extensive intake interview, and when doubts arise, testing the story.

(e) **Clients who want control**
Clients who claim to know better than their lawyer how to manage the engagement, and who demand to direct the lawyer's every action, are problematic in several ways. First, they cause much unnecessary work – for which they are likely later to object to paying; and second, they are often wrong, which in turn causes friction and more wasted time. Have your antenna out for suspect motives – clients out for revenge will be problematic. And avoid clients who will not listen. Yet again, a good intake interview will identify this characteristic.

(f) **Clients who want you to 'dabble'**
This group is the very antithesis of 'good' clients. They want the firm or its lawyers to undertake engagements for which they have no expertise or experience. This greatly increases the probability of errors and consequential malpractice claims. And even if the lawyers are successful, it will be at a disproportionate cost of time and effort, for which the client is sure to object to paying.

(g) **Clients who want joint representation**
Joint representations (which are sometimes unavoidable), when forced by otherwise 'good' clients, pose significant risks of conflicts that will arise in mid-stream, potentially forcing withdrawal, to the anger of all of the clients, and claims for fee

disgorgement and damages for harm caused by the impact of withdrawal on the ultimate outcome. Joint clients, who assure lawyers at the outset that their interests are identical, often fall out and become adversaries. In addition, problems can arise over the sharing (or failure to share) the individual clients' confidences, or over who will pay. When undertaken, these engagements should be premised on extensive discussions in advance with all the clients on the risks of these engagements, and then on a complete documented record of the disclosure made and of the clients' acknowledgement and consent.

(h) **Clients who want to litigate your firm's prior work product**
If the firm has negotiated a contract, or obtained a patent, and the product of those efforts later becomes the subject of a dispute, clients often expect the lawyers who did the underlying work – and who are presumably the most familiar with it – to take on the litigation. Often this may be problematic. If any part of the underlying work was done in error, by accepting the litigation the firm takes on the risk of a double-barrelled malpractice claim – one for the underlying error and the second for improperly litigating rather than resolving the problem to the client's satisfaction. Second, many courts will refuse to permit lawyers who may be witnesses in the litigation to act simultaneously as advocates, again potentially causing disqualification at a bad moment. And finally, in some jurisdictions, if the firm's underlying work is in issue, there may be problems in determining how (or even whether) the lawyer–client privilege will protect the litigation process. Careful independent analysis of the underlying work, with discussion of all risks with the client, is essential before undertaking this kind of engagement.

(i) **Clients who have had other lawyers on the file**
There are many reasons why clients change lawyers in mid-engagement, but only one – unlikely – is positive: that the last lawyers were incompetent or out of their depth. Much more likely are that the client failed to pay the prior lawyer's bills, or that those lawyers belatedly discovered that they were 'bad' clients for any one of the reasons enumerated here and cut their losses. Before taking on a client in these circumstances it should be the invariable practice to obtain a written direction from the client to prior lawyers that they must speak with prospective new lawyers, and then ask prior counsel very specifically both whether prior lawyers were paid in full, and why they think the client wants to substitute new lawyers. In one case, for example, the defendant was a law firm that was the sixth firm whom the claimant had instructed in succession, in each case to pursue claims against another predecessor firm. Counsel succeeded in having most of the claim against firm six struck out. This, however, led to a claim against the seventh firm.

(j) **Limited retainers**
If a client is trying to divide up aspects of the legal work for a larger project among multiple professionals, it is critical to determine whether the reason for doing so is legitimate, or if the client is in fact trying to create a screen of lawyers behind which it is seeking to engage in unlawful activities.

(k) *Clueless clients*

Clients who do not even know what they would consider a suitable outcome are likely to turn out even more unhappy – and to have all the characteristics of 'bad' clients – than clients with explicit but unrealistic expectations. Once again, an extensive intake interview will establish whether a client falls in this group.

(l) *Can't pay, won't pay*

Clients who cannot or will not pay fees are certainly 'bad' clients. There are numerous ways to identify them in advance, in addition to establishing that they have realistic expectations about achievable outcomes, and the likely amount of the bill. Basic online research will often show a prospective client's propensity to litigate instead of paying its creditors, the nature and extent of its indebtedness, its prior bankruptcy history and other problematic credit information. Other indicators of future problems in collecting fees include proposals regarding payment that are in any way unconventional.

(m) *'Partnership' proposals*

Be sceptical if clients say that they want their lawyers to be their 'partners', so that they are fully 'invested' in the client's success. Two separate risks are inherent in these arrangements. First, they necessarily involve significant conflicts of interest – and the greater the success of the client often the greater the conflict. Second, for every Steve Jobs (the founder of Apple Computers), venture capitalists' – and lawyers' – offices are littered with failed start-ups.

4.2 Al's Story

When you are a new lawyer, it seems any client should be welcomed with open arms. More mature lawyers know that is not necessarily so.

A friend of ours, Al, used to practise law in Columbia, South Carolina, and had a New Year's ritual of choosing clients.

Every year, Al gave himself a present. Late in the afternoon on New Year's Day, he'd settle into a rocking chair looking out over his back garden, a glass of George Stagg whisky in his hand. Rocking gently, Al would take stock of the year and consider how his firm had fared. How he had done. Not so different from you or us, but Al's annual ritual had a punch line. As he sipped his whisky, he considered each one of his clients – which had been the most difficult, the most challenging to manage, the least pleasant to work with.

Al reckoned there were always a few clients who took more energy than everyone else put together, who were constant trials. Clients whom he could sense would enjoy complaining about him, or even suing him. Clients who were not worth the trouble.

He would pick one of them. And he would fire that client.

It was always an enormous relief to make the decision. Later, he would wind down the work for the client, finish the last transaction and, with the final bill, send a letter confirming that the attorney–client relationship was at an end.

In this way, year after year, Al struck one client from the list without regret. Over time, his client list came more into focus. These were the clients whose work he enjoyed, clients who became friends, who paid on time and who valued his work. These clients became the backbone of a very successful firm. And a key part of his firm's success was Al's annual ritual of client choice on a winter's afternoon overlooking the garden.

You do not have to go to Al's lengths. But regularly taking the time to focus on client selection – and deselection – should be part of every lawyer's discipline.

Law practice gurus tell us that being rigorous about client selection not only is good for risk management, it's also good for the bottom line. And it's good for lawyer happiness.

It certainly worked for Al.

4.3 Due diligence

Practical advice for lawyers wanting to do due diligence on prospective clients is found in Chapter 4 of the Law Society of England and Wales Practice Note on Money-Laundering of October 22 2013.[8] It sets out a risk-based approach to due diligence which could be usefully adapted to other jurisdictions, bearing in mind the local requirements of money-laundering and anti-terrorist legislation. It is particularly helpful on how to deal with clients with whom one does not deal face to face.

Recommendations for due diligence include the following.

- Do not dabble with elderly and vulnerable clients – Representing the elderly, infirm and incapacitated is a specialised practice, requiring experience both of the applicable law and interaction with other professionals and other family members – all of which present further issues regarding confidentiality of information and privilege. Such engagement should be avoided by the uninitiated, as they are likely to lead to claims – often by individuals whom the lawyers never intended or understood to have an interest.
- Instructions by third parties – Whatever the circumstances, such engagements involve significant risk. Lawyers, as agents themselves, should never undertake work for undisclosed principals or disclosed principals, even if there is a clear trail of written communication from the principal as to the scope of the intermediary's authority. Even accepting the payment of fees by someone other than the client requires clear documentation that the actual client exclusively directs the lawyer, and that the lawyer will preserve the client's confidences as against the paying party.
- Testator's child – Here again, the problem arises as to what confidences from the testator may be shared with the child. Such engagements should be avoided unless both testator and child explicitly agree in writing how their respective confidences will be handled.
- A sub-contracted will drafter – just say no to accountants advising clients on tax and trusts who want the lawyer to draft a deed or will with the lawyer

---

8   Found at www.lawsociety.org.uk/advice/practice-notes/aml/customer-due-diligence/. Similarly, Chapter 11 of the Practice Note sets out money-laundering warning signs.

having minimal contact with the actual client. You will be an additional defendant if anything goes wrong.
- Fraud by email – The Internet has proved an all-too-fertile ground for criminals to prey on lawyers eager to take on what looks like a simple piece of work, such as collecting a debt. There is a simple rule. If it looks too good to be true, it almost certainly is a scam. Be extremely sceptical about any contacts that come from strangers via email or social media.

In the end, the victim in these schemes is likely to be either the lawyers themselves or their clients, while the criminal gets the lawyer to pay over funds that were not, as expected, covered by funds collected from the scamming client. As likely as not, the claimant will be the lawyers' bank, or their other clients. And these cases also often result in regulatory action against lawyers for not following with care and precision trust account rules.

4.4 **Avoiding fraud**
One of the best sources for up-to-date information on scams and fraudulent emails targeted at lawyers is a blog maintained by Tim Lemieux and Dan Pinnington at LAWPRO (Lawyers' Professional Indemnity Company, the primary insurer for lawyers in Ontario, Canada). It is called http://avoidaclaim.com and publishes detailed listings of known scams in areas such as commercial debt collection, business loan collection, separation agreement scams and breach of intellectual property, copyright or franchise agreements.

The scams work by encouraging a firm to act for someone outside its jurisdiction who claims to be owed money in its jurisdiction. The firm will be asked to accept a substantial sum into its trust account. Emergency circumstances will loom – and urgent emails will require you to transfer funds out to a third account. Of course, the initial cheque deposited into the trust account will bounce (the deposit being fictitious), and the law firm will have transferred real money to an account that proves untraceable.

Each year, law firms lose millions to fraudsters because lawyers are not suspicious and do not check. The http://avoidaclaim.com blog has an excellent search feature that lets you check out names and the text of emails. Encourage your lawyers to check it regularly.

4.5 **Limiting liability**
Jurisdictions differ widely on whether it is permissible to insert a limitation of liability provision into retainer agreements. And even where it is acceptable, many clients balk at agreeing to them. But where and to the extent they are permissible, they are an important tool in protecting lawyers and their firms from what might otherwise be catastrophically large claims and liability.

(a) *Structural mechanisms*
Retainer agreements (sometimes referred to as engagement letters) are an essential tool in protecting lawyers from bad clients. The defence of malpractice claims

becomes much easier when the scope of work and client expectations are clearly defined in a retainer letter. These should describe the client and the mandate, and exclude any additional duties to related parties such as affiliates. Confirm client decisions in writing, particularly if your advice is not accepted. Include details of how fees will be calculated in the retainer letter. Specify that once your mandate ends, so will your duties. Unless a new mandate is a repetitive clone of prior work (eg, intellectual property registrations) retainer agreements should be required for each matter, and not simply when an entity becomes a client for the first time. More claims can be traced back to a lack of communication than any other cause. So ensure that the client is kept informed, return calls within 24 hours and provide regular progress reports.

(b) *Retainer disclaimers*

To avoid, or at least limit, a client's ability to assert claims against their lawyers, some basic precautions should be adopted in a firm's standard retainer terms. Make it absolutely clear who is the client (and who is not[9] – if others, such as owners, investors, family members, company constituents, could claim that the lawyer owes them a duty of care); limit the scope of the services to be provided so as not to become liable for advice or work for which the firm is not accepting responsibility; and spell out other details for which disclosure is appropriate, such as conflict waivers.

(c) *Do not accept liability to third parties who are not clients*

Even jurisdictions that prohibit lawyers from obtaining advance waivers of liability to clients do permit avoidance of future liability to non-clients. In some instances, as where the lawyers are aware that their advice or instruments will be viewed by third parties, it may be essential to notify those third parties – perhaps on the face of the documents – that the lawyers are responsible only to the named clients, and that the third parties should obtain their own lawyers, and may not rely on the lawyers' work for their own protection. Even then, if the lawyer knows that his opinion will be relied upon by third parties, in some jurisdictions that may not suffice to avoid liability. In addition, in England and Wales, a lawyer who drafts a will defective in content or execution may be liable to disappointed beneficiaries. In practice little can be done to mitigate this risk.

(d) *Risks on third-party transaction opinions*

One area of exposure for large firms comes from the requirement for third-party opinions in major transactions, confirming corporate formalities and the effectiveness of the contractual arrangements. In major common-law jurisdictions, a complex literature has developed setting out generally acceptable formulations that satisfy markets while minimising risks. A useful article published by the ABA in 2008, entitled "Courting the Suicide King"[10] by Don Glazer and Jonathan Lipson, analyses

---

9 Good precedents for 'I am not your lawyer letters' can be found in English at www.cba.org/CBA/groups/conflicts/toolkit.aspx and in French at www.cba.org/abc/groups_f/conflicts/ toolkit2.aspx.
10 Donald W Glazer and Jonathan C Lipson, Courting the suicide king: closing opinions and lawyer liability, Business Law Today 17.4 (March–April 2008): 59. Available at www.abanet.org/buslaw/blt/

the client risks posed by opinion practice. These are opinions for the benefit of third parties, generally lenders, rather than clients. The third parties want the borrower's own counsel to confirm the legal aspects of the transaction. Glazer points out that in National Bank of Canada, Enron and Dean Foods, American law firms have been sued on such opinions; one Canadian case concerning opinions about Canary Wharf[11] shows that major UK firms face similar risks. The amounts claimed in these cases ranged up to $1 billion, although the fees charged by the firms were a tiny fraction of these amounts. Settlements have been rumoured to be in eight figures, although cases are rare, and it is virtually unheard-of for a case to go to judgment and damages to be awarded.

Because law firms are seen as having deep pockets with substantial insurance coverage, they are tempting targets for plaintiffs seeking to recover. They may even face greater liability than the clients, who stand to gain if the transactions are profitable. In many jurisdictions, law firms are not permitted to limit their liability exposure to their own clients. Glazer stresses the importance of internal review of all such opinions, the need to have fees that reflect risk, and the irrationality of hazarding the future survival of the firm on the arcane details of formulaic opinions in a marginally profitable area of practice.

(e) *Insurance coverage*
Bad clients will slip through even the best intake procedures. Lawyers are human and make mistakes. It is critical for lawyers to purchase professional liability (malpractice) coverage (and perhaps other coverage, such as that for the increasing risks of cyber liabilities and losses). What are appropriate levels of coverage, deductibles, and terms are highly complex questions. Even lawyers doing work for individual clients, such as in the decedents' estates field, have exposure that may be measured in the size of those estates, or of the tax liabilities of the estates. There are specialist brokers in almost every jurisdiction who can advise on these vital questions. It is critical to use their services and purchase coverage appropriate to the firm's practice and the scale of risk entailed.

(f) *Record keeping*
Anyone who defends malpractice claims knows that good records are golden. The obligation to maintain and preserve client documents and files is fundamental both to providing competent service, and to every lawyer's duty to preserve client confidential information. In the technocentric universe in which lawyers operate, it is a fundamental obligation to have software and hardware appropriate to those tasks, and to be competent to manage that technology.

(g) *Managing client expectations*
In the last analysis, whether clients are 'good' or 'bad' will depend in large measure on the degree to which lawyers maintain open and regular communication with all their clients. Memory is fickle. If clients becomes disgruntled, their memory of

---

11   *National Bank of Canada v Clifford Chance*, 1996 CanLII 8219 (ON SC) http://canlii.ca/t/1w9j9.

events, perhaps a long time earlier, may differ in critical and material ways from the lawyer's best recollection. The solution is simple: communicate regularly and in detail, and especially at important moments in the engagement. Very few claims against lawyers succeed where there is a complete record of what transpired, and where the client was kept aware of developments all along the way.

4.6 Withdrawal

In each jurisdiction, rules of professional conduct set out constraints on when it is permissible for a lawyer to terminate a client relationship. You may well have an ethical obligation to see a matter through to completion if there is unfinished business or serious prejudice to the client. The rules tend to balance the client's expectation interests against the lawyer's need to comply with professional norms. The client cannot be dropped on the eve of trial, for example, or on the eve of closing. But a lawyer who continues to act when she or he realises that a client is lying, or using the lawyer to commit fraud, risks the most serious of consequences.

4.7 Retention of foreign lawyers

Be aware of risk management issues when hiring local counsel in foreign jurisdictions. Check out their reputations in Chambers or Martindale Hubbell. Ask local contacts in your network. Ask what level of insurance they carry. In some jurisdictions, lawyers do not carry any malpractice insurance so you will need to arrange it, or accept the risks yourself.

5. Firm policies

Client risks, left unaddressed, can pose serious challenges to law firms – indeed, firms have been plunged into crises because of them. For example, Enron was only one of the clients of Vinson & Elkins, yet Enron's name seems inevitably to occur early in any discussion of the law firm. A firm's reputation is necessarily affected by the clients it chooses to serve.

The best time to deal with a crisis is long before you ever think of it as a crisis. Anticipating risk and planning for it can pay dividends. Firms that require a consistent and professional approach to issues that raise liability exposure tend to reduce both the incidence and the severity of issues that could become crises. Key to their mitigation strategies is the development of firm policies that set aspirational standards and guide firm behaviour. Such policies, when applied to client matters, will tend to match firm's strategic goals more closely than the personal preferences of rainmakers or individual partners. They can also avoid speculative risk.

Law firms cannot avoid risk – it is inevitable in competitive markets and in zero-sum areas like litigation where one party will inevitably be unhappy with outcomes and the expense accompanying the undesired result. The key is to understand acceptable levels of risk, communicate that acceptability across the firm and to have objective processes in place so that a specific client or mandate does not exceed that level.

Some commentators note the dangers of having policies and procedures that are not scrupulously observed. They point out that a policy which only exists on paper provides any malpractice plaintiff with a road map for applicable standards of care, and an avenue for devastating cross-examination. We disagree about the dangers. The exercise of developing specific policies and procedures will focus the firm's attention on its special vulnerabilities and challenges. Learning from others, if only through checklists, profits from experience.[12] Subsequent training can help to internalise the firm's preferred approaches. If a lawyer falls short, the lapse is the lawyer's. When a firm has no policies, the entire firm has lapsed.

5.1 Client review and file management

Lawyers love to attract new clients. They claim credit for that achievement. Even in firms that stress team practice, individual egos will rise to justify their personal achievement. The luxury of such a distributed approach becomes riskier as firms grow. Any firm of over 200 lawyers needs to have a consistent approach to evaluating potential clients, assessing their profitability and their propensity to be problematic, locating the clients within a wider strategic view of the firm's business focus. It is not a question of stamping out entrepreneurial initiative but rather ensuring that such initiative is assessed objectively, lest the firm be exposed to financial and other risk.

Institute an independent review on file opening. The firm needs to build a process through which an independent group of partners assess each potential client. This cannot be a bureaucratic ordeal or bottle-neck, obstructing the new work that is the life-blood of any firm, but should involve a speedy review of the standard information required for new file opening, the business of the potential client, its legal needs and its fit with the firm's resources and strengths. If a special intake group is not established, this should be an expanded part of the mandate of the conflicts committee or conflicts review process.

What should be considered? Firstly, the applicable conflicts rules, whether prescribed by courts or professional regulatory bodies. If they are triggered, consider whether the rules permit management of the conflict through informed client consent, or if ethical screens or Chinese Walls are lawful in the jurisdiction, through the timely construction of devices to protect confidentiality and other client interests. Screen erection should build on established models and policies, so that they can be put in place within minutes. Larger firms may wish to consider proprietary technological solutions such as those offered by Intapp, which permit screens fully integrated with time, billing and document management systems, as well as ongoing auditing of the effectiveness of screens.

Conflict assessment should go beyond the strict rules, and consider the impact of any particular retainer on an important client or client sector. Whereas firms have become increasingly specialised, in only a few areas of law – such as management or union representation in labour relations or brand/generic representation in pharmaceutical work – is there an effective dividing line between law firms that

---

12 See Atul Gawande, *The Checklist Manifesto: How to Get Things Right* [London, Picador 2011) and John Gillies, The Checklist Manifesto and the Smarter Lawyer at www.slaw.ca/2010/02/24/the-checklist-manifesto-and-the-smarter-lawyer/.

represent competing interests. Nor do most jurisdictions recognise the existence of a special category of issue conflicts or positional conflicts. Nevertheless firms should be careful before taking on high-profile contentious matters to consider that major firm clients may react negatively to the firm's representation of a specific client. For example, acting on a plaintiff side class action case against a financial institution (a defendant that passed formal conflicts scrutiny) may cause a firm's existing bank clients to quietly express concern about their firm's choice of target.

Firms differ in their approach to financial risk posed by clients. Some will establish a threshold level of minimum annual billings (say $25,000 or £17,500) to divert smaller clients that are unlikely to contribute meaningfully to firm profitability. Others, perhaps tempted by the success of firms that back successful start-ups, will run credit checks, through firms like Dun & Bradstreet or Equifax, on principals.

Files that will become disastrous time wasters are not always advertised, but the warning signs are evident to experienced litigation counsel. Files that make particularly slow progress through the court system; frequent changes of counsel; stories that change dramatically: all require caution.

Conflict checks need to go beyond the specific client before you. Your client file opening records should also reflect the names of everyone involved. For the specific practice areas listed below, consider checking:

- litigation: the insured, insurance company, plaintiffs, defendants, legal representative or guardian *ad litem* (for the lawsuit), spouse, parent or significant family members, witnesses (both lay and expert), opposing counsel;
- corporate, business and real estate: owner/spouse, partners, shareholders, directors, officers, subsidiaries and affiliates, key employees, buyers or sellers, any opposing party in transaction, tenants and sub-tenants, and if real estate is involved, the property address and property registration number (if applicable);
- estate planning: executor, spouse or partner, children, heirs, personal representatives or those holding powers of attorney, testator;
- probate: the deceased, personal representative, spouse or partner, children, heirs, trustees, guardians or conservators;
- family law: spouse, prior married names and birth name, children and grandparents;
- criminal law: witnesses, victims, co-defendants and co-accused;
- bankruptcy and insolvency: spouse or partner, secured creditors and trade creditors.

5.2 Dealing with risky clients

The best advice, of course, is do not start.

A lawyer may not assist a client in conduct that the lawyer knows is criminal or fraudulent. And lawyers cannot engage in conduct involving dishonesty, fraud or misrepresentation. But short of that warning suspicions may occur: a client who is prepared to give any assurance and wave away any concerns.

But if you discover that you are dealing with a high-risk client, how do you

manage your own risk?[13] Your local rules may constrain your ability to fire the client. Recommended actions include:
- Bring in reinforcements. Do not handle a risky client by yourself. Get your worked checked by a colleague. Require second-lawyer review of major documents or higher-risk engagements. Bring in a senior partner whose judgment and experience you value. Rotate client relationship management responsibility.
- Document everything. Good contemporaneous notes will be invaluable if the deal blows up and scapegoats are sought.
- Attend to the detail. Check everything and ensure that the client knows that your commitment to your legal and professional obligations will not be compromised. You do not want to become the client's patsy.
- Be prepared for write-offs. The fact that a client is ethically challenged may alert you to the fact that paying your fees may be another responsibility to be dispensed with. So cash retainers, regular billing and careful monitoring of receivables is essential.
- Communicate with management and your partners.
- Do not isolate yourself. If there are risks, ensure that they are discussed with the firm's ethics counsel, management or a practice group leader.
- Ensure that the new client will pay your fees. Financially problematic clients can be red flags. Not merely are you likely to lose money, they are also more likely to sue you, or complain about your services or performance. A standard response to aggressive collection efforts is a counterclaim of negligence or malpractice.
- Carefully probe the potential client's financial situation. Do they baulk at the financial arrangements, a request for a cash retainer or the scale of hourly rates? And be aware that if you shoulder the economic risk (assuming the legality of contingent fee arrangements in your jurisdiction) you become the client's banker. Any worries at the initial interview can only get worse when the client sees an actual bill for legal services
- If you do not know the client, do some due diligence. Google Advanced News Search will permit you to run a search against its considerable news archive. Run the client's name and any business names through free legal databases such as the British and Irish Legal Information Institute (BAILII) or the Australasian Legal Information Institute (AustLII). You may see warning signs about insolvency, judgments or vexatious litigation. If the file is significant, consider running full searches for judgments or get a report from a credit agency such as Equifax.
- Trust your instincts at the initial interview. Is the client evasive or unduly

---

13 See Kirke Snyder, Andrew Surdykowski and Lino S Lipinsky, Why Roll The Dice With An Unethical Client? at www.metrocorpcounsel.com/pdf/2004/January/07.pdf; Ronald E Mallen and Thomas P Sukowicz, Protect yourself from suit: knowing when to say 'no' to a questionable client or case can shield you from legal malpractice claims, *Trial* 38.5 (May 2002): 42, at www.justice.org/cps/rde/xchg/justice/hs.xsl/4938.htm; and Mary Beth S Robinson, Putting Clients to the Test: Careful screening at initial interview can minimize malpractice risks, at apps.americanbar.org/legalservices/lpl/downloads/journalnov98.pdf.

nervous? Has he or she had other lawyers? What was the story there? Why did it end? Why is the old lawyer not acting?
- And do not forget to consider issues when an existing client wants you to take on a new matter. A client who came in for a simple will or forming a company may raise issues as a litigation client. Do not neglect the conflicts checks.

6. **Risk management**

The central message of this chapter is that the management of client relationships must be informed by attention to risk, that the individual lawyers with those relationships may be too close to be objective, and that firms are well served by having policies and procedures that align risk to the firm's strategic goals and appetite for speculative investment.

Precedent databases and knowledge management

Martin Schulz
German Graduate School of Management and Law
Luis Felipe Mohando
SORAINEN

1. **Introduction**

    As law is a knowledge-intensive business, knowledge management (KM) has long been considered an important efficiency and risk-reducing tool for the legal industry.[1] However, a successful and sustainable implementation of KM still remains a challenge for many law firms and other legal service providers.[2] After introducing some of the current challenges to law firms resulting from the changing legal landscape in a dynamic business environment, this chapter explains the goals and benefits of developing an effective KM system for law firms. Special emphasis will be placed on developing a suitable KM strategy for law firms, including the complex task of creating a culture of knowledge sharing (the so-called 'KM culture'). After outlining the benefits of an effective KM system, we will explain how to build a precedent database, which typically forms a core part of a law firm's KM system. In addition to some practical suggestions regarding design and useful features of such databases, the reader will be provided with a guide to content management.

2. **Importance of KM and current challenges to law firms**

    Numerous divergent definitions of KM exist,[3] but for the purpose of this chapter we suggest taking a pragmatic approach and define KM as a continuous process of systematically collecting, analysing, organising and distributing know-how relevant to legal practice.[4] Empirical evidence documented by extensive academic research carried out over many years has indicated that enterprises can benefit greatly from leveraging their know-how and the skills and competencies of their partners and employees: According to the so-called 'knowledge-based view' of the firm, companies

---

1   Our thoughts and comments in this chapter are based to a great extent on our practical experiences in the field of KM but we will also refer to selected literature such as Gretta Rusanow, *Knowledge Management and the Smarter Lawyer* (ALM Publishing, 2003); Matthew Parsons, *Effective Knowledge Management for Law Firms* (Oxford University Press, 2004); Martin Schulz and Marcel Klugmann, *Creating a Culture of Knowledge Sharing in Law Firms*, in KD Althoff *et al* (eds), *Professional Knowledge Management*, Lecture Notes in Artificial Intelligence (Springer, 2005) pp 386–391; Martin Apistola and Petter Gottschalk, *Essential Knowledge and Management Issues in Law Firms* (Universal Publishers, 2011).
2   The focus of this chapter will be on law firms but will in most cases also apply to KM in legal departments or other legal service providers. For KM in legal departments see Rusanow (note 1), pp 399–436.
3   See, eg, Rusanow (note 1), pp 7–9; Parsons (note 1), pp 19–26.
4   See Schulz and Klugmann (note 1), p 386. But see also Rusanow (note 1), p 7, who uses the following, broader definition: "knowledge management is the identification, capture, dissemination and use of your firm's knowledge to meet your business objectives".

may significantly improve their capabilities by organising knowledge as a basis for competitive advantage.[5] Lawyers are considered typical knowledge-workers, since they sell specific know-how to their clients in the form of legal advice.[6] Furthermore, lawyers are constantly flooded with documents and information concerning new case law, new legislation and new regulations. This know-how[7] represents an invaluable part of knowledge which should be effectively collected and organised.[8] Thus, many law firms have long discovered the need for organising this codified knowledge by using, for example, document management systems or intranet solutions. Therefore, the legal profession can greatly benefit from effective KM.[9]

2.1 Increased information demands by clients and the courts

Building and maintaining an effective KM system, does, however, remain a challenge, since the legal landscape and the business environment for law firms and other legal service providers have changed quite dramatically over the years.[10] As mentioned above, lawyers have been traditionally flooded with information resulting from new legislation, court decisions and new developments in legal practice, but the speed and complexity of change have increased at both a national as well as at an international level.[11] For example, when advising clients on their business strategy, lawyers regularly need to take international legal options into account and therefore also need to consider international or foreign legal sources and regulatory frameworks.[12] In addition to such higher complexity of legal tasks, clients have also increased their demands, in particular in terms of speediness and efficiency of legal services. Clients also expect a sense of cost consciousness and a proactive approach from their legal advisors, without any compromise on quality.[13] Moreover, client expectations (as well as legal malpractice rules) are often built on the

---

5   For an account of the knowledge-based view of the firm see, eg, David Wagner, Gabriele Vollmar and Heinz-Theo Wagner, The Impact of Information Technology on Knowledge Creation, 27 *Journal of Enterprise Information* (2014), 31–44, with numerous references to academic research and literature. For the impact of this view on KM in law firms see Apistola and Gottschalk (note 1), pp 188–189.
6   See Schulz and Klugmann (note 1), p 386; see also Rusanow (note 1), Introduction, p vii: "Law is a knowledge-based business" and p 341: "Knowledge is at the core of the business and practice of law". See also Parsons (note 1), p 13: "Law firms and lawyers have been 'doing' knowledge work, and knowledge management, since lawyering first began."
7   This so-called 'explicit knowledge' is usually contained in written documents such as contracts, expert opinions, statements of claims etc as opposed to the implicit knowledge to be found in lawyers' heads, regarding specific experiences and skills. See Rusanow (note 1), p 8 and Parsons (note 1), p 21.
8   Thus, lawyers are especially in need of professional KM, see, eg, Schulz and Klugmann (note 1), pp 386, 387.
9   A comprehensive compilation of benefits is provided by Rusanow (note 1), pp 343–356; Apistola and Gottschalk (note 1), pp 28–31.
10 For an analysis of the changing legal landscape and the business environment in particular for legal departments see Rusanow (note 1), pp 9–11; Schulz and Klugmann (note 1), p 386; see also Constance E Bagley and Mark Roellig, The Transformation of General Counsel: Setting the Strategic Legal Agenda, in Stuart Weinstein and Charles Wild, *Legal Risk Management, Governance and Compliance* (Globe Law and Business, 2013), pp 45–66; Leo Staub, Ausblick: Der In-house Legal Counsel und die Rechtsabteilung im Jahre 2020 – stetig wachsende Herausforderungen im Zeitalter der Globalisierung, in Sylvie Hambloch-Gesinn, Beat Hess, Andreas L Meier, Reto Schiltknecht and Christian Wind, *In-house Counsel in internationalen Unternehmen* (CH Beck, 2010), pp 33–49.
11 See, eg, Staub (note 10), pp 33–34.
12 This means that legal advice is often no longer limited to only one jurisdiction but may require also including foreign legal issues, as in the frequent case of cross-border transactions.
13 See Schulz and Klugmann (note 1), p 386; see also Rusanow (note 1), pp 9–11.

assumption that lawyers completely know the law and will use this profound knowledge in order to pursue their clients' interests. This assumption that lawyers have to know the law is also shared by many judges (notwithstanding the vast scope of law and regulations). Nevertheless, being confronted with information overload, lawyers may miss important information (and may be held responsible for this failure regardless of how realistic it actually is to cope with such information overload).[14] In light of these changes in the legal environment and the continuously increasing demands on lawyers' activities, KM can play a crucial role in helping a law firm to overcome these challenges.

2.2 KM as a tool for improving efficiency and risk management

KM can also form an important basis for improving efficiency and risk management in law firms.[15] KM activities can help to reduce a number of risks which are often part of lawyers' work. Firstly, when dealing with a specific matter and seeking all relevant facts and applicable law, lawyers may not be able to find all relevant information and know-how resources. This risk could be called the 'knowledge deficit risk'. KM activities can help to reduce this knowledge deficit risk by timely providing the lawyers with the relevant know-how or the right experts who possess this know-how.[16] For an effective management of this risk, KM should provide the right answer in the right format and at the right time.[17] Secondly, there is the well-known risk of reinventing the wheel if lawyers do not use existing knowledge resources and experience.[18] In order to be able to serve clients' needs in a speedy and efficient manner, it is paramount to systematically collect, classify and store experience from past transactions and court proceedings, for example. Being able to take advantage of available knowledge and experience can have a favourable impact on the profitability of the law firm by saving time and resources when working on recurring tasks and creating more capacity for working on more complex and sophisticated tasks.[19] Last but not least, KM activities can help to reduce the risks of loss of knowledge (eg, when experienced people leave the firm).[20] In order to reduce this risk, the experiences of colleagues and other law firm members should be regularly documented (eg, through interviews or so-called 'after-action reviews').

---

14 This risk of missing critical information has been clearly pointed out by Rusanow (note 1), p 12: "In this age of the Internet and other electronic information services, lawyers face a multitude of information sources, and an exponential increase in the amount of information they must digest." See also Apistola and Gottschalk (note 1), p 29.
15 See Rusanow (note 1), p 352; Apistola and Gottschalk (note 1), p 29.
16 Thus, effective KM can help avoid professional liability, see Rusanow (note 1), p 352; Apistola and Gottschalk, (note 1), p 29.
17 KM should enable effective information flows among experts and it should also provide tools in order to divide the sea of information into manageable pieces of knowledge that can be kept up to date on a regular basis.
18 This risk of reinventing the wheel includes the risks of inconsistent legal advice and the inability to provide fast and efficient answers. See also Rusanow (note 1), p 23, arguing that "stop reinventing the wheel" should be one of the knowledge management objectives that should be closely tied to the business objectives.
19 See Rusanow (note 1), p 349.
20 See Apistola and Gottschalk (note 1), p 29.

2.3 KM as a basis for an effective learning organisation

Knowledge management is also a fundamental requirement for companies striving to become a 'learning organisation', helping new joiners to learn the essential business skills.[21] KM activities are aimed at fostering knowledge sharing among the members of the firm and the systematic capturing and delivering of know-how constitutes the basis for an 'organisational memory'. Such collective memory will form the basis for sound and consistent advice and for continuous learning opportunities to the benefit of the clients.

2.4 KM as a quality management tool

Finally, an effective KM enables the creation and prompt delivery of sound, consistent and high-quality advice, which is an important asset of every law firm. If KM activities are combined with a content management strategy to keep the relevant knowledge up to date, KM can be used as a safeguard for continuous quality control and can help to provide valuable advice as a competitive advantage.[22]

3. The need for a KM strategy

3.1 Codification and personalisation strategies combined

A crucial requirement to be met in order to build an effective KM system is the task of developing a KM strategy.[23] With regard to the contents of the KM strategy it is helpful to follow the traditional distinction between a strategy of codification and a strategy of personalisation.[24] So-called 'codified' or 'explicit' knowledge will include memoranda, agreements and other transactional documents, and legal briefs. A KM strategy focusing on codification will thus seek to systematically collect, classify and distribute these knowledge components.[25] A KM strategy focusing on personalisation will, on the other hand, focus on building a framework to allow lawyers and other members of the firm to exchange their experiences (so-called 'tacit knowledge').[26] Since codified knowledge, as well as tacit knowledge, is valuable for legal practice, law firms should combine both strategic approaches when developing their KM strategy. However, the scope and effort of the activities resulting from these two

---

21   Rusanow (note 1), pp 206–207; Apistola and Gottschalk (note 1), pp 63–65. For information and knowledge management as an important basis to create a learning organisation see also Xavier Gilbert, From Information Knowledge – How Managers Learn, in Donald A Marchand (ed), *Competing with Information*, (John Wiley and Sons, 2000) pp 103–126 and Peter Senge, *The Fifth Discipline – The Art and Practice of the Learning Organization* (Image Books, 2006).
22   See Rusanow (note 1), pp 348–349; see also Martin Schulz, KM strategy – Proving your Worth, *KM Legal Magazine* (2011) 19–21.
23   See Rusanow (note 1), pp 261–288; Parsons (note 1) pp 77–95. As mentioned above, the legal business consists to a large extent of selling specific know-how to clients as legal advice. Thus, all lawyers will always need some KM in one form or another. For small firms, an individual lawyer's good memory, a simple and logical filing system or communication tool for exchanges with colleagues may suffice to receive and use the relevant know-how. However, if law firms grow in headcount, range of services and geographical presence, and the relevant legal markets become more mature and competitive, there will be an increasing need for professional KM.
24   See Morten T Hansen, Nitin Nohria and Thomas Tierney, What's your Strategy for Managing Knowledge? *Harvard Business Review* (March–April 1999) 106; see also Parsons (note 1), pp 161–173.
25   Cf Rusanow (note 1), p 308; Schulz (note 22), 19–21.
26   For developing a KM strategy for law firms see, eg, Rusanow (note 1), pp 261–88; Parsons (note 1) pp 77–95.

strategic options will necessarily depend on the initial decision regarding the amount of resources to be invested in KM activities.

3.2 Link to the business model

Since building and maintaining a professional KM system inevitably means investing in resources, it is important to develop a KM strategy that fits well with the firm's specific business model.[27] This means that all necessary KM investments and activities should always be in line with the business strategy of the law firm. If, for example, advising small and medium-sized companies is one of the main areas of activity, then an important step may be to set up an electronic collection of standard form documents and precedents on all matters pertinent to small and medium-sized companies (such as limited liability companies). Instead of randomly collecting any available information on a specific subject, management should first create a list of priorities (and corresponding prioritised knowledge resources). The KM strategy should also include an outline of the potential benefits of KM activities in supporting the firm's business and client work.[28] The specific business factors and clients to be targeted by the law firm (outlined in its general business strategy) should play a significant role when designing and building the know-how collections.[29]

3.3 KM resources and budgeting

The initial decision of the law firm management on the amount of investment in KM activities will inevitably determine the scope, and to some extent also the quality, of KM services and activities.[30] Although there are many different forms of KM organisation, one can typically find two paradigmatic models. The first model relies on practising lawyers performing non-billable tasks such as KM activities in addition to their fee-earning activities for the firm.[31] In this case, the amount of time that may be devoted by each lawyer to KM tasks (as non-billable work) should be clearly defined and agreed by law firm management and the partners. The second model relies on 'special KM forces' (often called professional support lawyers or PSLs) to perform KM tasks on a full-time or a part-time basis.[32] This model allows more resources to be devoted to KM in order to create and manage know-how assets. In

---

27   See Rusanow (note 1), p 267.
28   Ibid.
29   Ibid, p 268. It is therefore very important to include in the strategy a realistic outline of how KM activities are going to be structured and staffed. The necessary investment will depend on whether the law firm is considering establishing an independent KM function (in this case it will be necessary to find the right people to perform the KM tasks) or whether KM activities are considered a part of the fee earners' tasks. In this case, the law firm will need to consider the evaluation of KM work compared to fee earning tasks.
30   See Rusanow (note 1), pp 327–328.
31   The advantages of this approach include a potentially fast roll-out of a KM system (because no additional personnel hiring or career outlining is required), flexibility (as the balance of KM and billable tasks can be adapted relatively easily), and close connection of KM contributions to real practice. However, giving advice to clients and billing will generally have priority over KM activities, and therefore time and effort devoted to KM activities (including quality control of precedents and standard forms) will remain low and implementation of firm-wide KM policies may be difficult. In particular, KM activities that require extensive non-legal training (for example, dealing with document assembly software) may not be possible.
32   See Parsons (note 1), pp 64–65.

particular, PSLs will be able to create added value[33] by keeping track of legislation, case law and law review articles, by updating standard forms and precedents, by regularly training their colleagues in the efficient use of know-how tools and by allowing the use of sophisticated KM tools.[34]

4. Creating a culture of knowledge sharing in law firms

Creating and fostering a culture of knowledge sharing among lawyers and throughout the firm is one of the most important challenges.[35]

4.1 Specific challenges in law firms

KM systems are only as good as the contributions of their users. Regardless of whether or not a firm uses PSL to build and maintain its KM systems, if fee earners do not provide feedback on what is good and relevant for them, it is very unlikely that the KM system will contain useful knowledge that justifies the devoted time and effort. Likewise, if fee earners do not use the knowledge accumulated by the firm (provided either explicitly in KM systems or implicitly by exchanges of experience with other colleagues), KM cannot fulfil its risk reducing, quality improving and efficiency enhancing functions, even if the KM collections are of great quality. For KM activities to succeed, therefore, it is important that lawyers are prepared to share their knowledge and experience with each other and that they are willing to seek knowledge from their colleagues and the firm when they need it. However, despite the increasing importance of KM for enterprises indicated above, there is unfortunately often a lack of KM acceptance in law firms and there may be the following typical barriers to knowledge sharing.[36] Being overwhelmed by client work, lawyers are sometimes not willing to contribute to the KM system and some might even view KM as an attack on well-established practices and traditions. Although this attitude may seem paradoxical given the benefits of KM to law firms, it may be explained by the asymmetry of costs and visible benefits in the initial phase of KM activities. Like with most support functions, the positive effect of KM on profitability and risk management will often be indirect, and is thus difficult to measure. Moreover, although the aggregate benefit of KM in broadening the collective knowledge base may be large, at the individual level such benefits may seem marginal in the beginning. By contrast, the costs of KM, in terms of necessary investment in qualified personnel and IT systems, and in terms of opportunity costs for fee earners who devote time to KM activities, are clearly visible. Thus, the costs

---

33 For the value-adding functions of KM to be performed by PSLs see, eg, Schulz, (note 22), pp 19–21.
34 However, this model implies a high investment in highly qualified personnel who need to have an attractive job and career path within the firm in order to switch from fee earning and keep motivated. Such a model does also have some other potential challenges, such as the difficulty of (a limited number) of PSLs in covering multiple practice areas and jurisdictions and the need for PSL work products to reflect the demands of legal practice. As indicated above, practising law is always a knowledge-based business to be performed by all lawyers, so employing PSLs must not lead to the wrong assumption that KM tasks can be completely left to them.
35 See Rusanow (note 1), pp 187–220; Parsons (note 1), pp 96–115; Schulz and Klugmann (note 1), pp 386–391.
36 For a detailed analysis of typical cultural barriers in law firms see Rusanow (note 1), pp 192–206; Apistola and Gottschalk (note 1), pp 192–196; Schulz and Klugmann (note 1), pp 386–391.

involved with KM are immediately visible whereas the benefits that KM is providing are a long-term perspective.

4.2 Improving knowledge sharing – some suggestions

To overcome the problems mentioned above the following methods have proved successful.[37] Firstly, the law firm's management (ideally some of the senior partners) should convince their colleagues and employees of the importance and benefit of KM and should strongly support KM initiatives. The members of the law firm's management should prove their commitment towards the value of KM and should serve as role models, contributing to and using knowledge resources and systems themselves. Management should also help to communicate clearly KM initiatives and tasks with special emphasis on how KM initiatives would improve everyone's day-to-day work and benefit each individual lawyer. Secondly, the management team should consider creating incentives for lawyers and other firm members who contribute to and use the KM system. Incentives may take a variety of forms, from posting rankings of contributors and users based on objective database metrics, to monetary KM awards given to a team based on totally subjective peer voting, depending on the individual firm, KM initiative and target group. Incentives can be successful at highlighting the importance of KM to the firm and motivating contributions and use. However, they need to be adequately crafted in order to avoid generating too many contributions without regard to quality or unnecessary database searches or standard form adaptations. To reduce these risks, it is helpful for the lawyers to understand and agree in general that contributing and using KM systems is beneficial in its own right (regardless of the incentive), that the contribution and use are realistically measurable, that the criteria are clear and reasonable and that the management (or the individual partners) retain some discretion as to whether or not to grant the incentive. It should also be emphasised that knowledge sharing requires an atmosphere of cooperation and constructive criticism. Unfortunately, the notion that knowledge is power still prevails in many law firms, which may lead to a psychological barrier to sharing knowledge: lawyers with specific know-how will typically hope to enjoy a higher standing by keeping their expertise to themselves instead of sharing it and may fear becoming less important if they impart their particular knowledge.[38] In addition, some lawyers may fear criticism from their peers when contributing to the knowledge collection, especially in areas not at the core of their competences. It is therefore important to create an atmosphere of open and constructive feedback and criticism. Comments and suggestions on how to improve standard form documents and precedents should always be recognised as a chance to improve the know-how of the firm, and should not be regarded as a personal attack on the person who created the knowledge item.[39]

37	For these and more strategies and tools to overcome cultural barriers and foster an atmosphere of knowledge sharing see Rusanow (note 1), pp 208–220; Parsons (note 1), pp 106–115; Apistola and Gottschalk (note 1), pp 196–202; Schulz and Klugmann (note 1), pp 386–391.
38	Cf Rusanow (note 1), p 201; Apistola and Gottschalk (note 1), pp 192, 193; Schulz and Klugmann (note 1), p 390.
39	See Schulz and Klugmann (note 1), p 391.

5. Building an effective KM system – focus on standard forms and precedents

The design and implementation of a KM system typically establishes the core part of KM in law firms. In many cases, there will be a digital database in which all relevant know-how is systematically stored. This KM collection will include all relevant documents for legal practice such as contracts, memoranda and briefings. Depending on the KM resources available and the quality level of the contents to be achieved, a distinction can be made between so-called standard form documents and precedents. A standard form is typically defined as a document which is up to date, of high quality, and which can be used for various cases and transactions.[40] A precedent, on the other hand, can be described as any document (such as an agreement) being generated by or used in a legal transaction advised by a lawyer of the law firm.[41] Precedents will serve as examples of client work but will often not have the same strict quality requirements as standard forms – they will not be expected to be used as a kind of standard or role model for all other cases in a specific context. Since precedents serve as illustrations of typical case scenarios they will also not always be kept up to date on a regular basis.

6. Designing a useful precedent database – some guidelines

The precedent database (as part of the firm's KM system) should be tailor-made to the needs and demands of the users. Hence, it would appear useful that the KM system as well as the precedent database provides for easy access and a variety of search options.[42] Nevertheless, the following requirements should be met in order to avoid risk and help users to access and use the knowledge resources.

6.1 Be aware of relevant legal issues

Some legal requirements may initially have to be met before documents may be stored in the KM system or a precedent database for distribution to the users. For example, since precedents are created for particular clients and matters, they will often contain client-related information that may be confidential or subject to conflicts of interest. Therefore, it is necessary to systematically erase any client-related information before storing the precedent in the database. Other measures to be taken include closely checking documents for any copyright issues or asking the client or other involved parties for their consent when using documents for the precedent database. Since legal requirements such as applicable intellectual property laws, IT regulations, data protection rules and confidentiality obligations will differ from one jurisdiction to another, every KM activity should be checked closely for any legal requirements or standards to be met. As a result, it will often be necessary to consider certain restrictions regarding access and usage of the KM system.[43]

---

40 Examples of standard form documents include powers of attorney, contract forms and shareholder agreements. As standard form documents are created for multiple scenarios, they often feature additional items like placeholders for inserting information about the particular clients of transactions or alternative texts with optional wording, eg, to favour one party.
41 For a description of precedents see also Rusanow (note 1), p 76; Parsons (note 1) pp 37, 145.
42 For an overview of useful components and features of a KM system see Rusanow (note 1), pp 237–258.
43 For example, for confidentiality (or other legal) reasons. See Rusanow (note 1), pp 245–247.

6.2 Facilitate users' search with additional tools and information

An initial consideration when creating the KM system and the precedent collection is the usefulness of all documents. This should be analysed on the basis of the knowledge objectives and priorities set out in the KM strategy. Thereafter, the documents and precedents should be systematically organised and sorted according to their subject matter (eg, according to areas of legal advice such as corporate law, employment law or tax law). In order to promote the KM goals of enhancing efficiency and quality the precedent database should be equipped with some additional features and tools to make life easier for the user. A useful first step is to describe the precedents with certain meta-data[44] (such as name of the author of the document, title, applicable law, practice area, language, etc) before storing it in the database. Using these criteria methodically will have a positive impact on any searches in the database (provided these criteria are used consistently by any distributor of know-how[45]). In addition, it would seem worthwhile to think about a taxonomy (or classification system), in other words structured guidelines for the KM collection.[46] Such taxonomy could serve as an electronic table of contents for different areas of knowledge such as the precedent database. In terms of user guidance, such a classification system (combined with an option to search by classification) is a valuable addition to a full-text search in the KM database. When designing taxonomies it is important to bear in mind that users may have very different approaches to classifying and grouping subjects and concepts.[47] In order to avoid problems resulting from abstract taxonomies not being intuitive to the users, it might advisable to involve as many lawyers as possible in the design of the classification system, and to provide for flexible tools and options (such as a combination of a full text search option and a search option via the classifications system). Experience shows that some lawyers are more comfortable with full text searches, while others prefer to browse the database following the taxonomy tree, while yet another group opts to have links to a selection of favourite documents close at hand.

6.3 Provide convenient ways to contribute knowledge

A good KM system should provide efficient tools not just for users but also for contributors of know-how. With regard to the submission of documents (eg, precedents) to the database, the process should be as simple and convenient as possible. If a law firm has PSLs, they would typically help with storing know-how and ensure that the relevant meta-data and classification criteria are applied consistently to the knowledge contributions.[48] In firms without PSLs, the fee earners

---

44 See Parsons (note 1), p 234.
45 See Rusanow (note 1), p 244, emphasising the need to apply a common language to the description of knowledge.
46 See Rusanow (note 1), pp 243–245; Parsons (note 1), p 237.
47 See also Rusanow (note 1), p 243, pointing out that the assumption that knowledge will be described consistently across all systems and applications is a dangerous one. Hence, it is difficult to create one particular taxonomy or classification system that will be considered satisfactory or logical by all lawyers.
48 Fee earners would typically send their contributions to a PSL, who would erase any confidential information, check the document for further requirements, provide some user guidance and then upload it to the database applying the classification system.

would be required to perform these tasks, making it more difficult to create a consistent and uniform process of submission and classification. In such cases, it may be advisable to look for options for automatic tagging and classification of contributed documents. In addition, law firm management should give clear guidance on how to handle contributions to the database, for example by producing guidelines for knowledge contributions and by organising training sessions.

6.4 Include tools to capture tacit know-how

Standard forms and precedents are not the only types of know-how that could be managed. On the contrary, knowledge exists in a great variety of forms, often in the form of implicit knowledge or tacit knowledge stored in the heads of the lawyers.[49] Therefore, in addition to the collection of precedents and standard form documents described above, the KM system should also include so-called 'expert directories'. These directories will provide the systematic collection and registration of all special skills and qualifications of the individual lawyers in order to help the user to find legal experts for his questions even in cases where no precedents or other documents are available.

7. Keeping precedents up to date with content management

The lasting success of any KM system and, in particular, of a precedent database will depend on regular and consistent quality control.[50] Thus, every knowledge collection requires content management, which can be defined as a systematic process of ongoing selection, evaluation, reviewing and updating of know-how resources. Content management should start with a thoughtful and strategic selection of content.[51] The first task to be addressed (as part of the KM strategy) is the question of exactly which content really seems worth collecting and maintaining in the long run within the KM database. Instead of creating huge silos of data, it is better to think twice before storing too many know-how items. Only those items that best suit the business strategy should be considered worth storing (on the principle of less is more).[52] The primary goal of content management is to secure the usefulness and quality of the know-how collected. Accordingly, it is advisable to reflect on the criteria associated with high-quality information and know-how, such as accuracy, topicality, practical relevance and reliability.[53] Furthermore, it is necessary to establish review and control procedures on a regular basis.[54] One option is to create so-called 'know-how life cycles' and to implement review dates (which could be installed when the documents are uploaded to the system).[55] In law firms employing

---

49	Cf Rusanow (note 1), pp 72, 111, 119–120; Parsons (note 1), pp 161–173. As far as possible, this tacit knowledge should also be captured, made explicit and shared by writing it down in manuals, practice notes and guidelines, which are then stored in the database.
50	See Rusanow (note 1), pp 241–243; Parsons (note 1), pp 161–173.
51	See Martin Schulz, Content Management – A Fine Art – And a Knowledge Paradox, *Knowledge and Information Management Legal* (2008) 17–20; see also Rusanow (note 1), p 241.
52	See Schulz (note 51), 19.
53	*Ibid.* For an analysis of these and other criteria see Martin J Eppler, *Managing Information Quality* (2nd edn, Springer, 2006).
54	See Schulz (note 51), 19; see also Rusanow (note 1), p 242.
55	See Schulz (note 51), 19.

PSLs, content management will be one of their tasks. However, in law firms where KM tasks are performed by fee earners, quality control and update of precedents and standard forms may pose a significant challenge, since fee earners (and, in particular those most skilled and knowledgeable whose contribution would be most valuable) will often have no time for KM tasks, nor show any interest in content management activities. To overcome this challenge, it is paramount that all partners share a common understanding of the value of KM and 'walk the talk' by appropriately allocating KM tasks (including performing KM tasks personally) and providing resources for KM activities.[56] It will also be important to minimise the time necessary to perform KM tasks, by providing efficient tools for content management, for example, so that fee earners will not fear wasting time on quality control.[57] In order to secure input from legal practice when updating precedents and other know-how resources, the responsibility for updating should always be assigned to selected lawyers and partners who (together with a PSL where applicable) will decide on the reusability of know-how. Only if precedents (as with any other know-how) are regularly kept up to date, can KM serve its function and be recognised by its users as an efficiency driver and a valuable system.

8. Conclusion

Professional knowledge management has become an indispensable tool for law firms and other legal service providers to handle the information overload with which lawyers are regularly bombarded. An effective KM system can lead to significant gains in efficiency in the day-to-day running of a legal practice and can even lead to competitive advantages (knowledge advantage = competitive edge). However, implementing and maintain an effective KM system requires a strategic approach by law firm management and a long-term commitment by all lawyers. Above all, successful KM requires the sustained establishment of a culture of knowledge sharing which promotes an open exchange of knowledge and experience. Precedent databases can form an important basis of a law firm's KM system provided that the documents are carefully selected in alignment with the law firm's business strategy, checked for any reuse restrictions, stored systematically with helpful information for the users and are updated on a regular basis by way of a systematic content management.

9. Checklist

The following checklist may be helpful for the purpose of establishing and maintaining a KM system:
- Develop a KM strategy and decide which KM model to use: practising lawyers or PSLs.
- Assess and improve a knowledge-sharing culture in the firm.

---

56   For the importance of winning top management support in the context of content management see *ibid*, 18. For its importance regarding KM activities in general see Rusanow (note 1), pp 209–210; Apistola and Gottschalk (note 1), pp 195, 200.

57   Ultimately, there will be a trade-off between assigning more resources to KM (as extra fee-earner time or hiring PSLs) and the acceptable level of quality for standard forms and precedents.

- Drive initiatives to establish and maintain effective KM systems:
  - Define document types: standard form documents and precedents.
  - Define scope of KM documentation and check for restrictions.
  - Use meta-data to classify and group documents.
  - Capture also implicit knowledge (eg, by expert directories).
  - Consider developing a classification system (taxonomy).
  - Establish procedures to regularly update KM documentation.

Review processes and client satisfaction: handling high-risk cases

Tracey Calvert
Oakalls Consultancy Limited
Anthony E Davis
Hinshaw & Culbertson LLP
Richard Harrison
Clyde & Co LLP

1. Introduction

Achieving client satisfaction is critical to avoiding claims, complaints and even regulatory action against a law firm, and to upholding the reputation of the firm. A key element of ensuring client satisfaction is the putting in place of adequate review processes to ensure that work is being carried out for the client to the requisite standard, and that the client is being kept fully apprised of and involved in developments on any matter. This chapter will explore these elements, with a particular focus on the handling of cases which might be categorised as high risk. However, much of the discussion is also applicable to lower risk cases, in which achieving client satisfaction remains important for the management of the risks to the firm.

2. Identifying a high-risk case

As noted above, review processes and achieving client satisfaction are particularly important in cases that can be identified as high risk. Given the discussion elsewhere in this text, and the need for consideration to be given to review processes and client satisfaction in cases that might be categorised as lower risk, this section provides only an outline of the types of case in which particularly acute attention should be paid to ensuring that full and proper review processes are put in place and implemented and other aspects of seeking to ensure client satisfaction are given similar attention.

2.1 High-value cases

Cases involving substantial sums of money, whether in the form of (for example) the value of a property or corporate transaction or litigation in which substantial sums are claimed, give rise to particular risks for firms, for a multitude of reasons: for example, errors in these cases may cause such damage to clients that it is certainly worth their while pursuing claims, and they may give rise to claims in excess of a firm's professional indemnity cover, claims in excess of the deductible or excess for which the firm is itself responsible under that cover, or claims that will make the securing of future professional indemnity insurance more difficult or costly.

2.2 **The nature of the client**

The nature of the client will also be a relevant consideration as to whether the case is high risk, and what should be done to try to ensure client satisfaction. In England and Wales, the regulatory body for solicitors, the Solicitors Regulation Authority (SRA), regulates in an outcomes-focused style (Outcomes Focused Regulation or OFR) and its requirements are client-centric. OFR encourages flexibility but requires a firm to focus on the needs of its clients in terms of how it provides services. Different clients may trigger different responses from the firm and also present different risks. Some particular examples are discussed below.

(a) *Sophisticated v unsophisticated clients*

Is the client unsophisticated or sophisticated? In England and Wales this has specific regulatory significance. The SRA does not use the adjective 'unsophisticated', but does refer, in the SRA Handbook, to vulnerable clients, and there are regulatory obligations to consider the needs of such clients in terms of client care (SRA Code, Chapter 1) and when evaluating conflicts of interest (SRA Code, Chapter 3). The SRA does not define vulnerability for these purposes in the Handbook, but elsewhere there is reference to this. For example, in a news release of December 2011 the SRA warned firms to take care with vulnerable clients[1] and described vulnerability caused by physical, social or psychological factors; further, in other reviews the SRA has referred to vulnerability being caused by either personal characteristics or circumstance, with the implication that the latter may mean a widening of the work type which may be caught. The phraseology of 'sophisticated' clients is used in the Handbook in Chapters 3 and 4 of the SRA Code (Conflicts of Interest and Confidentiality and Disclosure). Again, this is not a defined phrase but it is taken to mean clients who are familiar with legal process and procedure and thus more likely to be corporate clients and/or clients with an in-house legal team.

The distinction between sophisticated and unsophisticated clients not only has regulatory implications as described above, but there is authority in case law on professional negligence in England and Wales that if the client is inexperienced the lawyer may be required to give more detailed advice than would otherwise be the case, and vice versa (see, eg, *Carradine Properties Ltd v DJ Freeman & Co* [1999] Lloyds Law Rep PN 483). Thus, in the case of an inexperienced client, it is likely to be particularly important to ensure that full and accurate advice is given and recorded in detail (and robust review processes will be necessary to ensure that this is done).

(b) *Long-standing v new clients*

Likewise, different considerations may apply depending on whether clients are new or long-standing clients of the firm.

Approaches from new clients raise a number of unknowns, such as whether and why they have ended a relationship with a previous lawyer, and whether they have the resources to pay reasonable fees. If a new client is accepted, the firm may well need to provide a particularly clear explanation of what work the firm will and will

---

1   www.sra.org.uk/sra/news/press/care-for-vulnerable-clients.page.

not carry out and the review processes must ensure that the client's expectations of the firm, the work it will undertake and the likely outcomes of the matter are clearly understood and managed.

Long-standing clients may also have expectations that need to be managed carefully, and complacency in this regard (which may arise from, for example, complacency in relation to such important matters as engagement letters) may cause significant problems for the firm, whether from a regulatory, liability or client retention perspective. For example, in the United Kingdom, even if a client is a regular customer of the law firm, it is not necessarily a conflict of interest to act against their interests. However, a long-established client may believe that this is the case. It is important that the firm's risk management system (including its review processes) ensures that clients are aware of this and are advised, at the end of the retainer, of the residual conduct duties of confidentiality owed to them in their capacity as a former client. The case of *Shepherd Construction Ltd v Pinsent Masons LLP* [2012] EWHC 43 (TCC) addresses some of the risks created by client confusion. The duties in respect of former clients are changed where there is an ongoing, rolling retainer or where the firm enters into a commercial arrangement and agrees not to act against the interests of a good, long-established client. Again, a client's knowledge of these matters needs to be built into the risk management strategies (including review processes) in place within the firm.

(c) *'Problem' clients*
There are other types of client who may pose a particular risk to the firm. Work for these clients may require particularly close attention and review.

(d) *Protecting the firm's credit risk*
The key risk posed by some clients is that they may not be able to pay the firm's bills as and when these fall due. Firms should be astute to carry out full and proper due diligence on clients' financial circumstances from the outset in the same way as anti-money laundering procedures and checks must be carried out on each matter.

(e) *Multiple clients and the involvement of third parties*
Cases involving multiple clients and with a third-party dimension present particular issues for firms, which must be confident that they are acting on the instructions of the client and not of some connected third party, and, where there are multiple clients pursuant to a joint retainer (such as a husband and wife, or a company and its directors), that they are acting properly in accordance with all such clients' instructions and are not acting in a position of conflict as between those clients. Such conflicts may arise during the course of a retainer, even where they do not exist or appear to exist at the outset of a joint retainer, and therefore it is important for firms instructed on a joint retainer to stay alert to the possibility that a conflict may arise. This is an issue on which proper supervision and review of work is particularly important, as lawyers working closely on a matter and with the clients may sometimes lose the ability to stand back from the case and appreciate that a conflict has arisen.

Again this issue has regulatory significance in the United Kingdom. The SRA Handbook definition of 'client' is the person for whom you act and, where the context permits, includes prospective and former clients. The identity of the client is clear where this is an individual and you are able to take instructions from them directly. This may be more difficult with corporate or trust clients or where you are acting for more than one person or entity in the same matter. Indicative Behaviour (1.25) in the SRA Code suggests that acting for a client when instructions are given by someone else, or by only one client when you act jointly for others, unless you are satisfied that the person providing the instructions has the authority to do so on behalf of all of the clients, tends to show that the client care outcomes in the code have not been achieved. Regulatory difficulties may also be created by the involvement of third parties, such as introducers, agents and family members. Duties of confidentiality are owed to the client (SRA Code, Chapter 4) and the client's consent must be obtained prior to discussion of their retainer with the non-client.

2.3 Constraints on the retainer

Here, we focus on two areas where the risks involved in a retainer may increase, namely where a firm is asked to carry out work against demanding timescales or for a limited budget.

As to timescales, if the work is accepted then, absent very clear communication that it will not be possible to meet the timescales or that certain work will not be done given the timescales, all reasonable skill and care must be taken to ensure that the deadline imposed by the client or inherent in the transaction is met and the work carried out with all reasonable competence. This is critical to avoiding professional negligence claims, complaints and client dissatisfaction generally. In addition, from a regulatory perspective, the SRA Code states at Outcome 1.4 that a law firm must have the resources, skills and procedures to carry out a client's instructions, and at Outcome 1.5 that the service provided to clients must be competent, delivered in a timely manner and must take account of the client's needs and circumstances. In reality, corners are often cut and mistakes made under time pressure, and the firm's risk management procedures, including its review processes, must be tailored to pick up such errors.

Likewise, if an agreement is reached to do the work for a limited budget or fixed price, it must be carried out competently even if to do so becomes loss-making for the firm. In reality, however, the attraction for lawyers to cut corners in such circumstances remains, and procedures must be put in place to ensure that they do not succumb to such temptation.

Another scenario in which a firm may be instructed under a limited retainer is where the client divides aspects of the legal work on a project or transaction among multiple professionals or organisations (for example, an outsourced service provider), or even keeps some of the work in-house. In such circumstances it is important to carefully discuss and agree in writing with the client the scope of the firm's responsibilities vis-a-vis those of any other law firms or organisations, so that work does not fall between two stools and the firm does not find itself being blamed for failing to carry out a task for which the client believes it was responsible or failing to coordinate the efforts of the different entities involved (unless a project management role has been expressly assumed by the firm).

2.4 Particular types of work

Claims experience has shown that particular types of work are particularly likely to give rise to claims and complaints. These include the following.

(a) *Tax, pensions and other financial planning work*

The sums at stake in this type of work can be high, and frequent changes in the law in this area can make mistakes or incorrect predictions by lawyers particularly prevalent. Where there were risks inherent in a transaction of this nature which were explained to a client, being able to produce a detailed record that such an explanation had been given (and the client nevertheless had decided to proceed) will generally be critical to the successful defence of claims or complaints, and review processes in these fields should be particularly attuned to ensuring that such records are kept.

(b) *Property work*

Errors in conveyancing transactions, such as the failure to carry out certain searches or enquiries or in analysing the results of such searches, are frequently regarded as negligence and have given rise to a high volume of claims in the United Kingdom and other jurisdictions. Review processes should not be forgotten in this field, even where the work might be regarded as volume work or is being done for a low fee.

(c) *Litigation*

Litigation is costly and stressful for clients. Clients disgruntled with the outcome of litigation may seek to blame their lawyers, frequently alleging that they have not been given adequate advice on the merits, settlement or likely costs of the litigation. Although, in the United Kingdom at least, the case law is relatively favourable to litigation lawyers in that it recognises that the giving of advice on the merits of litigation is an art rather than an exact science,[2] a critical feature of risk management procedures (including review processes) in this field is the giving of detailed and well-recorded advice.

(d) *Cross-border/international work*

The risks inherent in cross-border or international work are manifold. For example, firms with cross-border practices need to be acutely aware of the different rules in different jurisdictions on such matters as lawyers' conduct (including conflicts of interest) and disclosure. Lawyers qualified in one jurisdiction but working in an office of the firm in another jurisdiction may also miss nuanced points of local law, which may give rise to liabilities to clients as well as regulatory issues. For example, in the United Kingdom, the reference to competence in Outcome 1.5 of the SRA Code is relevant: an individual should not undertake legal work if they do not have

---

2   See, eg, *Langsam v Beachcroft LLP* [2012] EWCA Civ 1230.

the appropriate knowledge of the subject matter; in addition, when performing cross-border activities in Europe there is a need to comply with the SRA European Cross-border Practice Rules 2011, which are in the Specialist Services section of the SRA Handbook. Firms carrying out work on a transaction in which other correspondent firms in other jurisdictions are also involved must be careful to define their responsibilities vis-a-vis those of such other firms and to negative any implication that they might be adopting a coordinating or oversight role in relation to other firms.

3. Client satisfaction: overarching issues

3.1 Compliance with service level agreements or external counsel guidelines

Corporate or other major institutional clients will frequently require firms, as a condition of their instruction on a particular matter or their inclusion within a panel of approved lawyers, to comply with a service level agreement or set of external counsel guidelines (referred to collectively herein as an SLA). An SLA will set out the manner in which the client expects the retainer to be performed, and in particular will frequently include detailed requirements as to such matters as:

- the individuals, or type of fee earner, who may work on the matter;
- timescales for responses to communications;
- the points in time or triggers for reporting to the client, and methods of reporting;
- conflicts provisions;
- billing procedures and what types of work may or may not be billed for.

SLAs will frequently be signed agreements with contractual effect, and for this reason (and in any event in the interests of client satisfaction) it is crucial that they are complied with. This will require a detailed review of any SLA before its terms are agreed, in case some terms are considered unduly onerous or will be unachievable or impracticable for the firm. This review process should always involve partners and, where requirements are particularly unusual or burdensome, may also need to involve the firm's risk function.

Thereafter, proper dissemination of the SLA amongst all those who are to work, or may find themselves working, on matters for the client in question, is essential. The firm's intranet, or some other readily accessible central repository, should be used for this purpose. It is essential that the information held in this way is kept up to date.

The supervision and review processes in place in relation to any individual matter must ensure that any applicable SLA has been complied with. This is likely to involve, for example, careful diarising of all dates for action imposed by the SLA, and a robust system whereby all members of the project team may check that those dates have been complied with. In addition, it is likely to prove useful to put in place an audit system to measure compliance with SLAs, for example by the regular random selection of a sample of files which are currently being worked on, or have recently been worked on, for a particular client.

3.2 Reporting to the client and managing expectations

Even where specific reporting requirements are not expressly set out in an SLA or otherwise agreed with the client, reporting to the client and managing their expectations, for example on the prospects of success in a piece of litigation, is critical to client satisfaction. Expectation management starts at the very outset of the retainer, with terms of engagement and/or an engagement letter, which should set out clearly the work which will be done, for what price, in what timescales, and any limitation on the work to be done or the responsibilities of the firm (cross-referring where appropriate to any applicable SLA). Communications thereafter should be regular (including at important points in the matter, such as if an offer is received from the other side, or when the matter is about to progress to mediation or trial), detailed and recorded in writing. This should help the client feel satisfied that they have received a good service at the end of the retainer, even if the outcome has not been as they would have liked. It will also assist the firm in defending any professional negligence claim that may be brought by a client who becomes disgruntled.

Costs is a specific issue on which detailed information must be given at the outset of any matter, and monitored and actively managed with the client thereafter. A client is likely to be unhappy and refuse to pay fees, or make a claim or complaint, if at the conclusion of a matter the costs are significantly higher than the client expected or had been estimated, particularly where there has been no prior warning or discussion of this increase.

Again a number of the outcomes in Chapter 1 of the SRA Code reinforce these points. For example, Outcome 1.12 requires that clients are in a position to make informed decisions about the services they need, how their matter will be handled and the options available to them, and Outcome 1.13 requires that clients receive the best possible information, both at the time of engagement and when appropriate as their matter progresses, about the likely overall cost of their matter. Overall, compliance with these client care outcomes will also support achievement of the overarching SRA Principles. These are described by the SRA "as the key ethical requirements on firms and individuals who are involved in the provision of legal services". In terms of client care, the SRA Principles of particular significance are the requirement to act in the best interests of each client, and to provide a proper standard of service to clients. The Law Society has published a practice note on client care, which contains best practice guidance.[3]

In England and Wales, the need to provide detailed costs information at the outset in litigation matters and to monitor this closely throughout has been heightened by new provisions in the Civil Procedure Rules, introduced in April 2013, requiring the production, at an early stage of litigation, of a detailed costs budget, which the court will consider and (if approved) set as a budget for the litigation, with any departures from the budget requiring specific court approval sought promptly once it becomes apparent that the budget will be exceeded.

---

3 www.lawsociety.org.uk/advice/practice-notes/client-care-letters/#cc14.

4. The supervision and review of work

4.1 The risks of allowing matters to be handled by individual lawyers without oversight

There are many reasons why claims, complaints and regulatory issues may arise where individuals are allowed to handle matters without any or adequate oversight by others. These may include, for example, the individual having insufficient experience to handle the matter or particular issues arising during the course of the matter, an inability to 'see the wood for the trees' in a complex or long-running matter, or an overly close relationship with the client leading the individual to fail to spot conflicts of interest or to believe too strongly in the merits of the case as presented to him by the client and therefore to fail to give sufficiently objective advice. Some of these issues may apply equally to partners as to more junior fee earners. It is therefore important that adequate procedures are put in place to provide oversight and support to lawyers at all levels.[4] Although in the case of partners it may be unrealistic to expect work to be supervised, on particularly high-risk cases it may be prudent to involve more than one partner (indeed, the workload demands of such cases may require multiple partners to be involved in any event), and firms should in all cases implement an open-door policy, which (subject to any information barriers in place) encourages even senior individuals to talk difficult points through with their colleagues.

In England and Wales, the SRA places significant importance on supervision arrangements. SRA Principle 8 states that lawyers must run their business or carry out their role in the business effectively and in accordance with proper governance and sound financial and risk management principles. Chapter 7 of the SRA Code supports this Principle by setting outcomes in terms of the management of the business (ie, the firm). For example, Outcome 7.1 provides that there must be a clear and effective governance structure and reporting lines; Outcome 7.6 provides that individuals working in the firm must be trained to maintain a level of competence appropriate to their work and level of responsibility; and Outcome 7.8 provides that there must be a system for supervising clients' matters, to include the regular checking of the quality of work by suitably competent and experienced people. The Law Society of England and Wales has published a practice note on supervision containing best practice guidance.[5]

4.2 Structuring the internal team

How the team working on any particular matter should be comprised and structured will depend on the demands of the particular matter in question. However, some general points may be made.

As noted above, on particularly large or high-risk matters it may well be appropriate to involve at least one partner to head up the team, so that there is adequate scrutiny even of partners' work. On large-scale matters, a team of associates or equivalent fee-earning lawyers is likely to sit below the partner team. Within the

---

4 Of course, in the case of sole practitioners this will not be possible; the discussion in this chapter focuses on the position of firms with multiple partners and other fee earners.
5 www.lawsociety.org.uk/advice/practice-notes/supervision/.

associate team, it may well be prudent to establish a hierarchy for review purposes, with one or more senior associates having responsibility for reviewing the work of other associates. This coordinating and review role will be particularly important where the scale of the matter is such that different tasks or elements of the matter have to be allocated in a rather discrete way to different associates in order to ensure that all relevant aspects are worked on in sufficient detail.

In addition to the associate team, large matters are likely to involve the support of a team of paralegals, who will generally have some legal knowledge and experience but no formal qualification as lawyers. On large matters, paralegals will frequently assist with volume work such as document review and compilation. The use of large teams of paralegals is becoming particularly prevalent, in the United Kingdom at least, in volume work and in order to meet clients' increasing demands for low-priced or fixed fee services. While a valuable and important way of resourcing matters at appropriate cost, the supervision of such staff presents particular risk management challenges for law firms, which are considered further below.

Firms must make sure that they put in place detailed arrangements for cover in the event of absences within the team and handover where a member of the team departs temporarily or permanently.

4.3   Setting and implementing review processes

(a)   *Methods of review*

In general, it is prudent for firms to apply a 'four eyes' principle, particularly when dealing with high-risk cases: in other words, two individuals within the firm should have sight of important work products or be involved in any decision-making process, and indeed should have overall oversight of the conduct of a matter. To achieve this, clear internal reporting lines should be set up on any matter, and internal protocols agreed as to when reporting and general matter review will take place. For example, will this be at regular intervals, such as weekly, or when particular trigger points are reached on the file (or both)? Reviewers and supervisors must ensure that they have adequate time to undertake their responsibilities in relation to the review of work, and also to have reasonable availability to provide guidance to more junior fee earners as and when sought. As noted above, an open-door policy should be encouraged as a general rule, so that even senior associates and partners can discuss points of concern with colleagues.

It should be kept in mind that supervision and review responsibilities may remain with the firm even where a member of staff is seconded to a client, particularly where the client does not have a substantial legal team of its own. Firms should be careful to agree responsibilities in this regard with the client at the outset of any secondment, and thereafter to put in place a clear system by which the review of work will take place, for example the copying of all work produced during the secondment to a partner at the firm and/or the setting aside of a certain period of time each week during which the secondee will return to the firm's offices to discuss with a partner the matters being dealt with by him for the client.

In addition to the formal and informal review processes that should take place during the lifetime of a matter within the team working on that matter, a system of internal file auditing may well be beneficial. This will involve the review (by someone outside the project team) of randomly selected files for such matters as compliance with SLAs or otherwise reasonable response times, the application of agreed or otherwise acceptable billing practices, and compliance with regulatory rules relating to the use of client funds and accounts.[6]

(b) *The review of third-party providers' work*
Careful review of third-party providers' work is also critical to minimising risks to the firm.

For example, the advice or other work product of barristers or other external counsel instructed on a matter must not simply be taken as read. In professional negligence cases in England and Wales, law firms may be able to rely on a defence of 'reasonable reliance on counsel' where they have been guided in their actions by the advice of counsel who has been properly instructed, but the authorities are clear that a solicitor must not rely on counsel blindly or unquestioningly, but rather must exercise his own independent judgment over the advice received and has a duty to reject counsel's advice if it is obviously or glaringly wrong (and if the law firm has specialist expertise in the area of law involved it may be more difficult for it to argue that the advice was not obviously or glaringly wrong).[7]

Reports of experts and other consultants should be closely scrutinised, as should the work of outsourced service providers. While a valuable and important method of providing cost-effective legal services (and therefore client satisfaction on cost) in many cases, legal process outsourcing presents a number of challenges for law firms in terms of delivering good client service and complying with regulatory requirements. Some of the dangers were underlined in, for example, the case of *West African Gas v Willbros* [2012] EWHC 396 (TCC), where a major City of London law firm found itself on the receiving end of severe criticism and a wasted costs order for the manner in which a disclosure exercise had been carried out by a third-party litigation support provider. Similar situations have arisen in the United States.

Again in the United Kingdom, the SRA has made outsourcing a regulatory issue. For example, outsourcing must be compliant with Outcome 7.9 of the SRA Code (firms must not outsource reserved legal activities to a person who is not authorised to conduct such activities), and Outcome 7.10, which provides that where legal activities or any operational functions critical to the delivery of legal activities are outsourced, firms must ensure that such outsourcing:

- does not adversely affect their ability to comply with, or the SRA's ability to monitor their compliance with, their obligations in the SRA Handbook;
- is subject to contractual arrangements which enable the SRA to obtain information from, inspect the records of, or enter the premises of, the third party, in relation to the outsourced activities or functions;

---

6   It should be noted that regular reviews can also be beneficial for wider risk, brand and reputation management purposes.
7   *Locke v Camberwell Health Authority* [1991] 2 Med LR 249; *Ridehalgh v Horsefield* [1994] Ch 205.

- does not alter their obligations towards their clients; and
- does not cause the firm to breach the conditions of its authorisation.

The SRA has concerns about a particular type of outsourcing, cloud computing, and the possible repercussions that this may have for compliance with the SRA Handbook. They and the Law Society have published guidance on this topic,[8] and the Law Society has published a practice note on outsourcing more generally.[9]

Key considerations for law firms engaging in legal process outsourcing will therefore include, at the outset, the conducting of robust due diligence on potential providers, including with regard to such matters as the preservation of client confidentiality, data security, conflicts of interest and their understanding of SRA regulatory requirements, as well as how matters are supervised and quality maintained within the provider. Thereafter, firms will need to consider carefully how to review the work of providers so as to ensure that clients are being provided with a good service: possibilities include sampling exercises in relation to a provider's work and regular meetings or conference calls between the law firm and the individuals responsible for supervising work within the provider.

(c) *Low-cost, volume and free client services*
As noted above, the use of teams of paralegals or other staff who are not fully qualified to perform tasks at a lower cost base than would otherwise be the case may be critical in some respects to providing a service a client wants at a price it is prepared to pay (or even at no cost to the client at all), but also presents risk management challenges.

Establishing efficient processes for dealing with particular work and providing robust training on these is an important starting point. Thereafter, the appointment of a partner or senior associate to act as project manager, with responsibility for coordinating the work of supporting staff such as paralegals, and (where appropriate) reviewing samples of their work, may well be prudent.

5. Addressing (potential) errors and client dissatisfaction

5.1 Addressing (potential) errors
Where review processes do pick up errors (or potential errors), there will be internal processes with which (depending on the jurisdiction) firms need to comply, such as informing the risk partner and/or (in the United Kingdom) the Compliance Officer for Legal Practice (COLP), as well as notifying professional indemnity insurers. In addition, obligations may be triggered to notify the client. In the United Kingdom, SRA Code Outcome 1.16 states that a lawyer must inform current clients if any act or omission is discovered which could give rise to a claim by them against the lawyer/firm. Further, under limitation case law in England and Wales, a solicitor who is negligent when acting for a client under a first retainer may, if subsequently

---

8   www.sra.org.uk/solicitors/freedom-in-practice/OFR/risk/resources/cloud-computing-law-firms-risk.page; www.lawsociety.org.uk/advice/practice-notes/cloud-computing/.
9   www.lawsociety.org.uk/advice/practice-notes/outsourcing/.

instructed to do work that, if correctly done, would reveal the earlier error(s), be held to have a duty at that later point to report the earlier negligence.[10]

Discovering such an act or omission may create a conflict between the individual or firm and the client and there is a need to consider whether there is an own-interest conflict thereafter, which would mean that the firm should stop acting for the client. Firms will need to carefully consider these issues, and how (and by whom) any issues are communicated to the client, in order to avoid further damage to the client relationship and further exposures to claims and complaints.

5.2 Client complaints

Firms should have fair and robust procedures in place for clients to make complaints if dissatisfied. In the United Kingdom, although the SRA does not impose a mandatory requirement to have a complaints policy (written or otherwise),[11] Indicative Behaviour 1.22 suggests that having such a policy will demonstrate compliance with the Outcomes in Chapter 1 of the SRA Code relating to complaints handling and the mandatory requirement to advise the client of their right to complain and of the right of redress from the Office of Legal Complaints. Further, the Legal Ombudsman, an independent ombudsman service to which clients may complain once they have exhausted any complaints system operated by the firm, will take into account how the firm has handled a complaint when reaching a decision about a matter referred to the Ombudsman. Failure to have dealt with a complaint properly may lead the Ombudsman to conclude that the firm has provided poor service, even if the initial complaint was unfounded. More generally, even if a client is initially dissatisfied with the work done by a firm, feeling that its dissatisfaction has been addressed by means of a proper complaints process may help to quell the client's feelings of dissatisfaction and therefore reduce the risk of further complaints, claims or damage to the firm's reputation.

Good complaints handling involves a number of elements.[12] Identifying the right person to handle a complaint is a key consideration, which is likely to depend on how the complaint is made: to adopt an example which has been given by the Law Society of England and Wales, a complaint about a failure to return a phone call might be resolved by the recipient promptly returning the call and apologising; but a complaint in the form of a formal letter to the partner responsible for handling complaints about the firm is likely to demand a more formal response from that partner or another senior member of staff. The involvement of an independent person to investigate and determine the complaint will frequently, though not invariably, be appropriate. It is therefore important that policies and training are provided to all staff as to when it is appropriate for them to resolve complaints themselves or when these need to be escalated.

---

10   See *Bell v Peter Browne & Co* [1990] 2 QB 495; *Ezekiel v Lehrer* [2002] Lloyd's Rep PN 260; *Gold v Mincoff Science & Gold* [2001] Lloyd's Rep PN 423.
11   The SRA defines a 'complaint' as an oral or written expression of dissatisfaction that alleges that the complainant has suffered (or may suffer) financial loss, distress, inconvenience or other detriment.
12   The Law Society of England and Wales has published guidance on complaints handling, available at www.lawsociety.org.uk/advice/practice-notes/handling-complaints/. The Legal Ombudsman's website, www.legalombudsman.org.uk, also contains best practice guidance and research on complaints.

The person dealing with the complaint should take time to understand the complaint and keep records so that the complainant does not feel that they need to repeat their complaint subsequently. If time is needed to investigate or resolve a complaint, the complainant should be informed of this, the reasons for this, what steps are being taken and the timescales within which they can expect a substantive response. Responses should in any event be timely; in the United Kingdom complaints should be responded to within eight weeks, otherwise the complainant may take the complaint to the Legal Ombudsman.

In the course of handling a complaint, if evidence of poor service is found, this should be acknowledged in the response and an offer of appropriate redress (such as an apology, compensation, putting things right or reducing a bill) considered. However, since such action may be construed as an admission relevant to a possible future negligence claim, firms may be well advised to liaise not only with their own internal risk functions but also (possibly via the risk function) with their professional indemnity insurers, before making any such acknowledgment or offering any such redress. If the outcome of consideration of the complaint is that no poor service has been found, the reasons for this conclusion should be explained fully and evidence set out as to why the service provided was reasonable. In the United Kingdom, as noted above, clients must be provided with details of the Legal Ombudsman and the timescales for contacting the Legal Ombudsman should they wish to progress the complaint (Outcome 1.10).

5.3 Learning from client feedback

Complaints may be a valuable source of client feedback from which firms can learn lessons and improve for the future. There is also much to be said for actively seeking client feedback as a matter of course. Such a process may both increase client satisfaction, as clients will feel that the firm values their input into the way in which its services are provided, and will provide the firm with information that it can use as the basis for future policy development, improvements in its working practices and training. The obtaining of such feedback may take the form of regular review meetings with repeat clients, 'de-briefs' at the ends of retainers, or more informal contact through key relationship managers.

6. Checklist

- Is the case high risk?
- Has an appropriate engagement letter been sent?
- Is a suitably resourced team in place for dealing with the matter, and are there clear reporting lines and supervision and review responsibilities within that team?
- Are adequate arrangements in place for the handover of work in the event of temporary or permanent absences by members of the team?
- Are the terms of any applicable SLA well known to all those working on the case, and are they being complied with?
- Is suitable reporting to the client taking place at appropriate intervals and stages in the case, and in accordance with the terms of any applicable SLA?

- Is the 'four eyes' principle being complied with?
- Is there an appropriate open-door policy to allow fee earners of any level to discuss concerns with colleagues?
- Is the work product of counsel, experts and other consultants subjected to detailed scrutiny?
- Have any providers of legal process outsourcing been the subject of adequate due diligence, and is their work being subjected to adequate scrutiny on an ongoing basis?
- Has supervision of any secondees been adequately considered?
- Have suitable review and supervision arrangements been put in place for any low-cost, volume or value-added legal services offered to clients?
- Do all staff know the applicable policies and their responsibilities, including who to contact within the firm in the first instance, where an error in the firm's work is discovered?
- Does the firm have a fair and detailed complaints procedure in place?
- Is feedback sought from clients as a matter of course, for example by way of review meetings or end of retainer de-briefs?
- Are complaints data and other feedback from clients properly analysed and acted upon?

Managing the client engagement

Tracey Calvert
Oakalls Consultancy Limited
Abhijit Joshi
AZB & Partners
Frank Maher
Legal Risk LLP
Angeline Poon
Rajah & Tann LLP

1. Introduction

Understanding what the client wants is critical to managing client engagement risks. It may be that the client's expectations are unrealistic, for example expecting to triumph in a litigation which is unwinnable. The sooner that is identified and communicated to the client, the less the risk of the client perceiving the lawyer as part of the problem.

An unhappy client may claim damages, make a complaint about poor service, take future business elsewhere, or share his or her dissatisfaction with others. Reputational damage may be the most significant.

In England and Wales, clients who are dissatisfied may, after complaining to the lawyer, complain to the Legal Ombudsman, who has power to award compensation. The Legal Ombudsman's reports give some insight into where lawyer–client relationships go wrong.

In Singapore, a client may lodge a complaint to the Law Society of Singapore for his lawyer's failure to meet one or more of the professional standards prescribed by the Singapore Legal Profession (Professional Conduct) Rules (PCR). The standards of professional service prescribed in the PCR include, *inter alia*, explaining to the client important developments in the case, example offers of settlement, explaining the manner in which the lawyer would charge for services and discussing the possible risks or expenses of proceedings arising from the case.

Those who are eligible to complain to the Legal Ombudsman in England and Wales include individuals, small businesses within certain limits, small charities and clubs. There are no eligibility requirements for complaints made to the Singapore Law Society. The Legal Ombudsman publishes statistics on complaints, though it should be noted that the restrictions on eligible claimants mean that large commercial clients do not feature in them. Notwithstanding the foregoing, issues giving rise to consumer complaints are often to be found in commercial work too. However, commercial clients are less likely to complain. They may simply take their business elsewhere.

In India, if the relevant State Bar Council, whether on receipt of a complaint (from any person, as there are no prescribed eligibility criteria) or otherwise, has reason to believe that an advocate on its roll has been guilty of professional or other misconduct, the case may be referred to the disciplinary committee. Courts in India have held that mere negligence unaccompanied by any moral delinquency may not amount to professional or other misconduct. However, as noted, a client may simply take business elsewhere.

The causes of complaints may partially differ from the causes of liability claims, but each can result in financial loss and loss of reputation. The lawyer who has to deal with a client complaint may not only lose future business from that client, but from others with whom the complainant shares his or her dissatisfaction.

Research by the Solicitors Regulation Authority (SRA) in England and Wales into the characteristics and risks associated with law firms in financial difficulty identified that while there was no direct correlation, poor quality service giving rise to complaints featured in 16% of firms in financial difficulty.[1]

The report commented:

In general, it is difficult to assert whether poor standards of service were the reason for firms starting to struggle, or the result of financial difficulty placing excessive strain on the wider operations of firms ... Examples of poor service quality tended to involve delays in completion of house sales, failure to attend court proceedings and overcharging.

It is important to document the relationship with the client at every stage. This may be by way of letter confirming what is agreed and the advice given, or by preparing a file note. Practice varies on the keeping of file notes. Commercial lawyers engaged in completion meetings and litigation lawyers in mediations and settlement meetings may find it particularly difficult to keep a full file note. It may be useful to have an assistant present for that purpose.

Practice may also vary from jurisdiction to jurisdiction. An English judge in one recent case noted, for example, that the practice of keeping attendance notes was not common among Greek lawyers.[2] However, as claims against lawyers become more common, the benefits of keeping proper attendance notes become more important. Where there is a conflict of evidence between the lawyer and the client, while the absence of a file note does not mean the lawyer's recollection is wrong, it has been the unhappy experience of many that a judge may prefer the evidence of a client for whom it is their only case, rather than that of a busy lawyer with many cases.

A Singapore Court of Appeal judge also commented on the importance of maintaining attendance notes in a case on conflicts of interest. He noted that while a court will not automatically accept attendance notes as conclusive evidence, they will be helpful in clarifying matters and corroborating a lawyer's testimony in the event of a factual dispute.[3] He also emphasised the importance of observing the practice of documenting the nature and scope of retainers with clients and maintaining reliable notes of discussions with clients.

---

1   SRA, Steering the course: Research into the characteristics and risks associated with law firms in financial difficulty, available at http://www.sra.org.uk/solicitors/freedom-in-practice/OFR/risk/resources/risks-and-financial-difficulty.page.
2   *Ostrovizky v Watson Farley & Williams* [2014] EWHC 160 (QB).
3   *Lie Hendri Rusli v Wong Tan & Molly Lim* (a firm) [2004] SGHC 213.

2. Initial instructions

If firms properly manage client engagement, a significant proportion of the related risks falls away. Consideration should be given to the competence of the firm to provide the services requested and having a clear agreement at the outset on the actual scope of the services to be provided, including any limitations imposed by either side and the billing process.

While clients remain the main source of claims, claims may also come from other interested parties, such as lenders, investors and beneficiaries. An important question to resolve at the outset is: 'Who is the client?' This may seem self-evident, but the question can arise in a variety of contexts. It can be relevant to the issue of the lawyer's authority to act, whether legal professional privilege applies to communications, to compliance with anti-money laundering legislation and prevention of fraud.

Instructions from third parties should cause particular concern. Examples in practice include elderly clients wishing to make wills or gifts of assets. Instructions may come from a child of the testator or donor.

The concern here is not limited to the authority of the child to provide instructions, but to whether the client has the mental capacity to make the will or gift and whether it truly reflects their wishes rather than the wishes of the child. There is also a significant risk of fraud. Particular care needs to be taken when dealing with vulnerable clients.

Problems can also arise where the lawyer purportedly acts for husband and wife, but only sees, and receives instructions from, one of the clients. An example of this occurred in the English case of *Penn v Bristol & West Building Society*.[4] In this case, Mr and Mrs Penn owned their house jointly. Mr Penn had considerable business debts, and plotted a fraud by which he would purport to sell the house to Mr Wilson, who was party to the scheme, and raise mortgage finance from Bristol & West on Mr Wilson's 'purchase' of the house. Mr Penn forged his wife's signature on the sale documents. She knew nothing about the sale. The lawyer took his instructions solely from Mr Penn. The judge set aside the transaction on the basis that it was void. He also awarded damages to Bristol & West against the lawyer on the basis that the lawyer had warranted that the firm had authority to act for both Mr and Mrs Penn, when it did not in fact have Mrs Penn's authority at all.

The growth in the incidence of identity theft since this case has exacerbated the problem. This has involved not only the theft of identity from purported clients, but also of law firms, with fraudsters cloning their websites, resulting in genuine law firms sending client money to the fraudsters and potentially being liable for doing so.

Lloyds TSB Bank PLC v Markandan and Uddin[5] was such a case. Lawyers acting for the buyer of a property and the mortgage lender sent the completion money to what purported to be a law firm acting for the sellers. The money was stolen and the buyer obtained no title to the property. The law firm was held liable to its lender client.

---

4 [1997] 3 All ER 470.
5 [2012] EWCA Civ 65.

The problem of cloning law firms' identity has become so serious that the SRA issued a warning in May 2012.[6] It advised firms to search their own names, and even those of partners and staff, on the Internet to ensure that false offices did not appear to exist. It also identified the need, worryingly, to check the firm's own details on the Law Society website to ensure that the firm's name had not been misused to set up a false office.

The warning gave some examples of factors giving rise to suspicion including:
- errors in letterheading – in one case the bogus office had a letterheading that misspelt the name of the town in which it was supposedly based;
- no landline telephone number – note that (in the UK) numbers beginning with 07 are mobile telephone numbers;
- inconsistent telephone or fax numbers with those usually used by the firm;
- telephone calls being diverted to a call-back service;
- a firm apparently based in serviced offices;
- email addresses using generic email accounts—most law firms have addresses incorporating the name of their firm; if in doubt, check the genuine law firm's website to identify its contact email address. You may well notice a difference;
- the sudden appearance in a locality of a firm with no obvious connection to the area, probably not interacting with other local firms at all;
- a firm appearing to open a branch office a considerable distance from its head office for no obvious reason;
- a firm based in one part of the country supposedly having a bank account in another part of the country – this is a strong indicator and has been seen several times;
- a client account apparently overseas – this is a breach of rule 13.4 of the SRA Accounts Rules and is a major red flag;
- a strange or suspicious bank account name – such as the account not being in the name of the law firm you are supposedly dealing with either at all or with some variation.

Questions of authority can also arise in commercial work. Sometimes commercial lawyers will perceive their role as being to act for 'the deal', without proper regard to the identity of the client, the source of their instructions or the source of their authority to act.

It is important to ensure that the person providing the instructions has the appropriate authority to instruct the lawyer. A case where this resulted in liability for the law firm was *Newcastle International Airport Ltd v Eversheds LLP*.[7]

In that case, the company instructed the law firm to draft new service contracts between it and its two executive directors. The instruction to the lawyers was given by one of the two executive directors. No separate advice was provided to either the full board or the remuneration committee.

---

6   See www.sra.org.uk/identitytheft/.
7   EWCA Civ 1514.

The contracts contained provision for bonuses of approximately £8 million to be paid to the executive directors and released them both from restrictive covenants that prevented them from working for certain competitor airports. The board and its remuneration committee, which was the committee with responsibility for reviewing these contracts, had failed to understand their effect.

As the lawyers had received their instructions from directors who had a personal conflict of interest, the Court of Appeal, allowing the appeal, found the law firm in breach of duty on the basis that it should have provided separate written advice explaining the terms and effect of the service contracts to the full board and to its remuneration committee. However, the court also found that had advice been given in this way, the contracts would still have been signed, and therefore awarded only nominal damages of £2.

When taking initial instructions, lawyers must be alert to the issue of conflicts of interest with existing clients, former clients (primarily in relation to confidential information) and the interests of the lawyer and his or her firm. The firm should have systems in place for checking for commercial conflicts as well as legal ones.

Care needs to be taken when acting for public authorities, as their powers and the ostensible authority of officials instructing the law firm may be narrower than for corporate clients. Examples of this causing liability on law firms have arisen in the context of local authorities entering into complex financial swap contracts.[8]

Lawyers need also to be alert to the risk of either assuming duties to non-clients, or of third parties assuming that the lawyers are acting for them. This may arise, for example, where the lawyer acts for a company in an employment dispute, perhaps arising from a claim for discrimination or harassment, and the supervisor against whom the allegations are made assumes that the lawyer is acting for him or her as well. At the outset, the company may be backing the supervisor and disputing the claim. Matters can become difficult when, further down the line, the supervisor admits privately to the lawyer that some of the allegations may be true, giving rise to conflict issues.

The question of whether duties are owed to individual shareholders and directors may also commonly arise. This should be considered when drafting terms of engagement. As well as identifying the client, it may also be prudent to identify individuals for whom the firm is not acting.

3. The engagement

It is important to clarify client expectations at the start of the engagement. This should cover what the client seeks to accomplish by instructing the lawyer, the expected timescale and the likely cost and recovery of damages or completion of a transaction, as the case may be. In practice, it may sometimes be difficult to identify timescale and cost but the lawyer, with more experience than the client, is better placed to warn of the likely parameters.

In some cases, particularly volume or repeat work, this may not be a significant issue. In other cases, however, lawyers could make use of data from previous

---

8   *Haugesund Kommune and another v Depfa Acs Bank and Wikborg Rein & Co* [2011] EWCA Civ 33.

instructions to assist in providing estimates of time and cost to new clients. If initial estimates of each instruction are also recorded, the information can be used to track how accurate their forecasting has been in the past and learn from that experience.

An important initial task will be to identify the scope of the retainer and record it in writing, either as terms of business or an engagement letter.

Where it is not possible to identify fully what the client needs at the outset, the lawyer should identify the initial exploratory work that will be undertaken and the point at which it will be reviewed. When the initial work has been undertaken and the position has become clearer, the scope and cost estimate should be revised and agreed with the client.

In areas where the lawyer does not intend to advise, it is prudent to record the fact clearly and exclude it from the retainer. If the lawyer is aware the client is receiving separate advice from another professional on a certain aspect of the matter or has not been specifically instructed by the client to advise, it should be noted in the retainer.

Leaving the issue silent makes the firm hostage to fortune. An example where this happened in practice was the English case of *Hurlingham Estates Ltd v Wilde & Partners*,[9] though on the facts of that case the judge expressed the view that the lawyer should not have taken on the instruction at all if he could not advise on the tax aspects.

It is also helpful to identify the fact, where appropriate, that the lawyer will not be advising the client on the commercial wisdom of a matter. Generally such decisions are matters for the client not the lawyer. However, the issue can enter grey areas as lawyers may increasingly wish to be seen to advise on the law in a commercial context, and their websites and other publicity may say they do. If it is their intention not to do so, they should ensure that their marketing is consistent with this.

An example where a claimant alleged that the law firm was under a duty to advise on commercial issues was one of the largest lawyer liability cases to reach the English courts. *Football League v Edge Ellison*[10] was a claim for £142 million arising from a contract for the sale of media rights for digital broadcasting of football matches. The bidder that acquired the rights was a subsidiary of a substantial company. The subsidiary became insolvent and the Football League alleged that the law firm should have advised them to negotiate a guarantee from the parent company.

The judge held that the retainer did not include provision for the consideration of, or advice upon, matters of bidder solvency, including questions relating to any need for guarantees. However, the claim cast a significant shadow over the defendant firm for some years, also attracting substantial press coverage. The express exclusion of commercial considerations from the retainer may assist in clarifying the parties' respective positions and making litigation less likely.

Clients instruct lawyers because they wish to transfer risk; prudence dictates that the parties should be clear as to which risks are transferred and which are not.

---

9 [1997] 1 Lloyd's Rep 525.
10 [2006] EWHC 1462 (Ch).

3.1   **Fee agreement and costs information**

A clear, written agreement on costs will help manage risk in a number of ways, as we shall see. In some jurisdictions, particularly in England and Singapore, it is also a regulatory requirement. Certain detailed requirements may also arise in relation to 'distance and off-premises contracts' following implementation of European Directive 2011/83/EU of the European Parliament and of the Council of 25 October 2011 on consumer rights, subject to implementation into the national law of EU countries.[11]

Costs may be an agreed fee, or charged on a time basis, or a combination of the two. If the fee is agreed, this will link into the scope of the engagement – making beyond doubt, one hopes, what is done for the price – but should also address the issue of what will be charged as extra, and the mechanism for charging for extra pieces of advice.

Written agreement on costs reduces the scope for the client to dispute what is due. Many claims against lawyers arise from fee disputes. Lawyers may sue for their fees, and clients use allegations of negligence as a reason for not paying, whether with good cause or otherwise. But the risk of such disputes is lessened where the costs are as expected.

There may be many cases where it is difficult to estimate costs accurately at the outset, but the lawyer should still provide the best estimate, and review the costs incurred against the estimate as matters progress. Lawyers acting for insurers are well used to this, as insurers are required by their regulators, and out of commercial prudence, to maintain reserves for anticipated expenditure on claims. It is also wise to inform the client when the next costs update will be provided.

It can be a useful exercise to keep a simple chart in a prominent place on the file, paper or electronic, tracking the costs incurred against the estimate, to provide a strong visual image and easy method of checking progress against budget. It can also be useful to monitor the accuracy of individual lawyers' costs estimates.

3.2   **The letter of engagement**

The letter of engagement is an important document. It will vary depending on the client, the type of work, the complexity of the instruction and the cost. For repeat business, it may be contained in a service level agreement or 'umbrella agreement'. There may be separate documents consisting of an engagement letter and terms of business, or they may be combined.

Ideally, the client would sign a copy of the letter and terms in every case to show that they had received them and agreed the terms. Practice varies. If it is impracticable to obtain a signed copy in every case, incorporating a provision that by continuing to instruct the firm, the client is deemed to have agreed to the terms will be helpful. It should identify who will carry out the work, who will supervise it and to whom the client may complain. Complaints procedures are a regulatory requirement in some jurisdictions, but even if they are not, it is better that the client has a clear route for raising concerns with the firm rather than taking their

---

11   http://eur-lex.europa.eu/LexUriServ/LexUriServ.do?uri=OJ:L:2011:304:0064:0088:en:PDF.

complaint, or their business, elsewhere. The complaint may, after all, be misconceived, and it may give the firm a chance to explain that, or it may provide an opportunity to put matters right and strengthen the relationship.

The letter of engagement should identify who is authorised on the client side to provide instructions. It should also make clear who may rely on the advice.

Government and institutional clients may seek to impose their own terms, sometimes referred to as 'Outside Counsel Guidelines'. These may seek to impose the clients' own ethical rules, including wider conflicts provision than applies under the general law and those of the lawyer's own regulator. Firms need to consider these carefully, as complying with them may present practical problems, particularly with conflict checking, and it is essential that there is central control on acceptance of such terms.

3.3 Limited retainers/unbundled legal services

A developing risk issue is that of clients who seek to reduce their expenditure on external lawyers by doing part of the work in-house, or by using a separate law firm or outsourcing provider that is not a law firm to provide specific aspects of the service, such as e-discovery (or e-disclosure) to deal with document-heavy matters.

The main risk is that a key issue will 'fall between two stools', with the client and the law firm each assuming that the other is dealing with a particular aspect. Clear project management with written allocation of tasks is needed to avoid this.

One of the authors acted for a large City of London law firm in a substantial multi-million-pound claim that arose from mergers and acquisitions work. The client was a major US-based multinational corporation with a small in-house legal team. It instructed the law firm to act on certain aspects of the purchase of the target company. The only significant asset of the company was its book debt which arose in a particular industry sector with some unusual characteristics.

There was evidence of an issue about whether the book debt was, as a matter of law, completely unenforceable. Both the client's in-house team and the law firm were immersed in the many issues which may arise on any acquisition and neither directed their minds adequately to the recoverability of the book debt.

In due course, after completion of the purchase, the difficulties in enforcing the book debt became clear. The inevitable claim ensued. Not only had the allocation of tasks been unclear, but the evidential trail of what instructions and advice had been given by each was poor, making defence of the claim almost impossible, though significant savings were made on the amount of the claim.

Another risk arises where the lawyer is not engaged in a complete transaction but is only producing an opinion on a particular issue. The client may seek to use the advice for some purpose other than that which the lawyer expects. Hence it is important to make clear the limited nature of the retainer and who may rely on it.

Outsourcing discovery (or disclosure) in litigation is a particular concern. The work may be done by a specialist company with paralegals who are not working under the lawyer's supervision. The lawyer, meanwhile, may be under a duty to the court as well as the client, and the risk of incomplete disclosure may fall on the lawyer.

4. Managing the client engagement

A carefully crafted letter of engagement specifying precisely the scope of the engagement will be to no avail if the lawyer then undertakes tasks which were not agreed. It is important therefore to monitor the scope of the engagement as the matter progresses and avoid 'engagement creep'. It is useful to keep a copy of the engagement letter readily to hand so that it may be reviewed regularly through the life cycle of the case.

Methods of communication with the client, whether through meetings, email or letter, should be agreed.

Communication with multiple clients needs care to ensure that the lawyer has effective instructions from them all. *Farrer v Copley Singletons*[12] was an English case where the firm acted on the purchase of a property by two couples, passing advice from time to time through one of the four individuals.

There were several problems with the title, including a public footpath across the front garden, a sewage disposal system under it used by several other properties, a difficulty over the boundaries, and a planning restriction which precluded the use of part of the property for bed-and-breakfast accommodation purposes.

These problems were communicated to one client, with whom the lawyers largely dealt, but not to the others. The lawyers were found liable for not communicating the problems to all the clients.

The strategy agreed with the client at the outset should be kept under constant review.

The risk that the lawyer, when instructed on one task, may, during the course of the retainer, identify that the client has another problem needing attention cannot be excluded. The lawyer may not be under a duty to carry out the additional task without client agreement, including terms as to the cost of undertaking it, but there may be a duty to warn.

In the English case of *Credit Lyonnais SA v Russell Jones & Walker*[13] the lawyer was retained to advise on the exercise of a break clause terminating a lease, and failed to advise that the payment required under the break clause was a condition precedent and that it was time critical. The claimant lost the opportunity to exercise the break clause and had to negotiate its way out of the lease on the best terms available. The judge was struck by the analogy relied on by the claimant's counsel:

If a dentist is asked to treat a patient's tooth and, on looking into the latter's mouth, he notices that an adjacent tooth is in need of treatment, it is his duty to warn the patient accordingly. So too, if in the course of carrying out instructions within his area of competence a lawyer notices or ought to notice a problem or risk for the client of which it is reasonable to assume the client may not be aware, the lawyer must warn him.

5. Dealing with weak claims

Lawyers may identify at the outset that a potential client's case has poor prospects of

---

12 [1998] PNLR 22.
13 [2002] EWHC 1310 (Ch).

success. In that event it is important to make clear in writing to the potential clients that they do not wish to accept the instructions.

Consideration should also be given to warning the potential claimant that there are time limits for bringing proceedings, although it may not be possible to identify with certainty when the time limit expires on the first meeting because the client may have given the wrong accident date, for example, which can only be ascertained on examining the evidence, such as medical records, or the client may for some reason be entitled to claim an extended time limit, depending on the applicable law.

Some lawyers find it difficult to tell a client that they do not have a good case, yet they are only storing up problems for the future that are better addressed at the outset. On a purely practical level, a realistic warning as to the likely cost of litigation can temper the enthusiasm of potential clients who may initially feel they have a point of principle to establish.

6. **General files**

General retainers, under which the lawyer provides advice from time to time on a variety of topics, may be hazardous for many reasons: the scope of the engagement, may not be agreed (though it could be done as each issue arises), costs may not be addressed properly, and, most importantly, it may mean that normal procedures for new client or matter inception, such as anti-money laundering and conflict checks, are not carried out. Some firms prohibit general retainers completely, others require a new matter to be opened annually and some may impose limits on what can be done under a general retainer, for example no transactional advice and no matter requiring more than an hour's advice. It is a matter for firms to consider based on their own experience and client base.

7. **Dealing with unrepresented third parties**

Unrepresented third parties are problematic for lawyers. Lawyers may be reluctant to appear unhelpful, and a judge may criticise them if they are unhelpful, but they have to tread a fine line between acting in the best interests of their clients and not assuming duties to the third party. It is also necessary to ensure that there is no perception that the lawyer is taking advantage of the unrepresented party.

8. **Duties to non-clients**

Duties to non-clients have been established in a number of cases in England and are increasingly being asserted in the courts of the United States. In England, for example, it has been held that duties are owed to the beneficiaries of a testator's estate when the lawyer has drafted a will negligently and in breach of the testator's instructions.[14]

More difficult are the cases where an opposing party may assert a duty. In the English courts, it has been held to be arguable that a duty exists where the lawyer has made a representation to an opponent and, in so doing, assumed a duty of care. An example would be replies to enquiries before contract in a conveyancing matter,

---

14   *White v Jones* [1995] 2 AC 207.

where the replies were those of the seller's solicitor rather than the solicitor's client.[15]

In India, Part VI Chapter II of the Bar Council of India Rules lays down Standards of Professional Conduct and Etiquette, which is divided into four sections dealing with the duties of an advocate towards the court; the client; an opponent; and colleagues. Advocates are required to comply with these prescribed duties, even in relation to non-clients.

9. **The dangers of volume work**

Volume work can give rise to particular problems. A lawyer may think he or she has established an efficient process for dealing with a particular category of work. However, if there is a defect in the process, it will be replicated across the entire book of business.

Examples are legion, and have resulted in mass litigation against law firms. The oft-cited case of *Investors Compensation Scheme Ltd v West Bromwich Building Society*[16] arose from disastrous financial products secured by mortgages on clients' homes, sold to mainly elderly investors. The products were missold by financial advisers, but the mortgage work was undertaken by solicitors. The financial advisers were uninsured, and the Investors Compensation Scheme, an industry body set up to compensate in such cases, brought recovery action against the law firms. Many were defended successfully at trial, but the judge found that one firm had given inadequate advice in its standard letters, which were replicated across thousands of cases.[17]

There have also been similar cases arising from personal injury litigation and other areas of practice.

10. **High-value matters**

In theory, the issues arising on high-value matters are no different from any others. However, where the stakes are higher, the risk to the firm is much greater, particularly if a successful claim were to exceed the firm's insurance cover, or make it difficult for the firm to take up insurance in future.

It is sensible, therefore, to have procedures in place to identify such matters. It may be appropriate to involve the firm's management in the decision to act. Additional supervision should be put in place to protect the interests of the firm.

It is often assumed that additional professional indemnity insurance can be put in place for the one-off, high-value instruction, but this is not generally the case. Insurers want a basket of risks, not adverse selection. Even if insurance were available, in most jurisdictions it is written on a 'claims made' basis, so it would be necessary to incur the annual cost of maintaining the additional cover for many years.

---

15 See *Wilson v Bloomfield* (1979) 123 Sol Jo 860, CA and *First National Commercial Bank v Loxleys* [1997] PNLR 211, CA.
16 [1997] UKHL 28.
17 See the judgment at first instance for the facts: *Investors Compensation Scheme Ltd v West Bromwich Building Society* [1999] Lloyd's Rep PN 496.

11. **The wider interest and duties to the public, creditors and others**
    Lawyers owe duties to uphold the rule of law, which will generally take precedence over the duty to act in the best interests of clients. It is important therefore to be alert to clients who may be seeking to use the lawyer to pursue an unlawful purpose, which may in some cases carry the risk of involvement in money laundering or risk bringing the profession into disrepute, for example where the client is seeking to take unfair advantage of vulnerable third parties.

12. **Managing files across international offices – ensuring local compliance**
    Firms with cross-border practices may be instructed to handle matters from more than one office. They need to be aware that the lawyers in each jurisdiction may be subject to different conduct rules, and this is particularly so with conflicts of interest, where the firm may be permitted to act in one jurisdiction but prohibited in another.

    Complex international firm structures may mean that the offices are different legal entities. It is therefore important to ensure that the client has consented to sharing confidential information with another legal entity.

13. **Checklist**
    The following points relating to the management of the client engagement should be considered in order to mitigate risks:
    - Are both the lawyer and the client clear about what the client wants?
    - Have the client's expectations about the likelihood of achieving a successful outcome been managed appropriately? Recognising that mismanagement of a client's expectations about what is possible can sometimes create a perception that the lawyer is at fault and means that the lawyer's opinion should be well documented.
    - Is there evidence of communications with the client in order to demonstrate what advice was given, why certain actions were taken etc?
    - Has there been an adequate consideration of the firm's competence to provide the services requested by the client?
    - Is it necessary to impose limitations on the scope of the retainer and have these been adequately documented?
    - Is the scope of the retainer clearly expressed?
    - Has the client been correctly identified?
    - Have any high-risk scenarios been identified? For example, the risks attached to acting for a client where there may be capacity issues, or purportedly acting for joint clients but only receiving instructions from one?
    - Have steps been taken to ascertain that the firm is not being duped, either through a retainer with an individual purporting to be someone else or through working with a cloned law firm?
    - In commercial transactions have steps been taken to ensure that the client has been correctly identified and to be satisfied that the person giving instructions has authority to do so?
    - Have all possible conflicts of interest – legal, regulatory and commercial – been identified?

- Are costs clearly evidenced?
- Where it is necessary to provide an estimate, has this been set realistically and is it kept under review as the matter progresses?
- When working on a matter with a third party – perhaps the client's in-house legal team – are the respective roles clearly identified and checked to ensure that there are no gaps in coverage?
- Are client engagement procedures applied thoroughly when acting on matters on a general file or when the same client regularly instructs the firm?
- Have non-clients been identified and risks relating to that relationship been documented?
- Have high-value and/or high-volume matters been identified and appropriate risk measures implemented?
- Have procedures been agreed when a client's matter requires international or cross-border attention?

Data protection and privacy in the United States

Steven M Puiszis
Hinshaw & Culbertson LLP

1. **Introduction**

Data protection has gained immense importance. It used to be something no one really looked into, bar some specialists. Nowadays it is at the core of risk management.

Although data are genuine global players, data protection is not, and it seems rather unlikely that we will ever achieve something like global data protection. Hence, we look at data protection issues from the US perspective and the following chapter examines the European perspective. Of course this does not provide a complete picture. The purpose of this chapter is to shed light on some of the most important issues, and to raise awareness. Data protection rules can be a nuisance, in global firms in particular, but neglecting them is fatal.

Law firms are regularly entrusted with some of their clients' most sensitive and valuable information. Clients expect their lawyers to protect the information they provide.

The global technology revolution has complicated the statutory and ethical duties owed by a lawyer to protect information provided by a client. Rapidly evolving technology provides the means to bypass locked doors and filing cabinets and can be readily used to circumvent traditional methods to protect confidential communications between a lawyer and the client. Thus, data protection today presents a far more complex and difficult problem for law firms than ever before.

Large-scale data breaches are becoming more frequent, and it is clear that law firms have become a popular target of hackers.[1] While data breaches resulting from malicious hackers have grabbed headlines, more data breaches are the result of human error, lost or stolen mobile devices, bad disposal practices and computer glitches than the work of hackers.[2]

Data protection and cyber security are related risk management concepts for law firms. Both encompass protecting confidential information. Cyber security, however, has a more targeted focus and addresses how confidential or sensitive information can be compromised through the use of technology. Data protection strategies must address a broader range of risks.

---

[1] Mandiant, a cyber-security firm, estimated that in 2011 at least 80 major law firms in the United States had been hacked. See Michael Riley and Sophia Person, China-based hackers target law firms to get secret deal data, Bloomberg, January 31 2012, available at www.bloomberg.com/news/2012-01-31/China-based-hackers-target-law-firms.html.

[2] Ponemon Institute, 2013 Cost of Data Breach Study: Global Analysis, at 7, available at www4.symantec.com/mktginfo/whitepaper/053013_GL_NA_WP_Ponemon-2013-Cost-of-a-Data-Breach-Report_daiNA_cta72382.pdf.

There is no one-size-fits-all approach to how law firms protect data. Variables such as a law firm's size, its geographic footprint, office structure, practice areas, technological sophistication and available resources are all factors that influence a law firm's approach to protecting its data. Today, data protection has long-term strategic implications for law firms around the globe. Clients, especially those in regulated industries such as banking and healthcare, are increasingly inquiring about the security measures a law firm takes to protect their data and, as part of their compliance programmes, are requiring that various data security measures are employed by their law firms.[3] Law firms that cannot meet or at least commit to satisfying a client's data protection requirements will lose future engagements to law firms that can meet those requirements. Thus, law firms should view data protection from a strategic perspective.

2. Overview of the US approach to data privacy

Unlike the comprehensive approach to data privacy adopted in the European Union through the EU Data Protection Directive (95/46/EC[2]),[4] there is no one federal law or regulation in the United States that broadly protects the privacy of sensitive personal information. The United States has taken what some have described as a sectoral approach to data privacy and protection. Various federal statutes, and accompanying regulations, involving the healthcare[5] and financial services industries[6] attempt to broadly protect personally identifying, medical[7] and financial information. Under the authority of the Fair and Accurate Credit Transactions Act of 2003 (FACTA),[8] the Federal Trade Commission promulgated its Red Flags Rule,[9] which also requires certain financial institutions and creditors to develop a written identity-theft programme aimed at detecting, preventing and mitigating the risk of identity theft.

The Privacy Act of 1974[10] applies to the collection, use and dissemination of any

---

3   Matthew Goldstein, Law Firms Pressed on Security for Data, The New York Times, March 26 2014, available at http://dealbook.nytimes.com/2014/03/26/law-firms-scrutinized-as-hacking-increases/?_php=true&_type= blogs &_r=0.
4   Directive 95/46/EC of the European Parliament and of the Council of October 24 1995 on the Protection of Individuals with Regard to the Processing of Personal Data and on the Free Movement of Such Data, 1995 OJ (l.281) §VIII Art 17.1, available at http://eurlex.europe.eu/LexUriServ.do?uri=CELEX: 31995L0046:en:HTML.
5   In 1996 Congress enacted the Health Insurance Portability and Accountability Act (HIPAA), Pub L 104-91, August 21 1996, 110 Stat 1936, which set a federal privacy floor for personally identifying information in health records. Subsequently, in 2009 Congress adopted the Health Information Technology for Economic and Clinical Health Act (HITECH Act), Pub L 111-5, Div A, Title XIII, Div B, Title IV, 123 Stat 226, 447, which among other things, extended the HIPAA obligations of physicians, hospitals, group health plans and other covered entities to protect protected health information (PHI) to business associates. The HITECH Act's final regulations were published in January 2013 as the HIPAA Omnibus Final Rule in (Omnibus Rule). Business Associates were given until September 23 2013 to comply with the Omnibus Rule. A law firm that receives, transmits, uses or maintains PHI in the course of providing legal services to a covered entity or another business associate generally qualifies as a business associate under HIPAA and must comply with its applicable privacy and security requirements.
6   See Gramm-Leach-Bliley Act (GLB Act), Pub L 106-102, 113 Stat 1338. The GLB Act's Privacy Rule encompasses many businesses not typically considered financial institutions.
7   HIPAA's Privacy Rule protects all individually identifiable health information in any form, whether electronic, paper or oral. This is commonly referred to as PHI.
8   15 USC §1681m(e).
9   16 CFR §681.1.
10 5 USC § 552.a.

item, collection or grouping of information about an individual[11] maintained by certain federal agencies in a "system of records".[12] The Act prohibits the disclosure of information encompassed by the Act unless written consent of the individual is obtained or the disclosure falls within one of twelve exceptions. The Driver's Privacy Protection Act (DPPA) requires states to protect the privacy of personal information in an individual's state motor vehicle records.[13] The Children's Online Privacy Protection Act (COPPA) attempts to protect the privacy of children under the age of 13 by, among other things, requiring parental consent for the collection of any personal information by websites or their operators.[14]

Data security standards for the protection of credit-card information that globally apply to all merchants or organisations that store, possess or transmit cardholder data have been promulgated by the payment card industry.[15] Compliance with these standards is no panacea or guarantee, however, as the Target Corporation data breach in 2013 amply demonstrates.

A hodgepodge of state laws also protects discrete categories of personal information such as social security numbers,[16] credit card information,[17] biometric data[18] and genetic testing.[19] Additionally, 47 states, the District of Columbia, Puerto Rico, Guam and the Virgin Islands have enacted data-breach laws, which require that individuals be notified when unauthorised access to unencrypted computerised data that contain personally identifying information about them has occurred.[20] Law firms with offices in one of these states are subject to its data-breach law. Additionally, approximately 30 states have laws addressing the disposal of paper or electronic records containing personal information.[21]

---

11 5 USC § 552a(2) (defining an individual as a US citizen or an alien lawfully admitted for permanent residence).
12 *Ibid* at § 552a(a)(5) (defining a system of records as a group of records from which information can be retrieved by a person's name or individual identifier).
13 18 USC § 2271, *et seq*. The information protected includes an individual's name, address, phone number, driver's licence and social security numbers, photographs, as well as medical and disability information.
14 15 USC § 6501, *et seq*. COPPA prohibits the collection of children's names, home and email addresses, telephone and social security numbers, and any other personal identifiers about a child or the child's parents including IP addresses.
15 See Payment Card Security Standards Council, available at www.pcisecuirtystandards.org. The Payment Card Industry (PCI) security standards include a data security standard applicable to any entity that stores, processes or transmits data (PCI-DSS); personal identification number (PIN) entry device security requirements applicable to entities that specify or develop device characteristics or manage PIN entry terminals (PCI-PIN); and a payment application data security standard (PA-DSS), applicable to software developers, sellers and users of applications that store, process or transmit cardholder data.
16 While there are significant variations between them, the laws of most states in the United States prohibit publicly posting or displaying a person's social security number.
17 Nev Rev Stat Ch 603A.215 (Nevada); Minn Stat Ch 325E.64 (Minnesota); RCWA Ch 19.255 (Washington).
18 See, for example, Illinois Biometric Information Privacy Act, 740 ILCS 14/1, *et seq*.; Texas Business and Commerce Code, Chapter 503 (requiring informed consent for collecting and disclosing biometric data, defined as "a retina or iris scan, fingerprint, voice print, or record of hand or face geometry").
19 See National Conference of State Legislatures, Genetic Privacy Laws, available at www.ncsl.org/research/health/genetic-privacy-laws.aspx.
20 See National Conference of State Legislatures, State Security Breach Notification Laws, available at www.ncsl.org/research/telecommunications-and-information-technology/security-breach-notification-laws.aspx.
21 For a list of state data disposal laws with links to each state's law go to: www.ncsl.org/research/telecommunications-and-information-technology/data-disposal-laws.aspx. These laws generally require the records to be shredded or erased or that personal information be redacted before they are disposed. Violations of these laws can trigger civil penalties. A full discussion of these data disposal laws is beyond the scope of this chapter.

The concept of what constitutes personally identifying information protected under these states laws is generally not nearly as broad as the concept defined in the EU.[22]

In the United States, these various state and federal laws and regulations apply to law firms' clients. Several, however, also directly impose obligations on law firms operating in the United States, including the obligation to report a data breach. While many of these statutes and regulations involve a system of self-reporting, several, such as HIPAA and GLBA, authorise audits for compliance and the imposition of potentially significant fines for non-compliance. Additionally, several state data-breach laws increase the fine or penalty that can be imposed if the report of a data breach is delayed. Accordingly, it is important for law firm general counsel or compliance counsel to be familiar with these laws and their reporting requirements.

Superimposed on this patchwork of laws and regulations are the ethical obligations imposed by state rules of professional conduct that require lawyers and law firms in the United States to maintain the confidentiality of information provided to them by their clients and to safeguard any property with which they have been entrusted. A lawyer's duty of competence under the Model Rules of Professional Conduct requires that "reasonable efforts" are taken "to prevent the inadvertent or unauthorized disclosure of, or unauthorized access to information relating to the representation of a client".[23] Factors to consider in assessing whether reasonable efforts were taken to protect information from inadvertent unauthorised disclosure or access include:

- the sensitivity of the information;
- the likelihood of disclosure if additional safeguards are not taken;
- the cost of employing additional safeguards;
- the difficulty of implementing the safeguards;
- the extent to which the safeguards adversely affect a lawyer's ability to represent a client;
- whether the client required special security measures to be taken or provided informed consent to forego security measures that might be required under this rule.[24]

Additionally, Rule 1.15 of the Model Rules requires a lawyer to adequately safeguard a client's property, and the comments to Rule 1.15 explain that a lawyer "should hold property of others with the care required of a professional fiduciary".[25] Against this backdrop, the remaining sections of this part of the chapter take a closer review of the statutes and regulations that provide the primary protection for data and informational privacy in the United States.

---

22   Article 8 of the EU Data Protection Directive 95/46/EC includes "special categories" of information defined as "personal data revealing . . . political opinions, religious or physical beliefs, trade-union membership".
23   Model Rule 1.6(c).
24   Comment 18 to ABA Model Rule 1.6.
25   Comment 1 to ABA Model Rule 1.15.

3. **Gramm–Leach–Bliley Act 1999**

Section 501 of the Gramm–Leach–Bliley (GLB) Act requires "financial institutions" to protect the integrity, security and confidentiality of non-public information about "consumers" and "customers". Federal banking agencies are required to establish consistent regulatory standards that financial institutions must implement to protect the security and confidentiality of customer records and information against unauthorised access or use. Lawyers and law firms engaged in the practice of law, however, are not subject to the GLB Act's requirements.[26] However, to the extent that lawyers and law firms become custodians of information in connection with engagements for clients that are subject to the regulations, the clients are increasingly insisting that their lawyers treat that information with the same degree of protection as is required by the regulators of the clients themselves.

4. **Health Insurance Portability and Accountability Act**

The Health Insurance Portability and Accountability Act (HIPAA) of 1996[27] addresses the privacy and security of personally identifiable health information (PHI). As required by the statute, the US Department of Health & Human Services (HHS) published regulations that are commonly known as the HIPAA Privacy Rule and Security Rule protecting the privacy and security of certain health information.

The HIPAA Privacy Rule establishes federal requirements for the protection for PHI held by covered entities and their business associates, and provides patients with a number of rights with respect to that information. BAs can be held directly liable for failing to comply with HIPAA and include lawyers and law firms whenever they receive information required to be protected under the regulations.

HIPAA defines a business associate as an entity or a person who is not a member of a covered entity's workforce, who either:

- creates, receives, maintains or transmits PHI; or
- performs functions or activities on behalf of a covered entity, or provides services for a covered entity that involves the access, use, or disclosure of PHI that is received from the covered entity, or another business associate of the covered entity.[28]

Thus, a law firm that receives, transmits, uses, discloses or maintains PHI from a covered entity or business associate, in the course of providing legal services for that covered entity or business associate qualifies as a business associate under HIPAA. As a result, when a law firm represents a covered entity or business associate, and that representation involves the use of PHI received from that covered entity or business associate, the law firm must comply with HIPAA's privacy and security requirements.

In many ways, HIPAA's privacy and security requirements for PHI mirror the approach taken under the GLB Act to protect the privacy and security of non-public

---

26 See *American Bar Association v FTC*, 430 F.3d 457 (DC Cir 2005).
27 Pub L 104-91, August 21, 1996, 110 Stat 1936, codified at 42 USC §§ 300gg, 29 USC § 1181, and 42 USC § 1320d, *et seq*.
28 *Ibid*.

financial information. HIPAA also has a Breach Notification Rule,[29] which requires covered entities and business associates to provide notice following a breach of unsecured ePHI. Additionally, business associates, including law firms, must appoint a security official who is responsible for the development of written policies and procedure required by HIPAA's Security Rule.[30]

4.1   HIPAA's Security Rule

HIPAA's Security Rule contains administrative, physical and technical safeguards to ensure the confidentiality, integrity, security and proper access to ePHI. HIPAA's Security Rule requires measures to guard against the unauthorised access to ePHI when it is electronically transmitted.[31] Generally, this is accomplished through email encryption, but if a covered entity or business associate determines that email encryption cannot be reasonably accomplished, it must document that determination and implement an alternative measure to protect the transmission of ePHI.

4.2   HIPAA's Breach Notification Rule

HIPAA's Breach Notification Rule[32] requires that covered entities and business associates provide appropriate notification following a breach of "unsecured" PHI. Unsecured protected health information is defined as PHI that has not been rendered "unusable, unreadable, or indecipherable to unauthorized persons through the use of technology or other methodologies".[33]

A breach is defined as an impermissible use or disclosure of PHI that compromises the security or privacy of that PHI.

Both covered entities and business associates must provide notice of a breach to the affected individuals, the Secretary of HHS and in certain instances to the media. Business associates must also notify a covered entity of the breach.

The failure to comply with HIPAA's Privacy, Security and Breach Notification Rules can result in the imposition of civil and criminal penalties.

5.   Payment card industry standards

The payment card industry (PCI) has developed a data security standard (PCI-DSS) to serve as a set of baseline requirements for protecting cardholder data. The PCI-DSS applies globally to any entity involved in the processing of payment card information. This standard also applies to any other entity that stores, processes or transmits cardholder or authentication information.

6.   State data breach laws

While there are many common elements to the state data breach laws in the United

---

29 See 45 CFR §§ 164.400-414.
30 45 CCFR § 164.308(a)(2). Covered entities are obligated to also name a person responsible for developing privacy policies and procedures. See 45 CFR § 164.530(a).
31 45 CFR § 164.312(e).
32 45 CFR §§ 164.400-414.
33 45 CFR § 164.402.

States, there are also significant variations between them. So it is critical to carefully review the law in a given state.[34]

Generally, state data breach laws are directed at unencrypted computerised data that include personally identifying information.[35] Typically, these laws apply to persons or entities that own or license the data and conduct business in the forum state.[36] However, they also apply to companies that maintain or control personal information owned by others.[37] These statutes are generally triggered upon the discovery of a breach or when the entity has been notified that a breach has occurred.

A breach requiring that notice be provided is generally defined as the unauthorised acquisition or access to unencrypted personal information that compromises the security, confidentiality or integrity of the personal information.[38] Personal information is typically defined as a person's first name or initial and last name, coupled with one or more of the following: the person's social security number, driver's licence number or other state identification number, financial account number, credit or debit account number in combination with any required security code, access code or password that would permit access to a financial account. Several states include biometric data[39] in the definition of personal information, as well as certain types of health insurance information such as policy or subscriber numbers, or information in the person's application or claims history.

When notice is required, typically it must be provided in writing to the affected persons in the most expedient manner possible and without unreasonable delay.

Some states permit an enforcement action by the State Attorney General for the violation of its data breach statute.[40] Actual damages and a civil penalty may be sought by the Attorney General in an enforcement action.[41] Various states have included a penalty provision in their law for failing to comply with the notification requirements.[42] Several calculate the penalty by the length of the delay in providing notice.

---

34 Currently, only, Alabama, New Mexico and South Dakota have no data breach notification law. For a link to the data breach laws in the other 47 remaining states, the District of Columbia, Guam and Puerto Rico go to: www.ncsl.org/research/telecommunications-and-information-technology/security-breach-notification-laws.aspx. The footnotes in this section of the chapter are only intended to provide representative examples and are not intended to be a list of every state law with a particular data breach requirement.
35 Ariz Rev. Stat Tit 44, Ch 32, 44-7501(a) [Arizona]; Col Rev Stat Tit 6, art. 1 § 6-1-716 [Colorado]. Several states, however, also require notice when the breach involves personal information in paper records. Alaska Stat Tit 45, Ch 48 § 10 et seq [Alaska]; SC Code Ann § 39-1-90 [South Carolina]; Ind Code § 24-4.9 et seq. [Indiana].
36 Conn Gen Stat. 36a-701(b) [Connecticut]; Tex Bus & Com. Code § 521.03 [Texas].
37 Ill. Comp Stat 815 ILCS 530/1 et seq [Illinois]; Iowa Code, §§ 715C.1 [Iowa]. The Kentucky data breach law applies to information holders. HB 232 (eff. July 1 2014) [Kentucky].
38 Illinois; California; Colorado; Connecticut; NY Gen Bus Law § 899-aa [New York].
39 Neb Rev Stat, §§ 87-801 et seq; Iowa; Texas.
40 Arizona; Iowa; Texas.
41 Arizona (actual damages and a civil penalty not to exceed $10,000 per breath); Del C, Tit 6, Ch 12B, §101 et seq [Delaware] (appropriate penalties and damages); Massachusetts (civil penalty of $5,000 for each violation); Michigan Comp Law § 445.72 (civil penalty of up to $250 for each failure to provide notice with a limit of $750,000 per breach); New York (civil penalties of the greater of $5,000 or up to $10,000 for each failure to notify capped at $150,000); Or Rev Stat § 646 A. 600 et seq [Oregon] (penalty $1,000 per violation with each day a separate violation with maximum penalty of $500,000).
42 Arizona, for instance, provides for a civil penalty not to exceed $10,000 per breach.

7. Data protection principles

Information security requires an organisation to determine the types of information in its possession, where that information is stored and the format in which it is held. A law firm should assess the sensitivity of that information and carefully evaluate how access to that information can be obtained. With that basic information, a risk assessment can be performed that considers foreseeable internal and external risks and threats to the firm's information, the likelihood that those threats could occur, and the resulting harm. A law firm should implement reasonable and appropriate security measures in light of that threat assessment. They should consider heightened or additional security measures for highly sensitive data. A law firm's security measures should also take into consideration the security requirements of any laws or regulations applicable to the types of information in its possession, and any specific security requirements of the client. Because security threats are not static, law firms should view data protection as an evolving process and should periodically reevaluate their security measures and take into consideration new risks and threats.

While reasonable and appropriate data security measures are no guarantee against a data breach, they are an important element of a law firm's risk management programme in light of the potential harm and damage that can result from a data breach. A data breach can cause reputational harm and the potential loss of clients. It can also result in potentially significant compliance and notification costs, as well as administrative fines and penalties. Lawsuits filed against organisations failing to take reasonable and appropriate measures to secure their information are becoming commonplace.

To protect confidential information, irrespective of its format, law firms should consider a layered approach to security. At a base level, it begins with an evaluation of the physical security of any location or facility where sensitive or confidential information is located. It is critical that a law firm physically protects its facilities, equipment and the information in its possession from unauthorised physical access, tampering or theft. A failure to do so effectively will cause any security measures to ultimately fail.

Visitors to the firm should be accompanied at all times and their access limited to specific areas within the firm for specific purposes.

Physically controlling information inside the firm's walls is also critical. Lawyers should not leave sensitive and confidential information unattended where it could be viewed by a visitor, cleaning staff or contractors working in the firm. A firm should consider adopting a requirement that confidential information is always put away when it is not actively being used, and depending on the sensitivity of the information, it should be secured in a locked room with controlled access.

Strong controls should be developed that limit those who can access electronic information on the firm's network. This should include unique user identification procedures, which validate a user's identity before granting access to the firm's information or email systems. The use of strong passwords that are frequently changed are also necessary. Security rules should prohibit the sharing of passwords, storing them in clear text files on a computer, or writing passwords down and leaving them where they can be easily found.

Access to information should be on a need-to-use or least privilege basis. Law firms should limit access to confidential or sensitive electronic information to only those lawyers or staff who need it to complete their work. Firms should consider limiting access to sensitive information such as PHI at the file opening stage and build ethical walls for any engagement that will allow electronic access only to those lawyers or staff who need to access that information for the engagement.

Law firms should also have a process in place to immediately terminate access to its network and all information systems for any lawyer or employee who resigns or is dismissed by the firm. Whenever an employee changes departments or a lawyer changes practice groups, the firm should consider whether that person's access rights should be changed or modified in light of his or her new position or practice area.

To the extent possible, law firms should limit electronic access between the firm's network or any information system and any of its contractors or business partners. This will help limit the risk that remote access to the firm's network can be obtained by third parties successfully hacking into the system.

Another layer of security involves the segregation of duties and the development of clearly defined responsibilities for all employees. No single person should be able to modify any of the firm's network security features.

Protecting against the risk of a malicious insider is another security consideration. All new lawyers and partners should undergo a careful vetting process that includes a background check to determine if the prospective lawyer has ever been convicted, declared bankrupt, or had any lawsuits or disciplinary actions filed against him or her. A law firm should also consider having all employees and contractors that have physical access to the firm sign non-disclosure agreements.

Records and data should be kept no longer than necessary. Firms should develop a record retention schedule and develop procedures to retain information in accordance with that schedule. Any remaining records should ultimately be disposed of in a secure fashion.

Data protection requires careful and proper disposal of client records. Paper records should be shredded and electronic records should be erased or rendered unreadable. The proper disposal of any equipment such as copiers or fax machines that store electronic information should include memory erasure before being sold or returned. The same steps should be taken for mobile devices before they are sold or reused by the firm or its lawyers.

If a law firm supplies mobile devices (eg, smart phones or tablets) to its lawyers and employees, the firm should limit the use of those devices to firm business and prohibit the downloading of any applications that are not approved by the firm. A surprising number of mobile device applications contain malware or malicious code.

A firm that adopts a bring-your-own-device (BYOD) policy has less control over mobile devices, but can impose requirements on their safe use as a condition of granting access to the firm's email or information systems. A law firm should consider using a mobile device management system that keeps work and personal email separated. Additionally, law firms should have rules and policies on the use of public clouds. This should include prohibiting lawyers or staff from backing up sensitive or confidential information to a public cloud or their home computers.

Firms should also address the use of applications like Dropbox or Google Docs that routinely store information outside the firm's control in public clouds.

Law firms should also consider the use of web filters to warn or block access to various websites via firm computers. Web filtering tools develop lists of websites that have downloaded malware or suspicious code.

Information can be lost or stolen and malware can be loaded onto a firm's networks through the careless use of flash drives. Controlling the use of flash drives is a security measure that should also be considered by law firms. Encryption should be used to the fullest extent feasible or practical. Encrypting the hard drives of laptop computers and mobile devices protect information stored on them should they be lost or stolen. Email containing sensitive or confidential information transmitted over public networks should be encrypted whenever possible. The use of unsecure public Wi-Fi hot spots presents a major hacking risk that should be avoided by a firm's lawyers.

The use of properly configured firewalls, installing and regularly updating antivirus software, and the prompt application of security patches from vendors are critical features of a secure network. Law firms should also consider the use of applications that monitor its network and intrusion detection applications that scan the network for anomalies. A law firm should also consider periodically testing its physical and electronic security measures and evaluate those measures in light of those test results.

While technology can provide a perimeter defence, even the best technological solutions can be compromised by employees who deliberately ignore or unintentionally bypass a law firm's security measures. Accordingly, training all lawyers and staff is a key element of any security programme. Security awareness training which, among other things, addresses requests to borrow passwords and other suspicious behaviour by colleagues, and trains lawyers and staff to recognise spear phishing techniques which involve emails that appear to be from a trusted source, is an important feature of a law firm's security programme. Lawyers and staff should be trained to report the inappropriate use of the firm's equipment or its information systems, suspicious incidents or requests, and potential data breaches to appropriate individual(s) at the firm.

A firm's security programme should include a statement that the violation of the firm's security procedures and rules can result in discipline up to and including dismissal. That rule should be consistently applied and enforced in order for the security programme to be effective.

Data protection and privacy in Europe

Silvia C Bauer
Silke Gottschalk
Luther

1. **Introduction**

In Europe the right to privacy is highly developed and part of the EU privacy and human rights law. Basically, everybody has the right to decide for themselves if and for what purpose their personal data will be collected, processed or used. The objective of the privacy law is to protect the persons concerned (data subjects) against infringement of their right of privacy as the result of the handling of their data.

In 1995 the European Commission created the European Data Protection Directive 95/46/EC, which regulates the conditions for the collection, processing and use of personal data within the European Union. It has been implemented in the national laws of all EU member states.

In January 2012 the European Commission decided to replace the Directive with a new European Data Protection Regulation (the Regulation) in order to harmonise the different national data protection laws. As a regulation it will be directly applicable to all EU member states without a need for national implementing legislation. The drafts of the Regulation are highly disputed so it is not expected to come into force before 2015.

Currently, companies such as those based in the United States and processing personal data in an EU member state have to comply with the applicable national legislation of each member state. If they process data in different member states, they have to comply with the different laws. Even if the national laws are quite similar, companies need to check if country-specific rules have to be observed.

At the moment offences for example in Germany may attract fines up to €300,000. In future, according to the new European Regulation, illegal processing of data will be sanctioned with fines of up to 5% of a company's global turnover or €100 million. Therefore, for companies or law firms doing business in Europe, it is highly recommended to comply with the applicable law.

2. **Basics of the collection, processing and use of personal data**

Article 2a of the Directive defines personal data as:

any information relating to an identified or identifiable natural person ("Data Subject"); an identifiable person is one who can be identified, directly or indirectly, in particular by reference to an identification number or to one or more factors specific to his physical, physiological, mental, economic, cultural or social identity

As a consequence, any information related to a data subject is considered as personal data. This includes, for example, personal data of clients or employees, such as name, address, credit card numbers or email addresses.

The company, law firm, public authority or any other body that alone or jointly with others determines the purposes and means of the processing of personal data is considered as the controller. Every legally independent body is considered as a controller. Even if it is part of a (company) group each of them is considered as a single controller.

Each controller is responsible for the lawfulness of the collection, processing, transfer or usage (together referred to as processing) of the personal data. Processing of personal data includes its recording, alteration, transfer, blocking and erasure.

2.1 Basic principles: data avoidance, specific purposes, transparency

Only personal data that are necessary should be processed. It should be considered carefully whether the personal data in question are indeed needed by the controller or by a party to whom data are transferred. If possible, personal data should be anonymised or processed using a pseudonym.

Furthermore, at the time of collecting personal data, the purpose for which they are processed has to be determined. Changes of purpose are only allowed in specific cases (eg, overriding justified interests of the controller). A purpose could be the contractual relationship with a client or an employment contract with an employee.

If the personal data are no longer needed for the purpose for which they have been collected and/or there is no other legal ground available (eg, a necessity to archive personal data on the basis of tax provisions), they must be deleted.

The data subject has to be informed of the purposes for which personal data are processed, and of the recipients of the personal data. Usually, the information is given in a data privacy policy, in general terms and conditions or in the contract concluded with the data subject. Only if the data subject receives knowledge by other means or if the controller can expect the data subject to know the purpose for which the personal data are used is it not necessary to inform him.

Furthermore, the data subject has several information rights (eg, which data are stored and for which purposes) and the right to demand the rectification, deletion or blocking of personal data that are incomplete, inaccurate or are not being processed in compliance with the applicable data protection law.

2.2 Legal grounds: data protection law and consent

Any collection, processing or use of personal data is only lawful if a statutory legal basis is available or the data subject has given his explicit consent.

In Europe, the processing of personal data is usually allowed by the law (a) if it is used for the contractual purposes for which it has been provided, or (b) if the collecting party has a justified interest in processing the data and the affected data subject does not have an overriding legitimate interest in preventing such use.

As a consequence, the use of a client's personal data during the term of a contractual relationship with a client is allowed by the law. Hence, it should be considered carefully whether the use or the transfer of the data is indeed necessary for the contractual relationship. The use of personal data for marketing purposes (eg, newsletters, cold calls, invitations to events) is only allowed under specific conditions. Furthermore, a transfer from one controller to another controller requires a legal basis – even if they are part of a group of companies.

If there is no applicable statutory provision available, the consent of the data subject has to be obtained. A valid consent requires a free decision on the part of the data subject, who always has the right to withdraw consent. Furthermore, the declaration of consent itself has to state clearly for which purpose the personal data will be processed. If the consent is part of a text (eg, a job arrangement) it has to be highlighted. Best practice is to ask for a separate signature as proof of an explicit consent.

2.3 Data processing on behalf

If a controller (eg, a law firm) employs a data processor such as an IT service provider or a marketing agency to process the controller's personal data under the controller's responsibility this is considered as data processing on behalf. The controller needs to ensure the legal basis for the processing of the relevant data and the data processor has to follow the instructions of the controller when processing the data. A data-processing-upon-commission relationship needs to be laid down in a written agreement which has to contain some minimum requirements (eg, scope of the processing, information about the personal data processed, obligations to return data, obligation to implement specific security/technical and organisational measures). The disclosure of personal data within a data-processing-upon-commission relationship to a processor located within the European Economic Area (EEA) is not considered a transfer of personal data in the legal sense requiring a separate legal basis. The disclosure is privileged by law even if sensitive data of clients are exchanged. Besides, such a disclosure is not considered as a breach of the lawyer–client privilege. If the data processor, however, is located outside the EEA some further requirements have to be fulfilled.

2.4 Transfer of data outside the EEA

According to the European data protection law, the transfer of personal data to third parties from an EEA member country is usually only allowed to companies that are seated in a country with an adequate level of data protection. Usually, countries that are not members of the European Union or EEA provide lower levels of data protection than required by European law. A transfer of personal data to companies in third countries (eg, the United States, China, Russia) not having an adequate data protection level may nonetheless take place under certain additional conditions, if, for example:
- the data subject has declared his consent to the transfer;
- the transfer is necessary for the performance of a contract;
- public interest, the establishment, exercise or defence of legal claims, or the protection of a vital interest of the data subject justifies a transfer;
- the data protection authorities have authorised a transfer of personal data, if an adequate standard of protection is confirmed under contract or by means of applicable binding corporate rules, for example; or
- the Standard Contractual Clauses (SCCs) issued by the EU Commission according to Article 26(4) of EU Directive 95/46 are in place.

2.5 Binding corporate rules

In the past, multinational groups that have their headquarters in Europe have increasingly implemented binding corporate rules (BCRs) for all members of the company group in order to facilitate the group-wide international transfer of personal data. Group-wide transfers can result, for example, from the use of worldwide employee management software or customer relationship management programmes. Implementing BCRs ensures that all transfers of personal data within a group benefit from an adequate level of data protection.

If a company applies for authorisation of its BCRs, it has to follow a defined procedure: the applicant company designates the so-called 'lead European Data Protection authority' and drafts the BCRs. The lead authority reviews the draft and provides comments. As each EU member state has its own data protection authority, the lead authority circulates the draft of the final version of the BCRs among all authorities seated in the EU member states in which the BCRs will be applicable (ie, member states in which the group companies are located). In order to speed up the review proceedings, most of the European data protection authorities are part of a mutual recognition procedure. If the lead authority considers that the BCRs meet the requirements of the law, the other European data protection authorities under mutual recognition accept this opinion as sufficient basis for providing their own national permit. Those authorities that are not part of the mutual recognition procedure have to release the circulated version of the draft. Nonetheless, the proceedings are very time-consuming, so many companies still prefer to enter into SCCs.

2.6 Standard contractual clauses

An adequate level of data protection can be ascertained on the basis of the SCCs that have to be concluded between the data exporter and the data importer.

The European Commission has approved two alternative sets of SCCs for use in transferring personal data to a controller outside the EEA.[1] A controller can decide for itself what personal data to collect and how to use them. The 2004 SCC set is perceived to be more business friendly, in particular concerning litigation, allocation of responsibilities and auditing requirements.

Furthermore, in 2010, the European Commission approved SCCs[2] to be used when transferring personal data to a "processor". A processor (upon commission) performs operations on personal data on behalf of the (exporting) controller and according to its instructions (see section 2.2(c) above). Business process outsourcing in a non-EEA country is a common context for using SCCs to protect employee and customer information or other personal data furnished by a European company.

When using SCCs, it has to be kept in mind that in some EU member states it is necessary to apply for authorisation of the SCCs to the competent data protection authorities.

---

1   Commission Decision (2004/5271) of 27 December 2004, amending Decision 2001/497/EC as regards the introduction of an alternative set of standard contractual clauses for the transfer of personal data to third countries and Commission Decision 2001/497/EC of 15 June 2001.
2   Commission Decision (2010/87/EU) of 5 February 2010 on standard contractual clauses for the transfer of personal data to processors.

2.7   **Safe Harbour Programme**

As a further alternative, personal data may be transferred to companies seated in the United States on the basis of the Safe Harbour Programme. In 2000, the European Commission adopted a Decision determining that an arrangement put in place by the US Department of Commerce known as the Safe Harbour Programme provides adequate protection for personal data transferred from the European Union to the United States. If a US company participates in the Safe Harbour Programme it is a further means of legitimising such data transfers.

Due to criticism concerning enforcement deficits in implementing the Safe Harbour principles and due to the National Security Agency scandals, for example, the European Commission and the European Parliament are currently discussing the termination of the programme. Besides, the European data protection authorities ruled in 2013 that EEA companies must verify certain minimum requirements of the Safe Harbour certification (eg, the presentation of a certification document, the certification not being older than seven years and evidence documenting compliance with information duties). As a consequence, European companies abstain more and more from transfers of data to the United States on the basis of Safe Harbour.

3.   **Formal requirements**

Law firms doing business in Europe and acting as a controller must observe and implement several formal data protection requirements:

- In some EU member states (eg, Germany) a controller must appoint a data protection officer, who must have specialised knowledge and the necessary reliability to carry out his or her duties. The main duty is to ensure compliance with the applicable data protection obligations within the company.
- Several member states of the European Union (eg, France or the United Kingdom) require prior authorisation (registration or notification with the competent data protection authority) as well as notification of security incidents.
- Furthermore, for transparency reasons, in most EU member states the controller must list its data processing activities and provide – if requested – at least an overview about those activities (eg, to the public or persons concerned).
- Employees processing personal data must be bound to confidentiality and the secrecy of the data, and must be trained in data protection matters.
- The controller must implement adequate technical and organisational measures. It must ensure confidentiality and the availability and integrity of the personal data. In particular, the controller must protect its processing systems against unauthorised or accidental destruction, accidental loss, unlawful use, unauthorised alteration, copying, access or other unauthorised processing. The technical and organisational measures must be adequate, in reasonable proportion to the desired purpose of protection and must be reviewed periodically.

4. Risk management

4.1 Data protection procedures and audits

In order to minimise risks based on illegal data processing or breaches of the formal requirements mentioned earlier it is recommended that a data protection policy is introduced in each law firm or company. Even though this is not currently mandatory, the situation might change in the future: According to the planned European Regulation, controllers will need to provide to the data protection authorities information about their data processing procedures or policies, for example.

Currently, it is best practice to implement data protection policies and operation instructions to be observed by all employees.

Furthermore, the implementation of a data protection policy requires the nomination of persons responsible for data protection in the company itself and in each department. These persons must be trained extensively in data protection issues, must collect and exchange all relevant information and be responsible for such matters as concluding contracts, obtaining consents from data subjects and giving notification of data protection breaches.

An increasingly important means to ensure compliance with the law is to carry out an audit of data processing activities and policies. Up to now, no uniform guidelines for such auditing have been adopted in the EU. Therefore, carrying out an audit is optional. In practice, companies conduct private audits in order to check if they comply with the applicable data protection law and to increase their level of data protection.

4.2 Whistleblowing hotlines and ethical codes

Section 301 of the Sarbanes-Oxley Act 2002 requires audit committees at Sarbanes-Oxley-regulated companies to establish hotlines for the submission of employees' concerns or complaints regarding questionable accounting or auditing matters to their employer (so-called 'whistleblowing hotlines'). In practice, internationally operating Sarbanes-Oxley-regulated companies as well as many non-Sarbanes-Oxley-regulated companies offer such hotlines to all employees, clients, suppliers and so on of the company group (even if they are located outside the United States). The purpose of the hotlines is usually to implement anti-corruption programmes or ethical and behavioural codes.

As part of such a hotline, personal data about the notifying and the accused persons is likely to be processed. Even if such processing is required and allowed in the United States, this is not necessarily the case in Europe. Therefore, if a company in Europe offers such a hotline, the company as the controller has to comply with the respective data protection law. The European data protection authorities in the different member states provided several statements regarding their concerns and guidance regarding the legal requirements of such a hotline. According to this guidance the hotlines should only be available to employees to report concerns relating to specific issues including criminal offences, audit/accounting fraud, banking and bribery issues. Issues related to ethical standards of the company should not be included. Anonymous whistleblower calls should only be allowed on an exceptional basis and generally should be discouraged. Under certain specific circumstances the competent data protection authority will need to be notified of the existence of the hotline.

Money laundering

Sue Mawdsley
Legal Risk LLP
Suzie Ogilvie
Freshfields Bruckhaus Deringer LLP

1. **Introduction**

    With a growing international focus on tackling money laundering, terrorist financing and other financial crime issues, the risks of lawyers finding themselves acting for clients whose assets are tainted by criminal association have become an important area for continuing consideration and vigilance.

    Local legislation varies, but broadly, there are detailed requirements for legal professionals to implement and employ risk-based and appropriate systems and policies to prevent and detect them being used to further the aims of money launderers.

    Money laundering occurs when the identity of illegally obtained money is concealed so that it appears to have come from a lawful source. Criminals adopt different techniques to conceal the origins and ownership of this dirty money and lawyers may be targeted by criminals to assist in this process.

    While criminal offences concerning terrorist financing are distinct from money laundering, the opportunity has been taken to use the framework required to prevent and detect money laundering to similarly address terrorist financing risks.

    It is difficult to estimate how much money is laundered annually, but the United Nations Office on Drugs and Crime has estimated that the value is between $800 billion and $2 trillion, or 2 to 5% of global gross domestic product. Consequently, the Financial Action Task Force (FATF), an inter-governmental body, which was mandated to develop and promote policies to protect the global financial system against money laundering and terrorist financing, has sought to strengthen anti-money laundering regimes around the world. A number of these standards apply to legal professionals.

    This chapter examines the background to money laundering and other financial crime risks and seeks to identify how risk may be effectively managed within a firm's risk management systems.

2. **FATF and the standards applicable to legal professionals**

    FATF has issued 40 recommendations on combating money laundering and terrorist financing, which are recognised as the global anti-money laundering standards and have been endorsed by over 180 countries. The first recommendations were published in 1990 and were reviewed again in 2006. After the terrorist attacks in September 2001, the scope and mandate of the recommendations expanded and subsequently a total of nine Special Recommendations concerning terrorist financing were developed.

The recommendations were most recently revised on 15 February 2012 to fully integrate counter-terrorist financing measures with anti-money laundering controls, address emerging threats and clarify and strengthen many of the obligations. However, the 40 Recommendations continue to be built on the core concept of risk-based regulation.[1] Thus, whereas the requirements for higher risk situations were strengthened, the recommendations made it clear that countries should adopt a flexible set of measures in order to target their resources effectively and apply preventive measures that are commensurate to the nature of risks. This chapter focuses on the 40 Recommendations, as amended, although at the time of writing, the process of incorporating the revisions to the Recommendations into the laws of all FATF countries is well-advanced but not completed.

It is also useful to note that FATF has issued two additional reports specific to the legal profession as follows:

- FATF Risk Based Approach Guidance for Legal Professionals issued in October 2008 (the "RBA Guidance for Legal Professionals"[2]), which the writers understand will be updated to reflect some of the changes introduced by the revised 40 Recommendations; and
- FATF Report: Money Laundering and Terrorist Financing Vulnerabilities of Legal Professionals, June 2013 (the "FATF Typologies Report").

It has always been acknowledged that the work of lawyers varies considerably[3] and that an individual legal professional's or firm's particular risk-based processes should be determined based on the activities undertaken by the legal professional, the existing ethical rules and supervisory structure to which the professional is subject and the susceptibility of a legal professional's activities to money laundering and terrorist financing in the particular countries in which it operates. Under the revised 40 Recommendations, in addition to the requirement on countries to identify, assess and understand the money laundering and terrorist financing risks for that country, relevant businesses, including law firms, are also required to take appropriate steps to perform such a risk assessment. In addition, firms should have policies, controls and procedures that enable them to manage, monitor and mitigate effectively the different risks that have been identified.

The 40 Recommendations, among other things, explicitly require legal professionals to undertake customer (or client) due diligence (CDD)[4] and report suspicious transactions,[5] where they prepare or assist in carrying out specified transactional activities for their client.[6] These points are covered below.

---

1 FATF Recommendation 1.
2 Available at http://www.fatf-gafi.org/media/fatf/documents/reports/RBA%20Legal%20professions.pdf.
3 RBA Guidance for Legal Professionals.
4 Recommendation 10.
5 Recommendations 20 and 21.
6 The Recommendations state that the following types of transactional work are caught:
   (a) buying and selling of real estate;
   (b) managing of client money, securities or other assets;
   (c) organisation of contributions for the creation, operation or management of companies;
   (d) creation, operation or management of legal persons or arrangements; and
   (e) buying and selling of business entities.

The more limited application of the 40 Recommendations to the activities of legal professionals (together with a recognition of the application of legal professional privilege or professional secrecy[7]) seeks to balance the fundamental rights of society in obtaining legal advice on their rights and obligations without interference from the money laundering regime, while requiring legal professionals to report transactional matters in which there is a perceived increased risk of money laundering occurring. It is recognised that in certain jurisdictions, legal professionals remain concerned that the balance may not have been adequately achieved but this chapter does not seek to go into detail on these issues.

3. Risk assessments

From a wider risk management perspective, the introduction of requirements to initiate and maintain a system and procedures to prevent money laundering has had a valuable impact on the client/matter inception processes employed by many law firms. For example, the need to undertake effective due diligence has led to more informed thinking on client intake. In the writers' view this has helped in the development of improved client selection as it focuses on reputational risk among other things. It may also assist in the earlier identification of conflicts. The requirement to maintain ongoing monitoring of business relationships has again put sharper focus on a continuous risk assessment process throughout the entire client relationship.

As highlighted above, one of the key elements of compliance introduced by the revised 40 Recommendations is to undertake risk assessments. These are required at both a national level to determine country risk, but it is also best practice (and in some countries a requirement) for a legal professional to conduct an assessment of the risk of money laundering in his/her business. The RBA Guidance for Legal Professionals seeks to assist legal professionals further in understanding the risk-based approach in the context of the legal profession. In addition, some national Law Societies and Bar Associations have made available materials to assist in the risk assessment process.

In order to understand risks, a risk assessment should include consideration of the following matters:
- a consideration of the legal professional's client demographic including consideration of geographical and industry risk; and
- a review of publicly available materials regarding money laundering typologies and risks against the type of services offered by the legal professional, including an analysis of clients and matters categorised as higher risk.

3.1 Client demographic

This should include an analysis of the type of clients for whom a law firm typically

---

[7] There is a 'privilege exception' to the reporting requirement, contained in Interpretive Note 1 to Recommendation 23. There is no requirement to report suspicious transactions if the relevant information was obtained in circumstances where they are subject to professional secrecy or legal professional privilege.

undertakes work and the risks associated with them. For example, law firms predominantly undertaking high-value transactional work for high net-worth individuals associated with higher risk jurisdictions are likely to need to regularly apply enhanced due diligence. Similarly, firms acting for well-known international companies advising in relation to their activities in mining and minerals in high-risk jurisdictions will face similar challenges. Verification of identity may feature as an issue in the former case. In the latter the risks are likely to lie in the work itself.

A law firm's exposure to politically exposed persons (PEPs) is also a major consideration. The PEP may feature as the client or a beneficial owner. The work to be undertaken in each circumstance will affect the risk profile. Political exposure is considered in the section on client due diligence below.

The stability of client relationships, how far the lawyers will be meeting the client or clients and detailed knowledge of their operations and associations are relevant factors, as are the complexity of the client's structure and availability of reliable information on that client.

Cash businesses are frequently highlighted as presenting risks but given the wider international focus and extra territorial issues surrounding anti-bribery and corruption laws in some jurisdictions, firms have to take into consideration the elevated risks attached to certain industries.

Country risk issues feature prominently in any consideration of money laundering risks. The robustness of anti-money laundering legislation and practice in any particular jurisdiction should be routinely considered in any risk evaluation process. FATF provides a source of valuable information on the relative risks associated with particular jurisdictions in its system of Mutual Evaluations,[8] which provide an in-depth description and analysis of each country's system for preventing criminal abuse of the financial system, and in providing its regularly updated list of high-risk and non-cooperative jurisdictions.[9] Information is also publicly available on bribery and corruption risks in different jurisdictions.[10]

3.2   Review of publicly available materials

The 40 Recommendations require countries to carry out a risk assessment at national level and to make the findings available to regulated firms to help them conduct their own risk assessments. The quality of such risk assessments may vary from country to country and it is not clear how much of the risk assessment will be devoted to the legal profession. However, these national risk assessments should not be ignored when firms are drawing up their own assessments. Firms should consider the materials available for the countries in which they operate and factor in any relevant information into their own risk assessments.

Otherwise, there is limited information in respect of the risks of money

---

8   See www.fatf-gafi.org/topics/mutualevaluations/.
9   See www.fatf-gafi.org/topics/high-riskandnon-cooperativejurisdictions/.
10   Transparency International regularly publishes several surveys and indices which measure corruption: the Corruption Perceptions Index (CPI), Global Corruption Barometer (GCB) and the Bribe Payers Index are helpful tools in analysing country risk: http://www.transparency.org.uk/corruption/measuring-corruption.

laundering in the legal profession. Many local Bar Associations provide domestic guidance on compliance to a greater or lesser degree. At the time of writing, the most recent study is the FATF Typologies Report.

The FATF Typologies Report does not focus solely on the unwitting involvement of lawyers and was drawn up with the dual purpose of assisting the legal profession in identifying risk areas, as well as assisting law enforcement. In addition, the report presents examples with the benefit of hindsight and the examples can appear stark, in circumstances where the situation developed incrementally over a period of time. There have been some discussions in private sector fora regarding the need for additional typologies to assist the legal profession in its understanding of the situations in which money laundering may occur unwittingly. In this chapter we have tried to highlight the areas where the report identifies risk areas for unwitting involvement in money laundering and how you might address these issues.

The report identifies the key money laundering methods that commonly employ the services of a legal professional as:

- misuse of client accounts;
- sale/purchase of real property;
- creation of trusts, companies and charities;
- management of trusts and companies; and
- sham litigation.

We have summarised in Table 1 on the following pages the key risks, red flags and how you might mitigate against such risks. This list is not exhaustive and we would recommend that you also review the red flag indicators set out in Chapter 5 of the FATF Typologies Report.

3.3 Client due diligence and ongoing monitoring

The application of CDD measures and ongoing monitoring of business relationships is at the centre of the regulatory requirements in most jurisdictions to implement effective anti-money laundering systems. This is also a key risk management control for any organisation.

The obligation is to undertake CDD on all clients with whom the firm forms a business relationship or for whom they conduct occasional financial or property transactions.

Client due diligence generally consists of three elements, which include verification of identity, but also a clearer consideration of the risks any new matter will present, so:

- identifying the customer and verifying the customer's identity on the basis of documents, data or information obtained from a reliable and independent source;
- identifying, where applicable, the beneficial owner and taking risk-based and adequate measures to verify his or her identity so that the institution or person is satisfied that it knows who the beneficial owner is, including, as regards legal persons, trusts and similar legal arrangements, taking risk-based

Table 1: Key risks, red flags and mitigation

Area of concern	Key issues	Red flags/issues	Mitigation methods etc
Misuse of client accounts	Transfer of funds without legal services.	Unlikely to be unwitting involvement but be aware of clients that put pressure on you citing their long-standing relationship with you or other financial pressures.	Impose strict procedures to ensure the client account is used appropriately. Use of client account without the provision of accompanying legal services to be prohibited.
Misuse of client accounts	Payments into legal professional accounts and subsequent abandonment of transaction in order to clean the money.	Requests to pay on account. General lack of interest in progressing the transaction. A transaction abandoned soon after instructions often with no apparent concern for fee levels or there are no or unclear reasons for abandonment.	Carry out thorough client due diligence before taking money on account, including understanding the transaction. Ensure appropriate checks are made and the rationale for a transaction is clearly understood before any third party payments are accepted into the client account. Where money is accepted into the client account in respect of a transaction or from a client on account and the transaction is aborted, carefully consider the level of risk analysis and CDD conducted at the outset, the legitimacy of the transaction and the parties to it, and the circumstances of the aborted transaction. You should not return funds unless you are comfortable that the reasons for the abandonment of the transaction stand up to scrutiny. Furthermore, you should return funds to the original sender of those funds and not to any other designated person.
Sale/purchase of real property	Investment of the proceeds of crime in property. Laundering money through property sales.	Use of cash in property transactions/ inadequately explained levels of private funding. Back-to-back sales, involvement of similar parties in such transactions. Use of intermediaries, trusts or other methods of obscuring ownership or funding, including convoluted explanations of funding. Inflated prices.	Perform thorough client due diligence checks. Keep up to date with emerging issues – it may be useful to tap into resources from law societies or bar associations in other countries to supplement knowledge in this area if law enforcement in your country does not provide up-to-date information. Provide information and/or training, where appropriate, to staff on these updates so that they are better equipped to spot issues. Information overload can also be a warning sign as launderers attempt to inundate the legal professional with information so that they do not spot the issue or become convinced.

Area of concern	Key issues	Red flags/issues	Mitigation methods etc
Creation of trusts, companies and charities	Disguising the real owners and parties to the transaction.	Use of intermediaries for no apparent reason. Lack of clear rationale for the setting up of an arrangement in a particular way. Limited information provided as to purpose. Lack of understanding of source of funds or reason for the level of funding.	Perform thorough client due diligence checks. Be aware of higher risk jurisdictions where ownership may be concealed. If the entity is set up in another country, investigate whether nominee shareholders are commonplace. If a prospective client simply requests you to undertake the mechanical aspects of setting up a trust, company or charity, without seeking legal advice on the appropriateness of the company structure and related matters, further investigation should be conducted into why this is the case. It is advisable to understand all aspects of the transaction, particularly as, even if there are no money laundering issues, you can expose yourself to professional negligence claims.
Management of trusts/ companies	Use of legal professionals in the management of companies and trusts to provide greater respectability and legitimacy to the entity.	Lack of clear rationale for the transaction. Unexplained speed and general lack of interest in the advice being rendered. Limited information provided as to purpose. Lack of understanding of source of funds or reason for the level of funding.	If you are asked to be involved in the management of a trust or company which goes beyond legal advice, you should consider why you are being asked. Is there a legal reason or is it customary to have a legal professional on the board of an entity in the relevant country? Be aware of other risks such as your own personal liability and conflicts of interest which may arise with other clients. Perform rigorous checks on the entities concerned to minimise the money laundering risk. Provide information and/or training, where appropriate, to staff on possible red flags.
Sham litigation	Fabricated disputes to allow the transfer of money (which would normally fall outside the anti-money laundering requirements).	Restricted involvement of lawyers in the matter/unclear instructions or limited information provided on the issue. Sudden settlement agreements made and requests to settle through the client account.	Some firms may choose to apply client take-on processes to all clients, not just those subject to formal anti-money laundering requirements to assist in identifying sham litigation. Consider carrying out background checks on the counterparties. Ensure that you have reviewed all relevant documentation relating to the claim so that you can assess its legitimacy. Consider whether the request to advise and the level of work involved is commensurate to the work that your firm would normally undertake. Provide information and/or training, where appropriate, to staff on possible red flags.

and adequate measures to understand the ownership and control structure of the customer;
- obtaining information on the purpose and intended nature of the business relationship.[11]

(a) *Identifying the customer and verifying the customer's identity*
Verification goes beyond identification. Identification can be a client merely confirming his or her name and address whereas verification consists of taking steps to check that information through reliable, independent sources. The firm will need to verify that the client is who he or she claims to be. If it cannot do so, it cannot undertake any business with the client or accept any money from him or her.

What constitutes appropriate verification of client identity depends on whether the client is an individual, a company, partnership, trust or some other legal entity, as well as the risks associated with that client or transaction. Firms should consider again such issues as the geographical risk associated with the location of the potential client or the business to be conducted, the type of business that it conducts or the manner in which the client came to request legal services from the firm. For example, a local client, who comes to the firm through recommendation from another long-established client and who the lawyers will regularly meet will have a different risk profile from a client resident abroad who they are unlikely to ever meet and who originally contacted them after finding the firm's name in a directory, even if they instruct the firm in relation to a similar type of transaction.

It is also worth considering some form of negative press searching on prospective clients to assist in the risk assessment process.

Law Societies and Bar Councils provide sector-specific guidance to lawyers within their own jurisdictions and some are responsible for supervision and compliance of their regulated lawyer community for this purpose.

(b) *Identifying the beneficial owner*
Client due diligence generally requires that when a legal professional or law firm is dealing with a client who is acting on behalf of another person, entity or arrangement, they need to identify the beneficial owner as well. This is considered key to understanding the ownership and control structure of the client, and in essence, for whose benefit any transaction is being undertaken.

Beneficial ownership and verification tends to have a specifically defined meaning within money laundering legislation and regulation. Some guidance on these considerations is set out below.
- *Agency arrangements:* Where there is an agency arrangement, CDD information needs to be obtained in respect of the client and the agent. Where the client is a company, partnership or trust, there is a need to ascertain whether there are any beneficial owners whose identity needs to be verified.

---

11   FATF 40 Recommendations, Recommendation 10 (formerly Recommendation 5 under the October 2003 set of recommendations).

- *Individuals:* Where a person is acting on behalf of another individual as agent, for example because the client lives abroad, there is a requirement to verify the identity of both. The ultimate client would in effect be a beneficial owner.
- *Companies:* A beneficial owner is a natural person who ultimately owns or controls the client or on whose behalf the transaction is conducted. In relation to a company a shareholder who owns more than 25% of the company's shares or voting rights (whether through direct or indirect ownership or control, including through bearer share holdings) is generally a beneficial owner for CDD purposes. Anyone who otherwise exercises control over the management of the company is also considered a beneficial owner. In higher risk situations, care should be taken to understand whether the information provided is fully comprehensive and firms should not necessarily focus simply on ownership information. Firms should consider whether the country of incorporation of the client permits nominee shareholders and should consider asking detailed questions regarding decision-making powers, entitlement to profits and source of wealth or funds.

It should be noted that the requirement to obtain beneficial ownership information does not generally apply to companies whose securities are listed on a regulated market.

- *Partnerships:* Similarly, in the case of a partnership, beneficial ownership extends to any individual who controls more than 25% of the capital or profits of the partnership or more than 25% of the voting rights in the partnership, or who otherwise exercises control over the management of the partnership.
- *Trusts:* Beneficial ownership issues are complex in respect of trusts and the term does not generally carry its conventional meaning in relation to money laundering legislation. There are three defined categories of beneficial owner:
  - individuals with specified interest – those with at least a 25% specified interest in trust capital;
  - the class of persons in whose main interest the trust operates;
  - individuals who control a trust.

Generally speaking, in respect of trusts, whilst the legislation treats beneficiaries and those who control the trust as beneficial owners, it is prudent to understand where the trusts funds have originated so it is advisable to understand more about the settlor of the trust, particularly in higher risk situations. Lower risk situations would generally extend to a variety of family and protective trusts whereas trust structures at the top of a corporate chain may require closer scrutiny.

Higher and lower risk situations: Local legislation in many jurisdictions, including, for example, successive EU Money Laundering Directives, has provided for enhanced or simplified due diligence in relation to certain client categories and situations:
- typically, where information on the identity of the customer and the

beneficial owner of a customer is publicly available, or where adequate checks and controls exist elsewhere in national systems: financial institutions that are subject to requirements to combat money laundering and terrorist financing consistent with the 40 Recommendations and that are supervised for compliance with those controls;
- public companies that are subject to regulatory disclosure requirements;
- government administrations or enterprises.

In such instances, the legal professional could place reliance on being satisfied that the client falls within one of those categories.

In addition, much practical use has been made in assessing risks associated with particular jurisdictions of lists provided by, for example, FATF on equivalent jurisdictions and risk ratings, adjusted accordingly.

Equally, in certain higher risk situations, enhanced due diligence is required. By way of example, in dealing with PEPs as clients or where there are additional risks in terms of the risk of identity theft, where the firm does not meet the client. In such instances additional documents, data or information are needed to satisfy the CDD requirements together with supplementary measures to verify or certify the documents supplied.

It remains to be seen how this area develops following the updated 40 Recommendations of February 2012, as there is a move away from the promotion of white lists and black lists towards individual risk assessment in all circumstances on a case-by-case basis.

Politically exposed persons: The existence of individuals with political exposure in a transaction is seen as a heightened anti-money laundering risk.

Pursuant to the 40 Recommendations, it is necessary to have risk-based measures in place to determine whether a client, or the beneficial owner of a client, is a PEP. Additionally, senior management must approve the relationship, the source of wealth of the client must be determined and ongoing monitoring of the relationship will also be required. Where the PEP is the beneficial owner of the proposed client, it appears likely that it is the source of wealth and funds being used in the transaction (which may be the client's funds) that need to be assessed, rather than the PEP's wealth, although ultimately this will require further analysis, depending on the circumstances.

Previous iterations of the 40 Recommendations confined the obligation to determining whether there is a politically exposed element to any relationship with a foreign PEP. The assumption had been made that it was more unusual for such persons to be transacting business in another jurisdiction. However, the 40 Recommendations expanded their remit to require closer scrutiny of domestic PEPs on a risk-based approach to address the risk that a domestic PEP might be involved in illegal transactions in his or her home jurisdiction.

Developments at European level: While it is intended to look at money laundering issues on an international scale it is worth looking at some of the developments at

European level as they may set a precedent for other countries implementing the 40 Recommendations.

On February 5 2013 the European Commission released its proposals for a Fourth Money Laundering Directive,[12] which seek to give effect to the revised 40 Recommendations and also some of the recommendations set out in a review conducted by the Commission on the implementation of the previous Directive. There are a number of developments which will affect the way in which firms should conduct CDD, summarised in the next paragraphs. Although, at the time of writing, the proposals are still the subject of further negotiations, unless otherwise stated, the key points highlighted below are unlikely to change.

The proposals move away from the current system of specified exemptions from customer due diligence requirements based on third country equivalence. This is a shift away from defining specific categories of low risk to an approach that requires regulated entities to consider guidance that is expected to be issued by each member state on lower risk categories in their jurisdictions and consider on a case-by-case basis the nature and severity of the customer or sector risk. It remains to be seen how these provisions will be implemented in each of the member states and whether these measures actually result in an increase in red tape and compliance activity for little added benefit.

The subject of much debate at European level is the desire for a requirement on member states to maintain publicly available ultimate beneficial ownership registers for corporate entities and trusts. This goes beyond the 40 Recommendations, which stopped short of imposing such stringent requirements and left it for countries to implement appropriate measures to ensure that beneficial ownership information would be made readily available to law enforcement. In the European Commission's initial proposal itself, the Commission had proposed to address the beneficial ownership issue by requiring all companies, legal entities and trustees to hold adequate, accurate and up-to-date information on their beneficial owners. However, a proposal for beneficial ownership registers, particularly for companies, has gained a substantial amount of support among politicians, particularly in the United Kingdom,[13] such that it is highly likely that it will feature in the final version of the text.

A question mark remains over the controversial issue of beneficial ownership registers for trusts, which the United Kingdom has been reluctant to fully endorse, but for which there is a significant body of support among a number of politicians from civil law jurisdictions, who view trusts with a great deal of suspicion. Trusts are widely used in common-law countries to give effect to family arrangements to provide for dependents and the vulnerable and in the vast majority of cases there is a very low money laundering risk. An all-encompassing trusts register would have some unfortunate unintended consequences for citizens' privacy in all member

---

12 Proposal for a Directive of the European Parliament and of the Council on the prevention of the use of the financial system for the purpose of money laundering and terrorist financing /* COM/2013/045 final – 2013/0025 (COD) */ available at http://eur-lex.europa.eu/legal-content/EN/ALL/;jsessionid= gMzLTjbKppGJXj57QjLn18hpvszJ70v0gqY6r5X2s241jD88VBPG!632333948?uri=CELEX:52013PC0045.
13 See www.gov.uk/government/news/the-uks-g8-agenda-increasing-trade-fairer-taxes-and-greater-transparency and www.gov.uk/government/news/public-register-to-boost-company-transparency.

states, with limited additional benefit in the anti-money laundering and counter terrorist financing fight. How this issue will be resolved remains to be seen.

Whereas the introduction of such registers ostensibly assists regulated entities in complying with their due diligence obligations, it is not clear how the information in the registers will be checked and verified. The success of any such register must be coupled with a drive to crack down on company service providers who turn a blind eye to due diligence requirements or are actively facilitating individuals who wish to hide their ill-gotten gains. Firms may therefore need to continue to assess the risk of the accuracy of the data provided when conducting CDD.

(c) *Obtaining information on the purpose and intended nature of the business relationship*

Client due diligence also includes a requirement to obtain information on the purpose and intended nature of the business relationship. This requires a consideration of the rationale behind any particular piece of work and a risk analysis.

The aim is to help identify more easily where there is something suspicious about the client. It involves using common sense in identifying whether there is anything unusual about the transaction. For example, a client from a high-risk jurisdiction seeks to instruct a law firm to assist him in transferring his investments to London. He has been working in a moderately paid occupation and is said to have investments worth many millions of pounds. In such an instance clarification on the source of funds should be sought as well as considering the client's source of wealth. Consideration should also be given as to whether or not the client may be a politically exposed person.

From a risk management perspective, the completion of the steps in the CDD process creates a risk profile that should be revisited as any client relationship progresses. This exercise and the requirement that a risk-based approach is adopted are often best evidenced on client/matter inception by the lawyer with conduct of the matter. Larger firms may have a designated team to facilitate the process. Law firms increasingly require an overall risk ranking for money laundering, terrorist financing and other financial crime risks.

These risk rankings can provide a wealth of information for risk managers and should allow for higher risk clients and matters to be more quickly identified to receive additional scrutiny as they progress.

(d) *Ongoing monitoring of business relationships*

The ongoing monitoring of business relationships forms an integral part of the CDD process and continues the requirement to understand the associated risk on a continuous basis throughout the client relationship. In general terms it includes:
- a scrutiny of transactions undertaken throughout the course of the relationship (including where necessary the source of funds) to ensure that the transactions are consistent with the acting lawyer's knowledge of the client, their business and the risk profile; as well as
- keeping the documents, data or information obtained for the purpose of applying CDD up to date.

Responsibility for compliance with these requirements, in many ways, will rest upon the legal professionals handling the matters, as they will have a close relationship with the client. They must remain alert to suspicious circumstances that may suggest money laundering, terrorist financing or the provision of false CDD material. While they will also be in the best position to assess whether the CDD information for existing clients is up to date, it may be prudent to set up an appropriate system for ensuring that this information is checked at appropriate intervals. What is appropriate may depend upon the risk that the client presents to the firm and the size or geographical reach of the firm.

4. **Financial sanctions**

    Although not strictly falling within money laundering and terrorist finance legislation, financial sanctions have recently become more prevalent. Given that sanctions connected with clients can arise as part of the CDD process or as a result of the legal professional's risk profiling on client inception, this area often falls to be dealt with within CDD. In addition, in many jurisdictions, it can be an offence to deal with the funds or resources of sanctioned individuals so it is vital that this issue is identified at the outset.

    Organisations providing certain types of services to clients must therefore also check the appropriate list of sanctions applicable to its area of operation before dealing with clients or beneficial owners in all types of work. It can additionally be an offence under various pieces of legislation to deal with designated individuals or entities listed on the relevant sanctions lists. Whether beneficial owners of corporate client entities are caught by the sanctions will depend on the level of ownership and control and the provisions of the applicable sanctions regime.

    By way of an example, the UK Treasury maintains a consolidated list of targets listed by the United Nations, European Union and United Kingdom under legislation relating to current financial sanctions regimes. It is a criminal offence to make available funds or economic resources and, in the case of Terrorism Orders, financial services, directly or indirectly to or for the benefit of these targets. Additionally, in the United States, the Office of Foreign Assets Control of the US Department of the Treasury maintains financial sanctions lists, which must be checked when dealing with US-related matters or if US persons or persons located in the United States will be involved in the advice.[14]

5. **Reporting**

    The obligation to report suspicious transactions is specific to lawyers on a jurisdiction-by-jurisdiction basis. As highlighted above, it will generally only apply in the context of the specific transactional circumstances referred to in the 40 Recommendations. However, there are differences in the interpretation of what will constitute proceeds of crime for the purposes of money laundering legislation: in some countries (eg, the United Kingdom) an 'all crimes' test will be applied, whereas other countries will only include offences carrying a minimum sentence or penalty.

---

14 See www.treasury.gov/about/organizational-structure/offices/Pages/Office-of-Foreign-Assets-Control.aspx.

The most recent FATF amendments recommended that tax crimes be specifically included in the offences that would be caught.

Another important consideration for any legal professional considering whether a reporting obligation arises is professional secrecy or privilege. Due to the differing nature of legal systems, professional secrecy and privilege apply in different ways.

It is therefore not possible to provide in-depth analysis on the application of the reporting requirements and the application of professional secrecy or privilege. You should ensure that you have considered both aspects carefully before submitting a report.

Legal professionals hold a special position in that they are entitled to advise their clients to cease from engaging in criminal activity. The 40 Recommendations make it clear that the legal prohibition on disclosing ('tipping off') the fact that a suspicious transaction report has been made does not prevent a legal professional seeking to dissuade a client from engaging in illegal activity.[15]

6. Conclusion

Money laundering, terrorist financing and the threat of serious organised crime is such that international and national bodies will continue to increase their efforts to counter the threat. Anti-money laundering and counter-terrorist financing compliance will continue to be a reputational and regulatory consideration for firms across the globe. It is constantly evolving and requires continued focus on emerging areas of risk. In a more globalised world, this focus requires an understanding not just of local risks and legislative requirements, but of international issues. Fortunately in the age of the Internet, information can be more easily accessed, but it continues to be a challenge for firms to keep up to date with emerging information and information systems and there will be cost and resource implications. The key for firms is to find the correct balance so that they can manage their money laundering risks in a cost-effective manner.

The obligation on firms to continuously develop and update their anti-money laundering risk management systems continues to provide opportunities for firms to enhance their overall systems and policies aimed at managing risk.

---

15 Interpretive Note 4 to Recommendation 23.

Hiring – identifying the key risks

Ruth Bonino
Chris Holme
Clyde & Co LLP

Hiring people, or rather the right people, is crucial to the running of a successful law firm. It enables a firm to grow and to continue to serve its clients when staff leave. But hiring needs to be planned carefully, and a firm needs to ensure it is carried out properly and in alignment with business strategy. Having its business strategy in mind will help the hiring firm target the right candidates, ask the right questions and therefore avoid potential costly mistakes.

The staffing needs of a law firm range from the lawyers (partners, associates, trainees and paralegals) to the support staff (covering IT, HR, marketing, finance, secretarial, reception and administration).

In this chapter, we consider the general risks to law firms when hiring staff (this includes the legal risks such as those in relation to discrimination claims and data protection responsibilities). There are particular risks involved in hiring partners and senior lawyers and these are indicated where relevant.

In the next chapter, we outline the process involved in hiring partners and their teams. Trends in partner lateral hiring vary across the world, with the most active markets historically being those in the United States and the United Kingdom, but with the ongoing growth of international law firms and the focus on developing markets, the lateral hire of a partner or group of lawyers is often the best way to enter a new market. Lateral hiring of partners has increased significantly in the past 10 to 20 years, and now occurs regularly internationally – the days of a partner automatically staying put in one firm for life are long gone. However, not all lateral hires are successful.

The risks associated with hiring staff can be significant, ranging from obvious direct costs, such as recruitment costs and wasted management time in hiring the wrong person, to less obvious hidden costs such as the impact on team morale, reputation and firm culture. Understanding where these risks lie will help law firms avoid potential pitfalls and issues in the hiring process.

1. **Impact on existing staff**
   Firms should first consider the reason for hiring, and whether hiring is necessary. Do you hire at all – or should you grow from within? If you have the talent within the firm, will hiring close off the space into which those staff can grow? If so, hiring can be a more expensive and short-term measure, which demotivates the ranks, sending out the wrong signal to junior lawyers, taking away their partnership prospects. In addition to this, a lateral hire who is the wrong cultural fit can have a major effect

on team morale and can be a strong influencing factor in a junior lawyer's decision whether to remain at the firm or to leave.

2. Loss of management time

Failure to plan properly in a hiring process can result in a huge amount of wasted time with interviewing and researching the wrong person. It is important to conduct the right checks at the right stage of the hiring process. For example, getting to interview stage only to discover the candidate does not hold the right qualifications for the particular jurisdiction (which could have been checked weeks earlier by the firm's recruitment team) can mean hours of wasted time talking to the candidate and preparing for interviews.

Undisclosed reputational issues can also result in significant loss of management time, and may completely scupper a deal once discovered. These issues might include professional liability insurance claims, professional conduct records, outside interests that could damage the firm's reputation or standing in the market. The quicker these issues are uncovered, the more time can be saved.

Firms should therefore ensure they have a proper plan in place for checking the administrative side of the recruitment process. Do not rely on the external recruitment consultant; and frontload these enquiries as far as possible to save time.

3. Exposure to claims

Failure to carry out proper checks and due diligence can lead to exposure to claims.

3.1 Legal action by candidate's current employer

It is common for partners in law firms to be subject to restrictive covenants preventing them from competing with their previous firm in a particular area or, more commonly, from soliciting clients and employees of the previous firm within a certain period after leaving. Failure to investigate the extent of the candidate's restrictions, or having done so and choosing to ignore them, can lead to claims by the former firm, both against the lateral hire and the recruiting firm. Whether the restrictions are enforceable in the courts will depend on how they are drafted and the jurisdiction in which they are to be enforced. However, often the power in practice behind them is not in their legal enforceability but in their threat value. The threat of legal action might not necessarily prevent a lawyer leaving their old firm but it might well deter them from taking instructions from previous clients once they have moved.

A spat over covenants in front of clients the new firm is trying to attract can also be seen as unprofessional, and can sour the relationship before it begins. Conducting proper checks so that the recruiting firm fully understands the position will enable the firm to assess the risks, evaluate the promises made by the candidate of a likely client following and make fully informed recruitment decisions.

When recruiting a team of lawyers, there are additional risks, such as where the hiring firm has obtained confidential details of team members from an individual in breach of obligations to their current firm. In the United Kingdom, for example, this could even bring into prospect the previous firm attempting to obtain an injunction to prevent the recruiting firm from recruiting the team.

3.2 Discrimination claims by the candidate

In many jurisdictions, there are laws preventing less favourable treatment of job applicants on the grounds of certain protected characteristics. The most common of these are sex, race, age and disability. Discrimination may occur at any stage of the recruitment process, for example:

- in the job advertisement (eg, advertising for a young lawyer, or a lawyer from a particular part of the globe, would be age/racial discrimination);
- in the job description (eg, "fit and active person required" could eliminate disabled candidates);
- in the application form (eg, asking excessive or broad questions about disability or family commitments which are not relevant to performance of the job);
- in short-listing candidates for interview and in the selection process (eg, an online questionnaire that asks whether the candidate has the right to work in a particular country could amount to racial discrimination if a negative response then precluded the candidate from continuing with the application process);
- the location and timing of interviews (eg, could be sex/disability discrimination);
- assessment techniques and the selection criteria used (eg, imposing unnecessary requirements that the candidate needs to follow a certain faith; imposing excessive continuous service as this may discriminate against women who have had breaks for childcare reasons).

In many jurisdictions around the world (and certainly in Europe), there is a distinction between direct and indirect discrimination. Direct discrimination is relatively obvious and easy to avoid. For example, an advertisement that requests only female applicants clearly treats male applicants less favourably and so is directly sex discriminatory. Indirect discrimination, however, may be less obvious. Under European law, it generally occurs when a firm has an apparently neutral requirement that applies to all equally, for example a requirement to attend every evening client functions that include alcohol. Although apparently neutral, this actually disadvantages certain groups of people, such as women who have primary childcare responsibilities, or those of certain religions who do not drink alcohol. This indirect discrimination is permitted only if it is justified – which essentially means that the requirement is for the business and there is no other way to achieve that requirement.

Firms need to take particular care in recruitment to ensure there is no direct discrimination (which should be easy to avoid) and also no indirect discrimination. For this reason, equality and interview training for all involved in the recruitment process is essential.

Another tricky issue concerns the need for cultural fit, which is generally understood to be about matching the norms and values of the organisation with those of the individual, as well as fitting co-workers with their supervisors. For example, an introvert might not work well in a department where team working is key; an open-door policy or open-plan office space might be unsuitable for that sort of individual. However, there may be discrimination risks associated with asking the candidate questions to explore cultural fit. Taking the example of the open-plan work space; if this is dominated by loud extroverts who are predominately male, it would amount to sex discrimination if the firm were to prefer male candidates because they might fit in better.

If cultural fit is about hard work, putting clients first, and supporting team mates – this is most probably fine. But it can all too easily be interpreted as 'someone who is the same as me' in the hiring of partners: 'I want someone who looks like me, likes the same activities as me, and has the same priorities as me'. This can very easily lead down a path where discrimination occurs either sub-consciously, or even consciously – with those with the same characteristics (sex, religious belief, race) as the hirer having an advantage over those who do not. Not only does this create discrimination risk, but it also means a firm could miss out on the best person for the job.

Firms therefore need to be very careful in communicating the need to fit in with a culture – and be sure that they themselves understand what that means and that the hiring partners understand what it means. This should be clearly discussed and taught in equality and recruitment training.

4. **Data protection**

In many jurisdictions there are controls on how personal data is stored and processed. This is particularly relevant in the recruitment process where personal information is collected and stored. The hiring firm should ensure that it understands the local laws as to how personal data can be stored and processed. Independently of the more thorough analysis of data protection issues elsewhere in this book, the following general points should be noted.

- Members of the firm involved in the recruitment process should be trained in data protection compliance.
- Application forms should make clear the identity of the recruiting firm and how their personal data will be used; the form should not require information which is irrelevant to the recruitment process and the process of submitting the form should be secure.
- Where third-party verification of information provided by the candidate is needed, the candidate should be informed how the checks are to be carried out and their consent should be obtained.
- Where psychometric tests are used, they should only be interpreted by trained staff to avoid discrimination claims.
- Interview notes may contain personal data so they should only be kept for a reasonable amount of time; interviewers should be aware that interviewees may have the right to see interview notes.
- Pre-employment vetting such as asking third parties about the candidate's background should be carried out with data protection laws in mind. Generally these checks should only be carried out if necessary and proportionate and the candidate should be informed that vetting is taking place; vetting should take place at the appropriate stage of the application

process so that any comprehensive vetting is left to the last stage of the process. Nowadays, it is becoming increasingly common for clients to specifically request that this information is obtained as a condition of them instructing the law firm.
- Records should be kept for no longer than is necessary and should be securely stored or destroyed.
- International firms also need to be careful about sending personal data between countries, where particular restrictions can apply.

5. **Confidentiality**

The candidate's duties of confidentiality towards their current firm and clients will give rise to certain risks for the recruiting firm. At the recruitment stage, confidentiality obligations might be breached by an enthusiastic candidate eager to impress at interview, or in the information revealed in the candidate's business plan or lateral partner questionnaire. Information that is subject to confidentiality obligations is likely to be defined in the candidate's contract of employment or partnership deed but commonly it will include details about individual client charge-out rates, revenues and names of team members. The hiring firm also needs to be sensitive to a candidate's confidentiality obligations, particularly when conducting its own due diligence about the candidate. Once a potential candidate has been identified and contacted, take great care in undertaking diligence about that candidate among clients. If the client reports back to the candidate's law firm, this could have potentially disastrous consequences for the partner who will no doubt be in breach of his confidentiality obligations to his current firm for having disclosed confidential client information to a competitor.

There is also a risk that once the candidate is recruited, they will be tempted to use confidential information from their old job to help develop new business. So that the hiring firm can mitigate its risks in relation to this, it must do what it can to ensure this does not happen. Thus, any offer of employment should be made conditional on compliance with confidentiality obligations and the candidate should be reminded in writing of the need to observe any confidentiality obligations owed to their previous employer.

6. **Hiring the wrong person for the job**

Failure to meet each other's expectations can be a key factor in failed lateral hiring, particularly in relation to hiring senior associates and partners. Did the candidate fully understand the job and the compensation package (including bonus, tax and social security implications)? Did the hiring firm fully understand what the candidate needed to develop and be successful? Did the candidate oversell their expertise resulting in them being hired at the wrong level with salary or drawings too high for billing rates? Asking the right questions in the interview process is vital to ensure both parties are fully informed and fully understand each other's requirements.

One of the most common issues in relation to the hiring of partners relates to client following. A recruiting firm should always be extremely wary about being seduced into believing a candidate's promises about the clients they are able to bring. It goes without saying that a recruitment agent's statement that a partner has a following of "US$2 million" should not be taken at face value.

There may be a variety of reasons why candidates are unable to fulfil their promises, including:

- Large international law firms tend to diffuse client relationships across the firm's various departments (and a number of partners), making it far harder for one partner to take that client away from the firm.
- A large client may be embedded not only with the departing partner but also a group of associates at the old firm, making it easier for the old firm to retain them, simply putting a new partner in place but with the same team of associates.
- Fee rates – the candidate may be moving to a firm with higher charge-out rates than the client is used to at the previous firm.
- Conflicts of interest – once on board, the candidate and the hiring firm realise that the firm has either a legal or a commercial conflict which prevents it from acting for that client.
- The promised client is already bound by panel agreements.
- Failures in integration – the candidate may be unable to develop the practice they need because they have inadequate access to other sector or practice group lawyers in the new firm.

Cultural fit has already been mentioned in the context of discrimination risks above. Hiring a person who ends up being the wrong cultural fit can be extremely damaging to the dynamics of the existing team members.

Detailed and precise questions should be asked at interview and in a questionnaire, aimed at establishing not only general matters, but also the 'risk profile' of that individual generally: for example, whether they have been involved in a negligence claim or any regulatory action, and their attitude towards various risk issues. Find out about the candidate's values and behaviours; what drives them; how they deal with their colleagues; and how they manage people. Do they show ethical duties towards their current firm at interview? Do the candidate's personal values fit with the firm's values in matters such as honesty, integrity, respect for others and professional mastery? It may be difficult to find out why a person is moving on, particularly if the reason relates to personality issues. It will usually be legally problematic in most jurisdictions to make enquiries of third parties without the candidate's consent, unless those enquiries are made on a no-names basis (eg, by asking a client who they rate in a certain practice area). However, subtle questioning during the interview may uncover some relevant information.

Cultural fit from a risk point of view is important, and therefore hiring firms may well also wish to consider what information is available about the risk culture of potential joiners' previous firms and the extent to which this is compatible with their own risk management culture. Although a good recruitment consultant will be of assistance in these areas, it is prudent for firms to carry out their own due diligence.

In this regard, it is worth mentioning here one recent innovation that is becoming more popular in relation to the lateral hiring of partners: the use of external objective due diligence reports. These are usually compiled by the research teams of search firms. They will identify 50 to 60 individuals to contact from clients, ex-clients, colleagues, former colleagues, recruiters and so on to get a perspective on the candidate, not usually by name but by asking who they would recommend in a particular area of expertise and what they enjoy about working with them and what challenges they see. Often the candidate's name will be mentioned or if it is not when it should, then that reveals a great deal. When carried out properly, these reports can be very helpful; if they are done early enough in the process they can save a lot of time and effort by disqualifying the candidate. These reports may be costly, but set against the total investment for a lateral partner hire they can be good value.

Lateral hiring of partners – the hiring process

Ruth Bonino
Chris Holme
Clyde & Co LLP

In this chapter we concentrate on the lateral hiring of partners, outlining tips for success and considering, in particular, the due diligence process, which should of course be a far longer and more detailed process than when hiring associates.

It is also worth remembering and considering the amount of due diligence that is carried out by most large firms now in relation to internal candidates for promotion. These commonly involve multi-day assessments, interviews, examination of business plans and sponsors' reports. Given the amount of background work put into internal candidates – whom a firm already knows well – firms should consider whether their work and due diligence on external or lateral hires start to look a little light.

1. **Reasons for failure in the hiring process**

   The success rates for the lateral hiring of partners are often poor. There are a variety of reasons for this. They may be attributable to failures by the hiring firm, the candidate or the recruiter. Identifying, being aware of and analysing these reasons will help law firms to minimise the risk of failure.

   Key law firm failures from a business point of view include failures to:
   - develop a proper strategy, especially if it is a new practice area for the firm;
   - understand the impact the lateral hire will have on firm culture and existing clients;
   - conduct proper due diligence;
   - properly integrate the lateral hire;
   - examine the profitability of the lateral hire; and
   - adequately identify legal and commercial risks.

   Key law firm failures from an administrative (HR team) point of view include:
   - not reading the recruiter's terms and conditions properly and then being caught out later in the process;
   - not respecting the fact that they should move at the candidate's pace; some want a fast approach, whereas others want a slow one;
   - not obtaining comprehensive interview notes from all the interviews so that future interviewers have a full picture;
   - not describing the process in sufficient detail to the candidate;
   - not planning the production of paperwork for approvals early enough in the process.

Key candidate failures include failures to:
- appreciate the constraints in bringing clients over to the new firm;
- operate to an achievable business plan;
- consider and address potential conflicts early;
- explore and verify promises made by the hiring firm;
- do due diligence on the hiring firm including on cultural fit.

Key recruiter failures include:
- saying to candidates they represent a firm when they have not been instructed;
- failing to be flexible on fee arrangements in difficult market conditions;
- not being realistic in relation to the candidate's potential following;
- sponsoring the candidate to a number of firms at the same time, leading to horse trading;
- carrying out insufficient research on the hiring firm's strategy and culture;
- trying to negotiate too hard on behalf of the candidate's package;
- approaching partners at the hiring firm directly and excluding other personnel at the firm who deal with lateral hires (such as the managing partner or the HR team).

2. Tips for success

2.1 Planning

Before embarking on the hiring process, it is vital to have a plan. The planning stage involves making a strategy and a business plan which may identify the need to hire in order to develop a new practice area, increase capacity in an existing area or set up in a new geographical area.

Many firms practice opportunistic hiring strategies, believing that if you recruit the right people the right clients will either come across with them or be attracted to the team because of the reputation of a particular individual. This may work but it is important that this approach does not replace proper planning and strategic thinking. A client or sector-focused strategy will ensure that the hiring strategy fits with the firm's core business, ensuring that new clients meet the firm's profile, rather than making the firm ever more diverse and fragmented, which will result in the firm losing its focus on the sectors and clients it aims to work in and for.

There should be a departmental or a sector group business plan. The main reason why firms engage in lateral hiring of partners is to increase turnover by expanding the firm's client base. It is therefore advisable to have a business plan that includes an analysis of the client market and the clients the firm wants to target within it. This will assist the firm in analysing the candidate's business plan and CV.

Recruitment priorities should be aligned to the sector group business plan to ensure the right specialist legal advisors are recruited to service that sector.

2.2 Consider if hiring is really the best solution

Hiring is not always the best quick fix – at least not by itself. Problems are often best fixed before hiring. If the department is not profitable, it may need a complete overhaul, which will take time and effort. This alone may be all that is needed but in some instances an overhaul coupled with a lateral hire may provide the best solution. Indeed this may be needed to attract the right candidate – after all, why would a candidate with a good following want to join an unprofitable department?

It is also important to consider the politics of hiring. Reaching consensus about hiring with the other partners is by far the best way forward since to do otherwise could impact negatively on other partners and may cause more problems than it solves.

2.3 Choose recruiters well

Hiring people is not easy. Firms hang on to good lawyers and good lawyers often do not have time to job search. Finding the right method of recruiting the right people will depend on the nature of the law firm, the particular practice area and the candidate sought. The hiring firm may choose to use a head hunter (the search method). The advantage of this is that it allows the firm to target its approach and thereby enable the recruiter to convince the candidate that they are only one of a small number of candidates the firm is considering. The disadvantage of this method lies in the psychology of the process: you are seeking the candidate and therefore trying to sell yourself to the candidate. This is fine for large firms with well-known brands, but becomes more difficult for less well-known firms. The other main disadvantage of this approach is that it can lead to some complacency from the candidate. Because the firm has approached them, they may not expect tough questioning or to have to make a sales pitch. Further, there is a risk that the hiring firm, so taken with the political kudos of successfully hiring the hard hitter, fails to conduct the proper due diligence processes and follow the business plan.

The alternative approach is where the law firm advertises the vacancy and the candidate therefore has to sell themselves to the firm, putting greater emphasis on the candidate's business plan. The downside of this approach is that the best potential candidate may not see or respond to the advertisement. The individuals who respond may well be people looking to move already and may not necessarily be the best lawyers or the best fit.

Whatever method of hiring is chosen, choosing the right recruiter is key. Firms are advised to keep the recruiter on side, for the sake of their candidate. For those law firms which would not automatically come to the top of a recruiter's short list, having an excellent recruitment process that the recruiter knows will impress at interview could make all the difference and get that law firm on the recruiter's list. Firms should therefore ensure that they educate their recruiters effectively, and impress and encourage them with proper briefings.

2.4 Consider direct sourcing

Direct sourcing is invariably the preferable way to recruit lateral hires rather than using recruiters, particularly if a firm is seeking to expand a niche practice area. Very often the partners already practising that area of law will know of the main players, and a lot of recruiting is often initiated by networking, for example at conferences. Many recruiters will simply refer the people they rate or know. Direct sourcing has the added advantage of not having to pay a hefty fee. Nevertheless, the risks remain the same, whether or not the candidate is known to the recruiting firm, so it is still vital to conduct proper due diligence.

2.5 Conduct due diligence

It is vital that, before entering into any contract, the recruiting law firm has carried out full due diligence on every individual it is proposing to hire. The risks of not carrying out proper due diligence, or doing it badly, have been explored above and a due diligence checklist can be found in later in this chapter.

Team hires present additional issues. Clearly, all team members should be investigated individually by the hiring firm. Relying on a 'recruiting sergeant', who is often a senior partner in the team, is very dangerous, both practically and legally. From a practical point of view are they objective enough? Is every team member really required, or are some merely included out of loyalty? From a legal point of view, by acting as recruiting sergeant the senior partner will undoubtedly be in breach of various obligations to his or her current firm.

2.6 The interview process

The interview should include assessments of:
- cultural and commercial fit; and
- expertise.

The first interview will probably be a general fact-finding exercise before preliminary conflict checks are made and a business plan requested. It will often be hosted by the sponsoring partner and a member of Human Resources who has previously reviewed the candidate's CV and carried out administrative checks. The first interview will establish whether the candidate has potential and whether it is worthwhile making further enquiries and checks, but it is also a good time to weed out completely unsuitable candidates, whether in terms of experience, client following or cultural fit.

Assessing whether the candidate has the right cultural fit should be one of the main objectives of the first interview. The firm should be assessing whether the candidate's personal values fit with the firm's values in matters such as honesty, integrity, respect for others, and professional expertise. It will also want to know about the candidate's personal drivers, whether money, recognition, power, legacy or developing others, for example.

In terms of expertise, this would be covered briefly at the first interview and explored in more depth at second interview stage, where questioning should be designed to uncover whether the candidate has the skills and experience needed to run the business and integrate it properly into the firm's existing business.

There may be a number of interviews. For all the interviews, it is best to:
- structure the interview so that you can compare candidates properly – a checklist and an interview template will assist with this;
- decide what message you want to get across, but whatever the message, treat the process as a marketing opportunity – it is a small world and if you fail to impress, word can get round;
- consider if tough interviewing is necessary – probing interviews will give a

good impression to the candidate but asking irrelevant questions will have the opposite effect;
- include human resources to encourage and reinforce a strategic approach to hiring;
- above all, be disciplined and keep to time to avoid frustrating (and potentially losing) a candidate. Once the interview process is complete, keep the candidate on side by being clear on the next steps and the timing of them, factoring in any additional due diligence that needs to be carried out.

3. Checklists for partner and team lateral hires

Set out below is a detailed checklist of the background checks that would normally be made and the documentation to request. Also set out below is a list of questions that a firm should ask in the form of a questionnaire and, most importantly in relation to partner lateral hires, an outline of the detail needed in the business plan. The information contained in the questionnaire and business plan can then form the basis of more detailed discussions – usually at the second and third interview stages.

3.1 Identification of and negotiation with potential candidates

- Request from any candidate a copy of, or more likely due to issues of confidentiality, an extract of their contract of employment, partnership/ shareholders' agreements, share schemes or other documentation relevant to their obligations to their employer/ex-employer/firm. If the candidate is unable to do this, ask the candidate to inform you about matters such as the restrictions they are subject to and notice they are required to give. Seek legal advice on the enforceability of any restrictive covenants that might restrict the candidate's activities after termination of employment and any other legal obligations that may be relevant to the hiring process.
- Remind candidates that they are expected to comply with their legal obligations to their employer or ex-employer, particularly confidentiality obligations. Any offer of employment could be made conditional on compliance with existing obligations to the candidate's ex-employer.
- When targeting a team of lawyers, check how the target team or individuals have been identified. Have names been obtained from an individual in breach of their obligations to their current firm? The hiring firm should ensure that it does not ask for, or receive names of members of the target directly from the main target or other team members. Consider appointing a well-regarded recruitment consultant to assist at arm's length with the recruitment process. Take legal advice in relation to risk here.

3.2 Conducting due diligence

(a) Background checks

Establish what can be lawfully carried out in terms of background checks in the jurisdiction concerned. Common checks include those listed below, although do check what is lawful in each country:

- Immigration – does the candidate have the right permissions to live and work in the relevant jurisdiction?
- Regulatory – does the candidate have the right qualifications and regulatory approvals to practise law in the relevant jurisdiction?
- Internal conflicts – check that the clients the candidate is promising to bring do not present any conflict issues with the firm's existing clients.
- Social media – a quick Google search and some more digging online could prove a useful source of discovering more about the candidate's character and outside interests.
- Psychometric tests – ensure that these are carried out and evaluated by trained personnel.

(b) Documentation checklist
- candidate's CV;
- business plan/lateral partner questionnaire;
- recruitment partner's/sponsor's report;
- report by management board or committee set up for selection purposes;
- client references.

(c) Business plan/lateral partner questionnaire

At interview there should be particular focus on the candidate's business plan and cultural fit. In relation to partner hiring in particular, analyse the key documents: the candidate's business plan, references and sponsor's report. Key details that should ideally be shown in the business plan are as follows, although you need to consider in each jurisdiction whether certain items of information would breach confidentiality obligations or fiduciary duties to the candidate's current employer with respect to information which the employer may regard as proprietary:
- client work, billings and business development information to include historical billing and collection rates in the current year and the preceding three years;
- a description of billing methods such as any discounts, premiums, blended rates, or other special fee arrangements currently used;
- estimated portable amounts – to include a list of named clients, the nature of the relationship, the fees collected over a two-to-three-year period and the expected future fees;
- the candidate's requirements in terms of the team required for the candidate's practice;
- a description of the candidate's target market, and potential new clients within the target market;
- business development activities undertaken by the candidate recently;
- the candidate's current compensation package;
- the candidate's concerns about running conflict checks on the candidate's named clients;
- practice restrictions such as restrictive covenants and notice for withdrawal;
- chargeable and non-chargeable hours including current charge-out rate for the candidate and any members of the candidate's current team.

(d)   Candidate questionnaire
It is vital to ask the right questions and these are best covered initially by a formal candidate questionnaire, which the candidate should complete before the second interview. The types of question that should be covered include:
- the nature of the restrictive covenants that the candidate is bound by – as evidenced by the relevant documents;
- business activities outside the candidate's legal practice;
- outside positions such as director, trustee, public office;
- legal permission to work and practise;
- professional liability insurance – whether any insurance cover has been refused or declined;
- professional conduct – has the candidate ever been subject to any investigation or had a sanction applied by a professional regulatory body?;
- involvement in civil proceedings or in any insolvency process;
- criminal history;
- references – contact details of at least two current clients who can be contacted for a reference.

3.3   Making the offer

- When making any offer, either of employment or to join the partnership, the offer should be made subject to client references.
- Take into account the candidate's obligations to serve notice and whether the candidate's firm is legally entitled to require the candidate not to perform any duties while serving notice (known as 'gardening leave' in many jurisdictions), bearing in mind there may well be restrictions on the candidate's ability to contact clients during this period.
- Make the offer conditional on compliance with existing obligations towards the candidate's existing firm.

The following additional steps should be undertaken in conjunction with making the offer to a partner lateral hire:
- Make sure all internal conflict checks are done before making the offer.
- Ensure the relevant internal approvals are obtained before obtaining appropriate board/partner approval for the hire.
- Offers should be drafted in conjunction with the appropriate partner and business service unit, department and support staff responsible for the recruitment of the partner.
- Consider carefully in relation to the financial aspects of the offer the psychological impact of offering too much or too little, and of whether to accede to demands for a guarantee. If a guarantee is so important to the candidate, the firm might ask itself whether the candidate is really worth hiring (after all, a guarantee hardly stimulates performance); on the other hand, turning it down might lead to resentment and internal turmoil.

3.4 Pre-litigation steps

- Think carefully how to react to any Letter before Action received from the candidate's previous employer or firm. Any such letter may require the hiring firm to give undertakings to protect the previous firm's business interests, such as confidential information and customer connections. Giving such undertakings might avoid future litigation but it could mean the new hirer gives more than is legally required, for example, if the restrictive covenants are not enforceable.

Integration of lateral hires

Anthony E Davis
Hinshaw & Culbertson LLP

1. Identifying the key risks

Anecdotal evidence indicates that the success rate of lateral hiring by law firms is dismal. This is demonstrable by three measures.

1.1 The laterally hired lawyer leaves very quickly after joining

Most firms report that fewer than half of all lateral hires are still at the firm after two years. As a New York judge once remarked, lateral hiring is a "revolving door" process – once a lawyer has done it, he or she can see how easy it is, and can repeat the process at will. Since almost invariably the financial risk is almost entirely on the shoulders of the hiring firm, the laterally hired lawyer can be on a perpetual search for the firm where the grass is greenest.

1.2 Long period before the laterally hired lawyer is profitable

Inevitably there is a time lag of at least months before the laterally hired lawyer begins to generate revenue at all, and frequently it takes a considerable amount of time – sometimes years – before the lawyer is performing up to the anticipated level of profitability. If the due diligence process was inadequate, sometimes the promises are never fulfilled, and true profitability is never achieved.

1.3 Laterally hired lawyer proves to be a disruptive force within their practice group or the firm generally

Law firms' due diligence tends to focus on the financial promise of a potential hire, not on the personal or cultural fit. This can prove to be a huge and costly mistake. Corporations frequently engage in and require significant personality and psychological tests to determine compatibility prior to significant hires. Law firms are fearful of losing a potential catch simply by suggesting such a review, or because of the delays this process would cause, and because a rival firm with no such requirements will snap up the prospect. While many firms profess to have a 'no screamer' policy, the limitations on the ability (or willingness) to check personal references frequently prevent firms from discovering that they have imported a troublesome individual until it is too late. Disruption can come in many ways. A lateral hire who refuses to follow the hiring firm's client intake or practice management protocols can cause huge expenditure on management time and effort in doing after-the-fact clean-up of problems these disruptors have caused. A look at malpractice claims against larger law firms in the United States would show that a very substantial proportion involve lateral hires who were not effectively integrated into the firm and were left alone without adequate oversight.

2. How to manage these risks in practice

Assuming that there has been adequate due diligence, and the hiring decision is itself prudent, there is one, fundamental and all-encompassing solution to managing these risks with respect to every laterally hired lawyer (or group of lawyers) – a comprehensive written integration plan, having the following characteristics:

- it must be prepared in advance of the hiring;
- the contents must be agreed in advance by the prospective laterally hired lawyer and by the practice group or team leader, who will be responsible to the firm's management for the success of the hire; and
- both the lateral hire and the practice leader must be accountable (in terms of ultimate compensation) for following through on all of the elements of the plan.

2.1 Goals of each party

It is critical that both parties identify and agree in advance the definition of success, in terms of the integration of the lawyer into the group and firm, the integration of the hired lawyers' clients into the firm (so that they become the firm's clients, not the lawyer's clients) and the involvement of the lawyer in work for the firm's existing clients. The fundamental objective is to create a plan that jams shut the revolving door so that the lateral has no need or incentive to move on. An important component of the definition of success will be to establish clear parameters for advancement, professionally and in terms of income, as the integration process proceeds. Career options – of counsel or full partnership, for example, should be discussed, as well as variations on work schedules, career paths, client mixes and compensation packages.

2.2 Merits of a formal, organised approach to support

There is simply no substitute for a written plan that meets all of the criteria discussed above. It is the only way to assure both parties that the hiring will be supported in a way that is most likely to secure success for everyone – the individual and the firm. The sink-or-swim approach taken by many firms on the arrival of a new lateral hire: "Here is your office, here is your computer and here is the secretary whom you will share with (however many) other lawyers – now go and make money for us" is at least as likely to fail as it is to succeed.

(a) Planning integration – what should be involved?
The firm should develop a template or form for all lateral hires. It should require the input of the human resources department, the practice group or team leader and, in larger firms, a geographic, industry or practice leader. The template should be discussed and modified as needed with each hire individually, so they know what to expect – and what is expected of them.

(b)   Responsibility and accountability

Someone in the firm must be responsible, and accountable for the implementation and follow through of the integration plan. While some firms view it as a human resource function, the better approach is to make the practice or team leader, or someone they designate from within the practice, to be responsible. The role of that person is to follow through on every aspect of the agreed plan, such as integration of clients in both directions and integration of the individual into every aspect of the firm, including compliance with firm policies and procedures. This will involve significant time and effort in attending meetings and in preparing regular written reports to senior management regarding progress towards the agreed objectives.

(c)   Integration budget

The plan must account for, and reward, the time and effort spent by the designee of the firm and the lateral in putting the plan into effect. Similarly, the plan should define the metrics of success along the way, and ultimately, including the matter of income and professional status.

2.3   Additional ways to improve success rates

(a)   Upgrade the oversight of the integration processes

Create a project team to assess, review and continuously upgrade the firm's induction procedures. The team should interview recent hires and the individuals responsible for the integration plan. Find out what could be improved, and update the metrics, including a checklist of expectations of what the laterally hired lawyer should achieve within designated time frames.

(b)   Senior management to oversee and remain accountable

Senior management must remain involved in overseeing and managing the accountability both of the lateral hire and the person designated to oversee the integration plan. It is very important that the firm reviews, analyses and tracks the success of the lateral hiring programme generally, and the progress of each individual hire. If senior management is not prepared to make this investment of effort, it should not be investing in the lateral hire in the first place. Senior management should have its own role in the integration plan, in terms of responsibility for involving the hire, by seeking input on firm decisions and involving them in social and professional events.

(c)   Two-way process

Underlying everything in this approach is that it must be two-sided. It should not be founded on the "we're paying you a lot of money, now it's up to you to deliver". Rather, it is all about how to work together most productively to integrate lateral hires and their clients, introduce them to the firm's clients and make them feel valued members of the firm. This can only be accomplished for every hire if there is a process and a system in place that always includes a written plan with the characteristics described in this chapter.

Personal development policies

Jaime Fernández Madero
Fernández Madero Consulting

The first stage of implementing a law firm's risk management strategy is to put in place policies setting out the rules and procedures that individuals working in the firm must observe. These may include, for example, policies that deal with anti-money laundering, anti-bribery, conflicts, confidentiality and data protection, information technology and whistleblowing. This chapter considers how a firm can encourage individuals in the firm to observe these policies and therefore reduce the firm's exposure to risk. For this purpose, it is necessary to consider three key areas when planning and implementing a risk management strategy: culture; evaluation and rewards; and coaching and training.

1. **Culture**

When seeking to enforce compliance with these policies and procedures, a firm needs to recognise and bear in mind collective and individual perspectives:
- The collective perspective recognises that the general environment (legal, cultural and managerial) in a particular jurisdiction exerts significant influence on these matters, since effective compliance is dependant to a large extent on the voluntary adherence of individual professionals to the whole system. Compulsory measures may play their role and are needed, but a high reliance on the enforcement system will not produce the expected results.
- The individual perspective recognises that a risk management policy is ultimately applicable to individuals and that individual compliance is what makes it successful or not.

Culture is something that affects both collective and individual behaviours, and has a significant influence in all management matters, including risk management. It could also be argued that culture has a different influence depending on the characteristics of the particular jurisdiction. Looking at the case of Latin America, for example, countries have traditionally found it difficult to maintain a stable legal environment at both regulatory and court-decision levels, although with differences among them. Among many possible reasons for this phenomenon is a lack of confidence and respect for the legal system, which produces a culture where citizens feel less protected, and obliged by the applicable law and therefore find ways to get around it.

Latin American lawyers are also part of this culture, which becomes apparent in different ways when they have to practice law and participate in organisations such as law firms. Although there are regulations in each country that provide standards for the practice of law and punishment for violations, there are relatively few cases when breaches of the law have been penalised harshly. As a consequence, risk management policies could be taken mainly as a set of best practices for 'hygienic purposes', aimed at having the appearance of protecting relationships with clients and/or as a group of principles and values that ethical lawyers should comply with. If legislation and the courts are not very active in establishing and applying clear limits, more aggressive firms might be tempted to look the other way.

What the Latin-American example shows is that firms that wish to establish risk management policies should first consider carefully how they will handle the cultural part of the equation. When lawyers do not feel compelled to observe the rules, and when top-down enforcement only has a limited effect, a strong culture will be needed to compensate for those limitations. Culture should provide a set of beliefs, values and behaviours that individual lawyers will incorporate progressively as their own, giving sense and direction to their daily practice. When culture is strong, lawyers comply with internal policies because they believe in them. However, if a culture is intended to work to support a set of rules, then that culture needs to be realistic and well embedded in the society in which the firm is operating. If a firm fails to appreciate this limitation, it risks trying to develop a culture which becomes more a set of abstract ideals than a concrete guide for behaviours to which lawyers may relate.

In order to develop an effective cultural environment there needs to be intense communication at every relevant level of the firm, by means of internal training and presentations, and also team and individual coaching. The objective is to achieve an appropriate understanding by all participants of how the system works, but also of its sense and purpose. A strong culture provides peer pressure, which might be more effective than formal regulations.

2. Evaluation and rewards

It is very important that a firm builds into its risk management policies rewards for compliance and penalties for non-compliance. Regardless of how formal or structured an evaluation system is put together, it is vital that lawyers are rewarded for compliance and penalised otherwise.

By evaluating behaviours and setting rewards, the firm is telling its lawyers that it means business. A push for cultural change would probably prove ineffective if the firm does not reflect it in its reward system, which is where the firm's management demonstrates its real values. But for the reasons explained above, the rewards system should work to help professionals embrace the underlying reasons behind, and the values of, a risk management system, rather than using it to punish non-compliance. If professionals feel that the reward system is unfair and inflexible, it will probably be ineffective in the long term. A clever system will find a balance between lenience and intolerance, depending on the particular circumstances. Although you cannot always work on a case-by-case basis, in its first stages some flexibility should be allowed so the firm can adapt to new standards and the culture can develop and become more embedded in the organisation.

Very often, an evaluation system is structured in a negative way with only penalties for non-compliance. If the professional commits a breach, there is a penalty; but there is no reward for a positive contribution to the risk management system. By rewarding positive contributions, the system will assume a higher sense of importance, and therefore obtain higher engagement and commitment from the lawyers. A risk management system based exclusively on the fear of sanctions will rarely produce high-quality performance.

The principles mentioned above are applicable both to career advancement and compensation policies. Whatever system the firm uses, risk management policies will have a much better chance of success if they have an impact on compensation and career progression. An interesting question is whether different management approaches and policies could be better structured to support risk management policies. It may be argued, for example, that rewards and career systems that prioritise a firm's objectives above individual ones, and long-term goals above short-term needs, would give stronger support to risk management policies. This is because a risk management policy should not be confined to encouraging individual benefit or short-term achievement, especially when you find relatively relaxed standards in your jurisdiction regarding these matters.

3. **Training and coaching**

Any risk management programme should provide for adequate training and coaching for all lawyers from the very beginning. Induction programmes for new and young lawyers should provide training sessions on risk management, including not only the technical aspects of the system but also its purpose, values and objectives. Since risk management systems are not very common in some jurisdictions, and are likely to face resistance from lawyers, it is important to build sense around them to help lawyers understand and balance the additional burdens they normally bring to a lawyer's practice.

Lawyers do not like to dedicate long hours to management matters, so it is key that training is well organised and not too time consuming. This is made easier if the rules themselves are simple to understand and apply. In addition to formal training, a coaching system should be established whereby professionals with different seniority can provide coaching on specific circumstances that appear as the system is applied. If firms want to have an effective coaching system, it needs to be part of the firm's culture and its reward system. It is suggested that higher management in the law firm, like the managing partner or relevant partners in charge of practice areas, are involved in some way in the communication and training process. This would send a very clear message of how important the matter is for the firm. If risk management programmes are just handled by technical personnel, it is likely that lawyers will consider them part of the administrative and bureaucratic part of their job.

Where a risk management system is simultaneously supported by a strong culture, a consistent reward and career system, and an adequate training and coaching programme, the chances of success increase significantly even in less developed jurisdictions such as Latin America.

Financial risk management in law firms

Anthony E Davis
Hinshaw & Culbertson LLP
Frank Maher
Legal Risk LLP
Wolfgang Weiss
University of Applied Arts, Coburg

1. **Criminal conduct**

   Sadly, although both the most recent and certainly the most dramatic example, the demise of Dewey & LeBoeuf is not the first law firm failure where prosecutors or regulators have alleged criminal conduct of its leadership. In England, for example, the Solicitors Disciplinary Tribunal struck off Jonathan Gilbert, saying that this was one of the worst cases that had come before it;[1] Gilbert accepted that he had improperly paid away funds held on behalf of lenders and it appeared that the losses, arising from multiple acts of dishonesty on some 43 property transactions, were likely to be around £50 million. His firm, Willmett Solicitors, was a small practice with four offices and about 60 staff and closed as a result, with innocent partners made bankrupt as well as Gilbert.

   In New York, in 2008, Dreier LLP closed after the arrest on fraud charges of its principal Marc Dreier, who was later convicted and sentenced to an extended jail term, which he is still serving.

   But the story of Dewey & LeBoeuf's collapse has significant risk management lessons for lawyers, their leaders and management – not to mention their lenders. Although the indictments recently handed down in New York against the firm's leaders do not tell the entire story (which will surely take some time to unfold and has yet to be proved), they show how prosecutors allege that frauds were committed, against whom, and how they went unnoticed for perhaps as many as five years.

   The prosecutors' allegations centre on interrelated frauds being perpetrated simultaneously, as follows:
   - first, that the firm's partners – many of whom had not been receiving the share of profits to which they thought they were entitled over several years – were repeatedly lied to about the state of the firm's finances and when their shares would be paid; and
   - second, that the lenders – both the firm's bankers and those to which bonds were sold – were also lied to about the state of the firm's finances over several years.

---

1   SDT Case 10532-2010.

There appear to be two explanations alleged by prosecutors as to how this may have been possible at all, let alone over a period of years. The first is that there was a total lack of transparency between the three senior managers and the rest of the firm, as well as its lenders. Even members of the committee of partners supposedly responsible for oversight, it is said, were never given accurate numbers and never insisted on regular and comprehensive distribution of the firm's financial information to all partners. The second is that it is alleged that the staff working under the direction of those managers were willing to accept direction to 'cook the books' on a regular and continuous basis.

Although the firm was, it seems, audited regularly, the three allegedly responsible for fraud apparently succeeded in pulling the wool over the auditors' eyes for several years. But the heart of the problem appears to have been that neither the elected committee of partners designated to oversee the three leaders nor the partners generally ever took the initiative to insist on the distribution of all of the firm's financial information on a regular basis. A critical reason for the firm's failure, then, was a total lack of transparency – and a total lack of insistence by the partners (and, it would appear, the lenders and auditors) on receiving transparent, comprehensive information on a continuous basis. The charges are not yet proved at the time of writing.

2. A review of other law firm failures

2.1 The US experience

The United States has seen the demise of a considerable number of law firms. Below are some of the more prominent firms to have failed in recent years, with a brief explanation of the principal cause of their demise:

- Howrey (2011) – a bad year, made worse by complete lack of transparency to the partners. Rapid expansion; overhead expense growing faster than revenue; and an excessive focus on litigation and reliance on contingency fee cases combined to weaken the firm. But it failed only a year after the most profitable year in its history – arguably because, like Dewey & LeBoeuf (but without any allegation of corrupt motive), the firm's leadership kept the partners in the dark about the growing financial problems until the last possible moment, so that when the financial numbers were finally announced, a group of the firm's biggest rainmakers exited in quick succession, making it untenable to continue to operate and bringing the firm down.
- Thacher Proffitt & Wood (2009) – over-dependence on a single practice area. The firm was almost totally dependent on one practice area, securitisation, so when the financial crisis hit and that business died, so did the firm.
- WolfBlock (2009) – over-dependence on a single practice area. A real estate-heavy firm in a real estate downturn sustained large year-to-year profit decline, resulting in partner departures and loan covenant defaults. The firm decided that it was better to dissolve in an orderly way than risk further firm operations.

- Thelen (2008) – a failed merger. This led to a rash of partner and practice group defections resulting in law firm failure.
- Heller (2008) – over-dependence on a single practice area. A litigation-heavy firm saw major cases settled in rapid succession, resulting in profit decline, partner departures and ultimate failure.
- Jenkens & Gilchrist (2007) – failure of management to act on a recognised risky practice area. Rogue partners in the tax practice of the firm in an office far from its traditional headquarters were involved in a fraudulent tax-shelter scheme – which was known to the firm's leadership, but was so profitable that they delayed taking steps to rein in the rogues. The firm was brought down when the regulators came on the scene.
- Testa Hurwitz (2005) – no succession plan in place when the founding and dominant managing partner died suddenly. The unexpected death of a dominant managing partner, the lack of a succession plan and dissension among the remaining partners resulted in firm dissolution.

There are some overarching lessons from the failure of these firms, all to a greater or lesser extent linked to management. Whether it be a failure to keep the partnership informed of developments affecting the firm (transparency), failure to address the problem of over-reliance on a single practice area or the flow of work, failure to develop and implement a succession plan, or treating a merger as a solution to institutional problems instead of addressing the problems – all of these failures are, at root, the result of a problem common to many law firms: insufficient time and resources devoted to managing the firm, and lack of trained and skilled managers. Law firm management is not for amateurs; rainmakers are rarely effective managers and in today's hostile environment, any management failure can be fatal.

2.2 The UK experience: Halliwells, Cobbetts, Manches and smaller firms

There have been many high-profile law firm failures in the United Kingdom in recent years. Lawyers often fear the professional liability claim exceeding their level of insurance, yet this is rarely – indeed, almost never – the cause of law firm failure.

Many of the UK failures were the London offices of well-known US firms, such as Altheimer & Gray, Coudert Brothers and Heller Ehrman; but in 2008 the legal community was rocked by the collapse of Halliwells LLP. It was ranked number 38 in the *Lawyer* Top 100 in the United Kingdom and, although solely a UK practice, was substantial by European standards.[2] In 2009 it had a turnover of £83 million and 154 partners.

Chambers magazine had reported that in 2006 the Halliwells managing partner had set out his vision to the annual partners' conference in Prague. Profits had grown by 25%. Using an overhead projector, he had predicted profits continuing to grow exponentially. The economist Nassim Nicholas Taleb, in *The Black Swan*,[3] observes how sales projections in Excel spreadsheets can grow effortlessly *ad infinitum*, and once on a computer screen they take on a life of their own, assuming a façade of reality.

---

[2] In 2005, before its period of dramatic expansion, it had been ranked number 90 in Europe by *The Lawyer*.
[3] Nassim Nicholas Taleb, *The Black Swan: The Impact of the Highly Improbable* (Random House, 2007).

There was much press comment about a property deal relating to Halliwells' opulent landmark office, designed by internationally renowned architect Norman Foster, under which the equity partners received £16 million personally and a further £5 million paid to the firm, leaving the firm with a heavily inflated rent bill. The firm had grown largely without recourse to borrowing, but in 2008 it arranged an £18 million loan facility. This was then followed by substantial bank borrowings to fit out the premises. When the firm went into administration it owed the bank nearly £18 million, and the members had nearly £13 million capital invested in the practice, of which approximately £10 million was funded through further bank loans. The projected return from the sale of parts of the business was less than £10 million.[4] Subsequent press articles reported that there were unsecured claims of over £191 million, but these included sums due on the balance of the office leases.[5]

One of the joint administrators was reported as saying, "Whilst that money [the £16 million from the property deal] would have been a lifeboat for the firm (had it not been paid out), it was not the principal cause of the failure. Halliwells' business model put it very much at the cutting edge of transactional activity and when this pipeline was affected by the downturn, it was badly impacted, so I'd say it was equally to blame."[6]

At first, the perception in the profession was that Halliwells was a one-off and, regardless of the business issues the practice had faced, many focused on the property deal as the prime cause.

It was after Halliwells' collapse that the Solicitors Regulation Authority (SRA), which regulates solicitors' practices in England and Wales, began to engage with firms through a programme of relationship management with named relationship managers for each of the larger firms. They began asking firms questions about their financial stability, but in the early days this was quite superficial. Gradually, it emerged that several firms were in significant financial difficulty.

It became apparent that there were firms borrowing not only from their main bankers, but from secondary lenders in order to cover short-term needs, such as tax, and professional indemnity insurance. Some firms were even borrowing to pay partners' drawings – against profits which may never have been realised. It has also become apparent, with the passage of time, that firms were even propping themselves up with substantial amounts of money collected from clients to pay for fees for barristers and professional expert witnesses, which are required to be kept in a separate client (trust) account.

The next large firm to fail was Cobbetts, again in the top 100 UK firms and established for over 200 years. In 2012 the firm called in administrators. The liabilities were in the order of £90 million; though as with Halliwells, these figures

---

4   See *In the matter of Halliwells LLP* [2010] EWHC 2036 (Ch).
5   Luke McLeod-Roberts, "Halliwells' Administrators Seek Funds to Cover £200m of Debts", *The Lawyer*, February 15 2011, available at www.thelawyer.com/story.aspx?storycode=1006976&PageNo=1&SortOrder=dateadded&PageSize=50#comments.
6   Chris Barry, "Halliwells' Payout not Sole Cause of Failure says Administrator", *The Business Desk*, July 22 2010, available at http://www.thebusinessdesk.com/northwest/news/27993-halliwells-property-deal-not-sole-cause-of-failure-says-administrator.html?utm_source=newsletter&utm_medium=email&utm_campaign=NorthWest_22nd_Jul_2010_-_Daily_E-mail.

were inflated artificially by the liability to pay rent for the duration of office leases. Even so, the firm's primary bank was owed £6 million. Unsecured creditors are expected to recover a mere 2% of what is owed to them.

As with Halliwells, the firm had suffered from the decline in corporate and property transactional work. Its turnover had shrunk from £60 million in 2008 to £44 million two years later. A significant issue was that the firm's impending failure came as a surprise to the majority of the partners – only four involved in management had had any detailed knowledge of the firm's predicament prior to its collapse.

Many smaller UK firms have failed due to economic circumstances – a combination, to varying degrees, of competition, reduction in work due to the economic situation (particularly in relation to property work), cuts in public spending on legal aid, significant reductions in the fees allowed on personal injury claims, competition with larger firms and poor business management. These have not been countered by any significant increase in litigation and insolvency work during the recession, which might have been predicted by some.

A significant number of firms have had problems with rogue partners and staff – in many cases people who were dishonest, but we should also include in this category those who take levels of risk beyond that which is acceptable to the partnership as a whole and do so surreptitiously. There have been rogue partners in a number of large and eminent firms, but those firms are big enough to survive. When the same issue occurs in a small firm, it frequently results in the firm either closing immediately or withering and dying within a couple of years. In the United Kingdom, this has been linked to the regulatory requirement to buy insurance: firms that have had these problems frequently find that insurance becomes either unavailable or unaffordable, and without insurance they are forced to close.

The failure of Dewey & LeBoeuf referred to above gave a new dimension, because this was a successful London office pulled down by the liabilities of its US parent. This highlighted a risk that the SRA later referred to as "group contagion".

Most recently, in 2013 Manches, a London-based firm with a £27 million turnover, failed. The administrators' report noted that turnover had fallen and that the decline had been exacerbated by the departure of one of its high-earning members, which in turn had led to cash-flow difficulties. By 2013 the firm had become unable to meet members' tax liabilities.

Availability of professional liability insurance, compulsory for all firms, has also been an issue for smaller firms, coupled with the failure of several insurers that provided cover predominantly to small firms.

3. **Financial management**

As we have seen, proper financial risk management is essential in partnerships. Law firms have been established by lawyers who are trained to and want to provide excellent legal advice. Most do not have an (additional) business administration background and are not used to financial management. Financial management is sometimes regarded as a necessary evil to deal with, but not to spend much time on. The client (ie, the legal work) always has priority.

Most law firms are established as partnerships. It is the spirit of a partnership that characterises the firm. Trust is an important value, and within such an environment control is difficult to achieve. Therefore, in order to avoid a breakdown, it is necessary to operate within the framework of best practice and follow a few principles of conservative financial management, as set out below.

3.1 Solid balance-sheet structure

In former times, a partnership used to be a life-time commitment and firms used to be small. Therefore, the partners used to own the office they operated in. Nowadays, the benefits of purchasing real estate do not fall together with the potential profits of selling the property many years later. Therefore, the partnership as a matter of principle should not own long-term assets. As it does not need significant capital to produce its services, the partnership should focus on the necessary IT infrastructure and office equipment. Whatever has a dual use, such as company cars or company flats, should be owned not by the partnership, but the partner who primarily uses it. That approach limits the depth of the balance sheet, which will consist of the above-mentioned equipment and accounts receivables.

All long-term assets on the balance sheet should be fully covered by equity. As a partnership typically does not have significant long-term assets, the duration of the long-term liabilities, such as loans, should be synchronised with the economic life of the assets purchased or can be taken off the balance sheet and leased (especially office equipment or computers).

The financing of accounts receivables could be covered either by a bank facility or, more conservatively, by deferred partner compensation or equity. As we will see later, the value of the accounts receivable might not always be their face value. Clients might withhold payments because of a series of reasons (see section 3.2 below). Therefore, the most conservative method would be to use paid-in capital, as this will not put pressure on the management to compromise in order to maintain liquidity. Alternatively, the firm could withhold distributions of profits (probably on an individualised basis) until the final payment of the accounts has been received. It is sound practice to make distributions to partners only when the accounts receivable have been paid and cash is in the bank account.

In principle, the partnership could also use a bank overdraft or short-term credit facility to fund its working capital. A credit line could be established and guaranteed by a percentage of the accounts receivable. This will limit the use of the facility. It should be used only on a temporary basis (in the case of defined growth or as a bridge in case of dispute on the worth of the receivables) as working capital to fund the wages of employees and office rent while the open receivables cannot be collected from the client. If there is no connection between the credit line and a defined use, there is a risk that it might be misused.

Mid and long-term loans to (newly elected) partners could be arranged in order to advance their equity contribution. There is no risk to the firm, as the partner will guarantee the payment by his work. Other long-term debt, especially to fund partners or associates for non-business related activities, such as private investments (excessive debt), should not be borrowed. The partnership should focus its funds on the absolute essentials of doing business. The partnership is not a bank and should not act like one. Therefore, retirement benefits should also be funded outside the firm's balance sheet.

3.2 Professional debtor management

As the main assets of the firm are accounts receivable, one should assume that clients will be good customers and all receivables will be paid after the agreed payment term or immediately in cases where no payment term has been agreed. The reality can sometimes be very different. The narratives of the invoices must be reviewed and entries negotiated. Sometimes due payments are not being paid by clients, as clients expect the law firm to wait until deals are closed (especially in private equity transactions) or share the (break-up) risks of transactions. Partners are hesitant to collect due invoices, because they are afraid that they might not be considered for the next transaction by the client. Also critical are discounts. Clients put leverage on firms. Compared with other industries, debt collection is typically less professionally managed in law firms and can result in significant write-offs. One reason for this is the fact that the partner who has been working on a deal is most often responsible for the debt collection. Because of the very special relationship between partners and their clients, there should be an institutional division of work. An independent finance person should help to review and manage the debtors. In cases of disagreement, an escalation to the practice group head as a negotiating partner might neutralise the pressure and also help to solve issues between the firm and the client.

Especially in smaller firms, concentration on one or a few very large clients can lead to uncovered fixed costs and can result in associates being under-used, and finally might result in losses if the client chooses to change law firm. Another area of concern within the debtor structure is an unexpected departure of a client. That might lead to an inability to divert the affected practice groups to other areas of work, or a lack of time or funding to do so.

Under competitive pressure, firms do not always ensure creditworthiness of new clients or limit the exposure to defined amounts. In the absence of a good payment history, the risk of overdue payments exists. Some clients might also want to use a law firm as a creditor. That increases the risk of write-offs. Some clients might use the firm only once, leaving a history of unpaid invoices. The market spreads the news, but it might be too late for the firm to react.

3.3 Solid cost management

Excessive costs are a significant reason for the failure of law firms. It could be the purchase of expensive real estate, excessive rent, excessive partner and associate remuneration or guaranteed payments for new joiners, all of which are beyond what the firm can afford. Symptoms are a rapid decline in profitability. There is no general rule pertaining to what a firm can afford. Firms are in competition and pressure is high to achieve good results.

The firm might pay more to associates or lateral hires then it should. One way to avoid this problem is to benchmark what successful competitors are paying (and demanding). Payments could be linked to results and be made only when these milestones have been reached.

With respect to rent, there are cycles in the markets. One should not enter into a long-term lease arrangement at the peak of the market. It is better to split arrangements into smaller pieces, which can be terminated at different points in time. Psychology can be an issue,[7] as most of these long-term rent agreements were signed at the peak of the market.

Another important factor in the cost calculation of any law firm is the imputed cost of partner work. Compared to other industries, this is a very substantial amount, as all partners are also key fee earners and their distribution is not shown in the profit and loss statement. Therefore a significant amount (between 30% and 50%) should be deducted from the sales volume in order to reach a realistic figure of a firm's true profitability.

3.4 Other principles, especially liability coverage

Another issue is the amount of insurance coverage. Too often, especially with large law firms, the amount necessary to cover the firm is not easily available in the insurance markets. The premiums being asked for the insurance coverage are very high and in some cases too expensive. In those cases the firm covers the obligatory liability and leaves a significant amount of consultancy volume uninsured. In other cases, firms with a poor track record of recent liability claims are forcing insurers to increase their premiums. If the firm cannot afford these, the firm has to shut down its activities even if it is operationally profitable. Even worse are law firms that operate while being uninsured or not adequately insured. This is not just an offence against supervisory rule; it leaves the clients without any protection in cases of malpractice.

A second area of concern is organisational inefficiencies with respect to financial reporting. In firms controlled by an inner circle of senior management, financial information may not be shared with operational partners. Partners are without knowledge of their firm's recent financial status and therefore unable to articulate and manage their own affairs.

4. Business management

Changes in the business environment and markets did cause some of the breakdowns of law firms. In some cases these changes came unnoticed. In other cases firms recognised these changes but were simply unable to respond quickly enough to them. In this section we differentiate between collapses caused by external forces and those caused by internal management failures.

4.1 External factors causing law firm failure

(a) Disaggregation of work

A huge trend in the last few years has been the disaggregation of work, driven by the purchasing departments of large corporations replacing general counsel in the procurement of legal services. While historically law firms used to charge by the hour and therefore built up their sales volume, the introduction of commercially proven

---

[7] On the psychology of markets, see Robert J Shiller, *Irrational Exuberance* (2nd edition, Princeton University Press, 2005), p 159.

purchase departments into the purchasing process destroyed the relationship between lawyers (order and supply) focused on legal issues and those focused on the type of work performed by the law firm. In the first step all kinds of non-legal work (eg, preparation of data rooms, management of purchase processes), formerly performed by paralegals within law firms, was moved to non-legal service providers. In the second step the type of work has been classified and reassigned from one law firm to several firms, each specialised on a certain level of legal work. Thus the price was readjusted to the firm with the lowest offer. Both steps led to a reduction in legal volume and reduced overall sales volume. Business management had to respond by either reducing headcount to the new sales volume or reducing price. Both activities reduced margins, and for those with already thin margins it caused shutdown or a reduction of operations.

(b) *Auction procedures*
Another threat was the competitive pressure resulting from the introduction of auction procedures that replaced traditional pitch processes in the purchasing procedure. These auctions led to reduced – sometimes unhealthy – pricing. Relatively inexperienced firms which had no routine in place to manage those processes were hit the hardest. Furthermore it was introduced in a phase of overcapacity, leading to unhealthy competition and losses in many firms. Some agreed on multi-year outsourcing contracts, which froze unfavourable prices and caused losses in segments for years. Renegotiation of prices is difficult in these circumstances.

(c) *The financial crisis*
The reaction of governments to the financial crisis created substantial work in regulatory practices. It reduced sales volumes in markets where complicated structured financial products had been designed and some of the real estate practice work simply vanished. Not all law firms had the ability to re-train lawyers or move them into areas where their expertise was needed. Some law firms that specialised in the high-volume, pre-crisis work went out of business quickly.

(d) *Volatile markets*
Other threats include over-dependence on highly volatile M&A-driven markets (investment banking) or special sectors, and clients which reduce their order volumes. In the M&A segments the unavailability of financing caused hundreds of transactions to be halted. If a firm was solely specialised or focused in this volatile work, it needed to cut back overheads and fixed costs quickly. Some of the costs, such as long-term leases or rent arrangements, could not be terminated without substantial penalties driving firms into losses.

All these external influences need to be monitored by business management, and when discovered need a quick response. In these volatile areas of work, flexibility in managing costs can be achieved by having a flexible workforce using the following measures: part-time arrangements, the introduction of sabbaticals and/or learning breaks. These measures have helped to overcome the 'dry' periods for law firms. The key is to quickly reduce fixed costs in order to avoid or minimise losses caused by unexpected sales cuts.

(e) **Liability claims**

A frequent reason for shutdowns is the threat of a serious liability claim from a client, regulators, etc. Even in cases where the claim might not result in damage payments, the threat that this might be realised causes some partners to leave a firm in search of a safe haven, which will result in cash losses and/or the withdrawal of other clients because of reputational reasons. This situation is the most difficult to manage. It will help if a liability cap has been agreed for this mandate and the insurance fully covers the damage up to that level. The reputational damage can be managed only by openly addressing the issue and active press handling, building confidence in the ability of the firm to manage and survive this threat.

4.2 Internal management causing law firm failure

(a) *Taking on new partners and employees*

Law firms try to grow their market share. If that is not possible by organic growth, management tries to accelerate the growth by developing new business segments with lateral hires, individual partners or teams. This approach is successful only if the law firm can identify candidates who are willing both to integrate into a new culture and to continue to work hard. In the cases where firms failed, investments in new partners were made with compensation guarantees disproportionate to their previous income levels, not measured by milestones agreed in a business plan, overly positive estimates and no adjustment possibilities in the process. Proper business management would accompany such a negotiation with a sound business plan covering the market potential (clients to keep/to win), prospective deals, transaction volumes, the cost involved in running the practice and prospective margins. With scenario planning, several options will be evaluated and results connected to the assumptions.

(b) *Entering new markets*

Another driver for losses is entering new markets without sufficient networks and experience of the relevant business practices. It can be geographical markets with closed market segments or sectors with strong players and deep relationships with their key advisers. Entering such an environment needs financial commitment, but even with this, a firm might be forced to give up the plan after several years of work. In order to fund such an activity, either cross-funding possibilities within one sector or a financial commitment to the plan is needed. If these are not available, losses are the inevitable consequence.

(c) *Failing to monitor business plans and empower supervisors*

Insufficient monitoring of business plans and empowerment of supervisors might prevent the recognition of losses. Decisive and brave actions are needed once the business has spun out of control. Sometimes management reviews the situation without taking action quickly and radically enough. Speed is often better than perfect solutions, especially in a situation where losses might lead to serious consequences for a whole firm.

(d) **Leavers**

The unplanned exit of partners might result in the loss of a client, which moves with that partner. That might cause the loss of business or sector expertise and prompt additional partners to leave, creating a 'stampede'. That leads to the inability to cover fixed costs with the shrunken sales volume and consequently to financial losses. In these cases, it is very hard to quickly replace the teams, especially as the market sees this as a reason not to join a firm. The situation might be accelerated by the lack of adequate succession planning.

The unplanned exit of associates reduces the ability to submit work in time and therefore might lead to unfinished or poor-quality work, or the exodus of more associates as they do not want to cover the work of unfilled posts. Preventive measures are regular (360-degree) feedback to associates to monitor their satisfaction levels and, if necessary, open discussions with the management about work changes.

5. New trends in regulation, rules and practice: the UK experience

5.1 Reasons for regulatory concern

The experience outlined above with the failure of Cobbetts, Halliwells and Dewey & LeBoeuf, compounded by the folding of a number of large regional firms and many small ones, some of which had been in existence for decades or even centuries, was – and is – a major issue for the profession in England and Wales. There is an added dimension which does not necessarily feature in other parts of the world, and that is the role of the SRA in maintaining financial protection for the public. The SRA has wide statutory powers to intervene in (ie, close down) a solicitor's practice in order to protect the public. It also maintains a compensation fund in order to compensate clients, primarily where there is dishonesty or other failure to account for money – both of which feature prominently where law firms have failed. These provisions impose a regulatory burden on the SRA to take action when a firm is failing. It is simply not an option to let a firm fold, leaving the clients unrepresented. A significant burden and major cost shouldered by the SRA is ensuring the safe storage of client files: firms that have failed to manage their file retention policies may have files going back many decades.

5.2 The regulatory response

As a result of the experience and regulatory obligations outlined above, the SRA took a number of steps to raise awareness of the need for financial management of law firms and ensure that it received appropriate regulatory attention where needed. The issue was addressed in a consultation paper in 2010,[8] which identified a combination of external and internal factors contributing to firms' problems.

External factors included poor trading conditions, interdependency with other

---

[8] SRA, Outcomes-focused Regulation – Transforming the SRA's Regulation of Legal Services, Annex B, Why the SRA is considering the financial stability of firms, April 30 2010, available at www.sra.org.uk/sra/consultations/ofr/annexb-firms-financial-stability.page

sectors in difficulty, availability of credit and economic conditions, changes in social behaviour or legislation, and competition.

Internal factors identified were ineffective financial management and controls, poor partner and staff retention and management, over-dependence on a single market, client or contract and poor business planning.

Further action included contacting the largest firms, discussions in meetings between the firms and their nominated SRA supervisory managers, starting with a pilot in January 2011,[9] raising the profile of the issue in public seminars, thematic reviews of personal injury firms, which were believed to be particularly at risk due to the impact of legislative changes substantially reducing costs[10] and prohibiting the payment of referral fees for their work.[11]

5.3 Professional duties to manage the practice

Solicitors in England and Wales have long been required, through professional conduct rules, to manage their businesses, but the spate of high-profile collapses increased the focus on this obligation and the attention it receives from regulators. The current provisions are set out in Principle 8, which requires solicitors to "run your business or carry out your role in the business effectively and in accordance with proper governance and sound financial and risk management principles"; and in Chapter 7 of the SRA Code of Conduct 2011,[12] which contains more detailed requirements for business management, including financial stability and business continuity.

5.4 Financial stability review

Aware of increasing numbers of firms in difficulty, the SRA embarked on a programme of intensive supervision of 160 firms. Further investigations were carried out on 2,000 firms. Firms were targeted using a risk-based approach, which took account not only of the SRA's perception of firms that may have been in difficulty, but also of large firms that would have a significant impact in terms of client protection and the cost of SRA intervention if they were to fail.

A questionnaire sought confirmation that firms had complied with their obligation to report to the SRA any indicators of serious financial difficulties relating to the authorised body, such as an inability to pay professional indemnity insurance premiums, rent or salaries, or a breach of bank covenants. They were asked whether they had negotiated time to pay tax liabilities. The questionnaire also asked whether any single client, group of clients or referral source accounted for more than 20% of turnover.

5.5 Regulatory guidance

SRA guidance[13] noted that some firms focused on work volume rather than

---

9   See the Relationship management pilot report, October 21 2011 at www.sra.org.uk/rm-pilot/.
10 The 'Jackson reforms', following the review by Lord Justice Jackson – see www.judiciary.gov.uk/publications/review-of-civil-litigation-costs/.
11 See sections 56–60 of the Legal Aid, Sentencing and Punishment of Offenders Act 2012.
12 See http://sra.org.uk/solicitors/handbook/code/part3/content.page.
13 See www.sra.org.uk/solicitors/handbook/code/part3/rule7/resources.page.

profitability. It identified a number of indicators of poor behaviour learned from its work with firms that suffered severe difficulties, and some good behaviour for which firms should aim, as follows.

(a)   **Poor behaviours**
- Drawings exceeding net profits.
- High borrowing to net asset ratios.
- Increasing firm indebtedness by maintaining drawing levels.
- Firms controlled by an 'inner circle' of senior management.
- Key financial information not shared with rank and file partners.
- Payments made to partners irrespective of cash at the bank.
- All net profits drawn, no reserve capital pot retained.
- Short-term borrowings to fund partners' tax bills.
- VAT receipts used as cash received, resulting in further borrowings to fund VAT due to Her Majesty's Revenue & Customs.
- Partners out of touch with office account bank balances.
- Heavy dependence on high overdraft borrowings.

(b)   **Good behaviours**
- All partners regularly receive full financial information including office account bank balances.
- Drawings are linked to cash collection targets and do not exceed net profits.
- Provision is made to fund partners' tax from income received.
- A capital element is retained from profit, and a capital reserve account built up.
- Premises costs are contained.
- Profitability levels are tested and unprofitable work is (properly) dropped.

In late 2013 the SRA published further guidance in two papers, "Navigating stormy seas: Financial difficulty in law firms",[14] and "Catching a chill: law firms and risks of group contagion",[15] the latter being of particular relevance to international firms.

---

14   See www.sra.org.uk/solicitors/freedom-in-practice/OFR/risk/resources/financial-difficulty-law-firms.page.
15   See www.sra.org.uk/solicitors/freedom-in-practice/OFR/risk/resources/law-firms-risks-group-contagion.page.

Non-lawyer ownership of law firms and outsourcing of legal services

Anthony E Davis
Hinshaw & Culbertson LLP
Heather Hibberd
Legal Practitioners' Liability Committee
Frank Maher
Legal Risk LLP

1. **The movement from protectionism to competition**

This subject is among the most fraught and contentious for lawyers everywhere. Essentially, it comes down to this: are lawyers uniquely qualified and entitled to regulate who may practise law, or should they be compelled to submit to outside regulation to determine the conditions under which they must operate? Until the third quarter of the 20th century, almost everywhere in the world, the answer was 'yes' to the first question and 'no' to the second. As a result, in most places lawyers regulated themselves (perhaps under the oversight of the courts), and determined whether and how they could operate alongside and share legal fees with others.

But then some chinks began to appear in the protectionist armour of the profession. In Europe, the EU regulators opened the door to hitherto unheard-of competition – at least to the extent of forcing the unwilling separatist legal professions in each member state to recognise that their peers in the other states were (really!) lawyers, and had to be given reciprocal rights of admission and practice in each other's domain. To the surprise of many, the sky did not fall.

In Australia, beginning with a simple move to permit lawyers to practise in a corporate business structure, something previously almost unheard-of happened – lawyers and law firms were permitted (subject to appropriate regulation) to accept non-lawyers as owners of and investors in law firms. Again, to the surprise of many, the sky did not fall.

Perhaps most dramatically, at the beginning of the 21st century, the legal profession in England and Wales found itself caught in a pincer attack from two sides – a public movement attacking the scandalous failures of the profession's own regulators to deal with its bad apples, and antitrust (monopoly) regulators who charged that the profession was rife with restrictive trade practices which hampered access to justice and kept prices artificially elevated. After several public commissions, the government forced the profession to swallow the pill of the Legal Services Act 2007, two of whose core values were attention to the needs of the consumer (not 'client'), and the promotion of competition in the provision of legal services. As a result, England and Wales became home, in short order, to a new creature – the alternative business structure (ABS) – where, as in Australia (but subject to much more heavy-handed regulation), non-lawyers were permitted to own and invest in law firms. As of the time of writing, 282 ABS entities had been approved by the Solicitors Regulation Authority (SRA) and established,[1] and applications for scores more were under review. Forty three had been licensed by the Council of Licensed Conveyancers, some of which are substantial practices (and the Institute of Chartered Accountants in England and Wales will shortly be authorised to grant licences, which is a potential game-changer). Yet again, as far as anyone can see, the sky has not yet fallen.

In Canada, the provinces are each actively (but in slightly different ways) considering what lessons are to be found in the Australian and English models and how (rather than whether) to open up the provision of legal services in Canada to non-lawyer ownership.

In Europe, the individual professions of many EU member countries appear to be fighting what are likely to be rearguard actions to stave off the arrival of anything that looks like an ABS. But inroads are already apparent and the strong policy of promoting competition will likely prevail so as to compel the separate professions across Europe to adapt to and accept the new models.

In the United States, protectionism still reigns. Traditionally, the problem of non-lawyer ownership of law firms has been controlled through two separate rules of professional conduct. In every state except the District of Columbia (DC), lawyers have always been and remain prohibited from sharing legal fees with non-lawyers. DC changed its rule some time ago under pressure from lobbyists and law firms themselves, to permit non-lawyers to be partners in law firms and to share fees and profits. But every jurisdiction has rules requiring that the independence of the legal profession be maintained, which has hitherto been interpreted to mean that only lawyers may own and operate law firms. The subject was first addressed on a comprehensive basis by an American Bar Association (ABA) Commission on Multi-Disciplinary Practice, which issued its final report in July 2000.[2] Although the commission recommended significant (albeit highly regulated) movement towards permitting non-lawyer ownership of and investment in law firms in the United States, the commission's report was roundly rejected by the ABA House of Delegates, at least in part because of fears that the accounting profession would 'take over' – fears which were further fuelled by the unfortunate timing of the Enron case and the demise of Arthur Anderson, during the period of these discussions.[3] Although the recent changes in Australia and in England and Wales have fuelled some further discussions, there is little enthusiasm within the organised bar to revisit the subject. And one jurisdiction's bar association (New York) has gone so far as to issue an opinion that the traditional positions must be so scrupulously maintained that no

---

1 As at July 10 2014. Some of these firms have subsidiaries with additional licences increasing the overall figure on a strict analysis.
2 See www.americanbar.org/groups/professional_responsibility/commission_multidisciplinary_practice.html.
3 See the link to the debate of the ABA House of Delegates in 2000, and the Recommendation to the individual States to reject efforts to introduce multidisciplinary practice in any form, both referenced in note 1 *supra*.

New York lawyer may enter into a partnership in a law firm that has non-lawyer owners in other jurisdictions, even if such arrangements are permitted in those places. While this position is untenable – given that not just England and Australia, but also DC permit such arrangements – it demonstrates the power of the traditional model within the US profession, and its resistance to change.

The perceived risks to the profession in the United States from any form of non-lawyer ownership and investment appears to be driven by the argument that lawyers' professional independence will be compromised, and, much more fundamentally, by plain and simple protectionism. While the jury is still out on whether the independence of lawyers is in any danger within ABSs in England and Wales, the evidence from Australia – with its longer experience of corporate entities providing legal services – is, to the contrary, that clients are being well served. It appears that there are fewer complaints of poor service and unethical conduct than before the introduction of the present regulatory regime.[4] It is an open question whether the positive benefits that appear to be flowing to clients, and the improved access to justice for the public at large that appears to be developing – particularly under the ABS regime in England and Wales – will at any point move the bar in the United States to moderate its opposition.

However, some chinks in the protectionist armour of the US legal profession have appeared in recent years, operating to some extent as an escape valve from the rigid operation of the traditional rules. First, many states permit law firms to share profits (as carefully, but arguably ultimately meaninglessly distinguished from fees) with non-lawyers, as long as the non-lawyers are employees of the firms rather than outsiders. This was the inevitable result of the introduction of professional (but non-lawyer) managers into law firms. Second, many states have adopted rules based on the ABA's Model Rule of Professional Conduct 5.7, which permits law firms to own and operate "ancillary businesses" that provide non-legal services. So although non-lawyers cannot own law firms, lawyers can own businesses (and share ownership and profits) with non-lawyers, as long as the businesses do not practise law.

2. Outsourcing[5]

2.1 Background

One of the consequences of the historic resistance from within the profession everywhere to competition in the delivery of legal services was the development of a process of disaggregation. Clients, disenchanted by the restrictions described above, have demanded that tasks formerly undertaken within law firms – and charged out at law firm rates – that were not strictly required to be performed by lawyers, should be given to non-law firm service providers, who came collectively to

---

4   See Adopting Law Firm Management Systems to Survive and Thrive: A Study of the Australian Approach to Management-Based Regulation of Law Firms (solicited for the Symposium on Empirical Research on the Legal Profession) (Susan Saab Fortney and Tahlia Gordon) 10 *University of St Thomas Law Journal* 152 (2012).

5   The author of this section, and the editors, are indebted to Michael Downey, on whose chapter on this topic in his book, *Satisfying Ethical Obligations When Outsourcing Legal Work Overseas, in intellectual property strategies for the 21st century corporation*, John Wiley & Sons, Inc (2011), this section is based.

be grouped under the heading legal outsource providers (LPO's). Initially, many of these were established not only outside law firms, but offshore. They began by handling document review in litigation and transactional contexts, but this has expanded very greatly, and in a variety of ways. For instance, some support functions that were traditionally handled internally within firms have been farmed out either to entities owned by the firms themselves or to third parties. Perhaps most interesting, given the resistance of the US legal profession to change, has been the recent development of non-law firm legal service providers in the United States, offering services well beyond those provided by the original LPO's.

2.2   Recent developments

In a February 14 2014 article in the online journal *Tech Cocktail*, author Joshua Kubicki reports that in the previous year almost $500 million was invested in the United States alone in companies providing services that either might once have been provided by law firms, or that are designed to replace outright law firm provided services. Among the examples he cites of new investment or acquisitions in this period are:

- LegalZoom and RocketLawyer, both online legal services platforms;
- Axiom Global Inc, which provides legal services from its virtual platform directly to corporate legal departments;
- Anaqua, a software company that helps law firms to improve their IP practices;
- Modus and Cicayda, both e-discovery technology and services providers;
- Judicata, which is building a new legal research platform that may be positioned as a competitor to the leading research tools offered by the industry giants of Thomson Reuters and LexisNexis;
- Modria, an online dispute resolution platform led by a two former eBay executives;
- Lex Machina, an online patent research analytics platform;
- Shake, a company trying to enable anyone to create, read, and sign contracts via mobile devices; and
- DocStoc, an online document library offering individuals and businesses customisable legal forms.

2.3   Ethical issues

Whatever the precise services being outsourced and acquired, either by law firms on behalf of clients or by corporate law departments directly, significant ethical issues must be addressed – by law firms, law departments (which are treated by regulators like law firms) and, consequently, the providers themselves. Since a very high proportion of this outsourcing work (reportedly about 90%) is done on behalf of clients in the United States and the United Kingdom, a body of ethics opinions and reports has developed to discuss these issues. The leading opinions and reports are:

- ABA Formal Opinion 08-451;
- Colorado State Bar Opinion 121 (2008);
- Los Angeles County Ethics Opinion 518 (2006);

- New York City Bar Opinion 2006-3;
- North Carolina Formal Ethics Opinion 12 (2007);
- Ohio Supreme Court Bd of Commissioners on Grievances and Discipline, Opinion 2009-6;
- San Diego Bar Association Opinion 2007-1; and
- the August 2009, New York City Bar Report "Report on the Outsourcing of Legal Services Overseas", available at www.nycbar.org/pdf/report/uploads/20071813-ReportontheOutsourcingofLegalServicesOverseas.pdf.

While each of these opinions generally addresses the same issues, they are not always consistent in their conclusions.

(a)   *Permissibility*

Each bar group that has considered outsourcing has found it permissible under the applicable rules of professional conduct. ABA Formal Opinion 08-451, for example, pronounces: "There is nothing unethical about a lawyer outsourcing legal . . . services, provided the outsourcing lawyer renders legal services to the client with the 'legal knowledge, skill, thoroughness and preparation reasonably necessary for the representation,' as required by [Model] Rule 1.1.'" Interestingly, that opinion even recognises the significant cost savings that legal outsourcing may offer to clients.

(b)   *Need for investigation and supervision*

An interesting clash is developing between law firms and their corporate clients regarding the duty to supervise the work of outsourced service providers. Under the ethics rules in place in many jurisdictions (including all of the states in the United States), a supervising lawyer is required to establish reasonable safeguards and then make reasonable efforts to supervise subordinate lawyers and non-lawyer assistants. ABA Formal Opinion 08-451 makes clear that this obligation applies even when a non-lawyer assistant is not working directly with or for the lawyer. However, with increasing frequency, client law departments are imposing conditions on their outside lawyers as to when and which providers are to be used, and that the client will not permit – or pay for – lawyer time spent supervising the outsourcer's work. This presents significant problems for lawyers in terms of liability for the ultimate work product that may contain the fruits of the work of the outsourcer, and in terms of responsibilities to courts to which such work is presented.

All of the opinions and reports agree that the supervisory responsibilities are heightened, not reduced, by the fact that the outsourcer may be offshore, have a different language in its normal operations and be subject to a different (or no) regulatory regime. Without question, except where a lawyer is acting under the specific direction of a client, particular care is required in vetting the project and LPO provider, and directing and overseeing the work.

In this context, the mere fact that a provider has been approved for one kind of service does not negate or reduce the same obligation to vet and oversee the provider if, later, services of a different kind will be sought.

Another area of risk, as well as of potential conflict between law firms and their clients, relates to the risks (and, in some cases legal restrictions) of sending data offshore. An example of a law in this context are the import-export controls contained in the US International Traffic in Arms Regulations, which prohibit certain defence and military related technologies from being shared with non-US persons and corporations.

There is no uniform standard for evaluating outsource service providers.

In addition to reviewing information about the provider and its employees, it may be critically important to determine in advance whether the country's legal system will provide adequate protection for privileged and confidential information, as well as adequate means for recourse if needed. Further, as well as assessing the competencies of both management and staff who will work on the requested lawyer's project, the outsourcer's compliance controls, financial resources and availability of applicable insurance or bonding may be critical.

Supervision of the work on a project needs to be continuous and ongoing throughout the project, and may involve much more than occasional phone calls to discuss progress, perhaps including site visits or even on-site supervisors from the firm or entity engaging the services.

But the issue of single greatest concern in selecting an outsource provider will relate to the security of communications, and the protection of client confidential information. Notably in this context, ABA Opinion 08-451 suggests that: "In some instances, it may be prudent to pay a personal visit to the [LPO provider's] facility, regardless of its location or the difficulty of travel, to get a firsthand sense of its operation and the professionalism of the lawyers and non-lawyers it is procuring." Lawyers engaging outsource service providers should also seriously consider having the provider execute a confidentiality agreement that requires the LPO provider to have and maintain adequate safeguards for information, notify the hiring lawyer if a problem occurs with such safeguards, and maintain the confidentiality of all client-related information that the LPO provider receives, regardless of the source. Such agreements should also make clear how the LPO provider should handle information at the end of the engagement, including if the engagement ends due to payment or performance problems of either party.

In England and Wales, the SRA makes clear that that outsourcing does not relieve lawyers of their professional obligations and arrangements must be "subject to contractual arrangements that enable the SRA or its agent to obtain information from, inspect the records (including electronic records) of, or enter the premises of, the third party, in relation to the outsourced activities or functions".[6]

Finally, lawyers engaging outsource providers need to ensure that written documents governing the outsourced project spell out and secure the necessary warranties and commitments regarding the project and all of the information provided during the review process.

(c) *Conflicts of interest*

It is of critical importance to ensure that the LPO provider and the people who will work on the project, both lawyers and non-lawyers, have no conflicts of interest. For

---

6   Outcome 7.10.

these purposes, the rules of the jurisdiction where the work product will be used must be applied.

(d) **Payment for outsourced services**

Where law firms engage LPOs on behalf of their clients, ethical issues arise as to whether the services must be charged to the client as a disbursement, with no mark-up, or whether the firm may charge fees in connection with engaging the provider over and above the actual cost incurred. ABA Formal Opinion 08-451 provides that there are two ways a law firm may bill for outsourced legal services. First, the law firm may bill for the legal services through the firm, as the firm does other legal services, and add a reasonable surcharge as appropriate to account for additional costs incurred because of the outside lawyer. Absent the client's agreement to the contrary, ABA Formal Opinion 08-451 indicates this surcharge should include only the law firm's "actual cost plus a reasonable allocation of associated overhead, such as the amount the lawyer spent on any office space, support staff, equipment, and supplies for the individuals under contract". ABA Formal Opinion 08-451 notes that in the outsourcing context normally such additional overhead costs would be "minimal or non-existent", thus limiting the surcharge.

Alternatively, the law firm may bill for the contract lawyer as if the contract lawyer were an expense, and simply pass through the cost of the outside lawyer. "If the firm decides to pass those costs through to the client as a disbursement... no markup is permitted" (ABA Formal Opinion 08-451).

(e) **Liability and insurance**

Finally, a client whose work is outsourced may face difficulties in recovering should the outsourced work be mishandled. When an intermediary law firm is used, the law firm's insurance policy may include temporary or contract attorneys within the definition of an 'insured'. However, the policy language or the nature of the outsourcing relationship (eg, that the outsourced service providers are located outside a law firm office and overseas or employed for lengthy periods) may exclude contract lawyers' actions from coverage. In addition, if care is not taken to review the language of the contract establishing the engagement, the law firm hiring the outsource provider may find – too late – that there is a limitation of liability clause that effectively nullifies any potential for recovery, even if the service provider actually has assets and is not in any event effectively judgment proof. Notably, such a limitation of liability may itself cause the hiring law firm's insurer to deny any coverage on the ground that by signing the agreement, the law firm rendered subrogation impossible, thereby violating the insuring agreement. Lawyers hiring outsource providers may therefore wish to ensure – probably in writing – that the provider itself carries adequate professional liability insurance, or to consider the absence of such insurance when deciding whether to outsource or what outsource provider to use.

(f) **Conclusion**

Disaggregation is upon us. In dealing with client needs and demands to use LPO's, lawyers need to take care to ensure that the specific tasks are appropriate to outsource, the LPO provider is appropriate to receive client information and complete the desired tasks, and the work is completed in a suitable manner. Only then should a lawyer believe that he has satisfied the ethical obligations that accompany legal outsourcing.

3. Managing the risk of non-lawyer ownership and outsourcing: England & Wales

The threats posed by non-lawyer owners and 'managers' (in effect, partners or directors)[7] in ABSs and outsourcing are similar in many ways – challenges to independence, and risks to legal professional privilege.

The SRA regulates most law firms in England & Wales. To date, most ABSs have been licensed by the SRA; a few have been licensed by the Council of Licensed Conveyancers, which can authorise firms for both conveyancing and probate services; and authorisation of firms by the Institute of Chartered Accountants in England & Wales will commence soon, which may potentially be a game-changer for corporate and tax work. However, the points which follow reflect the experience of SRA authorisation which commenced on March 27 2012.

A wide variety of firms has been licensed. Some look very little different from a traditional law firm – from the City firms which have appointed an accountant finance director as partner to the high-street sole practitioner who made his office manager, his non-lawyer wife, a partner. Others have introduced private equity finance or wish to be able to raise external capital by an initial public offering. One involved the acquisition of a UK practice by Australian-listed firm Slater & Gordon. Yet others are owned by insurance companies and claims management companies.

A detailed raft of legislation seeks to protect the public and the consumer of legal services. There must be one lawyer manager.

SRA Principle 3[8] – which came into force on October 6 2011, replacing similar provisions in earlier rules, and in common with many bar and law society rules – requires that those whom it regulates must "not allow your independence to be compromised".

Significantly, Guidance Note 2.7 explains – "'Independence' means your own and your firm's independence, and not merely your ability to give independent advice to a client. You should avoid situations which might put your independence at risk – eg, giving control of your practice to a third party which is beyond the regulatory reach of the SRA or other approved regulator."

The predecessor to SRA Principle 3 was Rule 1.03 of the SRA Code of Conduct 2007. After this was enacted, concern grew that with the anticipated implementation of the ABS provisions in the Legal Services Act 2007, some firms would jump the gun and reach agreements with non-lawyers which compromised their independence. There had already been experience of some firms doing so even before the act was passed and on occasions this resulted in disciplinary action.

---

7   For the full definition see the SRA Glossary http://sra.org.uk/solicitors/handbook/glossary/content.page#definition_M.
8   http://sra.org.uk/solicitors/handbook/handbookprinciples/content.page.

As a result, the SRA issued guidance in January 2009[9] and introduced additional guidance to the Code of Conduct on March 31 2009 which gave examples:

> *"Independence" means your own and your firm's independence, and not merely your ability to give independent advice to a client. Examples of situations which might put your independence at risk include:*
>
> *(a) finance agreements/loans to your firm with particular strings attached;*
>
> *(b) finance arrangements which suggest dependency upon an outside body, such as could, at that body's discretion, effectively put your firm out of business;*
>
> *(c) contractual conditions in agreements with referrers of business or funders which effectively cede control of your firm to the outside body;*
>
> *(d) granting options to purchase your interest in your firm for nominal value;*
>
> *(e) allowing a third party access to confidential information concerning your clients;*
>
> *(f) a relationship with an outside body which is not at arm's length, and/or which suggests that your firm is more akin to a part of or subsidiary of that body, rather than an independent law firm;*
>
> *(g) fee sharing arrangements which go beyond what is allowed under rule 8.02 [which permitted fee-sharing in a number of prescribed circumstances, including in return for introduction of capital or provision of services];*
>
> *(h) any arrangement for a third party to fund legal actions which lays constraints on the conduct of the matter which go beyond the legitimate interests of a funder.*
>
> *See also rule 3 (Conflict of interests) and rule 9 (Referrals of business).*

The guidance was used in support of action against a number of firms which were perceived to have jumped the gun and have subsequently obtained authorisation as ABSs.

All managers and owners who, broadly, have an interest of 10% or more either alone or with 'associates' (a defined term)[10] must obtain prior approval from the SRA. This is subject to the SRA Suitability Test 2011,[11] which contains a detailed 'fit and proper' test. This requires extensive disclosure of criminal convictions, civil judgments, insolvency history and action by other regulators.

The SRA Code of Conduct 2011 binds all managers and owners of ABSs, lawyers and non-lawyers alike.[12] Rule 8 of the SRA Authorisation Rules 2011[13] makes all managers responsible for compliance and an ABS's managers (including non-solicitors) must agree to be bound by the SRA Disciplinary Procedure Rules 2011.[14]

The Legal Services Act 2007[15] contains a number of provisions designed to ensure compliance.

Section 90 prohibits non-lawyer employees and managers from causing or substantially contributing to a regulatory breach by lawyers.

---

9   www.sra.org.uk/solicitors/code-of-conduct/guidance/guidance/preparing-for-alternative-business-structures---archived.page.
10 Schedule 13, Legal Services Act 2007
11 http://sra.org.uk/solicitors/handbook/suitabilitytest/content.page.
12 Chapter 13 http://sra.org.uk/solicitors/handbook/code/part6/rule13/content.page.
13 http://sra.org.uk/solicitors/handbook/authorisationrules/content.page.
14 http://sra.org.uk/solicitors/handbook/discproc/content.page.
15 http://www.legislation.gov.uk/ukpga/2007/29/contents.

Section 91 requires every firm to appoint a head of legal practice with wide responsibility for ensuring compliance and reporting all breaches, in the case of SRA-regulated ABSs, to the SRA. Section 92 contains a similar requirement for a head of finance and administration, with responsibility for compliance with the SRA Accounts Rules 2011, which provide protection for client and trust money. Further requirements on each are imposed by rule 8 of the SRA Authorisation Rules, which designates the appointees as "compliance officer for legal practice" (who must be a lawyer) and "compliance officer for finance and administration" respectively, and requires similar appointments in all traditional law firms too.

Finally, Section 190 makes provision in relation to the preservation of legal professional privilege, where a non-lawyer works under the supervision of a lawyer. The provision is complex and its potential limitations as yet untested.

Having looked at the legislative and regulatory framework, what is the experience in practice? So far, the author is not aware of any evidence of significant threats to independence or to the interests of consumers and the public. If there have been any incidents, they might equally have befallen a traditional law firm. There have been criticisms of delay by the SRA in authorising ABSs, which are being addressed, but it does mean that the slow trickle of authorisations has given limited opportunity to test the provisions in practice.

4. Non-lawyer ownership of legal practices in Australia

The move in Australia to allow lawyers to profit share with non-lawyers occurred first in New South Wales[16] in 1990 by allowing for incorporation of legal practices and multi-disciplinary practices, but there were very strict controls on voting rights and sharing of profits. The rules were relaxed in relation to multi-disciplinary practices in 1999, removing restrictions on voting and profit sharing. These structures were not widely used[17] and new legislation was introduced in 2001.[18] Requirements for more transparency under the legislation governing companies[19] at that stage meant that there was a sense that law firms would be better managed as companies. Incorporation of law firms in New South Wales has steadily increased since.[20]

New model legislation was agreed to by all attorneys general in Australia in 2004 which included the New South Wales regime for incorporated legal practices and multi-disciplinary practices. This legislation came in to operation in New South Wales and Victoria[21] in 2005. Queensland followed suit two years later,[22] Western Australia in 2008[23] and South Australia in 2014.[24] The legislation allowed profit sharing two ways; through incorporated legal practices (ILP) and through

---

16 Legal Profession (Solicitor Corporations) Amendment Act 1990 (NSW).
17 Steve Marks, *Notes on the listing of law firms in New South Wales and on the incorporation of law firms*, www.olsc.nsw.gov.au/agdbasev7wr/olsc/documents/pdf/notes_for_joint_nobc_aprl_aba_panel.pdf.
18 Legal Profession (Incorporated Legal Practice) Act 2000 (NSW).
19 Corporations Act (2001) (Cth).
20 Steve Marks, supra note 15.
21 Legal Profession Act (2004) (NSW), Legal Profession Act (2004) (Vic).
22 Legal Profession Act (2007) (QLD).
23 Legal Profession Act (2008) (WA).
24 Legal Practitioners Act 1981(SA) as amended by the Legal Practitioners (Miscellaneous) Amendment Act 2013 (SA) on July 1 2014.

multidisciplinary practices. ILPs are required to have at least one director who is a lawyer who holds a current practising certificate (an Australian legal practitioner) and it may have other directors who are not Australian legal practitioners. In a similar way, a multi-disciplinary practice must have at least one Australian legal practitioner partner but may have other non-lawyer partners.

The legislation places an onus on the lawyer directors or partners to ensure that appropriate management systems are implemented and maintained to enable the provision of legal services is in accordance with the obligations on lawyers. They are required to take positive steps to avoid such breaches if it becomes apparent (or should have) that they may occur. They are also required to ensure that the legal obligations on the employee lawyers are not affected by non-lawyer officers or employees. Lawyer directors or partners can be subject to disciplinary action for failure by the lawyer officers or employees to act in accordance with their legal obligations. They can also be in trouble if the conduct by the non-lawyer directors adversely affects the provision of legal services.[25]

The legislation makes it clear that the interests of the ILP become those of the legal practitioner director or employee for the purposes of the conflict of interest rules.[26] The legislation also makes it clear that its provisions prevail over any constitution or constituent documents of the ILP.[27] These provisions put the legal practitioners' duties to the court and administration of justice and their clients ahead of directors' general fiduciary duties.

The regulators in each jurisdiction have extensive powers to audit and call for documents of ILPs and multi-disciplinary practices, specifically in relation to compliance with relevant legislation and the management of the provision of legal services. The powers are not replicated for other legal practices owned solely by lawyers.[28]

The statistics in Victoria as at June 30 2013[29] show that 14.5% of private practice entities were ILPs and approximately 0.2% were multi-disciplinary practices. ILPs made up approximately one-quarter of the overall practice population in New South Wales[30] and 30% in Queensland.[31] Multidisciplinary practice structures have not ever been very popular.[32]

Anecdotally, most ILPs are the equivalent of small or sole practices, with only a few who have non-lawyer directors, many of whom are spouses of the lawyer directors, with some non-lawyer directors being business managers.[33] Many

---

25 See, for example, Sections 2.7.10 and 2.7.11 of the Legal Profession Act (2004) (Vic).
26 See, for example, Section 2.7.14 of the Legal Profession Act (2004) (Vic).
27 See, for example, Section 2.7.32 of the Legal Profession Act (2004) (Vic).
28 For further information on the obligations on ILPs see Patrick Oliver, *Incorporation – proceed with caution*, (2011) issue 85.08, *Law Institute Journal*, p 42, also available at www.lexcel.com.au/wp-content/uploads/2011/08/Lexcel-Article-August-2011.pdf.
29 Legal Services Board and Legal Services Commissioner Annual Report 2013, page 57 where private entities constitute sole practitioners, firms, ILPs, MDP (multidisciplinary practices) www.lsb.vic.gov.au/documents/2012-13_LSB+LSC_Annual_Report.pdf.
30 NSW Office of the Legal Services Commissioner Annual Report 2012-2013, p 18 www.olsc.nsw.gov.au/agdbasev7wr/olsc/documents/pdf/olsc%202012_2013%20annrep_final.pdf.
31 Queensland Legal Services Commission 2012-13 Annual Report at p 32 www.lsc.qld.gov.au/__data/assets/pdf_file/0014/216104/Legal-Services-Commission-2012-13-Annual-report.pdf.
32 Steve Marks, supra note 15, at p 3.
33 For example Hive Legal, http://hivelegal.com.au/.

practitioners set up their practice as an ILP for tax advantages on advice from their accountant. Notably, however, Australia has the first publicly listed law practice, Slater & Gordon, followed closely behind by Integrated Legal Holdings Limited,[34] both listed in 2007 and Shine Corporate Limited[35] in 2013. At the time of writing, they remain the only three publicly listed legal service companies.

---

34   Now ILH Group Limited, which operates its legal practice through Rockwell Olivier.
35   Operates as Shine Lawyers.

Mitigating law firms' cyber risks

Steven M Puiszis
Hinshaw & Culbertson LLP

1. Introduction

In November 2011, the FBI held a meeting with 200 law firms in New York where it explained that hackers consider law firms to be a "backdoor to the valuable data of their corporate clients".[1] One cyber-security firm estimated that at least 80 law firms in the United States were hacked in 2011.[2]

Of the attorneys who responded to the 2013 Legal Technology Survey conducted by the American Bar Association (ABA), 20% acknowledged that their firm had experienced a security breach.[3] In the United Kingdom, a survey conducted in 2012 revealed that more than 20% of the responding law firms acknowledged that they had been hacked in the preceding 12 months.[4]

The former Director of the FBI, Robert S Mueller III, in the keynote address provided a sobering assessment of the state of cyber security: "there are only two types of companies: those that have been hacked and those that will be. And even they are converging into one category: companies that have been hacked and will be hacked again."[5]

That law firms have become a target of hackers should come as no surprise. Today modern law firms function as large data centres, receiving and distributing sensitive information in the course of providing legal services. Hackers target law firms because of the concentration of valuable information accumulated by law firms and because law firms' cyber defences are perceived to be weaker than those of their clients. As a result, the computer networks of law firms around the globe are routinely probed for vulnerabilities, and hackers are repeatedly sending socially engineered emails with attachments containing malware,[6] or with links to malicious websites.

---

1 Michael Riley and Sophia Person, China-based hackers target law firms to get secret deal data, Bloomberg, January 31 2012, available at www.bloomberg.com/news/2012-01-31/China-based-hackers-target-law-firms.html.
2 Ibid.
3 Joshua Poje, Security Snapshot: Threats and Opportunities, ABA Techreport 2013, available at www.americanbar.org/publications/techreport/2013/security_snapshot_threats_and_opportunities.html.
4 Julius Melnitzer, Twenty percent of UK Law Firms Suffer Cyber-attacks, Legal Post, December 10 2012, available at http://hildebrantblog.com/2013/11/13/UK-law-firms-less-prepared-than-other-sectors-for-cyber-attacks-but-can-mitigate-risk-survey-says/.
5 Combating Threats in the Cyber World: Outsmarting Terrorists, Hackers and Spies, available at www.fbi.gov/news/speeches/combating-threats-in-the-cyber-world-outsmarting-terrorists-hackers-and-spies.
6 Malware or malicious software is any program, file, software or application that gathers information, or is used to disrupt the operation of, or gain access to or control over, a mobile device, a computer or a network. It includes viruses such as Trojan horses or worms, keyloggers, sniffers, ransomware, spyware, adware, scareware and rootkits.

A virtual cybercrime ecosystem has developed on the Internet involving an anonymous, virtual-currency-based point-of-sale system. There exists an internet black market where stolen personal information, credit card information, cracked passwords, and "off-the-shelf malware" can be purchased.[7] Hackers range from industrial and state-sponsored actors bent on corporate espionage[8] to tech-savvy criminals seeking financial gain. They also include 'hacktivists', motivated by geopolitical ideals, and teenagers who view hacking as sporting activity.

Today, no law firm is immune from being hacked. All firms are potential targets of cyber criminals seeking access to a firm's banking or trust account information, and any personally identifying information in their possession that can be sold to identity thieves. Industrial or state-sponsored hackers seek trade secrets, patents, intellectual property and other high-value information about new products, or information about high-stakes business deals. In one notable incident, seven Canadian law firms were the targets of highly sophisticated cyber attacks aimed at stealing sensitive information relating to a potential $40 billion-dollar corporate acquisition.[9] Whether a law firm becomes a target of hacktivism will depend on the positions taken by the firm's clients on political or social issues.[10]

While their motives may differ, and the tools they use have become more technologically sophisticated, the techniques employed by hackers fall into common patterns aimed at various human and network vulnerabilities. After studying over 93,000 security incidents, Verizon, in its 2014 Data Breach Investigations Report, concluded that 92% of all data breaches fall into nine basic patterns.[11] While hackers' motives are understood and their attack strategies are known, preventing successful hacks has proven to be difficult. Contributing factors include the inability to effectively patch network vulnerabilities, the failure to properly monitor network activity for the presence of malware, the growing use of mobile devices which have created new attack vectors to guard, the popularity of social media, which enables more sophisticated social engineering schemes to be directed at law-firm personnel, and the failure of law-firm personnel to follow the firm's security guidelines.[12]

Another difficulty with cyber security is that threats are never static, they are constantly evolving. Spam filters will capture some phishing emails, but hackers are trying new methods to evade those filters. Hackers are refining malware to evade

---

7   McAfee Labs Threats Report, Fourth Quarter 2013 at 4, available at www.mcafee.com/us/resources/reports/rp-quarterly-threat-q4-2013.pdf.
8   Allison Grange, US Charges Chinese Officers with Hacking Alcoa, Others, Law 360, May 19 2014, available at www.law360.com/ip/articles/539014/us-charges-chinese-officers-with-hacking-alcoa-others.
9   Jeff Gray, Major Law Firms Fall Victim To Cyber Attacks, The Globe and Mail, August 5, 2012, available at www.theglobeandmail.com/report-on-business/industry-news/the-law-page/major-law-firms-fall-victim-to-cyberattacks/article576152/.
10   Pierluigi Paganini, Hacktivism: Means and Motivations ... What Else? InfoSec Institute, available at http://resources.infosecinstitute.com/hacktivism-means-and-motivations-what-else/(explaining the term hacktivism was "derived by combining hack and activism" and refers to the "use of computers and any other IT system and network to debate and sustain a political issue"). The article explains that hacktivism "involves the use of computers to express dissent" but can also represent a dangerous threat that creates damage through cyber attacks.
11   Verizon, 2014 Data Breach Investigations Report, available at www.verizonenterprise.com/DBIR /2014/.
12   In its 2014 Internet Security Threat Report, Symantec reported: "Over the past decade, an increasing number of users have been targeted with spear-phishing attacks, and the social engineering has grown more sophisticated over time."

detection. So a law firm's cyber security measures must evolve as the threats they face evolve. Additionally, every time a law firm alters its network architecture, installs a new program, changes a server, a router, a switch or a firewall, a new vulnerability may be introduced. If a firewall is not properly configured, if systems that were once segregated become open, or group access rules are modified, new vulnerabilities to a firm's network can be created. As a result, periodic review of threats and vulnerabilities to the network are critical.

While industrial or state-sponsored hackers have employed headline grabbing ingenuity to breach an organisation's network,[13] many hackers simply look for the low-hanging fruit. And the unfortunate reality is that many successful hacks could have been avoided if a vendor-issued patch for a vulnerability had been timely applied, or if an employee had simply avoided clicking on a link in an email from a person he or she did not know. While there are technological solutions that can strengthen the perimeter and internal security of a law firm's network, frequently the weakest link in the security of any law firm is its personnel.

Many clients are reviewing their law firm's cyber-security measures.[14] For some clients, these reviews are part of a regulatory compliance scheme imposed upon them by federal law. For many others, however, these reviews are part of a larger data security initiative, and a prerequisite to obtaining and keeping their business. A number of state and federal laws are also directly imposing cyber-security requirements on US law firms.

Strong cyber security is more than simply a cost of doing business in today's global economy. A law firm that is successfully hacked will suffer reputational harm and may lose clients as a result. There is significant administrative time and expense involved in determining how a breach occurred and in re-establishing the integrity of a network. State and federal laws in the United States frequently require that notice be provided to government officials and any affected individuals following a data breach. Fines and penalties can be imposed on law firms under these statutes, and civil litigation following a data breach is becomingly increasingly common. Thus, cyber security has long-term strategic implications for all law firms.

This chapter is intended to acquaint the reader with basic information about how hackers operate, explain how unauthorised access to information can be obtained, and provide strategies to consider that will strengthen a law firm's cyber defences. There is no sure-fire method to protect a law firm from being hacked, however, and the security measures that any law firm chooses to deploy can be impacted by any number of factors unique to that firm.

---

13   Nicole Perlroth, Hackers Lurking in Vents and Soda Machines, New York Times, April 7 2014, available at www.nytimes.com/2014/04/08/technology/the-spy-in-the-soda-machine.html?_r=0.
14   Matthew Goldstein, Law Firms Are Pressed on Security for Data, New York Times, March 26 2014, available at http://dealbook.nytimes.com/2014/03/26/law-firms-scrutinized-as-hacking-increases/?_php =true&_type=blogs&_r=0 (explaining: "banks are pressing outside law firms to demonstrate that their computer systems are employing top-tier technologies to detect and deter attacks from hackers" and other companies "are asking law firms to stop putting files on portable thumb drives, emailing them to non-secure iPads").

2. How hackers operate

2.1 Reconnaissance

A successful hack does not just happen. There are methods and tools used by hackers to obtain information about the intended target. This is called 'footprinting' a network. A hacker will 'case' its target, like a bank robber, and gather any available information from the Internet. Because firms are electronically marketing their legal services and their lawyers' expertise there is a surprising amount of publicly available information about law firms on the Internet.

Hackers will review a firm's website, its web pages and lawyer resumés to obtain information about the firm and its personnel. Hackers will attempt to determine how the firm grants remote access to its lawyers and who at the firm has administrative privileges. They will seek out links to other related organisations and review information posted by lawyers on social media. This information will be used by hackers to develop phishing schemes, which are emails intended to trick a person into thinking the email is from a trusted source, not a hacker. Hackers also employ programs specifically designed to identify systems and devices that may lack appropriate security and authentication.

2.2 Enumeration

Once hackers have learnt as much as possible about a firm, they will scan its network looking for open entry points or ports. Hackers 'ping' a network because open ports can provide clues as to vulnerabilities in a network. Some hackers will also deploy a vulnerability scan of the network with a database of known vulnerabilities that is used to further evaluate network security. Hackers will begin to probe open ports in firewalls. They will sometimes do this by fragmenting information in an email packet which makes it harder for firewalls and intrusion detection systems to detect their scanning activity. They will also employ diagnostic tools that allow them to observe the path an email takes across the network. During this stage, hackers seek to identify valid user accounts on the network, and seek out users with weak or nonexistent passwords. They will also identify network vulnerabilities and poorly protected aspects of a network to exploit.

2.3 Exploitation

Hackers will next seek to exploit the weaknesses and vulnerabilities they have found. This can include the use of phishing schemes, compromising websites frequently visited by system users, or compromising the security of a third-party vendor with electronic access to the firm's network. It can include guessing or cracking weak passwords and exploiting applications found on a user's mobile device or weaknesses in the network. Once a hacker finds a way into the network, he will seek to install a remote back door that can be used to regain access into the system, and will seek to take control of a user's account from which the next step of the attack can be launched.

2.4 Escalation

The next step in the process involves an attempt to obtain additional network access towards the goal of obtaining administrative privileges over some aspect of the network. Some form of malware will be deployed depending on the type and level of access obtained. This can include keyloggers to steal passwords, sniffers to capture data as it moves across the network, or an exploit kit that will seek to surreptitiously gain administrative control over the network and will allow the hacker to remotely control any malware installed on the network. Modern malware will seek to temporarily suspend or alter network audit logs to hide this activity with the ultimate goal of transmitting data out of the network.

3. **Performing a cyber-risk analysis**

The first step a law firm should take to lessen its cyber risk is to conduct a risk assessment of the electronic information in its possession. The assessment should begin with an inventory of the various types of electronic information under its control, the format in which the information is stored, and all locations where the information resides or is stored on the firm's network. The firm should identify the various ways access to that information can be obtained, how it can be transmitted and how it flows across its network, as well as all persons who have access to each type of information. With that information, the firm can evaluate the threats and vulnerabilities to each type of information in its possession and assign a risk level to each type, based on the sensitivity of the information, and the likelihood that unauthorised access to, or disclosure of, the information might occur.

The law firm also should assess its cyber-risk profile when evaluating the risk level of the information in its possession. Not all firms have the same cyber-risk profile. A small firm located in the heart of Kansas is likely to have a risk profile far different than a mid-sized regional firm, which in turn has a different risk profile from an international law firm with offices in various countries in the EU and the Far East. The law firm's practice areas are another factor that will affect its risk profile. Firms that receive, use or transmit protected health information, financial information, trade secrets or intellectual property will have a higher risk profile given the sensitivity of that information. Similarly, firms with clients that are government contractors, or considered part of a nation's critical infrastructure, or that have an energy, technology, health-care or patent practice, or that handle mergers and acquisitions will have a higher cyber-risk profile than firms with other practice areas. The firm should evaluate the threats and vulnerabilities to its information in light of its cyber-risk profile. It should then apply available resources in a reasoned fashion, addressing the most critical vulnerabilities to mitigate the firm's cyber risk.

While the risk of being hacked poses a major threat to law firms, more information and data is compromised through lost or stolen mobile devices, inadequate disposal measures of equipment with hard-drive storage, such as copiers or fax machines, the use of unsecure Wi-Fi for its transmission and a lack of attention in the transmission of information.[15] So these threats, which are discussed briefly below, should not be overlooked in the firm's risk analysis.

---

15   Ponemon Institute, 2013 Cost of Data Breach Study: Global Analysis, at 7, available at www4.symantec.com/mktginfo/whitepaper/053013_GL_NA_WP_Ponemon-2013-Cost-of-a-Data-Breach-Report_daiNA_cta72382.pdf.

Given the proliferation of malware distributed via mobile apps, whether a firm supplies mobile devices or adopts a bring-your-own-device (BYOD) policy is another factor that will impact the firm's risk profile. While BYOD policies enable lawyers to work anywhere around the clock, they introduce new risks and present an ever-changing security perimeter. BYOD and cloud-based applications such as Dropbox and Google Docs allow confidential information to be transmitted, shared and stored in multiple locations, some of which are beyond a firm's ability to control. Mobile devices introduce additional attack vectors that have to be analysed and protected.

Modern copy and fax machines contain hard drives, which if not properly sanitised before disposal, could result in the unintended disclosure of confidential information. For instance, one organisation was advised by a representative of CBS Evening News that CBS had purchased a photocopier previously leased by the company which contained confidential medical information on the copier's hard drive. Over 344,000 individuals were affected by this data breach.[16]

Another threat to law-firm cyber security is the firm's partners and employees. Some lack a basic understanding of technology and the threats that technology can raise and how their actions can affect the security of the firm. Many value convenience over security and will look to work around any security policies.[17] A law firm's most tech-savvy lawyers, its Millennials, are the ones most likely to try to circumvent its security rules.[18] For many firms "[t]he battlefield upon which we engage cyber intruders has shifted from the server rooms and data centers to the space occupied between the desktop and the chair – to the lawyer's paralegals and administrative assistants".[19]

4. Designating a chief security officer

A law firm should designate a person to manage the firm's cyber risk and protect the information under its control. In the United States this is a requirement for law firms that qualify as a Business Associate under the Health Insurance Portability and Accountability Act 1996 (HIPAA). Additionally, the security of the law firm's information is not likely to improve without someone taking responsibility for it. Studies have demonstrated that designating a person to be in charge of information security is a factor that will lower the cost of a data breach.[20]

The person selected for this role does not need an IT background, but will need to have a basic understanding of how hackers operate, and the technological, administrative and operational measures that can be deployed to mitigate the firm's

---

16 HHS Settles with Health Plan in Photocopier Breach Case, August 14 2013, available at www.hhs.gov/news/press/2013pres/08/2013814ahtml.
17 Mark Hansen, 4 types of employees who put your cyber security at risk, and 10 things you can do to stop them, ABA Journal, March 28 2014, available at www.abajournal.com/mobile/article_war_ stories_of_ insider_threats_posed_by_unapproved_data_ services_and_device/.
18 Sarah Greene, Do Millennials Believe in Data Security? Harvard Business Review, February 18 2014, available at http://blogs.hbr.org/2014/02/do-millennials-believe-in-data-security/?utm_source=Social flow&utm_medium=Tweet&utm_campaign=Socialflow.
19 How Can We Guard Against Cyber-Attacks? Attorneyatwork, available at www.attorneyatwork.com/help-how-can-we-guard-against-cyber-attacks/.
20 Ponemon Institute, 2014 Cost of Data Breach Study: Global Analysis, May 2014, at 11, available at www.public.dhe.ibm.com/common/ssi/ecm/en/sel03027usen/SEL03027USEN.PDF.

cyber risk. If that person is not the law firm's general counsel, compliance counsel or head of the firm's IT department, he or she should have a close working relationship with those colleagues. The law firm's security officer should periodically report to management on the state of the firm's cyber security, and seek additional human and capital resources for the IT department when needed to mitigate vulnerabilities and threats to the firm.

While it is important to designate a person to be in charge of security, protecting information is the responsibility of all members of the firm's workforce. A culture of data security must be developed in the firm and fostering that culture is perhaps the single most important task of the firm's security officer.

5. **Draft an incident response plan**

Law firms should consider proactively developing a response plan to address possible security incidents or breaches of its network. Having a plan that outlines the basic steps to be taken will avoid confusion and will enhance the firm's ability to effectively respond to a breach of its network. Time is of the essence when a security incident occurs, and it is critical that the firm's response team act quickly to control and eradicate a threat and prevent information leaks from the firm.

The response plan should identify team members who are to take charge, along with back-up personnel if necessary. Team members should include the firm's general counsel, compliance counsel and/or chief risk officer. Appropriate individuals from the firm's IT, human resources and marketing or media relations departments should be included. The roles and responsibilities of each team member should be outlined in the plan, whose mobile phone or home telephone numbers should be included. The plan should also include an outline of the steps to follow in the event of a security incident, and if possible these should be rehearsed. Because the firm's network may have to be forensically examined, the person or entity to perform that work should be selected beforehand. The plan should identify who will perform any forensic examination and include necessary contact information.

The plan should require more than a simple containing and eradication of any malware found on the network. The plan should require that the team confirm that no 'back doors' were installed by the hacker. It is critical that the firm is able to confirm to its clients and any regulators that the integrity of the network has been restored. The firm must also determine whether any information was leaked and if so, identify what information was taken and when that occurred.

A law firm's general counsel or compliance counsel should evaluate any statutory requirements for data breach reporting, and determine whether and when the firm needs to provide notice to its professional liability or cyber insurer. The response plan should address the notification of the proper law enforcement agencies, clients and any other affected persons. Sample notifications should be drafted. The plan should identify who will serve these notifications, how and when. Law enforcement may ask a firm to delay notification to third parties and some state data breach laws provide that notice can be delayed to ensure that the integrity of the network has been restored. It is critical that the firm first determines how the breach occurred so that it is able to explain how it happened and what steps are being taken to prevent a recurrence.

The plan should also require an evaluation of whether there are security vulnerabilities that need to be addressed, procedures that should be changed, or whether new or different security measures are needed to prevent a recurrence. The Ponemon Institute's yearly studies of data breaches have consistently concluded that having an incident response plan in place is a factor that significantly reduces the cost of a data breach.[21]

6. **Best practice considerations for mitigating cyber risk**

The concept of defence in depth, or a layered approach to network security, should be adopted when possible. In its 2014 Global Threat Intelligence Report, Solutionary noted that anti-virus software failed to detect approximately one-half of new variants of malware,[22] which suggests the need for additional security layers to protect a firm's network. Law firms should focus on more than simply strengthening their perimeter security. They should consider intrusion detection tools that will detect threats and remedy any damage should malware gain a foothold in their network.

There are various steps that a law firm can take to lessen its cyber risk. What steps a firm should consider depends on a variety of factors such as its cyber profile, security measures already in place and available resources. There is no one-size-fits-all approach when it comes to security. However, a law firm's cyber security is only as strong as its weakest component. And the strongest security measures can be unknowingly negated by a firm's employees or lawyers. Therefore, training is a vital component to any mitigation strategy.

Outlined below are 30 steps to consider – several are low cost and do not involve technology. Several may seem basic, but are critical considerations that should not be overlooked. Several steps are offered as alternatives, but all are relevant considerations that can help to mitigate a law firm's cyber risk.

1. *Segment the computer network into sub-networks separated by firewalls.* This will allow the firm's financial and accounting functions and its human resource information to be separately secured from other less sensitive information. Additionally, network segmentation can help a law firm meet its compliance obligations by funnelling highly sensitive client information such as trade secrets or protected health information into a sub-network. Segmentation will not only help improve the overall performance of the firm's network, it provides flexibility to add additional layers of security to categories of information that warrant the extra protection. Additionally, in the event that a hacker is able to gain access into the firm's network, the entire network is not placed at risk. It will help slow down a hacker by not allowing direct access to the intended target, which will hopefully allow other security features built into the network to control and eradicate the malware.
2. *Harden a firm's network security.* System hardening should be an ongoing process aimed at reducing a network's vulnerabilities. System hardening

---

21   Ponemon Institute, 2014 Cost of Data Breach Study: Global Analysis, May 2014, at 11, available at http:www//public.dhe.ibm.com/common/ssi/ecm/en/sel03027usen/SEL03027USEN.PDF.
22   NTT Group, 2014 Global Threat Report, available at www.solutionary.com/research/threat-reports/annual-threat-report/ntt-solutionary-global-threat-intelligence-report-2014/.

includes taking steps such as removing unnecessary software, servers, protocols, features or scripts from the network and closing any unused open ports on the network.
3. *Maintain robust and properly configured firewalls.* Firewalls should have ports closed unless specific traffic is permitted. Blocking entry into the network unless permitted by a specific rule is a critical feature of network security. Firms should consider having a second firewall in the background in a 'fail over' mode that will be activated if the firm's primary firewall fails for any reason. Additionally, if a firm has a co-location facility that can be activated in the event of a failure of the network, consideration should be given for a separate firewall for the servers in that facility. Any redundant firewalls should be synchronised with primary firewalls.
4. *Deploy, maintain and update antivirus software with heuristic scanning capability and deep packet filtering.* Anti-malware should be deployed at network endpoints, such as desktop or laptop computers, within the network and on all systems. Antivirus protection should continuously operate and employ policy-based controls to prevent it from being altered or disabled. Antivirus protection should be regularly updated and configured to generate audit logs that can reveal malware activity and the reaction of the virus protection. Hackers are increasingly using sophisticated malware which makes its presence harder to detect and eradicate. Heuristic scanning provides the ability to flag not only known species of malware but also new variants. On its own, antivirus protection is not a panacea, but it should not be overlooked. Kept updated, it will generally identify at least 50% of the malware launched at a network.
5. *Incorporate intrusion detection/intrusion prevention tools that reside in firewall ports or within the network at switches and routers.* These tools will examine all network traffic and look for malicious activity or anomalies in the network. These tools can identify and quarantine email traffic suspected of containing malicious code. They can also identify an unusual increase in network traffic by specific users, which can be a sign that a user's account has been hacked, or activities by a user that should be investigated.
6. *Review audit logs.* Every server, router and switch in the network and every port in a firewall generates activity logs that may reveal an intrusion or breach of a network. These logs can produce thousands of entries and millions of lines of code for possible daily review. The timely and regular review of these logs can reveal the presence of a malicious intruder. Audit logs, however, provide little security if they are not regularly reviewed, and the failure to monitor network activity can trigger an HIPAA violation for law firms in the United States that qualify as Business Associates. Law firms should evaluate cost-effective solutions for reviewing these logs. An unusual increase or decrease in the volume of log data can suggest the presence of malware on the network, and developing an alert that is issued when there is a significant change in the volume of log activity can be a useful tool. There are also managed security service providers that employ technology to review

these logs and identify the presence of malware on the system. Sophisticated malware, however, will seek to alter log activity in an attempt to hide its presence. Log data must be protected and attempts to alter a log should generate a security alert. Technological tools are available to protect the audit logs, including file integrity monitoring and change-detection software, which scan the network for changes to critical files such as a network's audit logs. They are another security feature that should be considered when appropriate. Daily reviews of security alerts should be made and if possible, daily reviews should also be made of logs by any network components performing security functions.

7. *Implement a process to generate audit trails of network activity.* Audit trails enable a firm to determine who gained access to particular information on its network and potentially to trace malicious activities on the network. Audit trail logs should be segregated within the network to make them harder to find by a hacker, and should be promptly backed up. Firms should also synchronise all critical system time clocks on its network in order to be able to establish an accurate sequence of events should a breach of the network occur.

8. *Keep software current.* Firms should attempt to stay within one version of the latest release of all software applications used by the network, provided vendor support is still available.

9. *Develop a scheduled system for patching all security updates released by software vendors.* Hackers monitor security updates and the release of patches to fix vulnerabilities in the software used in networks. Failing to apply these patches in a timely way can leave a network vulnerable. Consider prioritising the application of patches to critical aspects of the network as soon as possible, followed by patches for lower risk components of the network. Do not overlook applying patch updates to network hardware, switches and routers. A recent study of the exploits contained in 61 popular exploit kits by a global security engineering research team concluded that 99% of the vulnerabilities targeted by these kits would be rendered useless and ineffective had available patches been properly applied.[23] There are third-party vendors that can help manage the process if a firm's IT department lacks the necessary depth or resources to promptly apply security patches to a system.

10. *Routinely change vendor-supplied default settings and passwords for any network component.* Frequently, these settings are published and are available to hackers. Failing to change a vendor's settings and passwords leaves a network vulnerable to attack.

11. *Use data-loss protection or content-filtering software.* These tools are designed to either detect potential data breaches or block sensitive data while it moves through a network or at its endpoints. This security tool is distinct from intrusion detection or intrusion prevention applications, which focus on

---

23 Chad Kahl, My Top Recommendations for Increasing Security, April 3 2014 available at www.solutionary.com/resource-center/blog/2014/04/patch-management/.

detecting intrusions into the system by hackers. The purpose of data-loss prevention software is to protect against the transmission of sensitive data, such as intellectual property. This is accomplished by scanning outbound network traffic and setting rules concerning the transmission of sensitive data. These security tools can encrypt, quarantine or block the transmission of types of data before it leaves a network.

12. *Use web filtering tools.* Web filtering is another layer of protection that can block an attack vector frequently used by hackers. Web filters use block lists or blacklists of internet protocol addresses and URLs of websites engaged in known or suspicious online activity. A web filtering tool will block employee access to identified or suspected malicious sites or warn employees about sites that are graded suspicious or inappropriate. These tools will help lessen the risk of drive-by downloads of malware that occur when these sites are visited.

13. *Evaluate and limit third-party electronic access to any part of the network.* All law firms work with trusted vendors and business partners who are granted electronic access to some aspect of their network. Key card security systems, electronic bill and payment systems, and call-centre personnel are examples. Every third party who has electronic access to some aspect of a firm's network provides a potential gateway for a hacker.[24] The breach of US retailer the Target Corporation was accomplished by hackers who used the credentials stolen from a refrigeration and heating, ventilation and air conditioning contractor that worked for Target that had electronic access to Target's network. Once hackers gained control of the contractor's system, they were able to exploit the contractor's external access to Target's network, upload malware and complete one of the largest breaches in retail history.[25] Permitting a third party to have round-the-clock electronic access to a network increases the chances of this type of unauthorised access. A firm should attempt to limit third-party electronic access to its network and consider allowing access only when needed and only at approved times.

14. *Use a secure email gateway.* Third-party vendors can provide a secure gateway that will scan inbound email for spam, phishing emails and malware. These gateways will identify and move spam or phishing emails into folders and block malicious email before it reaches the law firm's firewalls. These gateways can encrypt outgoing email traffic and can also scan and filter a firm's out-bound email traffic for malware or for specific items such as nine-digit patterns used for social security numbers or 16-digit patterns used for credit cards. Content filtering of outgoing email is one way to protect against deliberate or accidental leaks of certain types of confidential information.

15. *Encrypt mobile devices and the hard drives of portable laptop computers.* Studies of data breaches have revealed that approximately one-third of all breaches are

---

24 Perlroth, Hackers Lurking in Vents and Soda Machines (noting a security research firm, Ponemon Institute, concluded in 2013 that 23% of breaches were attributed to third-party negligence and "vendors are tempting targets for hackers because they tend to run older systems").

25 Krebs on Security, Target Hackers Broke in Via HVAC Company, February 14 2014, available at http://krebsonsecurity.com/2014/02/target-hackers-broke-in-via-hvac-company/.

the result of lost or stolen mobile devices. This is a risk that can be avoided through encryption and is well worth the administrative time and expense involved. A total of 47 states and several federal laws in the United States authorise the imposition of fines and penalties on law firms following a data breach. These fines and penalties can be avoided in many instances through the encryption of portable laptops and mobile devices.

16. *Use mobile device management tools.* When a law firm moves away from providing firm-supplied mobile devices to a BYOD environment, complete control over mobile devices is lost. However, firms can and should impose conditions on the use of personally owned devices in return for access to the firm's email and information systems. Firms should consider requiring full device encryption, the use of strong passwords, and the immediate reporting of lost or stolen mobile devices. Idle timeouts and password lockouts discussed below should be applied to mobile devices. Mobile device management tools are becoming an increasingly important security consideration. They will separate personal and firm email on these devices and can be used to remotely wipe a lost or stolen device. Firms should also consider prohibiting jail-breaking or rooting of phones, prohibit the backup of client information from those phones onto home computers or the cloud, and prohibit the use of a personally owned device in any way that allows third-party access to firm email or information stored on the device.

17. *Require the use of strong passwords and develop a strong password policy.* Requiring the use of strong passwords is a basic but important line of defence, since hackers will try to identify users with weak or nonexistent passwords. Passwords that are short, simple, easy to guess, or are dictionary words pose a security vulnerability for a network. Password policies should require passwords to have a minimum of 8, preferably 12 to 16 characters and require a mix of upper- and lower-case letters, and numbers and symbols. The use of phrases or the first letter of a phrase is a strategy that will help users to remember strong passwords. A firm's password policy should require that they be periodically changed every 90 to 180 days, and prevent prior passwords from being reused. A firm's password policy should prohibit the sharing of passwords with others, prohibit the storing of passwords in plain text and prohibit using the same password for different applications. This will prevent placing all applications at risk should a hacker be able to crack a user's password for a particular application. Educating all personnel on the firm's password policies is critically important.

18. *Include in the system of access control the use of ethical walls and group policies in active directories.* Individuals should only have access to the information, systems or applications needed to perform their work. One way to limit access to critical client information is through the use of ethical walls that limit the lawyers and other personnel who can access client information for a specific engagement. These walls can be set up during the file intake process. Group directories with specific rules can control who has access to sensitive information such as that held by the firm's accounting and human resource

departments. Properly authenticating system users and limiting lawyers and staff to only that information and applications on the network necessary for their work is an important security step. If a hacker takes control of a user's account, this type of access control will limit those areas of the network to which the hacker can gain easy access. A firm's system of access control should include a deny-all default that blocks access unless a policy or rule specifically grants a user access to specific applications or information.

19. *Incorporate two-factor authentication for remote access to the law firm's network by personnel from outside the network.*
20. *Block access to the firm's network following a set number of unsuccessful attempts to access the system.* Some hackers employ a brute force attack on a user's password via computers that can literally guess millions of passwords per second. Without this type of password lockout feature, a hacker could repeatedly attempt to guess a password either manually or through the use of a password cracking tool. Once a lockout has been triggered, access to the network can be granted to a user only after a set time, for example 30 minutes, or through a confirmation process that requires law firm administrators to confirm that an employee or lawyer is requesting reactivation of his or her access to the network.
21. *Employ idle timeouts on any computer or mobile device that has access to the network.* This timeout measure requires a user to reenter a password if that user's computer or mobile device has been idle for a set time period. Different time frames should be considered for desktop or laptop computers and mobile devices. This will prevent unauthorised access to the firm's network by non-firm personnel who have access to the firm's office on evenings or weekends or who gain access to a lost or stolen mobile device.
22. *Develop a process to immediately terminate electronic access to the network upon the resignation or termination of any person from the firm.* This procedure is a low-cost, low-tech practice that should be adopted and followed as a matter of routine. A surprising number of data breaches are the work of malicious insiders, and a number are the handiwork of former employees whose system access was not blocked when they left the firm. This risk can be mitigated by developing a procedure that mandates the immediate termination of network access rights or user accounts. A user account that is not regularly used becomes a target for a hacker because it is less likely that changes will be recognised. Therefore, firms should periodically disable or remove inactive user accounts on its network. Firms should also prohibit anonymous user accounts and any group or shared user accounts for this same reason.
23. *Restrict physical access to key components of the network.* This is an important security feature that should not be overlooked. Servers should be kept in locked rooms, and access to network jacks in public parts of the firm should be prohibited. Additionally, firms should develop policies to restrict physical access to wireless access points, mobile devices, networking and communications hardware to prevent unauthorised individuals from attempting to connect their own devices to the system and thereby gain

access to the network. Laptop computers in the office should be secured with locks and cables to prevent their theft when they are left unattended.

24. *Securely configure and monitor any wireless network developed by the firm and encrypt both user authentication and transmission of information over the network.*

25. *Restrict user flexibility on firm-owned computers and mobile devices and prohibit downloading of unapproved programs or applications.* The firm's IT department should screen and approve any program or application before it is downloaded on to firm-owned equipment. This can be accomplished by denying administrative rights to firm personnel over the firm's equipment. The development of a blacklist of prohibited programs and applications, or whitelists of approved ones, can help streamline the process. There are policies and third-party tools that can assist with this security measure.

26. *Control the use of portable USB flash drives.* Flash drives present several security risks for law firms. They provide a means to remove sensitive or confidential information by departing employees. Unencrypted flash drives containing confidential personal or protected health information that are lost can trigger an obligation to report the loss of that information. Additionally, hackers have loaded malware onto flash drives and either passed them out, or left them in places where they can be found by the employees of the targeted entity. When the flash drive is plugged into a desktop or laptop computer the hacker's malicious payload will be delivered into the network. The development of policies regulating the use of flash drives will not prevent employees from inappropriately using them. As a result, some law firms have physically or technologically closed USB ports on their computers, and others only permit the use of encrypted flash drives. Encrypted flash drives are significantly more costly than unencrypted drives, but there are technological tools available that firms should consider that will encrypt data before it is loaded onto a flash drive.

27. *Keep web browsers up to date and periodically evaluate the risks and benefits of third-party browser plug-ins such as Java and Flash.* Out-of-date web browsers frequently contain security vulnerabilities. Keeping browsers updated and applying security patches in accordance with a vendor's instructions will prevent browser vulnerabilities from being exploited. Java is a programming language that works across multiple computing platforms and is routinely found in plug-ins in web browsers. Java has a history of vulnerabilities. According to Kaspersky Lab, Java was responsible for 50% of all cyber attacks in 2012.[26] Symantec in its 2014 Internet Security Report indicated that "Java's platform had the highest number of reported plug-in vulnerabilities". When a user visits a malicious web page or a compromised website, the site will exploit a security flaw in the browser's Java plug-in and download malware onto the user's computer and potentially gain access to the network.

---

26 Kaspersky Lab, Oracle Java Surpasses Adobe Reader as the Most Frequently Exploited Software, December 21 2012, available at www.kaspersky.com/about/news/virus/2012/Oracle_Java_surpasses_Adobe_Reader_as_the_most_frequently_exploited_software.

Symantec indicated that hackers continue to "exploit Java vulnerabilities where users have not upgraded to newer, more secure Java versions".[27] It may be unrealistic for a law firm to disable the use of these plug-ins given their widespread use, but firms should upgrade to the latest version of Java and Flash, and periodically evaluate if network endpoints are being infected due to the vulnerabilities of browser plug-ins. If so, firms should evaluate whether additional security measures are warranted.

28. *Develop a system to protect all keys used for encryption (data encryption keys).* Otherwise, a hacker could gain access to the keys and will be able to decrypt the protected information. A number of data breach laws are triggered when unauthorised access to encrypted personal information is obtained and an encryption key is compromised. One way to protect data encryption keys is to encrypt those keys via a key-encrypting key. All key-encrypting keys should be stored in a separate location, away from the data encryption keys on the network to reduce the risk of unauthorised access to both types of cryptographic keys. Just as with passwords, cryptographic keys should be periodically changed or replaced to minimise the risk of being compromised. Access to the keys should be limited to the fewest number of firm personnel necessary, and when a firm employs a system of manual control over its data encryption keys, dual control over cryptographic keys should be implemented to prevent one person having access to the entire key.

29. *Periodically perform security audits on the network through an outside vendor.* This process should include network scans and penetration testing as well as testing a subset of systems and security measures deployed in the network. The purpose of penetration testing is to simulate a real attack on the network to determine how far a hacker is able to penetrate. The security audit should provide a detailed report of system vulnerabilities with action items ranked by severity. A firm should have a set plan to review and address issues raised in the security audit. There should also be a record kept of network or system changes since the last security audit and those should be an initial focus of any subsequent audit to ensure that those changes have not introduced a new vulnerability or threat to the network.

30. *Train and educate the firm's lawyers and employees on internet safety and cyber security risks.* A firm can have great technological safeguards built into its network and develop strong written security policies and procedures, but those efforts will be wasted if the firm's employees either do not know, or refuse to follow, the firm's security procedures. Building security awareness into the culture of the law firm for all personnel is a key part of any security programme. A law firm should consider including in its training programme how the firm's employees and partners can protect themselves against identity theft and the risk of being hacked. That approach should increase

---

27 Symantec Internet Security Threat Report 2014, p 59, Volume 19, April 2014, available at www.symantec.com/content/en/us/enterprise/other_resources/bistr_main_report_v19_21291018.en-us.pdf.

their receptiveness to the training, increase their security awareness and will ultimately help to protect the firm in the process. Topics to consider for any training programme include secure password practices, recognising phishing emails, internet and social media risks, understanding encryption and the risks of file transfer and storage in the cloud, risks associated with removable storage, remote access risks, mobile device and Wi-Fi security, foreign travel risks, acceptable use of firm systems and client information, as well as compliance with any governmental regulatory requirements such as HIPAA.

A law firm must ensure that its personnel understand the firm's security policies. To develop a culture of security in a law firm requires that its security policies and practices be routinely applied and consistently enforced.

The globalisation of legal services

Friedrich R Blase
Holland & Knight
Julia Graham
DLA Piper
James W Jones
Georgetown University Law Center

Globalisation is by now a well-established fact of modern life as dramatic changes have bound countries, economies and businesses more tightly together through better infrastructure, faster and more efficient communications systems, and closer trade and investment links.[1] It is also clearly one of the major factors shaping the legal market over the past 20 years. While the benefits of globalisation to the legal profession have been numerous, the increased risks associated with transnational practices have created new challenges for law firms actively engaged in international work. In this chapter, we review the rapid pace of globalisation in the legal market, describe many of the risks associated with the increasing globalisation of legal practice, and suggest some steps that firms can take to understand and mitigate the risks identified and convert them into opportunities.

1. Pace of globalisation in the legal market

Globalisation refers to the dramatic increase in international commerce that has occurred over the past two decades as a result of the confluence of tariff reductions, improvements in shipping and transportation systems, and technological innovations that have permitted the rapid and efficient transfer of money and assets throughout the world.[2] While cross-border business activity is, of course, as old as the idea of borders themselves, the distinct development of the past quarter of a century has been the dramatic increase in the scale of such business around the world, spurred by a combination of legal and technological developments that have made such transactions remarkably easy.

On the legal side, the growth of globalisation has been reflected in a lowering of trade barriers on an unprecedented scale. The momentum began in 1993 with the formation of the European Union, a development that was quickly followed by the signing of the North America Free Trade Agreement (NAFTA) in 1994 and by the

---

[1] See World Economic Forum Global Risk Report: Ninth Edition, a global view of risks produced in collaboration with Marsh & McLennan Companies; Swiss Re; Zurich Insurance Group; National University of Singapore; Oxford Martin School, University of Oxford; and Wharton Risk Management and Decision Processes Center, University of Pennsylvania (2014).

[2] See Thomas L Friedman, *The World Is Flat: A Brief History of the Twenty-First Century* (Allen Lane, 2005), a book that built on Thomas L Friedman, *The Lexus and the Olive Tree: Understanding Globalization* (Picador, 1999).

establishment of the World Trade Organization (WTO) in 1995 (the latter being the culmination of a decade of free trade negotiations). The formation of the WTO led to the rapid globalisation of trade beyond North America and Europe, to include large parts of Asia, Africa and Latin America. The subsequent addition of new members to the WTO – especially China (in 2001) and Russia (in 2012) – as well as the contemporaneous explosion in information and communication technology, has now resulted in a world that is more interdependent than ever before and growing more so day by day. Moreover, the pace of such globalisation is accelerating.

The lowering of trade barriers through the European Common Market, NAFTA and WTO, as well as other regional and bilateral agreements that mirrored them, resulted in an extraordinary surge in foreign direct investment activity. Indeed, global foreign direct investment stock (ie, the value of investments held by foreigners everywhere in the world) exploded between 1990 and 2012, from US$ 2 trillion to over US$ 22 trillion. Not surprisingly, this unprecedented increase in cross-border transactions quickly led to business for law firms and changed the profile of firms around the world.

Prior to the 1990s, large law firms had, of course, been involved in some international work, sometimes through their own overseas offices but most often working with local offices in other jurisdictions when necessary to serve a client's needs.[3] There were a handful of truly international firms like Baker & McKenzie (founded in Chicago in 1949), but for most firms revenues derived from international work were relatively modest. All of that began to change, however, in the 1990s.

Evidence of the dramatic expansion of globalisation can be traced through the growth of foreign offices of large US law firms over a period of 20 years. Among the National Law Journal 250 (ie, the 250 largest firms in the United States by lawyer headcount), 59 firms had overseas offices in 1988, compared to 102 in 1998 and 113 in 2008. More striking, however, was the number of overseas offices operated by these same firms – a figure that rose from 158 in 1988 to 383 in 1998 and 617 in 2008 – and the number of lawyers in those offices: 1,467 in 1988, compared to 4,883 in 1998 and a staggering 17,267 in 2008.

Similar growth patterns were seen among large UK firms during roughly the same period as they moved to consolidate a pan-European and Middle East presence, expand into promising Asian markets, and even try modest inroads into the United States. During the decade between 1993 and 2002, for example, Clifford Chance, Freshfields and DLA grew their lawyer headcount by over 100%, with much of that growth in non-UK offices.

Global law firm expansion is also evident in the growing number of international mergers in recent years. The record-breaking year for these purposes was 2012, a year that saw 96 cross-border mergers, substantially more than the 54 that occurred in 2011, the 44 in 2010, or the 48 in 2009. The trend continued in 2013, albeit at a more moderate pace. Moreover, many of these international mergers have been quite substantial, including:

---

3   Reflecting this activity, the International Bar Association was founded in New York in 1947, although it did not admit individual members until 1970.

- Piper Rudnick Gray Cary in the United States with DLA in Europe, the Middle East and Asia-Pacific;
- Norton Rose with Canada-based Ogilvy Renault;
- UK-based Ashurst with Australia's Blake Dawson;
- Australia's Mallesons Stephen Jacques with China's King & Wood;
- SNR Denton with Canada-based Fraser Milner Casgrain and Paris-based Salans;
- Norton Rose with Calgary-based MacLeod Dixon;
- Norton Rose with Fulbright & Jaworski;
- London's Herbert Smith with Australia's Freehills;
- K&L Gates with Australia-based Middletons;
- King & Wood Mallesons with London-based SJ Berwin; and
- Hogan Lovells with South Africa-based Routledge Modise.

While many of these cross-border mergers have resulted in one-firm combinations, in recent years a growing number of firms – including Baker & McKenzie, Dentons, DLA Piper, Hogan Lovells, King & Wood Mallesons, Norton Rose Fulbright and Squire Sanders – have opted to structure their global operations through a Swiss *verein* model that allows partner firms to maintain separate profit pools.

The substantial global expansion of large law firms over the past quarter-century obviously reflects strategic judgments on the part of many firms that they need larger global footprints to serve the needs of their rapidly globalising clients. At a deeper level, however, the trend may also mark a recognition of an important shift in global economic activity.

As shown in Figures 1 and 2 below, the International Monetary Fund and the Citi Investment Research and Analysis group predict that, over the next 40 years, there will be a dramatic shift in world economic activity, with developing countries (particularly in Asia) accounting for an increasing share of world GDP.

Figure 1: Composition of world real GDP, 2010

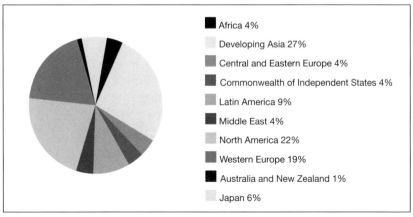

Figure 2: Composition of projected world real GDP, 2050

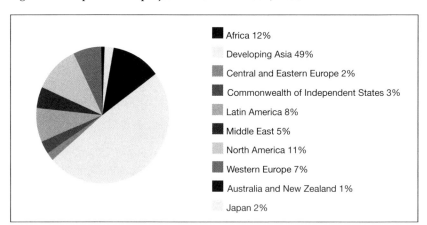

As a consequence, and considering the largely irreversible effects of the globalisation of commerce and trade that has dominated the world's economy for the past two decades, it seems inevitable that law firms will be increasingly drawn into the arena of global practice, with all of the potential benefits and risks that entails. At the same time, since the financial crisis of 2008, some economic commentators have talked of the potential for de-globalisation, as some organisations[4] transfer production back to their home countries. While this is more thesis than trend at the moment, law firms need to watch this scenario and take account of it as part of their strategic planning.

2. Risks associated with the increasing globalisation of legal practice

In the sections that follow, we address the various risks associated with global practice by looking at three broad categories: (1) law firm organisational and management risks (both internal and external), (2) regulatory risks and (3) new business risks. In each of these areas, there are special challenges that arise as firms move onto the global stage.

2.1 Law firm organisational and management risks

At the most basic level, law firms managing overseas offices, participating in networks of foreign lawyers, referring clients to firms in other countries or otherwise engaged in global practice face a series of structural and management challenges related to size, cultural diversity and uniformity of service delivery. They must also address financial and political risks not normally relevant to practices in their home jurisdictions, some of which may arise from other firms that are not under their direct control.

---

[4] Business Insider October 2013 – comment by Morgan Stanley head of global economics Joachim Fels www.businessinsider.com/economist-worries-about-de-globalization-2013.

(a)   **Size and organisational complexity**

It is perhaps obvious, but most law firms with significant global practices tend to be large and complex organisations, and their very size and complexity can make effective risk management more difficult. Such firms often have hundreds (or in many cases thousands) of lawyers practising in dozens of offices in multiple countries. Those lawyers in turn participate in scores of local and global practice groups and may be parts of regional, client or industry teams. The overlapping – and sometimes confusing – lines of authority in these matrix-type organisations can make it very difficult to impose common standards of quality and risk management across the entire firm. The problem can be exacerbated in cases such as the Swiss *vereins* where the overall firm comprises several more-or-less free-standing organisations that may be separate profit centres. Implementing effective risk management in such complex settings requires both careful planning and skilful implementation.

(b)   **Cultural and language diversity**

The risk environment in any organisation refers to the values, beliefs, knowledge and understanding about risk shared by a group of people with a common purpose, in particular the employees, teams or groups within an organisation. An effective risk environment is one that enables and rewards individuals and groups for taking the right risks in an informed manner.[5] An organisation's risk environment is strongly affected, however, by the culture or cultures in which it operates, since some cultures have a much higher tolerance for risk than others. Some countries, for example, have relatively few rules and controls, reflecting cultures that emphasise and tolerate individualism while being sceptical of conformity and authority. Other countries have highly structured rules and controls, reflecting cultures that emphasise conformity and deference to authority.

While common risk management standards are surely a worthy goal, law firms operating in many different countries and cultures often find that a single risk management system is inadequate, particularly if the system reflects only the cultural values and norms of the firm's home country. Just as marketing professionals must tailor their advertising and sales strategies to appeal to the tastes and preferences of local consumers around the world, so too must law firms adapt their risk management strategies to reflect the cultural sensibilities of their offices scattered around the globe.[6]

Carefully selected risk management language can allow an organisation to cut through management, functional and country silos to facilitate a common understanding of risk and to reinforce the organisation's key risk management principles. While there are various generic and legal risk management standards

---

5   The Institute of Risk Management, *Risk Culture under the Microscope: Guidance for Boards* (2012), available at www.protiviti.com/en-UK/Documents/Resource-Guides/Risk_Culture.pdf.
6   Similar issues can arise in respect of client expectations and behaviours as well. Differences in risk tolerance can sometimes be seen in business terms of reference and outside counsel guidelines from corporate clients located in different countries and cultures. Firms need to be mindful of these differences in reviewing such documents and in putting in place mechanisms to implement their requirements.

(including common definitions and glossaries) that firms can draw from, there is no standard risk management language that is essential. The key is that whatever language is used, it should reflect the usual management language of the firm, avoid jargon, and use only words and phrases that can be translated unambiguously into the different languages in which the firm operates around the world.

(c) *Service delivery standards*

The practical difficulties of dealing with organisational complexity and cultural diversity across wide global networks are particularly evident in the challenges faced by global firms in insuring uniform quality and service delivery standards. In today's legal market, clients are focused more than ever before on efficiency, predictability and cost effectiveness in the delivery of legal services. Obviously, consistent quality in service delivery is key to meeting these client expectations. Indeed, providing seamless service is often cited by firms as one of the primary drivers for establishing international offices or networks.

To address these challenges, some international firms have established service standards intended to apply to all lawyers and offices across their firms or networks. These standards are intended to insure that client work will be handled in a consistent way regardless of the location or subject-matter expertise that may be involved. Such standards might, for example, provide templates to be used in conducting due diligence reviews or preparing documents for certain corporate or financial transactions, protocols for use in international arbitrations, or common rules for billing or client communications. The point is to provide clients with the assurance that all work performed by a firm measures up to a common set of standards with work products that are complementary and of consistent quality. Providing such assurances in any firm is difficult enough, but in international firms it is particularly daunting.

As described above, the practices and work habits of lawyers around the world can differ widely and are influenced in important ways by culture and language. For example, the service standards of one global firm provide the following with respect to responsiveness to client inquiries: "Client calls or emails are answered as promptly as can reasonably be expected." The problem, of course, is that reasonable expectations can be very different in New York than in London or Tokyo or Rome. More importantly, such differences in cultures around the world can also influence the role, functions, and attitudes of lawyers – for example how deferential they may be to the wishes of their clients, how aggressive in pursuing inquiries in due diligence and other settings, or how active in influencing client behaviours. Such differences in practice have obvious implications for risk management.

The issue of service standards is further complicated by the growing tendency of clients to impose their own rules with respect to such matters. In particular, in recent years, multinational corporations have taken the lead in developing and imposing such standards in the form of customised terms of business and outside counsel guidelines. These guidelines mandate common practices for all of a client's outside law firms in a wide variety of matters from conflicts of interest and waivers to staffing, communications, reporting, budgeting, billing, information and data security, business continuity, legal and regulatory compliance, and many others. Again, while such guidelines pose challenges for firms in all circumstances, they can be especially difficult in international settings. Rules of practice or norms in various jurisdictions may often be at odds with those promulgated by the firm or mandated by client policies, as, for example, in the case of conflicts of interest, data security or privacy protections. In addition, the sheer size and complexity of global firms (such as issues arising in Swiss *verein*-type structures) can make it much more difficult to ensure that a client's requirements are achievable and, if so, strictly followed in all parts of the organisation.

(d)   *Financial risks*

Apart from internal risks associated with complex and diverse organisational structures, firms with offices in more than one country also face external financial risks related to currency fluctuations. First, there is the exposure to currency fluctuation that inevitably occurs because of the delay between the performance of the work and the payment for the work. In many firms, this conversion period can be 100 days or more. As long as the work undertaken by lawyers is paid in the currency in which they are paid by the firm (and in which the rent for their office space and other expenses are paid), the currency fluctuation risk associated with this time lag may be negligible and can usually be managed. In cases where there is a mismatch between the currency of revenues and expenses, however, the risk can be significant. Firms often choose to ignore this risk, either on the theory that it impacts a relatively small portion of their overall revenues or on the assumption that currency fluctuations will even out over time. Ignoring the problem can lead to larger issues, however, particularly issues related to partner compensation.

Where a firm has a single global profit pool that is shared with partners throughout the firm, currency fluctuation becomes a significant risk because performance and compensation must be denominated in a single currency. For example, a US firm would probably denominate its performance and compensation in US dollars worldwide. Partners throughout the world would be paid in that currency, even though they would need to convert their US dollars into local currency to meet their own living expenses. If, by way of example, the euro gained considerable value against the dollar in a given fiscal year, either the European partners or the firm or both would have to bear the risk of that appreciation. The problem is exacerbated by the fact that in many firms foreign partners' remuneration (ie, partners in a jurisdiction other than the one in whose currency the firm is denominated) is safeguarded by guaranteed exchange rates. While that approach provides certainty for foreign partners, it can have a high cost for 'home' partners, at least where a firm has a large number of foreign lawyers or where the currency swings are significant. Some firms have tried to adjust their guaranteed exchange rate mechanisms to mitigate their effects on home partners, but such moves are almost inevitably met with strong resistance from foreign partners who perceive that the compensation system is being changed to their disadvantage.

Since the significant fluctuations in major currencies that occurred in 2007, some large international firms have sought to address their currency risks by creating dedicated treasury functions that work with the firms' banks in developing hedging strategies for the firms as a whole as well as for individual partners. Given the continuing expansion of internationally oriented firms and their continuing exposure to currency risks, such an approach seems likely to spread.

(e) *Insurance risks*

For law firms with significant global practices, the purchase of compliant insurance programmes to protect their operations at both a local and global level can be challenging. The laws and regulations governing insurance policies and coverage vary dramatically around the world, and some of the regulatory regimes are far less clear than others. The resulting uncertainty, unpredictability and ambiguity of the legality and enforceability of global insurance programmes have been among the top concerns of global risk managers in many organisations for some years. Complying with regulatory requirements around the world can be extremely complex, particularly because the rules are so varied and they can be changed with little or no warning. Even some highly experienced insurance buyers admit that they often cannot be sure that their programmes are fully compliant, especially when brokers and insurers can have different interpretations about compliance for the same cover in the same jurisdiction. Solutions provided by third-party organisations[7] can help insurance buyers to conduct discussions with their brokers and insurers from an informed position. The consequences of non-compliance can be serious, including the prospect of fines, invalid insurance policies and reputational damage.

(f) *Geopolitical risks*

As organisations operating with people and assets throughout the world are vulnerable to rapidly changing political and economic conditions and the effect of foreign policy in many countries, global law firms face geopolitical risks and challenges that are far more significant than those confronted by firms operating in a single jurisdiction. Such risks can take many different forms and can often come from unexpected places. Events that lead to discontinuity of operations may include events as diverse as civil unrest and riots, bombings, kidnapping or detention by governments of firm personnel, economic collapses, imposition of currency controls or trading restrictions, harassment by local government authorities, and many others. The sheer variety of things that can go wrong means that global firms have to develop the capabilities to monitor geopolitical risks on an ongoing basis and be able to move quickly using honed and rehearsed business continuity and crisis management plans to address crises when they arise.

2.2 **Regulatory risks**

In addition to the organisational and management risks described above, law firms operating in multiple national jurisdictions face regulatory risks that can be far more

---

7   *Axco Information Services,* which offers information on regulation and tax compliance through a number of products, and services a database of regulatory and tax compliance information, a Q&A system to answer specific questions on regulation and compliance and regulatory alert emails.

complicated than those affecting firms practising in a single jurisdiction. These regulatory risks include national and international rules governing money laundering and related terrorism and political corruption issues, divergent national and international standards relating to data privacy, sometimes conflicting national standards for professional responsibility and ethics, and choice of law issues involving all of the above.

(a) *Rules governing money laundering, terrorism and political corruption*

In recent years, there have been numerous statutes, rules and regulations adopted by governments and quasi-governmental bodies around the world to address the particular threats posed by terrorism and political corruption. While these requirements apply to all law firms, they pose special risks for firms engaged in transnational practices.

Perhaps the most onerous of these regulatory schemes are the measures growing out of the recommendations of the Financial Action Task Force on Money Laundering (FATF)[8] aimed at detecting and combatting money-laundering activities and terrorist financing. The recommendations are reflected in the so-called '40+9 Recommendations' of the FATF,[9] recommendations that have been endorsed by more than 180 jurisdictions, as well as the World Bank and the International Monetary Fund.

The FATF recommendations, which now have the force of law in most jurisdictions,[10] include a number of 'gatekeeper' requirements aimed at lawyers and other professionals, such as conducting appropriate due diligence with respect to new clients, maintaining certain records and reporting suspicious activity to the appropriate authorities without alerting the client. The FATF recommendations apply particularly to lawyers who engage in:

- buying or selling real estate;
- managing client money, securities or other assets;
- managing bank, savings or securities accounts;
- organising contributions for the creation, operation or management of companies; or
- creating, operating or managing legal persons or arrangements, and the buying and selling of business entities.

Since the penalties for violation of FATF requirements in many countries can be draconian, firms must put in place comprehensive client due diligence systems and

---

8   FATF is an international organisation currently consisting of 33 countries and two regional associations. It was established by the G7 countries in 1989 to combat money laundering. In October 2001, FATF expanded its mandate to include efforts to combat the financing of terrorism.
9   The "40 Recommendations" address money laundering. They were adopted in 1990 and revised in 1996 and 2003. The "9 Special Recommendations" address efforts to combat terrorism financing. They were adopted shortly after 9/11 and revised in 2004.
10 In most jurisdictions, the FATF recommendations have been incorporated into statutes or regulations issued by governmental bodies. In the United States, for example, the recommendations have been implemented through the Bank Secrecy Act and the USA Patriot Act, and the provisions of the Bank Secrecy Act have been further clarified through regulations issued by the Financial Crimes Enforcement Network in the Treasury Department.

carefully monitor all of their practice activities that could give rise to FATF liabilities.

Also of concern to global firms are the various statutes and rules around the world designed to deal with political corruption. These include particularly various regulatory regimes adopted pursuant to the Anti-Bribery Convention of the Organisation for Economic Co-operation and Development (OECD), including, for example, the UK Bribery Act 2010. Under the latter statute, it is a criminal offence for any person or entity to bribe foreign officials. Moreover, the 'failure of commercial organisations to prevent bribery on their behalf' is also an offence for which violators can be punished on a strict liability basis. Similar, though somewhat less severe, is the US Foreign Corrupt Practices Act. To provide some shield against liabilities under these anti-bribery statutes, organisations (including law firms) must develop codes of conduct that reflect the prohibitions set out in the statutes and must be able to show that they have trained their staffs to comply strictly with the requirements.

(b) *Standards on data privacy*

As rapid changes in information technology have dramatically increased potential threats to privacy, governments around the world have imposed statutory and regulatory requirements to protect the privacy of individuals and sometimes organisations. The various schemes have widely differing requirements, however, and are sometimes even based on different philosophies, thus offering a significant challenge to organisations such as global law firms that operate – and hold and use data – in many different jurisdictions.

A prime example of the problem is the contrast between data privacy requirements in Europe and those in the United States. In Europe, under the EU Data Protection Directive adopted in 1995,[11] the processing of personal data within the European Union is strictly regulated. The directive incorporates seven principles originally articulated in the OECD Recommendations of the Council Concerning Guidelines Governing the Protection of Privacy and Trans-Border Flows of Personal Data in 1980. These are:

- notice: the requirement that subjects should be given notice when their data is being collected;
- purpose: the requirement that data should be used only for the purpose stated and not for any other purpose;
- consent: the requirement that data should not be disclosed without the data subject's consent;
- security: the requirement that collected data should be kept secure from potential abuses;
- disclosure: the requirement that data subjects should be informed as to who is collecting their data;
- access: the requirement that data subjects should be allowed to access their data and make corrections to any inaccurate data; and

---

11 On January 25 2012, the European Commission unveiled a draft European General Data Protection Regulation that will, if adopted, supersede the Data Protection Directive.

- accountability: the requirement that data subjects should have a method available to them to hold data collectors accountable for not following the above-described principles.

By contrast, the United States has adopted what it terms a 'sectoral' approach to data protection that relies on a combination of legislation, regulation and self-regulation, rather than on governmental regulation alone. As a result, the United States lacks any single data protection law that is comparable to the EU Data Protection Directive. Instead, it has adopted privacy legislation on an *ad hoc* basis as needs have arisen in particular sectors.[12] As a result, some commentators have suggested that in the United States data is assumed to be unprotected unless there is a specific law or regulation providing otherwise, whereas in Europe data is assumed to be protected unless there is a specific law or regulation making it public. It is easy to see why large organisations operating in both places find it difficult to create systems that satisfy both sets of requirements.

(c) *Standards for professional responsibility and ethics*

Of all of the risks that are exacerbated by a firm's international operations, one of the most nettlesome relates to differing national standards for professional responsibility and ethics. Lawyers are, of course, regulated by the national jurisdictions in which they practise (or, in some countries such as the United States, Canada, Australia and elsewhere, by states or provinces within those national jurisdictions). Where the local rules governing a particular lawyer vary significantly from the rules applicable to other lawyers in his or her firm, substantial issues can arise.

One of the most common examples of the effects of such conflicting rules of practice involves ethical conflicts of interest. In almost all US jurisdictions, a lawyer has an ethical conflict of interest if his or her firm is adverse in any way to a current client, even in a wholly unrelated matter.[13] In the United Kingdom, continental Europe and most of the rest of the world, an ethical conflict exists only if a firm is adverse to an existing client in a related matter. By way of example, if a US lawyer were representing a company in tort litigation in a US court and one of the lawyer's partners – say in the firm's London office – wanted to represent another client in an unrelated corporate matter that was adverse to the company, an ethical conflict of interest would arise under US rules (except for Texas) but not under the rules of the United Kingdom. If the London lawyer agreed to accept the representation, the US partner would be in violation of US rules and subject to disqualification or discipline.

Obviously, the problem described in the example above might be solved if the firm made it clear that US rules should be applied in all of its offices around the world (which a US-based firm might well do). But issuing such a policy and assuring compliance with it may be two quite different matters. In particular, lawyers based in jurisdictions around the world who are not trained to think of conflicts in the

---

12   See, for example, the Video Privacy Protection Act of 1988, the Cable Television Protection and Competition Act of 1992, the Fair Credit Reporting Act and the 2010 Massachusetts Data Privacy Regulations.
13   The only US jurisdiction not adhering to this rule is Texas, which has adopted the UK approach.

expansive way embraced by US rules might be less sensitive to circumstances that could give rise to US-style conflicts. Also, foreign clients not familiar with the peculiarities of US practice might be confused – or, indeed, even offended – to be asked for a waiver of a conflict that they do not believe even exists.

The conflict problem can also be complicated by the changing nature of a matter. Suppose, for example, that a firm takes on a financing in Hong Kong for a Chinese corporate client in a matter that is adverse to a UK client that the firm is representing in an entirely unrelated matter. Because both representations are occurring in jurisdictions outside the United States, the firm rightly concludes at the outset that no ethical conflict exists. In the course of the financing work for the Chinese client, however, suppose that the locus of the deal shifts to New York. The shift gives rise to an immediate ethical problem for the firm's New York lawyers, even though neither client is based in the United States.

Problems raised by conflicting national standards of practice are not, however, limited to conflicts of interest alone. They also extend to such issues as multidisciplinary practices, multijurisdictional practices, restrictions on law firm ownership, non-compete arrangements for professionals, fee-sharing arrangements and the payment of referral fees. In all of these matters, national (or state or provincial) rules of practice can differ significantly, sometimes posing very difficult problems for firms operating in many different national jurisdictions. An additional problem (often overlooked) relates to qualifications for admission in various jurisdictions. It is common practice in many large multinational firms to temporarily assign lawyers from one office to another, a practice often cited as helping to build cohesion and collaboration across the firm. Unfortunately, in many of these secondments, firms neglect to consider whether the lawyers temporarily practising in an overseas office may in fact lawfully do so under the rules of the relevant local jurisdiction. Since unauthorised practice in some jurisdictions may constitute a criminal offence, this is a risk that should be taken seriously.

(d) *Choice of law issues*

To deal with the issues described above, every law firm operating in multiple national jurisdictions has to make a basic decision as to which sets of national standards should be applied across the firm in various circumstances. Some firms try to resolve the issue by providing that the rules of a single (often the US) jurisdiction will apply in all circumstances except when applicable local rules are more restrictive, in which case the more restrictive rules will prevail. This approach has the benefit of providing some certainty to the choice of law process, but it can result in the application of more restrictive rules than are necessary in a given circumstance. Why, for example, should UK lawyers be forced to comply with US conflict rules in a matter involving only UK parties and entirely confined to the United Kingdom?

Another approach taken by some firms is to apply the rules of the jurisdiction having the most obvious nexus to the matter, with the proviso that if a matter has a plausible connection to a jurisdiction with more restrictive rules, the latter should prevail. This approach has the benefit of being more customised to particular clients and matters, but it forces separate determinations in each case, thus complicating the firm's intake process and running the risk of inconsistent decisions being made across the firm.

Whichever approach is taken, it is important that processes are in place to provide quick review and rapid decision making, typically through a firm's general counsel's office. As most of these issues must be initially resolved at the intake stage of a new engagement, delays in making decisions can be detrimental to both the firm and its clients.

2.3 New business risks

In recent years, there has been an explosion of non-traditional, law-related entities and business models that have created a dramatically different market for law firm services. Indeed, there is mounting evidence that such non-traditional competitors are increasingly siphoning off business that was traditionally sent to law firms.[14] While this development poses challenges for all law firms, there are particular risks for firms engaged in international practices.

(a) Alternative business structures risks

Closely related to the regulatory risks described in Section 2.2 above are challenges presented by various alternative business structures (ie, non-traditional methods for delivering legal services) that are now permitted in England and Wales under the Legal Services Act 2007 and under similar statutes and rules in various other countries. Such alternative business structures might permit investment in or ownership of law firms by non-lawyers or other passive investors, might permit law firms to engage in multidisciplinary practices by offering legal services in combination with other types of professional and non-professional services, and might permit various fee-splitting arrangements involving lawyers and non-lawyers. All of these practices are considered unethical and illegal in some jurisdictions (most notably in the United States).

Where a firm is engaged in alternative business practices in a jurisdiction that permits them but also has offices in a jurisdiction that prohibits them, an obvious problem arises. To some extent, regulatory authorities have tended to ignore these issues, at least if the offending activity is confined to jurisdictions in which it is lawful. There is no guarantee, however, that the regulatory attitude will always be so benign.

Some have suggested that this problem can be solved through use of the Swiss *verein* format, on the theory that since *verein* members do not share profits, they effectively operate as separate entities for regulatory purposes. That argument has not, however, been tested in any major court decision and, in any event, is not as clear cut as it may first appear. In the first place, there are many ways in which some profit sharing is possible through the *verein* structure. Additionally, most firms that

---

14 As but one example of this phenomenon, it is estimated that the market share of legal process outsourcing companies grew from US$640 million in 2010 to US$1.1 billion in 2012; and it is projected that the market share will increase to US$2.42 billion by 2015. That represents an annual growth rate of 30% or more, considerably higher than the annual growth rates of most law firms. Source: The 2010 Legal Outsourcing Market Global Study and Thomson Reuters Strategic Analysis.

are organised as *vereins* aggressively market themselves as single firms throughout the world and emphasise their capabilities to deliver services seamlessly and consistently wherever required. Such 'one-firm' marketing would seem to cut against the separate entity argument.

(b) *Special risks in international outsourcing and off-shoring*
For firms that elect (or are asked by clients) to outsource certain legal and law-related functions to offshore companies, a variety of risks must be considered. First, there is the full range of questions as to the quality, stability and security of the outsourced entity and the environment within which it operates. While there are many competent and high-quality companies offering these services, there are also many others that may not meet minimal standards. As in all matters, due diligence is required, including site visits, reference checks and careful structuring of contractual liabilities.

A second concern with international outsourcing relates to data security. Under current laws in the United States, the European Union and elsewhere, the transmission of certain types of data outside the geographic territory of the governing jurisdiction can be a serious offence. Also, transmitting data to an outsourcing entity without adequate provision for the security of the data might well result in the loss of the lawyer–client privilege with respect to such data in jurisdictions where it would otherwise be available as well as loss or damage to the data itself if hosted in a potentially insecure environment.

To the extent that an outsourcing entity is asked to perform any legal analysis or research, it is important to remember that such activities could run foul of local rules of practice in the jurisdiction in which the outsourcing company is based. More specifically, it is possible that some kinds of research or analysis could be regarded by local bars as the unauthorised practice of law. This may be especially true in jurisdictions with highly protective and aggressive local bars.

Finally, firms must remember that while work can be outsourced and offshored, responsibility cannot. A process for the ongoing management and assurance of such work is key.

3. **Steps firms can take to mitigate the risks of global practice**
Given the broad range of risks faced by firms pursuing global practices, it is hardly surprising that a comprehensive and far-reaching approach is required to mitigate such risks. To implement such an approach successfully requires a firm to think more broadly about its risk environment than most firms have historically. From this point of view, risk management covers much more than just traditional concerns about ethics and rules of practice; it extends to every aspect of the firm's operations. This more comprehensive approach is generally known as enterprise risk management (ERM) or sometimes enterprise business continuity management.

Development of a successful ERM system requires a firm to develop and adopt a risk management framework specifying (i) how risk management will be governed in the firm, (ii) how the risk management programme will be implemented across the firm's various offices and sectors, (iii) how risks and controls will be monitored and reported, (iv) how the framework will be managed, and (v) how the framework will be reviewed and updated. Components of the risk management framework should include:

- the policies and processes that will be used to monitor and assess risk and controls within the firm;
- guidance for lawyers and employees as to how they can most effectively adhere to the policies and procedures;
- tools, techniques and metrics that will be used to measure risks and mitigation efforts;
- training, education and communication activities that will be used to foster a more risk-conscious environment; and
- steps that will be taken to assure compliance with risk management policies and procedures.

A key part of the risk management framework should be the identification of the specific risks and risk categories that the firm wishes to monitor and address. Typical broad categories might include financial and economic risks, legal services risks, operational risks (including health, safety, security), and competitive risks – all or any of which might affect the reputation of the firm. For risks identified in each risk category, it is then necessary to think about (i) the likelihood that the identified risk will occur, (ii) the consequence its occurrence would have on the firm, and (iii) the severity of the risk (impact multiplied by consequence). Qualitative and quantitative scales might be used in assessing each risk.

For the risks identified, the firm must then determine its risk appetite (the amount and type of risk that the firm is willing to take in order to meet their strategic objectives), and its risk tolerance (which is about what a firm can deal with and what it will not deal with).

The hallmarks of a high-quality ERM programme include:

- board-level commitment to ERM as a critical framework for the firm's successful decision making and for driving value;
- a dedicated risk executive in a senior position who drives and facilitates the ERM process;[15]
- an ERM culture that encourages full engagement and accountability at all levels of the firm;
- engagement of key stakeholders in risk management strategy development and policy setting;
- transparency of risk communications;
- integration of financial and operational risk information into decision making;
- use of sophisticated quantification methods to understand risk and demonstrate added value through risk management;

---

15   Some global firms have now created the position of Chief Risk Officer to manage their ERM programmes. Such positions, which have long been used in financial institutions and other businesses, can be a very effective way of keeping senior firm leaders focused on risk issues.

- identification of new and emerging risks using internal data as well as information from external providers; and
- a move from focusing on risk avoidance and mitigation to leveraging risk and risk management options that extract value.[16]

Firms have found it helpful to adopt one of the global risk management standards and many firms have started to adopt ISO31000, a family of standards relating to risk management codified by the International Organization for Standardization. The purpose of ISO 31000 is to provide principles and generic guidelines on risk management.[17]

Managing the risks relating to global legal practice, as described above, can be quite daunting. With proper risk management structures and processes, however, those risks can be effectively managed and, indeed, even turned to competitive advantage.

---

16   Source: Aon Global Enterprise Risk Management Survey 2010.
17   Source: ISO 31000 www.iso.org/iso/home/standards/iso31000.htm.

The effects of risk management on brand and reputation management

Georg-Christof Bertsch
Bertsch.Brand Consultants
Simon Chester
Heenan Blaikie LLP
Jane Hunter
Aon Risk Solutions

1. **How to use branding to positive effect**

    Long before the name for branding even existed, confident institutions and powerful people have leveraged its power. A classic example is the Roman Empire's Senatus Populusque Romanus (SPQR) brand and the strong promise it conveyed to Roman citizens. Sheltered within the imperial frontiers, everyone – whether citizens, freedmen or slaves – could feel secure and protected. Anyone outside the shadow of SPQR banners either feared for their lives or surrendered to Roman authority. Only submission would lead to the benefits of the empire's power, knowledge and technical progress.[1]

    Imagine a monochrome supermarket without brand names or product information. Picture an entire shelf of cereals without the slightest differentiating information, in either packaging or content. How could this supermarket survive? There is only one answer – competitive pricing of products, since quality factors are irrelevant. The best-priced products would sell out, while all other products would quickly be forced off the shelves. Prices would plummet relentlessly downward.

    With this in mind, let us look at the current legal market. Many lawyers feel like the products in our ghostly supermarket. Their law firms lack identity. They have no striking hallmarks to set themselves apart from their colleagues, battling for clientele without showing any distinctive merits. Once upon a time, you could survive in this scenario. After the World War II, the scarcity of attorneys ensured a nice income for anyone in practice. Today, we have a glut of lawyers competing for discriminating clients – a highly precarious situation; yet one which is ideal for applying branding principles, but with an understanding of risk management.

    What does branding mean for a law firm? Externally, it means a distinctive identity based on a promise of value that is different or distinct from any other. Internally, it can remind members of the firm what makes them special. One of the

---

1   Stefanie Hartung, Starke Marken (Strong Brands), Bonn, 2013, p 16.

few English words to come from Gaelic is 'slogan',[2] from the word for a war-cry sounded going into battle to unite the clan.

The strongest brands are those which arise organically from firm culture, not dreamed up by a Madison Avenue brand factory or a cool graphic designer. The best signify the shared identity of the firm. A telling example is the Cravath walk[3] – at a funeral of a lawyer at the New York firm of Cravath, Swaine & Moore LLP, all the partners will enter at the end, slow-marching two by two, in dark suits and polished shoes, in order of seniority. What does this funeral phalanx signify? A shared commitment, an elite attitude, precision, élan, a conservative tradition, a true partnership.

A firm trademark is a service brand. Defining the purpose of a service brand is no more difficult than defining the purpose of a product trademark, such as iconic soft drinks. To be noticed, both types of brand must stand out in cluttered markets. But a service mark conveys a considerably deeper and broader meaning than a product brand. By definition, a service cannot be stored or tasted; it can only be sampled by practical experience – by buying the service. Legal service is an abstract concept, but it is nonetheless a very important, often essential, service for clients.

When we refer to risk management, we are talking about reducing risk for both the law firm and its clients. Put yourself in the position of having to make a vital decision concerning a supplier. It is likely that you would base your decision predominantly on trust in renowned and proven brands. The more expensive, complex and weightier the decision, the greater the role that trademark dependability and trustworthiness would play. Clients are confronted with exactly the same difficult decisions when selecting a law firm.

1.1 What should my brand look like?

You may therefore ask yourself: "What should my brand look like?" The answer is to present yourself as you would like to be seen, highlighting your personal and professional qualities and abilities. Each individual is unique and performs each and every service distinctively. So it is all a matter of identifying your uniqueness. Many lawyers still endorse the idealised and naïve claim that excellent legal service is enough of a trademark and clients will come of their own accord. However, the client can choose from an enormous selection, at any time, anywhere and increasingly online.

According to an old rule of thumb, in the commodity industry, only companies or products that can invest more than €2.5 million annually in marketing on a national level can be considered to be trademarks in the true sense of the word. Under this definition, a legal firm can hardly be considered to be a trademark, although marketing measures and guidelines for smaller professional service providers follow the same basic rules that apply to global players. Not every firm can promote itself with a message like Allen & Overy's: "Our lawyers were ranked in Band 1 and 2 in 201 categories across all Legal 500 Directories, the highest of the global

---

2   Gaelic *sluagh-ghairm*, < *sluagh* host + *ghairm* cry, shout. A war-cry or battle cry; spec one of those formerly employed by Scottish Highlanders or Borderers, or by the native Irish, usually consisting of a personal surname or the name of a gathering-place.

3   James B Stewart, Death of a Partner, *New Yorker*, June 21 1993.

elite group of international law firms."[4] However, not every firm is globally active. The idea is to pinpoint the markets in which you are predominantly active and develop a marketing message, tailored precisely to your target audience.

1.2 Calculating brand value

What does branding cost? What is branding worth? Both of these are pivotal questions and cannot be answered easily. It is important to bear in mind that your brand not only has an impact on client procurement, but also affects investor relationships, potential mergers and acquisitions, and licensing/royalty rate setting, where applicable.

The advent of social media has changed the balance of opportunity and those who establish their unique attractions nimbly through social media may outpace those committed to traditional media.[5] A blog or a relevant Twitter feed may mark a lawyer or a law firm as knowledgeable and worth considering at minimal expense. But such a strategy needs focus, energy and commitment from the lawyers.

Since even large firms lack a broad empirical basis and it is exceptionally difficult to glean reliable market information from focus groups, the legal market depends on internal professional rankings. Examples include *Legal 500*, *Chambers & Partners*, *The Am Law 100* and *Juve* in Germany.[6] Clearly, firms are judged by their track record and measurement of such can differ for each firm, rendering comparison tables only superficially useful. This can result in highly volatile and potentially inconsistent market awareness (should you rely on it exclusively), since firms will not win the same awards every year; nor will they be consistently successful year after year. Therefore, in addition to the messages generated by awards, professional ranking tables and other measurements of success, other valid messages must be relayed, especially in less successful years. Relevant distinguishing characteristics might include awareness and knowledge of specific issues beyond professional topics, such as regional attributes, culture, habits and idiosyncrasies.

There are plenty of systems and methods for calculating brand value. One of the most effective is the Interbrand® model. Interbrand® is a globally active business and the most prominent international branding consultancy. It subdivides the relevant factors for brand success into internal and external factors. The internal factors are "Clarity, Commitment, Protection [and] Responsiveness"; the external factors are "Authenticity, Relevance, Differentiation, Consistency, Presence [and] Understanding".[7] Market segments are studied first and then financial data is analysed over a five-year period. Finally, the role that a brand has played in purchase decisions is determined. Tellingly, Interbrand's website does not mention a single law firm that has used its services.

---

4   See Allen & Overy at www.allenovery.com/publications/Pages/default.aspx.
5   These opportunities may be more easily exploited by individual lawyers or practice groups, than firms: see generally Simon Chester, "Thinking about social media in your law firm", *Law Practice*. 37.2 (2011): p 64; "How to create a law firm: social media policy", *Law Practice*. 38.1 (2012): p 50; "Social media networking for lawyers: how should law firms approach social media?" *Law Practice*. 38.1 (2012): p 26. Thomas Schwenke, *Social Media Marketing und Recht*, (Köln, 2014).
6   www.juve.de/handbuch and in English translation: www.juve.de/handbuch/en.
7   www.interbrand.com.

A different metric is applied by consulting firm Acritas when it measures the strength of law firm brands in the English-speaking common law jurisdictions. Surveys of brand recognition are notoriously unscientific and depend on asking a relatively small group of major clients when they think of law firms in a jurisdiction, as follows:

- What names come to mind?
- Which are most favoured?
- Which are considered for top-level M&A or bet-the-company litigation?
- Which are used most for high-level work?
- How far do the firm's values align with those of its clients?
- Is the firm known for technological savvy and innovation?

Whether this corresponds to the reality of brand recognition is an open question. The firms that dominate these surveys are closely correlated with size, largely due to the selection of respondents.

1.3 Case study: generating goodwill can reduce risk

Looking at the difference in public reaction to two similar incidents at companies Van der Falk and IKEA exemplifies how a strong image can reduce risk. Both companies were involved in construction accidents. While Van der Falk was probably considered in the public's mind to be an aggressive, rather unlikeable undertaking, IKEA was firmly established as inherently approachable and family oriented.

In February 2002, prolonged bad weather caused the roof of Van der Falk's Hotel Tiel to cave in. In August of the same year, the roof of the IKEA basement car park in Amsterdam also collapsed. Local authorities closed down the hotel in Tiel, launching a national investigation against Van der Falk. IKEA, however, apologised for the bad weather with irresistible charm and a week after the calamity, authorities allowed the branch establishment to reopen.[8]

2. How to develop a law firm brand

2.1 Make a bold statement

One of the most blatant dichotomies between the brand positioning of large companies and that of nearly all law firms is the reluctance of lawyers to provide any emotional content about their services in their marketing materials. This is surprising, considering that emotional capital is at the heart of the relationship between a private practice lawyer and his clients – namely, implied trust. The absence of this type of branding means that law firms are missing an opportunity to engage with clients. Price is not the only criterion for winning work; the impression that marketing material makes on a client is equally important.

Evidence can be found when taking a random sample of marketing material from the top 50 firms in Germany (2013) and comparing them with public presentations

---

8 Bronnen: Max Kohnstamm in Adformation, September 2002; Coebergh Communication & PR, PR advisors for IKEA in 2002.

or business reports from DAX companies. In many cases, for whatever reason, there is no statement whatsoever next to the firm's name. A rare exception is the range of services that Cleary Gottlieb puts forward on its title page:

> We are internationally active solicitors providing our clients with unmatched service transcending geographic regions and practice areas. Cleary Gottlieb seamlessly handles the largest and most innovative deals worldwide. Legal and financial publications across the board have only acclaim for Cleary Gottlieb's juristic excellence.

Why would you not want such an explicit statement on the front page of your publicity material?

These statements are more banal: "CMS Hasche Sigle, attorneys at law; tax consultants for successful growth", or "Noerr, excellence creating value" – but they at least convey a service commitment beyond merely "Solicitors XL – Your Solicitors!" The most ineffective cases are those firms whose graphic designers convinced them to completely forgo script on their title pages.

There appears to be a conflict of interest between a law firm's preference for informative brand messaging and a designer's preference for very clear, logical and minimalistic layouts over the largest surface possible. Lawyers wish to attract clients with words, their most powerful tool. Why, then, does language not appear on the cover of their brochures?

In this context, Shearman & Sterling's German office statement may appear rather dry, but it is also very informative:

> For two decades Shearman & Sterling has ranked among Germany's leading lawyers. Our German offices, in the finance and business centres of the country, provide our clients with comprehensive, flexible and practical consultation.

That is a pragmatic and clear statement that inspires confidence. Clear statements such as this greatly reduce the risk of misunderstanding.

Nonetheless, there is a deep rift dividing firms from their ideal clients. Large companies have known the value of market positioning for much longer than the legal profession has. Examples of strong corporate brand messages include:

- Henkel's "Excellence is our passion";
- the insinuation from Siemens that "Trust binds us";
- Bayer's "Science for a better life";
- Continental's "Values create value. Solidarity, a winning mentality, freedom and trust" (values that are easily transferred to a firm focused on service and value-oriented relationships with clients);
- German Telecom's "We believe in a future full of possibilities"; and
- Fresenius's "Being better than we have to is not only in our interest, it is the core of our corporate culture".

In the latter case, the client is included in the service provider's reflections, which provides an excellent launch pad for discussion with clients. "Not only in our interest" (in yours, too?) is a wonderful approach to a partnership.

2.2 **Simplicity is key**

Clarity and simplicity are essential when devising a brand message. Many are willing to pay a high price for an Apple iPhone because, in addition to its attractive features, it is primarily intuitive to use. Other mobile phones promise impressive performance and a multitude of applications, yet the iPhone outsells them all. The key is simplicity.

If a firm wants to convey its competence while keeping its brand messaging as simple as possible, it needs to try to encapsulate the essence of the firm succinctly. What counts is that a client can immediately recognise what your firm does, and that it does it well.

(a) **Font**

Clichés won't cut it. Lawyers are conservative by nature. Just as lawyers instinctively go for navy blue in dress and design, so they tend to pick the least attractive, most traditional fonts. Picking Times Roman will ensure that your brand looks just the same as everyone else's.

(b) **Colour**

The colour should be distinct. Since the bulk of law firms will choose navy blues, burgundy reds or bottle greens, firms which depart from those safe norms can get noticed. Two Canadian examples come to mind: a family law boutique appealing to a predominantly female clientele signals that message with a shocking and warm pink. A firm which prides itself on fixed fees, embedded lawyers and a non-orthodox approach to growth and governance signals that difference with a name that is a distinct abstract noun – Conduit – and a visual identity built on bright yellow.

(c) **Name**

Firms name themselves after their founding partners, which means something internally while the founders are alive, but scarcely anything externally. A few firms are now using descriptive nouns or made-up names, such as Conduit and Axiom. The alternate business structures promoted in England and Wales after the Legal Services Act 2007 are increasingly adopting names which speak to their markets about the nature of the firms and the services which they offer.

2.3 The importance of client trust

To assume that a client trusts you simply because you say "Trust me!" is rather naïve. Why should a client trust a solicitor more than a bazaar trader who swears, "Trust me! This carpet is worth €100,000"? Trust is a risky business. If you win a client's trust, you will have a powerful advantage over your competitors. For the client, trust means risk reduction. So despite or due to its arbitrary nature, trust can be seen as a solicitor's most valuable consultation asset.

2.4 Starting the branding process

Deciding on the firm's brand message will require consensus from the partners. This crucial group of stakeholders needs to decide on the firm's target clients, what they are prepared to invest to win new work and the risks they are willing to take to achieve these ends. They need to answer the questions: "What sets us apart from our competitors? What are our qualities, as well as our negative aspects?" These need to be followed up with: "How can we convey our uniqueness, according to Interbrand® factors, to our target groups?"

(a) *Identifying target groups*

Every branding process begins with defining your target clients. A suggested approach is to create a list of your largest current and previous clients according to categories such as public company, mid-sized company and sole proprietor. Assign each of these groups three specific objectives that are important to each, such as establishing market presence, avoiding litigation or increasing profitability. General objectives such as legal certainty, compliance and successful outcome are implied. Discuss as a group how you can satisfy these outlined client objectives. Once you have worked out your groups and their objectives, you are well on your way to defining your brand.

(b) *Brand ambassadors*

A firm's key asset is its lawyers. They must be brand ambassadors living up to the firm's brand pledge.

Ensure that the right lawyers are assigned to the target group objectives outlined above and that the lawyers and clients are optimally paired according to expertise, interest or background.

(c) *Unique selling proposition/positioning*

Now you are ready to address your unique selling proposition. What do you, and you alone, offer? Being the only employment law firm in a small city simply states the obvious; a corporate law firm in a large city has to delve deeper. Which target groups do you serve best? Which lawyers are best equipped for which potential clients? Brand positioning requires a clear vision of who you are and what you wish to achieve. After thorough and candid deliberation with all partners, generate a list of unique services offered by your firm. Do not be disappointed if the list is very short.

Setting out your quality proposition may appear to be a very simple thing: "We provide professional legal consultation in XXX law." That is not going to help you to secure clients from other firms. Any client looking for more than standard, bargain-priced legal services will expect you to scrupulously address its wishes. Refer back to your target groups as defined above and set out special qualities that set you apart from the competition. Effectively and strategically presented success stories are worth their weight in gold. They clearly and efficiently demonstrate your approach. A potential client will then understand your approach and make an informed decision against its needs. Here, the emotional aspect of trust and relationships comes into play. Only a lucid portrayal of how services have been rendered in the past can demonstrate how services will be rendered in the future, and an agreement on approach and methodology is a giant step towards risk reduction, for both you and your client.

You and your partners can best derive your unique characteristics from selected examples of previous work. This is not necessarily intended for publication, but is most suitable for your purpose. Recollect how you achieved these successes. Is there a discernible pattern? When you understand how you have done it, you can sell it.

(d) *Launching brand communications*
This might be the best time to bring in professional assistance – perhaps through consultation with a branding or public relations (PR) specialist to help you best represent your findings in a statement that proclaims your mission and vision. Discuss consultation results with your colleagues, taking them as a basis for changes in your firm. Mission defines the purpose of your firm and vision defines your business goals.

Alternatively, you may wish to engage a graphic designer or set up an in-house operation to generate, launch and maintain your brand communications. These include a website, brochures and press releases. Without the initial groundwork as described above, these media applications will be no more than a shot in the dark. This way, though, they will be the most effective way to reduce your business risks and the risk that clients expect something that you neither can nor want to provide.

3. The benefits of law firm branding

The concept of brand awareness within the legal industry is something with which we are familiar, but its common application is a relatively recent phenomenon. This is not to say that before the advent of PR and brand experts, a lawyer's reputation could not be damaged: it has always been the case that if a person holds himself out as offering a level of service on which he then fails to deliver, his reputation and market value are likely to suffer.

3.1 Responding to clients' needs

Ask a client the most important factor in selecting a law firm and reputation is likely to feature at the top of the list. There is nothing new about this, but what has changed over the years is the recognition that strong brands can have a significant influence on clients' buying decisions. The power of branding has grown steadily in the public consciousness. Living in a world driven by consumer demand, we have grown attuned to the notion of brand names and we relate to brand messages.

In today's strained economic climate, there is increased pressure on companies to drive down their legal spend and ensure even greater value for money from their lawyers. The legal market is crowded, panels continue to be reduced and clients are being very selective when considering their options. As a result, lawyers must expect close scrutiny of their service offering, negotiation over terms of engagement, resourcing demands, specific risk management procedures required to be in place and a general expectation of more for less. In addition, underpinning all of these requirements is the presumption of technical excellence at a fair price. If a law firm cannot meet these requirements in this competitive market, the client will simply take its business elsewhere.

3.2 The power of differentiation

Savvy, forward-thinking lawyers know that differentiating themselves through branding will help them to grow their client base, achieve competitive positioning and increase their market dominance. Pursuing a clear brand strategy, focusing on what is important to the client, will set a firm apart and help it to win and retain business.

The positive effects of a strong brand can have innumerable benefits for a law firm and its stakeholders. These can include work referrals, repeat business, positive client feedback and goodwill, high-calibre trainee solicitors and lateral hire candidates, and an impressive record in new business tenders.

A strong brand can be the foundation for internal and external marketing and can assist with a firm's growth strategy, increasing the likelihood of successful mergers and acquisitions and recruitment of lateral hires. It can be the bedrock of the firm's culture and values, and can set the tone for the firm's corporate social responsibility activities. It can be central to tender submissions in competitive situations and can assist with client presentations, industry fairs and conferences.

3.3 What's in a brand?

Although law firm branding might seem typically associated with logos, colour schemes, website design and straplines, it is much more multifaceted than that. It can be a comprehensive strategy comprising many elements, including the firm's profile, culture, behaviour and reputation. It incorporates everything that the organisation is saying about itself and how it is representing itself to the public.

Some firms might find they have a brand that has evolved over time without them even realising it. This might have resulted from years of doing a certain type of work, resulting in the firm becoming known as a specialist in that particular field. This type of reputation might have certain drawbacks, such as the firm being sidelined when attempting to make inroads into other types of work. Trying to change the impact of the current brand and alter the public perception of the firm will probably require a targeted rebranding exercise. This will take time. Creating a brand is not a quick process; it is a long-term investment which might take years to reap dividends.

Individual lawyers also have personal brands within their law firms that can affect the reputation of the entire firm. Law is a people-orientated business and a firm's reputation relies on the reputation of its lawyers. In the case of some smaller specialist firms, the entire firm's brand might be centred on an individual lawyer's profile and market presence. This can create problems when this individual leaves the firm.

Knowing your target market and how you want to be perceived by existing and future clients, employees and your competition will inform the messages that you need to convey when defining your firm's brand. As a result, the views and expectations of clients and prospects are vital and need to be kept under regular review. It is also important to think about the type of lawyers you wish to attract to join the firm and be the partners of tomorrow. A firm with an impressive reputation will be invited to compete for the most lucrative and high-profile work, attract the most impressive lawyers and retain key individuals. Key benefits of branding can therefore include client attraction, fee-earning capability, firm growth and sustainability.

A law firm's brand strategy might be based around enhanced client service capability, extensive international presence, sector knowledge, innovative pricing structure or approach to billing. With the advent of alternative business structures in certain jurisdictions, it might also be an increased service offering beyond the provision of legal services. Whatever is at the heart of the firm's brand strategy, it is critical that it resonate with the firm's client base and deliver on their expectations.

(a) **The risks facing law brands**
The high-profile law firms that crashed and burned over the last few years failed for a variety of different reasons. Every failed firm is subject to the *Anna Karenina* principle[9] – unhappy or failing for its own unique reasons. Some had generous compensation systems that would prove unsustainable if growth faltered for a second. Others faced defections of key practice groups – loyalty seems a dwindling virtue. Still others foundered on mergers which failed to gel – where loyalties endured to prior firms and the new firm never coalesced behind a shared vision or strategy. Some could not survive allegations of fraud, mismanagement or malpractice; their brand was irretrievably affected. Despite the noble history and significant achievements of Coudert Frères in France or Heenan Blaikie LLP in Canada, the circumstances under which they shuttered their respective businesses will mark their reputations in the future. And in the age of Google and Wikipedia, bad news is perpetual.

Comparatively few firms are sunk by negligence or malpractice liability. Of course, if the claim falls outside insurance coverage (eg, fraud), firms without limited liability can fall like houses of cards. More firms fail because they cannot mobilise collectively to respond to new challenges. Their leaders run out of steam. And their brands cannot save them.

How firms respond to crisis shows how robust their culture and commitment is. Firms that have grown quickly can collapse just as quickly. Structure may also be relevant. Firms which are the products of numerous mergers seem more fragile. A crisis in one foreign office can spread reputational contagion to other offices. That is why due diligence is so critical – not just whether the leaders are socially compatible, but whether the client base, the individual recruits, the entire cultures can match harmoniously.

One North American example demonstrates the point. A major regional firm decided to merge with a New York City firm it had frequently worked with. At a party to celebrate the merger, however, a serious scandal emerged: the senior name partner of the NYC firm – fuelled by alcohol, arrogance and assumed *droit du seigneur* (right of the lord) – attempted to engage in sexual misconduct with several female associates. All the potential good publicity was at risk of evaporating in a media frenzy. But the firm responded smartly. They started the response in the middle of the disastrous party – they acknowledged the problem, set in motion an objective review, renamed the firm (dropping from the letterhead the name of the offending

---

9   Jared Diamond, *Guns, Germs and Steel* (New York, 1999) p 157, Arm und Reich, *Die Schicksale menschlicher Gesellschaften* (Frankfurt, 2002).

lawyer) and stated publicly their commitment to equality and respect. Yes, they shredded a lot of paper, but they focused on the protection of the brand – which in the long run has only become stronger.

It is not just scandal or malpractice that firms need to worry about. Law firms are the most vulnerable enterprises to industrial espionage. You should have worked out in advance how to deal with damage resulting from IT security breaches and loss of confidential data. Computer use policies should also deal with social media issues and spell out the limits of personal use.

3.4 The threat of the big brands

The *Legal Services Act 2007*, which allows non-lawyers to own and invest in law firms, has changed the shape of the provision of legal services in England and Wales. Well-known brands such as the Co-operative Group, PwC and BT have entered the legal market within alternative business structures and, although there has been slow take-up since they were permitted on October 6 2011,[10] more big brands have expressed their intention to follow. Regardless of the market share that these new entrants will take from traditional law firms, the entrance of the big brands into an arena which was previously the preserve of private practice law firms will no doubt raise the profile of brand awareness as an important consideration within the legal industry.

With other international jurisdictions also moving slowly towards permitting alternative business structures, the presence of global brands in the legal market is only likely to increase in significance over the coming years, bringing a new perspective to brand globalisation within the legal services industry.

One of the most interesting experiments in recent years came in England and Wales with the opening of formerly closed markets for legal services to so-called alternative business structures, permitting external investment in law firms, and innovative business structures designed to meet the needs of underserved markets. These new firms seldom call themselves by the surnames of their managers or owners. Instead, they adopt names that are more like corporate brands that communicate their focus and their difference to potential customers for their services. An interesting example is a franchise firm called Quality Solicitors which engaged Saatchi Masius – the advertising gurus Saatchi & Saatchi – to develop a multimillion pound-campaign.[11] In a franchise, ensuring common quality standards is vital. The campaign raises expectations of such consistent quality. There were 2 million views, a significant number of potential inquiries and a flurry of interest from firms that wanted to be part of the franchise. The jury is still out on whether Quality Solicitors or any of the other new business structures will succeed in creating a meaningful and permanent brand. One English commentator, John Hyde, poured cold water on the very notion: "Law firms are a necessary evil to most clients, not a cuddly brand name to wear on a T-shirt. No amount of soft-focus advertising is going to change that any time soon."[12]

---

10   The Solicitors Regulation Authority (SRA) did not start accepting applications until January 2012.
11   www.youtube.com/watch?v=-SDE9GCJlVg.
12   www.lawgazette.co.uk/analysis/comment-and-opinion/slater-and-gordon-cant-be-a-household-name-its-a-law-firm/5037818.article.

A firm's corporate culture is reflected in everything it does – from the charities and community activities it supports to the art on its walls, its treatment of support staff and its attitude towards innovation and technology. This should inform the human resources function, especially the firm's approach to recruitment, as well as to potential mergers and acquisitions. Remember that younger lawyers will interpret a firm's hidebound traditional pamphlets and websites as stodgy and traditional. Involve younger lawyers in branding decisions – in particular, have them intimately involved in any social media strategy.

3.5 Global considerations

With clients becoming more international in their outlook, firms need to respond through their branding. Building a global brand is a significant challenge, requiring a focus on clients, quality control, trust, integrity, management and stakeholder buy-in.

In order to maximise the benefits of a firm's brand value on a global scale, it is important for firms to ensure that their brand translates well across different countries in which they and their clients have an interest or presence. However, care should be taken to ensure that messages that are acceptable in one country will not be interpreted as inappropriate, insulting or simply unintelligible in another.

A consistent message is important, although achieving uniform brand awareness across a firm's entire international office network will be almost impossible. In the Acritas Sharplegal *2013 Global Elite Brand Index*, some broad jurisdictional differences are highlighted, which brings the difficulty of consistency into stark relief. In the United States, responsiveness is considered to be a highly valued quality in a law firm; in the United Kingdom, clients are drawn more to the demonstration of a thorough understanding of their business; and in China, professionalism is the quality that is rated most highly.

A special problem faces international alliances of law firms sheltering under a common brand umbrella. Can the alliance provide seamless and high-quality service in more than one country? Can international clients expect the same service in all countries when they do business with law firms that use the same name or are members of an international network of otherwise independent law firms? For such alliances, common processes, training initiatives and service standards need to be continually strengthened. Clients need to have complete confidence that an alliance member in another jurisdiction will treat them with the same level of service as their local firm.

From a risk management perspective, mistakes or negligence on the part of an alliance member can have serious local consequences. Even if private international law principles or carefully constructed retainer letters insulate the local firm from legal liability for the faults of a foreign colleague, the reputational harm is less easy to deflect. Client disappointment will inevitably spill over.

That's why careful planning and due diligence are necessary before taking on new alliance members and sheltering them under the brand. Much can be learned from the major international accounting firms and how they integrate new national offices, and ensure the implementation of service standards. Accounting firms routinely share best practices and work product so that specialised expertise can be readily identified and cross-border working teams constructed.

3.6 Successful brand penetration

Firms' reputations are constantly susceptible to change; but in the United Kingdom and the United States, the largest, global law firms dominate the best law firm brand reports, compiled by companies such as Acritas and Eulogy. According to research carried out by these companies, the UK 'magic circle' firms and New York 'white shoe' firms appear to have an established position in terms of brand identity. These firms are likely to have well-resourced internal marketing teams, ensuring positive press coverage and social media activity. They also have extensive international reach, high-quality expertise and strong, established client relationships. This combination of factors makes these firms identifiable brands with unassailable brand image penetration that reaches considerably beyond the legal industry.

One firm to have taken a serious approach to branding is Irwin Mitchell – the largest UK law firm to have become an alternative business structure. Over the last few years the firm has invested heavily in a comprehensive and integrated approach to profile raising through all forms of media channels, including television advertising. This multifaceted brand strategy represents a new approach for law firms and recognises the fact that clients interact through a number of different platforms. The firm website says that it has a clear vision "to be the brand of choice". The firm will have its own means of measuring the success of its media strategy, but it has seen a sustained increase in profitability since raising its profile in this way.

3.7 Stakeholder benefits

Brand-aware firms know that all their stakeholders will reap a number of benefits from a strong brand image. It is therefore vital that everyone in the firm has a clear understanding of what the firm stands for, based on its history, culture or values. Feeling pride in one's sense of corporate identity will help to ensure commitment, teamwork and effort. All of these factors have a positive impact on a firm's reputation.

A firm's brand and its reputation are of utmost importance for firms or companies considering an involvement with a firm, whether as a provider of an outsourced service or a potential affiliate or associated firm. A firm seeking a merger partner or alliance should find it easier to find a willing party if perceived prestige value will derive from the association.

The contrary is also true. Why would you want to be connected to a firm with a brand message that is at odds with your own service offering or a firm with a dubious reputation? There are significant risks in being associated with a damaged brand. Factors such as the loss of a key client, a high-profile professional negligence claim, poor client care, a significant partner resignation or a number of departures across the firm can create a damaging momentum in public perception that is hard to control and even harder to reverse. The concepts of branding and reputation are inextricably linked with quality.

3.8 Branding opportunities

Mergers often present excellent opportunities for rebranding. Firms can significantly increase their brand presence through a high-profile merger. The Norton Rose Fulbright merger in 2013 represented the coming together of a large global UK firm, Norton Rose, and a Houston-based US firm, Fulbright & Jaworski. Norton Rose had merged with two Canadian firms in the years leading up to the US firm merger. The US merger had the effect of cementing the cross-border work between the Canadian and US parts of the business, which has now given the firm the benefit of significantly increasing its brand profile in Canada.

A change in business focus or the development of a new area of expertise, perhaps spearheaded by a new key partner recruit or team acquisition, can also present a good opportunity for a fresh brand strategy in conjunction with the firm's growth. The other side to this is the devastating effect that can be wrought on a firm losing a team that is pivotal to its success, and the external messages associated with such losses will need to be managed carefully.

A firm with no brand or with confused messages around its brand can be vulnerable to client loss, although such damage is unlikely to be immediate. Brand is important to clients. They will frequently base their purchasing decisions around their perception of a firm's brand. For a firm not to focus on this aspect of its business is to leave it exposed to potential client loss through poor perception and poaching from the competition, which might be on upward trajectories with their own brand strategies. This erosion of business will eventually take its toll on the firm's reputation in a tangible way and lead to eventual loss of market position.

With a link between a firm's reputation and client attrition, it may be possible to attach a financial value to brand and reputational damage, although the attribution will be inherently imprecise.

3.9 Using PR

Every organisation has the potential to increase its brand value. Spending money on good PR can help when building a brand. A significant increase in brand awareness can be achieved on the back of panel appointments, high-profile deals or litigation wins. It is worth remembering that a firm's reputation is not necessarily based on actual experience, but can be based on people's perception. PR can influence this and may also provide some benefit in offsetting brand damage. We look at this later in the chapter.

4. Exposures and risks to law firm brands

Every aspect of a law firm's business and every individual working in the firm can influence its brand and reputation. Both are relatively intangible concepts, based on perception, credibility and respect. They are difficult to define, measure and protect; yet they can be regarded as a firm's most prized assets, vulnerable to significant damage.

4.1 Brand stakeholders

Stakeholders in the firm's brand are extensive and include the management board, partners, employees, clients, outsourced legal and business service providers, associated or best friend firms, the regulator, the firm's bank, its accountant and auditor. Other parties also have an interest in the firm's brand, such as the firm's competitors, legal journalists, the public and the media.

4.2 The lawyer-client relationship

The most significant risks to a law firm's brand are those arising from the lawyer-client relationship. Consequently, the reason for the demise of many law firms is the erosion of their client base. At the heart of this relationship is a fundamental implicit trust. For the client, the lawyer is a trusted adviser, relied upon to resolve the client's problems at a fair price for the work. Underlying this level of trust is the quality of the firm's reputation. In the case of the lawyer, there is trust that the client will be open and honest and meet the fees upon conclusion of the matter.

There is a broad spectrum on which this level of trust and integrity can be damaged. It might start with a concern that, if unresolved, could develop into a breakdown and severing of the relationship. Damage at this irreparable end of the scale is likely to be something tangible and significant, such as a serious error in the handling of a piece of work, a major lapse in client care or a damaging regulatory breach. When trust in the relationship has broken down to this degree, it is hard to repair – even when there was previous inherent goodwill. A danger is that the breakdown of one client relationship might lead to another and result in a large-scale series of client departures. A strong brand might be unable to save a firm experiencing this kind of momentum; but it can certainly help it to withstand reputational damage.

4.3 Other stakeholders

A number of perspectives need to be taken into account: primarily the firm's stakeholders (not merely the partners as owners of the business, but also the employees and the clients). Ensure that everyone in the firm understands the firm's brand, what the firm stands for and the firm's approach to risk management: the most prudent strategy is to encourage all firm members to tell the risk partner if anything untoward is happening.

Next, be aware of the regulator's concerns (a firm's branding might conflict with regulatory objectives). The rise of law firm marketing and social media has led most regulators to be more comfortable than they once would have been with innovative branding. We say 'most' because some US states have restrictive rules that require careful attention: take care in Florida and Texas. In other jurisdictions, claims to special expertise or aggressive assertions of comparative merits ("We are better/cheaper/more successful than competitors A, B or C") will often be found to be misleading to the clients and the general public. This is especially important for law firms whose cross-border reach may lead to them being considered to be practising local law. A website which in one country would be quite unremarkable might constitute gauche and potentially unprofessional self-promotion in another.

Of course, clients are supreme. How lawyers respond to client demands can affect their credibility and reputation. Bad experiences do get talked about by in-house counsel. Over-promising and under-performing can be fatal. Consistency of commitment and performance across the firm is key.

4.4 General risks and exposures

Damage to a firm's brand and reputation can manifest itself in many ways. It might be caused by reduced levels of public confidence in the firm itself, structural instability after the departure of a key partner or concern for the firm's financial viability, possibly as a result of a damaging professional negligence claim or large client loss. These difficulties may develop to the extent that they result in the break-up or dissolution of the firm, or alternatively in insolvency, indebtedness, intervention by the regulator, damaging allegations or claims made by employees, partners or third parties. Any one or a combination of these factors can threaten the firm's brand and lead to the sad demise of what was previously a viable, well-known law firm.

Some negative aspects of a law firm's business are more likely to result in press coverage, such as loss of key partners, a high-value professional negligence claim or a serious employment-related allegation. Public airing of a bribery and corruption allegation, international sanctions breach, money laundering breach or an adverse finding or penalty imposed by a regulator can also all represent risks to a law firm's brand and reputation.

Recently, numerous high-profile whistleblowing cases have progressed through the courts, receiving extensive press coverage. Whether proven or not, the press coverage itself in these circumstances is unwelcome to any organisation.

These potential exposures are set against the sophistication and complexity of modern-day business, which increases the scope for damage to a firm's brand and reputation through a compliance breach.

We have witnessed a decline in the strength of law firm brands. Jordan Furlong is a Canadian commentator and consultant. He noted that a firm's brand "is shorthand for a repository of client trust. Its brand is essentially its marketplace ID, its industry access pass, its credit line of credibility. Lose that, and it loses everything".[13] Some of the most spectacular failures in recent years – Heller Ehrman, Goodman and Carr, Brobeck and Heenan Blaikie – are noteworthy. These firms were not incompetent or evil. Rivals expressed sadness at their demise and staff were disconsolate. What was notable was how quickly each firm collapsed, without evident warning signs. And once the process started, confidence and trust evaporated overnight. As analyst Jordan Furlong commented: "The marketplace suddenly stopped believing in them." Your brand is vital to survival.

4.5 Group contagion

The regulator of legal services in England and Wales, the Solicitors Regulation Authority (SRA), recently identified group contagion as a new potential area of risk for

---

13 Jordan Furlong, The Future of Law Firm Branding at www.law21.ca/2008/10/the-future-of-law-firm-branding.
14 Under the Swiss Civil Code, the *verein* structure lets lawyers create a legal person for the global partnership or association without transferring legal responsibility to that new entity. This means that individual members can be sued directly without liability attaching to the other members of the group. The structure is used by international law firms such as Baker & McKenzie and a few global accounting firms, such as KPMG and Deloitte. See Drew Hasselback at http://business.financialpost.com/2010/11/16/more-on-the-swiss-verein-system/. See also Megan E Vetula "From the big four to big law: the Swiss *verein* and the global law firm", *Georgetown Journal of Legal Ethics*, 22.3 (Summer 2009) p 1177-1192; Chris Johnson "The hustlers: law firm mergers and the rise of vereins create new players in the Global 100; more change is on the way", *American Lawyer*, 34.9 (Oct 2012) p 151-153.

law firms. It arises mainly as a result of the new and varied approach to firm structure that has been embraced by the United Kingdom with the introduction of alternative business structures and the increased popularity of the Swiss *Verein* model.[14]

Group contagion is particularly relevant to large, corporate-style structures comprising several firms and entities within a single group. However, the SRA recognises that it is a risk that any firm could face if a group structure exists. 'Direct contagion' is described by the SRA as financial harm that spreads through the structure from one limb to another – for example, financial crime within one part the group or business interruption within the group. 'Indirect contagion' is seen as the reputational impact on another subsidiary within the structure – for example, as a result of an ethical breach in part of the group. Indirect contagion is thought to have a slower impact than direct contagion, but it carries with it a far greater threat of harm to the public image.

The risk of group contagion can be observed when looking at the recent fortunes of the most high-profile alternative business structure in England and Wales. The Co-operative Group started to offer legal services under the banner of Co-operative Legal Services in March 2012. Unfortunately, its progress has been clouded by the crisis that has beleaguered the group's banking arm, which has resulted in well-publicised losses and component parts of the business being sold off. The legal services arm continues and at the time of writing is about to consolidate and restructure, despite its director of policy having left the company. It has given public assurances about structural contagion and continues to work hard on its brand image to counter any potential damage to its brand.

4.6 Risks associated with technology

One of the most critical risks when considering brand and reputation in today's climate is the advance of technology, which provides for the instantaneous relay of information and news on a global scale. Events are likely to come to the public's attention from wherever in the world they occur, rapidly and extensively, with potentially devastating impact. Social media exacerbates the prompt, widespread delivery of news and comment. As a consequence of modern technology and communication systems, a negative social media publication has the capacity to 'go viral' faster and more widely than ever before.

The increasing take-up of easily accessible platforms such as Twitter, online forums, blogging, media sharing such as YouTube and other forms of commonplace social media represents a significant area of exposure for law firms. Anyone can have their say, post their own content and share it instantaneously with the world. In the hands of those wanting to do damage to a firm's brand, these are powerful tools and the potential for damage is extensive. An ill-advised Tweet or Facebook entry by a law firm employee, whether malicious or entirely innocent, can result in damaged credibility to the firm and individuals.

Technology carries with it a multitude of risks for a law firm brand, from cyber-attacks and data loss to identity theft. In tackling these exposures, lawyers must apprise themselves of the extent of the risks facing their business, assess the strengths and weaknesses of their IT systems, understand the extent of the data they hold and know what is required of them according to relevant data protection legislation. A proportionate, risk-based approach needs to be adopted to maintain data security. An effective response will comprise resilient networks and communications systems, regular stress testing and protection of critical infrastructure. Vulnerability in a firm's cyber-security plan can destroy client trust, threaten the ongoing working relationship and result in serious damage to the firm's brand. Even with the most comprehensive approach to IT security, a mislaid laptop, disk, USB stick, handheld device or hard-copy papers can cause untold damage and be hugely embarrassing for the firm.

5. **Controlling and protecting a law firm's brand and reputation**

A law firm's risk management processes and procedures usually enable early identification, escalation and control of an issue. However, how can a firm plan for brand and reputation damage with any degree of accuracy given the relatively intangible nature of both, the difficulty of measurement according to usual risk frameworks and matrices and their potentially extensive impact?

When preparing a brand and reputation damage response strategy, a useful starting point is to arrange a meeting of relevant firm stakeholders to talk through what this type of damage might look like. Firms should be encouraged to think the unthinkable in order to prepare for all possible eventualities and put relevant contingency plans in place to address likely disruption to the business. Since reputational damage can arise from any aspect of the business, there is merit in initially involving representatives from all areas of the firm.

To ensure that the risks to the firm's reputation and brand are considered thoroughly, an appraisal can be undertaken against the firm's operational, financial and compliance risks using a risk register. Reputation and brand impact should form part of the strategic risk analysis conducted by the firm, in order to ensure that both are factored into the firm's overall business strategy and planning processes. If the firm adopts an enterprise risk management framework, this should encompass reputation and brand issues.

A foundation for protection of the firm's brand can be found in:
- a comprehensive approach to risk management;
- a strong risk manager and highly visible risk team;
- a broad suite of firm policies (kept up to date and reviewed regularly);
- a business continuity plan; and
- effective processes and procedures, especially for reporting breaches, complaints or concerns.

This would ideally be set against an environment of strong financial management, heavy investment in information technology, clear firm structure and effective governance, all of which play a role in controlling the firm's brand and reputation.

5.1 **The role of the risk manager**

The risk manager's role is pivotal in protecting and improving the business. It is a gatekeeper role at the forefront of the firm's ethical and risk-aware culture. In protecting the firm's core values, the risk manager enhances the firm's reputation and protects the brand. Involving the risk manager in all strategic initiatives under consideration by the board will ensure that all business planning projects are assessed according to risk management principles and provide another important layer of control and protection for the firm.

The risk manager or general counsel will be able to assist in using structural controls where these are appropriate to protect a firm from brand damage in a group contagion situation. Firewalls are a common control for direct contagion – for example, separate management boards or structures with limits on common membership, or policies to prevent financial and critical business information leakage across the group.

5.2 Internal risk and compliance policies

Internal risk and compliance policies should be integrated throughout the firm and adopted universally; they cannot exist in a vacuum with only limited use by pockets of the firm. They need to be communicated through a comprehensive approach to messaging and training, all as part of a process to embed a risk-aware culture across the firm.

Bear in mind that reputational issues might result in a regulatory investigation, so up-to-date policies and well-communicated processes will add another level of protection and control to a law firm's defences.

5.3 Effective firm-wide communication

Good communication within a firm is vital. Clearly, the greater the number of offices, particularly across different jurisdictions, the more attention needs to be paid to communication across the firm. There is also the issue of integration of different jurisdictional requirements, which serves to complicate the risk management function, resulting in added exposures to a law firm brand and necessitating increased protections. Areas of particular vulnerability can include the different approaches taken to bribery and corruption internationally. This aspect of risk management could cause particular embarrassment to a firm and have a damaging effect on its reputation.

5.4 Establishing a risk-aware culture

A risk-aware culture is important in preserving the firm's brand and reputation, ideally by providing a supportive environment. This might be through a mentoring, buddy or coaching scheme, an open-door approach to partner access or a no-blame approach to mistakes. Those firms which try to embed a risk-aware culture across the firm in a holistic way, based on enterprise risk management principles, position themselves most effectively to protect the firm's reputation and brand.

Everybody in the firm is a guardian of the firm's reputation and all employees need to understand the implications of this. Creating reputation awareness across the firm starts with a sense of corporate identity and a positive atmosphere around the firm's brand. This can be enormously helpful in generating a sense of pride in working at the firm and encouraging a sense of responsibility across the practice.

Management and senior level buy-in is critical to developing a risk-aware culture across the entire firm and establishing behaviours expected of others. This includes a diligent approach to regulatory compliance, which is an area prone to attempted circumvention.

Senior management can encapsulate the firm's values in some clear messages, which the partners should follow in an effort to set the tone at the top of the organisation. Some firms use brand champions to raise the profile of the firm's brand internally and externally.

A firm that makes an effort to capture its brand values and use them as a means to set the standards expected of its lawyers, possibly through a code of conduct, will reap dividends in terms of protecting and controlling the firm's brand and reputation.

Establishing good corporate behaviour at an early stage is important. The firm should ensure its brand values and expected behaviour are communicated clearly at the time of taking on new recruits as well as during the training programme for junior lawyers. Reinforcing brand messages at partners' meetings, practice group gatherings and annual retreats will provide further protection to the brand.

5.5 The value of training

Compliance training software packages tend to be purchased by law firms to ensure a comprehensive approach and ease of monitoring. This works well, but there is no substitute for face-to-face training where possible, especially with new starters, in order to convey the firm's cultural approach to risk management.

Quality control is critical within a professional services organisation concerned with preserving its reputation. High standards of best practice, up-to-date knowledge, comprehensive training and effective supervision will all support the overall quality of the firm's legal advice. Validation of approach can be sought using internal file reviews and/or external audits.

5.6 The role of the human resources department

Ensuring that the firm is using an up-to-date employment contract with new recruits, and that the staff handbook is current and accessible, is a good starting point in protecting the firm from claims by employees. Having a highly visible and supportive human resources department respond quickly to an internal complaint might contain an issue before it gets out of hand.

5.7 Managing client relationships

A prime exposure to the firm's reputation and brand image can arise from client complaints and claims. Ensuring the highest levels of client service, accurately scoping out the terms of engagement, adhering to agreed billing targets, submitting regular bills and providing frequent client updates will all assist in avoiding the most common types of client complaint and causes of professional negligence claims.

Investment in client relationships ought to be at the heart of the firm's business strategy. It is not just the firm's relationship partners who need to have a vested interest in good client relations. It is the responsibility of everyone in the firm to nurture client relationships and be alert to any possible dissatisfaction. The firm should have a formal procedure in place for reporting possible client complaints to relevant stakeholders as quickly as possible and a strategy for dealing with a developing issue before it becomes irretrievable.

Clients' needs will change over time. Monitoring client expectations and satisfaction levels through a process of feedback and evaluation will put firms in the best position to ascertain how the firm is perceived and identify a developing situation which might be capable of being contained. Complaints need not be regarded negatively; nor should they be ignored. Treat them instead as an important opportunity to be seen as responsive and accountable. A good strategy is to provide an immediate acknowledgement, offer to investigate and provide a constructive solution where possible. A commercial response might result in lost fees, but it might also preserve the relationship with the client and the firm's reputation.

As the client's trusted adviser, a law firm will be expected to protect the client's brand too. Firms which remain committed to making the lives of their clients easier and helping them to become more successful stand a better chance of retaining that client in today's competitive environment.

5.8 Data protection

Data protection is a critical part of a lawyer's business and a prime concern for clients. A number of controls, in the form of systems, processes and training, can be put in place to meet the increasing data protection requirements facing businesses nowadays.

A law firm should have a data protection policy in place that encapsulates the firm's procedures in handling firm and client data, in both electronic and paper form. A policy of ensuring that hard-copy data is not taken out of the office will assist with the latter. In the case of electronic data, steps can be taken to ensure the encryption and lockdown of lost or stolen devices.

If a firm's loss of documents or unencrypted data were aired in court, or reported by the press, this would cause considerable embarrassment for the firm and could have a damaging effect on its brand. The same would also be true of emails being sent to the wrong party or the public airing of compromising emails which were never meant to be seen by anyone except the intended recipient. It is a helpful reminder for every lawyer never to put into email anything that he would not be comfortable being read out in court.

5.9 Social media

No firm can afford to ignore the growth in importance of social media. The speed of dissemination and widespread impact of social media have the potential to seriously damage the reputation of a company built up over many years. Potentially negative confidential information can be leaked or a negative comment made through a social media outlet accidentally, deliberately or maliciously. Firms need to prepare in advance a response mechanism for all of these eventualities. Marketing departments can monitor social networking sites and blogs for mention of the firm and its lawyers, whether favourable or not, to provide advance warning of negative situations.

Firms can control their employees' use of social media in the office to a certain extent. They can restrict the internal use of social media outlets with blocks on employee access, as well as having a strongly worded policy and monitoring procedures to check appropriate usage. Additionally, the risk team can educate employees on the risks associated with the use of social media, damaging or embarrassing postings and potentially actionable content.

There is a growing school of thought that firms are putting themselves at a disadvantage by missing out on the opportunity to reach out to clients using social media. Firms can control their social media messaging if they choose to interact with their clients in this way. If so, this can help build their brand by adopting a distinctive style and approach.

What is more difficult for firms to control is the effect of a damaging Tweet, blog or forum posting, or a second or third-hand negative comment, which has become embellished in the re-telling. Planning a purposeful response before a crisis develops will mitigate the need for a potentially flawed knee-jerk reaction.

5.10 Reliance on goodwill

There will be times when the goodwill in a firm's brand can be useful to protect it against claims, allegations and negative comment in the public domain that on their face might appear dishonourable or dubious. A client complaint, allegation of professional negligence or claim by a disgruntled ex-employee may have great potential to damage a firm's reputation. If the firm has a strong, positive brand and an untarnished reputation, any such allegation is less likely to cause lasting damage to the practice. Obviously, the reverse is also true, and frequent publicly aired complaints will eventually start eroding the esteem in which a firm is held.

6. Managing brand and reputation damage

We have already examined the processes of risk planning, protection and control; but what steps can a firm take when its reputation and brand are under threat? Certainly, a proactive strategy will be far more effective in protecting the firm's reputation than a reliance on reactive crisis management.

When a problem arises, a firm will need to carry out a quick appraisal of the situation, assess the threats (risks) against the opportunities to the business, consider all available options and, for those risks anticipated, deploy an appropriate pre-planned strategy. In the case of unforeseen reputational damage, the firm might want to consider whether a public acknowledgement is appropriate in the circumstances.

Damage limitation and containment will be at the heart of a strategy for handling an issue. A firm's brand, reputation and profitability are at risk if the firm is unable to respond swiftly and decisively.

Depending on the type of damage to the firm's brand (eg, a damaging piece of journalism), specialist media lawyer input might be required to advise on protecting the firm's reputation using available legal rights. These might include an allegation of libel, malicious falsehood or negligent misstatement. Recourse might also be

---

15   The PCC is an independent self-regulatory body that deals with complaints about the editorial content of newspapers, magazines and their websites. It is currently in a stage of transition to a new, self-regulatory body – the Independent Press Standards Organisation (IPSO).
16   Ofcom is the communications regulator regulating the television and radio sectors.

available in the United Kingdom from the Press Complaints Commission (PCC)[15] or Ofcom.[16] Both regulators publish codes of practice that might be helpful.

The Ofcom Rules require broadcasters to alert people to their intention to publish potentially damaging articles about them and the PCC encourages newspapers to do the same. A challenge can therefore be brought in advance of the broadcast or publication if there is considered to be merit in taking this step.

Corrections or an apology may be possible in the case of published articles or broadcasts, although a firm might take the view that the damage to brand and reputation has already been done by the time any steps are taken via these routes.

To win a libel action, a claimant needs to prove that the words were defamatory, although the bar has been raised with the introduction in England and Wales of the Defamation Act 2013, which came into force on January 1 2014. The act has introduced a 'serious harm' requirement in Section 1 for claimants wanting to bring a claim for defamation. This section provides that a statement is not defamatory unless its publication has caused, or is likely to cause, serious harm to the reputation of the claimant. In the case of reputation to a company, the act makes it clear that there will be serious harm only if the harm to the reputation of the entity has caused, or is likely to cause, serious financial loss.

Negative news often appears to be much more pervasive in terms of impact and distribution than positive news. For that reason, a swift, purposeful response is often the best course of action to curtail a potentially damaging piece of journalism or social media commentary. An emphatic denial of an allegation might be considered the best approach or the establishment of a clear position on an issue.

Responding publicly can also represent an opportunity to reinforce the firm's brand message. A prompt, bullish retort can convey clear messages about the firm's culture and approach. It might be helpful to seek the advice of a PR company to assist in finding the right tone.

Online reputation management companies operate nowadays to assist organisations in protecting their brand online. They do this by offering to repair and manage a firm's reputation through web search results, ensuring that positive messages about the firm rank higher than negative stories when using search engines.

7. Conclusion

In this period of continued change within the legal sector, increased globalisation, further advances in technology and greater use of social media, it is more important than ever for law firms to be clear about their service offering and to communicate this effectively in order to differentiate themselves from their competition. At the same time, it is essential for firms to be aware of the risks associated with their brand and have a strategy in place to protect their reputation, however it might be damaged.

It is clear that no single solution can be relied upon to protect a firm's brand and reputation, and it is unrealistic to expect an organisation to eliminate all risks to its business. This is simply impossible. However, if a firm adopts a comprehensive approach to risk management that enables it to look after its clients and at the same time protect the business, it will thrive where others fail.

8. **Ten pointers to build a brand**
    - Create consensus among partners.
    - Define the firm's target clients: your differentiation, your uniqueness should matter to the market.
    - Address the firm's unique selling position, including:
        - unique services that the firm offers; and
        - special qualities that set the firm apart from competitors.
    - Your brand should be threaded through all communications.
    - The commitment to a brand must be one for the long haul: it is time-consuming, expensive and necessary.
    - Lawyers may think themselves omniscient and omnicompetent, but designing a brand is an area where lawyers need to engage specialist expertise. Check and refine the process with outside consultants and/or design assistance.
    - Think through your brand in all relevant media, including social media. Make sure it looks good on a smart phone.
    - Remember the regulatory perspective – your brand should not be false or tend to mislead the public.
    - Speedy and effective handling of client complaints is critical to preservation of relationship and reputation.
    - Defend your brand if it is under attack.

About the authors

Silvia C Bauer
Partner, Luther Rechtsanwaltsgesellschaft mbH
silvia.c.bauer@luther-lawfirm.com

Silvia C Bauer is a lawyer and partner in the IP/IT service line of Luther Rechtsanwaltsgesellschaft mbH in Cologne, and has worked for Luther since 2000. After vocational training as a business administration manager, she spent three years at Hoechst AG in Frankfurt as a country consultant. In addition, she studied economic sciences at the University of Applied Sciences in Mainz. She received her law degree at the University of Frankfurt.

Ms Bauer specialises in providing legal assistance in the data privacy field. She conducts data privacy audits and advises companies on the organisation of their data protection. She also provides assistance in evaluating the reliability of planned data processing, the introduction of whistleblowing hotlines or customer relationship management systems, the creation of contracts for processing personal data, data privacy policies and other relevant documents. Ms Bauer is the data protection officer at Luther and for several other companies. She is a guest lecturer at numerous events related to data protection and IT law.

Georg-Christof Bertsch
Principal and founder, Bertsch.Brand Consultants
georg-christof@bertsch-bertsch.de

Georg-Christof Bertsch is founder and owner of Bertsch.Brand Consultants (since 1995), one of the most renowned German brand consultancies for service industries. Since the early 1990s he has published books and essays on design, art, architecture and branding (both online and offline).

As a honorary professor at the University of Art and Design Offenbach (Frankfurt, Germany) Mr Bertsch teaches on and researches intercultural design projects, with a focus on intercultural teams. He is a member of the board of governors of the Bezalel Academy of Art and Design, Jerusalem and member of the board of the Museum of World Cultures, Frankfurt.

Mr Bertsch has delivered consultancy to commercial clients in Europe, Asia, Latin America for industries reaching from law, energy and information technology to logistics, banking and insurance.

Friedrich R Blase
Chief international officer, Holland & Knight
friedrich.blase@hklaw.com

Friedrich R Blase is chief international officer of Holland & Knight. He is responsible for the firm's relationships with major clients and law firms outside the United States, as well as the growth and operations of its foreign office network. Mr Blase is part of the firm's executive team.

Before taking on this role Mr Blase served as the firm's director of strategic initiatives, handling a variety of key projects to improve its competitiveness for clients and talent. He joined Holland & Knight in 2009 after consulting to major law firms on strategic business issues in Europe and the United States for a decade. Mr

About the authors

Blase started his career in international commercial arbitration before focusing on law firm management.

Ruth Bonino
Professional support lawyer, Clyde & Co LLP
ruth.bonino@clydeco.com

Ruth Bonino is a solicitor with extensive experience in employment law. She holds a master's in employment law and has specialised in employment law for more than 15 years.

Ms Bonino writes regular legal articles for external publication and is a contributor to a number of legal textbooks. She keeps the lawyers at Clyde & Co, and the firm's clients, up to date on employment law developments by writing client alerts, organising and preparing client training seminars and managing the team's internal training programme. As a fee earner, Ms Bonino was a senior associate at an international law firm based in the City of London where she handled a full case load of both contentious and non-contentious employment cases.

Ms Bonino is a member of the Employment Lawyers Association and PEN, the network of professional support employment lawyers.

Tracey Calvert
Director, Oakalls Consultancy Limited
tcalvert@oakallsconsultancy.co.uk

Tracey Calvert is a lawyer with many years' experience of working for the Law Society and the Solicitors Regulation Authority (SRA). She was a senior ethics adviser and, in her last role with the SRA, part of the ethics policy team which drafted the *SRA Handbook*.

Ms Calvert is now the director/owner of Oakalls Consultancy Limited and provides regulatory consultancy services. She has a varied portfolio of clients and interests and also writes regularly on regulatory topics. She has written six books (including *Ethics in Law Firms: A Practical Guide and Conflicts* and *Confidentiality in Law*

Firms), is a contributor to *Cordery on Legal Services* and sits on the editorial board of the Law Society's *Legal Compliance Bulletin*.

Simon Chester
Former partner, Heenan Blaikie LLP
rsgchester@outlook.com

Simon Chester is a law firm general counsel who has spent most of 2014 helping to manage the largest law firm dissolution in Canadian history. His earlier career included law teaching, government service, senior positions in bar associations and organisational consulting.

For 20 years he has helped law firms to navigate the complex and shifting landscape of professional regulation and to solve an array of professional crises that threaten regulatory compliance, liability risk and reputational harm. He is one of Canada's leading experts on conflicts of interest. With roots in three continents, he is a global lawyer, qualified in both Europe and North America.

Mr Chester is a frequent commentator, writer and master presenter, delivering high-energy, provocative presentations to legal conferences around the world about change in the law and the pressures that firms face.

A technological innovator throughout his career, he has earned an international reputation for his insights into the future of legal practice.

Anthony E Davis
Partner, Hinshaw & Culbertson LLP
adavis@hinshawlaw.com

Anthony Davis advises lawyers and law firms on legal profession and legal ethics issues, as well as on law firm risk management. He is a lecturer at Columbia University School of Law, teaching professional responsibility issues in business practice. He is the co-author of *Risk Management: Survival Tools for Law Firms*, published by the American Bar Association. In addition to his books, Mr Davis has written numerous scholarly articles and writes the bi-monthly "Professional Responsibility" column in the *New York Law Journal*. He is a past president of the Association of Professional Responsibility Lawyers. He received his law degree from Cambridge University and an LLM from New York University School of Law. He is admitted in New York and Colorado, and as a barrister and a solicitor (both non-practising) in England.

Jaime Fernández Madero
Founder, Fernández Madero Consulting
jfm@fmaderoconsulting.com

Jaime Fernández Madero is founder of Fernández Madero Consulting, a strategy and management consultancy firm for law firms in Latin America. He is associated with Hildebrandt Consulting. He practised law for 30 years and founded Bruchou, Fernández Madero & Lombardi, a leading law firm in Argentina, where he acted as managing partner for 10 years until he left the firm to start his consultancy practice.

Mr Fernández Madero has a master's in organisational studies from the *Universidad de San Andrés* in Buenos Aires (2011), for which his thesis was on organisational identification in professional service firms. He is the author of a book about managing law firms in Latin America (*Organizando Firmas de Servicios Profesionales. El caso de los Abogados*, ed *La Ley*, 2012). He writes articles in specialised magazines and for other publications sponsored by the Law Firm Management Committee of the International Bar Association.

Silke Gottschalk
Senior associate, Luther Rechtsanwaltsgesellschaft mbH
silke.gottschalk@luther-lawfirm.com

After finishing her law degree at the Philipps University in Marburg, Silke Gottschalk received an LLM in European law at the London School of Economics and Political Science, and worked under Georgious Gounalakis as a research assistant for the Faculty of Comparative Law. Following her legal clerkship at the Higher Regional Court in Cologne, she joined Luther and began working as an attorney in the IP/IT area. She has worked in compliance and quality risk since 2008.

Julia Graham
Director of risk management and insurance, DLA Piper
julia.graham@dlapiper.com

Julia Graham is a director in the international business of DLA Piper, based in London. She holds a BSc and is a fellow of the Chartered Insurance Institute and the Business Continuity Institute. She is currently president of the Federation of European Risk Management Associations and a member of the Technical Committee and Working Group for ISO 31000, the global risk management standard.

She is responsible for designing, implementing and managing an enterprise-wide risk management system at DLA Piper, and the design and procurement of International insurance programmes for all classes of insurance. She is a board director of the firm's captive insurance company.

Before her time at DLA Piper, Ms Graham worked in a variety of underwriting, management and risk management roles in the insurance sector.

Richard Harrison
Partner, Clyde & Co LLP
richard.harrison@clydeco.com

Richard Harrison leads the Lawyers' Professional Liability Group at Clyde & Co LLP and has 25 years' experience of English civil litigation in the High Court and appeal courts, as well as arbitration and mediation. He specialises in commercial dispute resolution relating to professional liability matters, disciplinary proceedings and investigations and insurance policy disputes.

Mr Harrison has extensive experience of handling complex claims involving law firms, with a particular focus on cases involving complex transactions, dishonesty and fraud. He has been involved in the defence of Solicitors Regulation Authority (SRA) investigations, advised law firms in relation to disciplinary matters and acted for UK law firms on significant civil claims and related SRA investigations. He regularly speaks on issues relating to law firm liability and risk management.

Mr Harrison is described in Chambers as "a leading light of the professional indemnity world" with "a reputation as a tough negotiator".

Markus Hartung

Director, Bucerius Center on the Legal Profession
markus.hartung@law-school.de

Markus Hartung is a lawyer and mediator. He is director of the Bucerius Center on the Legal Profession (CLP) at Bucerius Law School, Hamburg. He has a broad experience in managing law firms. From 1999 to 2008 he served as managing partner of Linklaters in Germany (and its predecessor firm) and as a member of the Linklaters global executive committee.

At the CLP, he focuses on legal market research and is responsible for the conception of executive education programmes (management and leadership) for legal professionals. His expertise lies in market development and trends, management and strategic leadership as well as corporate governance of law firms.

Since 2007 he is member of the Committee on Professional Regulation of the German Bar Association, chairing this committee since January 2011.

He is a regular conference-speaker on leadership, management and professional ethics and has written numerous articles and book chapters on these topics. He is co-editor and author of *Wegerich/Hartung: Der Rechtsmarkt in Deutschland*, a standard reference for the German legal market.

Janet M Henderson

Divisional director, Brit Syndicate 2987
janet.henderson@britinsurance.com

Janet Henderson is the divisional director of the global professional lines division of Brit Syndicates Limited in London. She has underwritten professional liability in the Lloyd's market for more than 25 years, during which time she underwrote for RA Edwards Syndicate 219 and St Paul Syndicate 1411, before joining Brit in 2003.

She is an actuarial graduate, an associate of the Chartered Insurance Institute and a member of the Professional Liability Underwriting Society. She has specialised in professional liability for law firms across the world for most of her career, covering a full spectrum of firm sizes.

She oversees four underwriting teams: three which split the global professional liability book for lawyers, accountants, architects and engineers, insurance brokers and miscellaneous classes on a geographical basis, and a fourth which is responsible for cyber, privacy and technology insurance worldwide.

Heather Hibberd

Chief risk manager, Legal Practitioners' Liability Committee
heather.hibberd@lplc.com.au

Heather Hibberd is the chief risk manager at the Legal Practitioners' Liability Committee (LPLC) in Melbourne, Australia. She holds degrees in law and science, and while in private practice specialised in professional indemnity insurance litigation for lawyers.

She joined the LPLC on secondment as a risk manager in 1999 and became a permanent member of staff in 2001.

As a risk manager, Ms Hibberd has written many articles and bulletins on a wide range of risk management topics for lawyers, she writes the LPLC's quarterly newsletter, *In Check*, and has spoken at many forums to lawyers, giving practitioners insights into what goes wrong as well as practical tips on how to avoid falling into the same traps.

Chris Holme
Partner, Clyde & Co LLP
chris.holme@clydeco.com

Chris Holme is an employment partner at Clyde & Co and works with companies and firms on the full range of employment issues that they face, from managing grievances and change programmes to resolving high-value employment claims. He has extensive experience of employment litigation, as well as advising on all employment issues and providing employment support in projects and transactions.

In particular, Mr Holme works with clients on partnership disputes; particularly in relation to dealing with alleged discrimination issues, partner hires and partner departures (whether individuals or teams).

Mr Holme's clients come from a variety of sectors, including a number of law firms and accountancy firms, as well as other professional services practices.

Mr Holme is a member of the Employment Lawyers Association, the Association of Partnership Practitioners and the City of London Solicitors Company.

Jane Hunter
Executive director, Aon Risk Solutions
jane.hunter@aon.co.uk

Jane Hunter is an executive director of Aon Risk Solutions, based in London. Admitted as an English solicitor in 1993, she practised as a defendant professional indemnity and insurance policy wording lawyer before moving into law firm management in 2001. Her managerial roles at Bird & Bird LLP and in the London office of US firm Squire, Sanders & Dempsey LLP comprised responsibility for insurance strategy and purchase, internal claims handling, regulatory and compliance and risk management issues.

Ms Hunter joined Aon in March 2011. Aon Risk Solutions' professional services practice provides specialised insurance brokerage and risk advisory services to lawyers, accountants, consultants, notaries, engineers, architects and other design professionals. Ms Hunter provides regulatory, compliance and risk management advice to Aon's professional services clients, in particular UK and US law firms.

Ms Hunter is also a qualified business coach.

James W Jones
Senior fellow, Center for the Study of the Legal Profession, Georgetown University Law Center
jim.w.jones2011@gmail.com

James W Jones is a senior fellow at the Center for the Study of the Legal Profession at the Georgetown University Law Center. He is also principal of Legal Management Resources LLC. Mr Jones is widely recognised as an expert on the US and global legal markets, having spent more than 40 years as a practising lawyer, law firm leader, corporate general counsel and management consultant.

Before his current positions, Mr Jones served as the managing partner of Arnold & Porter (1986-1995); vice chairman and general counsel of APCO Worldwide (1995-2000); and senior vice president and managing director of Hildebrandt International (2001-2011). He received his bachelor's degree from Trinity University and his JD from New York University School of Law.

Abhijit Joshi
Senior partner and chief executive officer,
AZB & Partners
abhijit.joshi@azbpartners.com

Abhijit Joshi, senior partner and chief executive officer, is one of India's leading corporate/mergers and acquisitions lawyers. He has advised Indian and multinational companies, and has been involved in many major and noteworthy transactions over the past 20 years. Mr Joshi is a qualified solicitor in India and England. He is the recipient of many accolades, including being named a leading lawyer for mergers and acquisitions in India in *International Who's Who Legal* for 2013 and 2014 and being named as M&A lawyer of the year in India for 2013 by *Finance Monthly*.

Hermann J Knott
Partner, Luther Rechtsanwaltsgesellschaft mbH
hermann.j.knott@luther-lawfirm.com

Hermann J Knott is a partner of Luther in Cologne, specialising in corporate transactions with a focus on cross-border deals, and has more than 20 years' experience. He is also the firm's risk managing partner.

He attended law school in Cologne, Geneva, Philadelphia (where he obtained his LLM) and Stanford, and wrote a doctorate thesis on international business law. He gained professional experience abroad working with firms in New York and Paris.

Frank Maher
Partner, Legal Risk LLP
frank.maher@legalrisk.co.uk

Frank Maher is a solicitor and partner in Legal Risk LLP, a law firm specialising in advice on professional regulation and professional indemnity insurance. Mr Maher is a committee member of the Association of Partnership Practitioners, a multi-disciplinary organisation of advisers to professional practices, and a member of the Association of Professional Responsibility Lawyers and of the Association of Regulatory and Disciplinary Lawyers.

He has more than 30 years' experience and his clients include many of the largest law firms in the United Kingdom, the United States and Europe, along with professional indemnity insurers of law firms and regulators of law firms.

Mr Maher is a frequent speaker at law firm risk management, compliance and insurance events and has spoken at events in Europe, the United States, Asia and Australia. He has written many books and articles on law firm risk management, professional indemnity and anti-money laundering.

Sue Mawdsley
Partner, Legal Risk LLP
sue.mawdsley@legalrisk.co.uk

Sue Mawdsley is a partner in Legal Risk LLP. She is a solicitor with more than 29 years' experience and advises law firms – from multinationals to high street practices – on risk management, claims prevention and regulatory compliance. She has particular expertise in anti-money laundering and in advising firms on anti-money laundering problems and compliance strategies, as well as extensive experience of developing bespoke procedures and systems for law firms.

Ms Mawdsley is noted in *Chambers UK* as a Key Individual in the firm and is recognised for her "encyclopaedic knowledge" of anti-money laundering regulations and "excellent support and advice". She is also noted in the *Legal 500 2013* as having "cutting-edge knowledge of anti-money laundering".

Ms Mawdsley has a diploma in anti-money laundering from the International Compliance Association and a practitioner's certificate in data protection. She is co-author of *The Money Laundering Reporting Officer's Handbook: A Guide for Solicitors*.

Ernst Millaard
Executive account director, Aon Global Risk Consultants
ernst.millaard@aon.nl

For more than 30 years Ernst Millaard has worked for Aon and its predecessors. At present, he works for Aon Global Risk Consultants as executive account director. In this role he is currently being deployed as risk and insurance manager in several Dutch and international companies.

From 2009 to 2013 Mr Millaard was responsible for the development and sales of insurance products for law firms and other professional services clients in the Europe, Middle East and Africa region. He assisted the local Aon offices in their client contact and developed insurance products that could be used in many European countries and even worldwide.

Previously, Mr Millaard had management responsibility for several departments of Aon Netherlands, such as professional services, commodity trades and global business manager.

Luis Felipe Mohando
Regional knowledge manager, SORAINEN
felipe.mohando@sorainen.com

Luis Felipe Mohando is associate and regional knowledge manager in SORAINEN. As part of the knowledge management team he designs, implements and manages systems and procedures enabling SORAINEN legal teams to organise, share and use know-how and experience.

Mr Mohando joined SORAINEN's M&A and private equity team bringing his international experience from the tax department of Ernst & Young in Buenos Aires, and from building up and heading the corporate and M&A practice in Leverone & Mihura Estrada.

He read law at Torcuato Di Tella University in Buenos Aires, and also holds LLMs from New York University, the National University of Singapore and Torcuato Di Tella University. He was called to the Buenos Aires Bar in 2002 and the Madrid Bar in 2010.

Since 2012 he is chairman of the Knowledge Management and IT Subcommittee of the International Bar Association Law Firm Management Committee.

Suzie Ogilvie
Head of anti-money laundering, Freshfields Bruckhaus Deringer LLP
suzie.ogilvie@freshfields.com

Suzie Ogilvie is the head of anti-money laundering at Freshfields Bruckhaus Deringer LLP. She advises both the firm and its clients on anti-money laundering issues and also has responsibility for managing reputational risk and ensuring that the firm has appropriate procedures in place in order to comply with anti-bribery laws and economic sanctions.

Ms Ogilvie is currently the chair of the Money Laundering Task Force of the Law Society of England and Wales and the UK delegate on the Money Laundering Committee of the Council of Bars and Law Societies of Europe. She assists in the coordination of the legal profession's policy positions on financial crime in the United Kingdom, and represents members of the legal profession at government committees in this area. She has also been involved in the lobbying efforts on the Fourth EU Money Laundering Directive.

Angeline Poon
Director, knowledge and risk management, Rajah & Tann LLP
angeline.poon@rajahtann.com

Angeline Poon is the director of knowledge and risk management in Rajah & Tann LLP, the largest full-service law firm in Southeast Asia.

She has more than 20 years' experience in the legal profession, having practised corporate finance law as a partner before her current specialisation in knowledge and risk management.

Before joining Rajah & Tann, she was the director of legal and compliance and knowledge management in another of Singapore's top law firms. Her current role at Rajah & Tann involves managing the firm's know-how and training, as well as advising on regulatory risk and compliance matters of the firm and its regional network.

About the authors

Steven M Puiszis
Partner, Hinshaw & Culbertson LLP
spuiszis@hinshawlaw.com

Steven Puiszis is a partner in Hinshaw & Culbertson LLP's lawyers for the profession practice group, representing lawyers and law firms in professional liability claims. He is the firm's deputy general counsel and its privacy and security officer. He has developed policies and training materials for e-discovery, social media and data privacy and security. Hinshaw was recently named *US News & World Reports'* Best Firm in Ethics and Professional Responsibility.

Mr Puiszis has taken numerous civil and criminal trials to verdict. He is the author of a book on governmental liability and constitutional law, now in its third edition. He has also written book chapters and law review articles on jury selection, e-discovery, the Class Action Fairness Act 2005 and the role of general counsel in law firm risk management.

Mr Puiszis is the secretary treasurer of the Defence Research Institute and serves on the Board of Directors. He is a past president of the Illinois Association of Defence Trial Counsel and a fellow of the American Bar Foundation.

Martin Schulz
German Graduate School of Management and Law, Heilbronn, Germany
martin.schulz@ggs.de

Martin Schulz is a professor of German and international private and corporate law at the German Graduate School of Management and Law (GGS) in Heilbronn. He studied law at the Goethe University, Frankfurt and the Yale Law School, New Haven, holding a PHd in law from Frankfurt and an LLM from Yale. His publications and main areas of work include German and international corporate law, compliance and compliance management as well as knowledge management for lawyers. In addition to his academic activities, Dr Schulz works as an attorney at law and knowledge management lawyer in the Frankfurt office of Freshfields Bruckhaus Deringer LLP.

The GGS is an internationally oriented university of applied sciences specialising in management and legal education. GGS programmes and research focus on future global market trends and international developments in business and legal practice.

Andrew Scott
Partner and general counsel, Clyde & Co LLP
andrew.scott@clydeco.com

Andrew Scott is a partner and general counsel at Clyde & Co LLP. He qualified as a solicitor in England in 1985 and has long experience of professional liability and disciplinary defence work, and of advising on professional regulatory and risk matters, principally for lawyers and accountants.

In his general counsel role at Clyde & Co, Mr Scott is a member of the firm's risk committee and has involvement in all aspects of the firm's risk and compliance functions.

Mr Scott edited *Risk Management for Accountants* by Clyde & Co's predecessor firm, Barlow Lyde & Gilbert, and has contributed to other publications and periodicals on risk management.

Richard Turnor
Partner, Maurice Turnor Gardner LLP
richard.turnor@mtgllp.com

Richard Turnor leads the professional practices group of Maurice Turnor Gardner LLP in London. He advises professional practices and their partners on constitutional documents, international structure, team moves, limitation of liability issues, internal disputes, governance, Solicitors Regulation Authority regulation, mergers, demergers and other similar transactions. His clients have included some of the largest global professional firms, onshore and offshore firms, boutique firms and financial services firms established as limited liability partnerships. He is a former chairman of the Association of Partnership Practitioners and is a regular participant in government consultations and speaker and contributor to publications on related topics. He is also a non-executive director of the Royal Marsden NHS Foundation Trust.

Wolfgang Weiss
Professor, HUK-Coburg endowed professorship,
University of Applied Sciences and Arts, Coburg
wolfgang.weiss@hs-coburg.de

Wolfgang Weiss holds the HUK-Coburg endowed professorship at the Business Administration Department of the University of Applied Sciences and Arts, Coburg. Before joining the university, he was head of management Germany at Linklaters LLP. In 2011 he received the Professional Management Network Award as Managing Partner/Chief Operating Officer for his work at Linklaters LLP. He holds degrees in law and business administration. His research focuses on knowledge-based service industries, especially in the field of financial and risk management. He has regularly published on this subject. Professor Weiss conducts research projects and consults on successful management and leadership of law firms. He is a member of the Advisory Board of the Centre on the Legal Profession of the Bucerius Law School in Hamburg, Germany.

Other titles in this series

Globe Law and Business

For further details and a free sample chapter go to
www.globelawandbusiness.com